Challenges to the Powe
in Early Greek Poe

CHALLENGES
TO THE
POWER OF ZEUS
IN
EARLY GREEK POETRY

Noriko Yasumura

B L O O M S B U R Y

LONDON • NEW DELHI • NEW YORK • SYDNEY

Bloomsbury Academic
An imprint of Bloomsbury Publishing Plc

50 Bedford Square
London
WC1B 3DP
UK

175 Fifth Avenue
New York
NY 10010
USA

www.bloomsbury.com

First published by Bristol Classical Press 2011
Paperback edition first published 2013

British Library Cataloguing-in-Publication Data
A catalogue record for this book is available from the British Library.

ISBN: HB: 978-0-7156-3678-7
PB: 978-1-4725-0447-0

Library of Congress Cataloging-in-Publication Data
A catalog record for this book is available from the Library of Congress

Typeset by Ray Davies
Printed and bound in Great Britain

Contents

Contents

Preface

It was a long time ago – indeed, as long as thirty years ago – that the idea for this book first came to my mind. In 1974-5 I was given the chance to study at Cambridge as a British Council Scholar under the supervision of the late Dr John Chadwick. Under his guidance I studied the Linear B tablets and found myself particularly attracted by the religious tablets from Pylos. They seemed to show that Zeus was just an ordinary god in those days – a god, no doubt, but one of no specific significance. This revelation was a great surprise: with my ideas so informed by Homer and Hesiod, I had never doubted Zeus' supremacy in the Greek mythological universe. I recognised now that the characterisation of Zeus had been transformed by the beginning of the Archaic period, and I became curious to know more about the strategies and processes underlying Zeus' progression to sovereignty. From this tiny germ of curiosity arose the idea for this book.

I was able to return to this theme and build on my preliminary ideas when I undertook a PhD at University College London under the supervision of Professor Richard Janko. He greatly encouraged my work and this book has its basis in this PhD dissertation, submitted in 2004.

I returned to Japan in 1998, having obtained a professorship at Kanazawa University. As I read Classical literature with my students, I found myself involved in many exciting and enjoyable discussions about my work. Moved by these dialogues, directly and indirectly, I wrote the article on Prometheus which forms the basis of Chapter V in this book.

One fascination has remained constant throughout this long journey: Homer. Whenever I read the Homeric epics, I find something new. I find myself deeply impressed by the profundity of thought, richness of artistic technique, and humour of the storytelling in these poems. Although the history of Homeric studies dates back to the Hellenistic Age, and unimaginable numbers of works have been published on the poems, I believe that it is still possible to tease out some hitherto hidden threads and reveal some obscured facets of the Homeric tradition. That is the aim of this book.

On various occasions in my life – some delightful, some sad and some inspiring – I have recollected and gained comfort from the Homeric poems. For example, admiring a beautiful snowfall in Kanazawa, I recalled the simile of the snowflakes used of the eloquence of Odysseus (*Il.* 3.222); when sad, I was reminded of the story of the two jars on Zeus' floor (*Il.* 24.527-33), or of Achilles' memorable resolve when contemplating his death, that 'even mighty Heracles could not escape death' (*Il.* 18.117). I have been encouraged, educated and restored by the Homeric verses, and it is as though the two epics have become my good friends. It has been my greatest pleasure to study them and I truly believe, as Xenophon so properly writes (*Smp.* 4.6), that everything relating to human life is in Homer.

I am often asked how Asian people could ever understand Classical Greek thought. But I have never doubted that we too can appreciate the profound ideas transmitted to us from the ancient Greek world. As Herodotus points out about those older times, interchange between East and West was constant and ongoing. Thus Greek civilisation has not been alien to Oriental people, nor does the Western world have a monopoly on its understanding. These ideas possess a value which is universal; and we are all part of this one world. Truly, the radiance of Greek thought should be shared and perceived by us all.

*

I could not have completed this book without the generous support of a large number of people who spared me their time and offered me invaluable insights and advice. I wish first to express my great gratitude to Professor Richard Janko, my supervisor at the University of London. I am indebted beyond measure to him for the time he has so freely offered in reading and commenting on my work. I will always be grateful for his support, innumerable useful suggestions and encouragement.

I am particularly grateful to Professor Pat Easterling, who kept me on the right track. From the time I first met her in Cambridge in 1994, her exceptional intellectual guidance has been as unfailing as the strength of her moral support. It has been my privilege to know her and enjoy all of the benefits of her generous nature. When I found the following verse in the fragments of Diphilus,

ὡς μακάριον φρόνησις ἐν χρηστῷ τρόπῳ
How blessed it is to have intelligence in noble character (Diph. fr. 113 K.-A.)

I thought that this entirely encapsulated Pat's finest qualities. I hope to dedicate this verse to her.

I would like to express my gratitude to my professors who taught me at the International Christian University in Tokyo and the Graduate School of Kyoto University for their guidance of my education when I was a student. The instruction which I received from them provided a firm foundation for my further studies. Without the enthusiasm of these teachers, I could never have dreamed of a career in the Classics. I owe a great debt to their thorough training and will always be grateful for their personal support.

Preface

Special thanks are due to my many friends who have always supported me greatly. In particular I wish to record my thanks to the late Professor Colin Austin who kindly read my manuscript and corrected my English translations of the ancient texts. I deeply regret his too early death. Professor Elizabeth Craik, Dr Natalie Tchernetska, Dr Naoko Yamagata and Dr Antonia Ruppel kindly read my manuscript and gave me many useful comments. I am grateful to them for their cordial friendship. I owe a debt of gratitude to Dr Akiko Tomatsuri for the preparation of the indexes. I have been greatly assisted by her diligence. Above all, I would like to express my deep gratitude to Dr Victoria Jennings and Dr Andrea Katsaros, who read my manuscript carefully, tirelessly corrected my English, and offered countless valuable suggestions. Their patience and warm support were indispensable for the completion of this book. I must also thank Ms Deborah Blake, my editor, for her great support. Since the time when the first contract for the publication of this book was made with Duckworth, she has continued to encourage me with kindness and tolerance. Any remaining errors are, of course, my own. Finally, I would like to thank my family for their unlimited empathy and patience. I am especially grateful to my husband, who is now seriously ill, for his profound understanding.

Kurihira   N.Y.
May 2011

To my family and friends

Introduction

In what follows my aim has been to offer an innovative interpretation of a number of early Greek epic texts in which I have found common compositional connections. One of the themes that links them is that of the accomplishment and maintenance of Zeus' Olympian supremacy in the face of challenges for cosmic domination. I examine the traces of this theme – the legacy of predecessors in the poetic tradition – manifested in early Greek poetry. In the earliest extant works of Greek literature, Zeus reigns supreme in the Olympian hierarchy. By the eighth century, it is clear, the concept of the Olympian 'family' had crystallised: they are the principal mythical figures in epic, and Zeus' power over them is already secure. However, there are indications that before this time Zeus faced and overcame challenges which threatened his rule over the universe. In the *Iliad*, Poseidon and Hera always appear in alliance against Zeus; and his son and daughters, Apollo, Aphrodite and Athena, are also problematic figures deserving of consideration for their roles in familial internecine conflicts. Furthermore, Prometheus, the 'cousin' of Zeus, stands out as the challenger of the power of Zeus in the realm of cunning intelligence.

Zeus' route to victory

There is no indication of Zeus' supremacy in the Mycenaean documents. The religious tablets from Pylos contain a great number of what appear to be the names of gods,[1] among whom Poseidon is clearly the most significant. For example, in Pylos tablet Tn 316,[2] there are fourteen or fifteen divine names, including Zeus, Hera, Poseidon, Hermes and Potnia, together with six shrines or holy places. One of the significant features of this tablet is that Zeus, Hera and the goddess called *diuja* (Zeus' wife?) are mentioned together, under the headline of the shrine of Zeus.[3] It is also surprising that there are eight other deities on this tablet who are unknown in the classical period, for example, *manasa*, *dopota* and *dirimijo*. A golden vessel is dedicated to each of these figures, and some of them are also offered a human dedication.[4] Poseidon's prestigious position in Pylos is attested by the fact that the shrine of Poseidon is listed at the top of the tablet and offered, specifically and exceptionally, two women. He is also an important deity on the other Pylos tablets: in the Es group of tablets, he receives annual contributions of grain (with three other uncertain figures),[5] and his offerings are by far the largest; in Pylos tablet Un 718 he

1

is the recipient of a long list of offerings including oxen, sheep, goats, pigs, wheat, wine, honey, unguents, wool and cloth.[6] From the perspective offered by these documents, Poseidon appears to be the strongest of all the gods in Pylos. This picture well suits *Odyssey* 3.43-4, which tells how Telemachus and Athena (disguised as Mentor) join in celebrating the festival of Poseidon at Pylos.

Compared with the importance of Poseidon, Zeus does not appear as particularly consequential in the tablet documents. Tablet Tn 316 records his ostensibly unexceptional nature: he is just an ordinary god, receiving the same quantity of offerings as the other deities, some of whom may have been only minor gods since they are already unknown in classical times (as mentioned above). Given Zeus' later sovereignty over the universe, it is undeniable that his characterisation has undergone a major transformation by the beginning of the Archaic Period.

If we attempt to delineate the significance of Zeus in the Linear B Tablets, it lies surely in his name: among the deities written on the tablets, only Zeus can claim to be etymologically Indo-European in origin. As I discuss in Chapter V below, many of the suggested etymologies for divine names of the Olympians are thought to be suspicious.[7] The fact that Zeus alone is exclusively the legitimate descendant of the Indo-European god is noteworthy with regard to his later supremacy among the Olympians.

It is not only Poseidon who must be considered a challenger of Zeus. A number of local deities, especially goddesses, received cult. As Campbell writes, 'wherever the Greeks came, in every valley, every isle and every cave, there was a local manifestation of the mother-goddess of the world whom Zeus, as the great god of the patriarchal order, had to master in a patriarchal way'.[8] The Mother Goddess is the embodiment of the fruitful earth, who gives life and fertility to plants, animals and men. Perhaps all the Greek female divinities are, more or less, variations of her role in cult. Aphrodite, whose origin I discuss in Chapter VII, Section 2, is surely one of such variants. The Zeus whom we encounter in Homer and Hesiod is the conqueror only after he has subdued all of these deities; and the texts of these poets preserve for us chance traces, albeit fragmentary, of Zeus' route to victory.[9] Actually, the Olympian gods are a heterogeneous collection, and Guthrie points out that their settlement as one family on Olympus is '*a tour de force*' of Zeus.[10]

The concept of the Olympian family over which Zeus rules as father can be seen as a consequence of the drastic changes of that period. In the course of the eighth century, when the *Iliad* came to achieve its final shape, the Greek world grew increasingly receptive to new influences, both internal and external. Internally, the movement towards Panhellenism became prominent; and externally, the influence of the Near East grew pervasive from the latter half of the ninth century onwards in response to organised colonisation.[11]

2

Panhellenism

The Olympic Games were organised in 776 BC, and the great sanctuaries of Olympia, Delphi, Delos and Eleusis were established in this period.[12] The Panhellenic character of the Homeric epics is obvious: the diverse epic tradition is synthesised into a unified Panhellenic model.[13] Since it was often performed on Panhellenic occasions, the epic theme itself is infused with and authorised by a Panhellenic spirit. For example, the death of Achilles is a theme officially celebrated in the 'paean' in the worship of Apollo at Delphi, one of the Panhellenic institutions. In addition, Achilles was traditionally mourned by the women of Elis in a ceremony that inaugurated the Olympics every four years, as reported by Pausanias (6.23.3).[14]

The ideas of the sovereignty of Zeus and of Panhellenism itself seem, indeed, to have proceeded hand in hand. In particular, the creation of the myth of the birth of Athena from Zeus' head would have been 'the great landmark'[15] in the establishment of a new kind of city-state. As I discuss below in Chapter IV, Section 3, for the ancient Greeks the fundamental perception of the state is as the 'fatherland' (πάτρα, πατρίς). The state is a family and the image of the ruler is one of a 'father'. Such ideology leaves no place for the daughter as sovereign heir; thus the daughter cannot be a threat. The concept of a strong alliance between Zeus and Athena fits perfectly both with Panhellenic ideals *and* with Greek societal and moral norms, and may have been a significant factor in Zeus' success.

Near Eastern influence

Near Eastern influence on Greek myth is nowadays widely accepted.[16] For one thing, many of the Greek gods are thought to be oriental in origin, including Prometheus, Apollo and Aphrodite, whom I deal with in Chapters V-VII. For another, the Near Eastern succession stories seem to have had a striking influence upon Greek myth.

The Hurrian story of Kumarbi and the Babylonian creation poem of the *Enuma Elish* share with Greek myth a similar presentation of the concept of strife between the gods over the possession of supreme power in the universe. In the course of the conflict for succession in the Hurrian myth, we find the motifs of swallowing, castration and other details which are peculiarly similar to the Greek succession myth.

The Babylonian epic *Atrahasis* represents the idea of the division of the universe, which is paralleled in the Homeric account of the three portions of the world shared by Zeus, Poseidon and Hades (*Il.* 15.187-95). Moreover, this epic offers features consistent with Greek myth: the gods have an assembly, and the mightiest god (Ea) among them determines the beginning and the end of the flood. It also deals with man's sins and his consequent punishment through plagues and the deluge which, notoriously, provides a parallel to the Biblical motivation for the Flood. The idea of strife among the gods for the highest power – the strongest god ruling over the other gods – is ubiquitous in Near Eastern epics.

Along with these parallels, there are also significant differences between the Greek and Near Eastern myths. The peculiarities of the Greek myth are, first, that the succession occurs through generational strife, and, second, that it is Zeus, a god of the third generation, who halts the cycle of strife.[17] These differences are precisely the essential characteristics of the Greek myth and, at the same time, clearly reflect the cultural and social conditions of their age. It was the time of pan-Hellenisation, when strong centralising forces were present in all aspects of Greek life. The *Theogony* represents the powerful and unchallengeable sovereignty of Zeus in response to this trend, which I discuss in Chapter IV.

We can also connect pre-Greek Indo-European poetic traditions to the tales of Zeus' sovereignty. For example, Dumézil analyses the cognate theme of war as the divine solution for overpopulation in the *Mahâbhârata* and in the *Cypria*.[18] Eliade discusses the cosmogonic and metaphysical significance in the *Rig Veda* of 'binding',[19] a theme also to be found in the *Iliad* and in Hesiod in connection with generational strife and cosmic sovereignty. I discuss the Near Eastern and pre-Greek Indo-European influences on Greek myth in Chapters IV, V and VII.

Generational strife and other challenges to Zeus

My investigation makes manifest the existence of two, often intertwined, thematic threads woven throughout these texts. The first is the threat of the mighty son with the potential to overcome and usurp his father. This image is perceptible in Book 1 of the *Iliad* – the subject of my Chapter I – and runs through the other texts under discussion. I discuss the story of the binding of Zeus (*Il.* 1.399-400) and Thetis' supplication (*Il.* 1.493-530), focusing on how the mythological theme of the threat of a son mightier than his father functions in the scene between Zeus and Thetis, and also throughout the *Iliad*. My analysis reveals, for example, that the birth of Athena (*Theog.* 886-91: see Chapter IV) is pivotal to Zeus' acquisition of supremacy because, as a maiden daughter born from Zeus himself, she breaks a recurrent pattern of menace. The *leitmotif* reappears in Chapter VII in my exploration of Aphrodite's disempowerment in the *Hymn to Aphrodite*: although she is not an explicit challenger to Zeus, her incorporation into the patriarchal Olympian family nonetheless entails the loss of much of her personal power. I demonstrate that a major theme of the *Hymn* is the celebration of the solidarity of Olympian society at the expense of Aphrodite's personal happiness. In my investigation of the *Hymn to Apollo* – Chapter VI – I illustrate how the theme of the threatening and mighty son operates on two levels in the twin stories of Typhon and Apollo. Against a background of generational strife – a motif casting its shadow over so many of the texts under discussion – Typhon, son of Hera, challenges the power of Zeus in a narrative which emphasises the antagonistic role of the mother *and* the son against the father. As the oppressive atmosphere of the *Hymn's* opening scene suggests, Apollo – another powerful son – might also have challenged Zeus. Instead, he establishes overall peace. Highlighting these parallels reveals, in my interpretation, that the central theme of this *Hymn* is the celebration of the reconciliation of father and son – or, rather, the father's successful deliverance from the son's potential threat.

Several kinds of family tension are universal story patterns of folklore. Particularly in Greek myth, the relation of son and father seems to have been of great importance. One example of this dissent between fathers and sons can be seen in the stories in which a father eliminates his son (Phoenix in the *Iliad* [9.447-84]; Hippolytus in the *Hippolytus* of Euripides; cf. other examples listed by Sourvinou-Inwood).[20] Generational strife is thus a conspicuous theme in Greek myth, and it constitutes a basic element in many Greek stories. As I argue in Chapter I, the story of Odysseus, like that of Oedipus, is at the very heart of this tradition. Secondly, I emphasise another theme of the challenges to Zeus, namely that of the dangers represented by the Olympians. My discussion concentrates, in particular, on the appearance of this theme of early Greek poetry in the alliance between Hera and Poseidon. In Chapter II, I interpret the myth of the golden chain of Hera (*Il.* 15.16-33) as a clear indication of the persistent struggle between Zeus and Hera, in which Poseidon, overtly and covertly, always supports Hera. This insight enables me to establish plausible links with the broad epic tradition, such as the *Gigantomachy* on which, I argue, Homer draws. The result is a proposal for the reconstruction of the plot of this lost epic. Further, in my discussion of the Theomachy (*Il.* 20.54-74; 21.385-520) in Chapter III, I identify and trace the latent logic underlying this antagonism between Zeus and Poseidon – Zeus' final challenger – and examine how this logic is integrated by the poet into his account of the process of Zeus' reordering of the universe. Fundamental to this process, as I see it, is the analogy presented in the *Iliad* between the destiny of Achilles and that of Poseidon.

In Chapter V, I also examine Prometheus, who is the only god in the *Theogony* to challenge the deceptive intelligence of Zeus. The myth of Prometheus is something of a mystery, both in the story itself and its location in the *Theogony*. My close reading of this text sheds fresh light on the conflict between the two great gods Zeus and Prometheus. My interpretations of the above-mentioned texts also underline the often overlooked significance of cosmic – i.e. divine – strife as a popular theme in early Greek poetry.

Zeus had to conquer these powers – dangerous sons, chthonic potentates and the crafty rival who battles with his wits – before he gained supremacy on Olympus. Among threats to his power we find not only the explicit challenger, such as Typhon, but also implicit challengers, such as Hera, Poseidon and Aphrodite. They might not have actually caused a war against Zeus, but our texts show that they in fact oppose him or at least behave insubordinately towards him. Opposition and insubordination constituted a subversive threat towards Zeus against which appropriate countermeasures were required. In this regard, in Chapter III, I also discuss Ares as an insubordinate challenger of Zeus. As we will see, there could be various types of challenge and various levels of threat. Zeus conquered all these threats before they became a real rebellion.

The order of the chapters

I structure my investigation chronologically, with regard to the likely date of composition of the texts: the *Iliad* (Chapters I-III), the *Theogony* (Chapters IV-V), the *Hymn to Apollo* (Chapter VI), and the *Hymn to Aphrodite* (Chapter VII).[21] As a consequence of my approach through generic and thematic integration, it is also possible to appreciate this analysis by considering the myths according to the sequence of challenges to Zeus' power: that is, (1) the birth of Athena; (2) Typhon, the son of Hera; (3) Prometheus, a god of foresight; (4) the threat of Thetis; (5) the golden chain of Hera; (6) the reordering of the Universe; and (7) the bitter sorrow of Aphrodite. I choose, however, not to emphasise this aspect, since such an approach would involve analysis of *all* the challengers to Zeus' sovereignty, and would expand this study beyond manageable limits.

Methodology

In each chapter, I view the text as primary, and approach it from the point of view of a literary critic, using the familiar techniques of philological analysis and close reading. My discussions are naturally related to what is known about the myths of the various gods, but my first concern is the texts themselves, not mythology. I deal mainly with early Greek poetry, and some tragedies only in passing.

I show how the quest of Zeus for supremacy received different treatments in different genres – the epic story-telling of Homer, the didactic style of Hesiod, and the hymnic poems. Nevertheless, the juxtaposition of these texts also demonstrates the existence of a significant degree of thematic cross-over and harmony. Therefore, when these results are reapplied to each text, their interconnections culminate in a more comprehensive understanding of each work both as an individual, generically structured epic, didactic, or encomiastic piece, *and* as a representative part of a broader, thematically linked corpus of mythic material. The insight characterising this study is, then, that an approach grounded, synthetically, in the scrutiny of each genre has the potential to offer an improved understanding of the relationship between different kinds of literature.

I began my study fascinated by the number of references to challenges to the power of Zeus, and the significance which these fragmentary traces assume in the poems on close reading. My analysis reveals that these apparently arbitrary references can be considered, paradoxically, *central* to the theme of each work in which they appear. Germane to this is Taplin's observation,

> As so often in Homer's narrative technique, a seed in the form of a passing hint or subtle implication grows, as the poem progresses, into a full-blown and explicit issue or theme.[22]

Identifying this cumulative or 'snowball'[23] effect can provide a possible reconstruction of events which appear, on first reading, to be discrete. The obvious implication is that the theme of the resolution of the challenges to Zeus' power was of greater importance to the poets than has hitherto been acknowledged. A further implication is that the frequency of allusions to this theme in different genres of early Greek literature indicates that the ancient Greeks were particularly fond of the theme. We can postulate some of the manifold reasons for this: for instance, the competitiveness of Greek society laid the foundation for people's acceptance that Zeus' achievement of supreme Olympian power implied the defeat of his ene- mies and rivals.[24] Alternatively, the Greeks' characteristically logical spirit of inquiry into the cause and processes of the phenomenal world made them receptive to the elaboration of the reasoning offered in the representation of these myths in extended narratives.

Some of the passages that I evaluate are so-called 'digressions' (Chap- ters I, II, IV and VI), which are often regarded as 'interpolations' or 'inventions'.[25] My own view is, however, that a consistent logic can be detected behind these digressions, which permits the evaluation of their overall thematic relevance. This methodological approach has much in common with Taplin's 'soundings' of the Homeric texts: '... tracing the coherence of foreshadowings, back-references, cross-references, interlock- ing sequences – the "cobwebbing" of motifs and ideas.'[26]

The aim of this study is to focus attention on the elements with which the ancient audience were familiar from their wide acquaintance with epic tradition, but which we, being unfamiliar with them, have not necessarily recognised.[27] Of course, we can appreciate the poems even without further knowledge of such elements; but, as I will try to demonstrate, further knowledge can only bring us closer, in interpretation and appreciation, to the poems' ancient audiences. In tracing the hidden or apparently lost logic of the epic legends underlying our extant texts, we achieve an improved understanding of early Greek poetry. As Clay notes of the *Homeric Hymn to Demeter*,

The hymn, then, appears to lack certain crucial links of logic and motivation. But what is especially remarkable about these narrative gaps and inconsequences is that other extant versions of the myth organize many of the same components and motifs into a coherent narrative sequence, in which each change of scene or transition follows with admirable logic and clarity from what has preceded. There is good reason to suppose that at least some of these versions do not constitute later rationalized revisions of elements found in the hymns but, rather, that they preserve traditions older than the hymn itself.[28]

An intertextual reading of this kind – a reading *between* the lines and *beyond* the text – must take into account two related elements. The first is the notion of a presupposed, 'ideal' audience receptive to the details of (and possibilities for) mythographic variants and/or to the wider epic tradition to which, I argue, the poet refers.[29] For example, I suggest that the assumption of this audience's knowledge can allow the poet to curtail full explication of the underlying core of material on which he draws (see Chapter VI). The question of audience 'appreciation' is vexed: as Taplin has noted, an audience is not 'homogeneous', though its members can possess much in common. Of course, not all audience members will appreciate every cross-reference or digression as the poet intended. It is the epic poets' achievement to be able to approach this group on 'many different levels' – and over such a long period of time.[30]

The second element which this methodological discussion must address is the poet's use of innovation within the 'given' existing cores of material, and/or his invention beyond this same core. In Chapter VII we note that the poet of the *Hymn to Aphrodite* prefers the Homeric version of Aphrodite's birth to the Hesiodic (which, even allowing for uncertainties over the dating of the *Hymn*, we may assume that he knew).[31]

In practice, of course, it is very difficult to determine to what extent traditional motifs remain in the Homeric stories, and to what extent these early poets are inventing. As Willcock has suggested, 'the parallelism between the mythological story and the immediate situation often appears to be the creation of the poet ... the poet was free to invent details within an already existing framework of legend. The background ... was there in the legends before Homer.'[32] While this is an important and valid assertion, it is equally valid to recognise the impossibility of distinguishing for certain between sheer invention and poetic allusion and innovation. 'Probability',[33] by definition, remains only that. Dating alternative versions is fraught with difficulties, and is often a futile exercise. In addition, it is clear that we no longer possess all of the material on which these poetic 'innovators' drew. Any exploration of the mythological themes and threads which run through the epic corpus must, therefore, be dependent upon recognition of the element of 'probability' implicit in any judgement of narrative intention. Of course, close readings of texts of such complexity offer an abundance of alternative interpretations, of which mine is but one.

I make mention of 'cores of material'. I do not suggest that these registers of mythological variations existed, for the epic poets or their successors, in the form of a unique 'canon'. The fall of Hephaestus, not the only case of inconsistency in the *Iliad*, offers a glimpse of this available repertory: at 1.590-1 he is thrown from heaven by Zeus; at 18.395-6 this expulsion is carried out by Hera. The latter version, as I discuss in Chapter VI, is the one followed by the *Hymn to Apollo*.[34] If we read the Iliadic 'inconsistency' in a positive light (i.e. not necessarily as a threat to the unitarian point of view), it brings into relief the kind of innovation that the poet was able to employ.[35] In my investigation I note a number of places where poetic innovation and/or invention serves to steer the narrative in a specific direction. To cite one example, from Chapter VI, the poet of the *Hymn to Apollo* chooses to depart from the convention, represented by four other versions, by assigning a female gender to the dragon, which enables the narrative to proceed along a carefully calculated path.

Homer and Hesiod are heirs to great variations in the epic tradition. As I will demonstrate, it is to be expected that among these traditional stories there existed tales of early strife among the gods over whom Zeus finally achieved overall rule. I suggest that both Homer and Hesiod would have known these tales, and both exploit this material to develop their characters' roles in relation to their poems' central ideas. As Lang rightly points out,[36] the various episodes or parts of episodes narrating the strife that preceded the Trojan War are not likely to have been invented independently in order to parallel details of the *Iliad* plot; rather, the divine strife of the *Iliad* story had its origin in such precedents as appear in the paradeigmata. The oral character of the epic tradition leads one to expect that these stories would be transmuted according to the perspective of each previous story-teller, and that Homer and Hesiod, too, would re-draw the stories from their own perspectives. What is remarkable is that both poets are extraordinarily consistent in their references to these previous stories. The use and modification of these stories are not arbitrary or random, but possess their own design. Particularly in the *Iliad,* we note that references to divine strife are so complex and so consistent that the poet seems to have in mind a coherent picture of the mythical past.[37] Bearing this in mind, it is my aim to trace this logic through the epic tradition.

The traditional nature of Homeric epic suggests that we need to apply a broader range of imaginative and hermeneutic skills if we are to increase our ability to 'understand' the stories lying behind and beyond the narrative *per se*. The so-called 'digressions' and 'paradeigmata' suggest a wealth of underlying pre-Homeric legends which are exploited by 'dynamic selection, combination, modification and revision of the myth'.[38] Some stories have been designated 'inventions' on the grounds of improbability, inconsistency or 'the lack of other parallel accounts'.[39] However, as I shall suggest, such stories may be revisions of earlier material.

For example, the myths associated with Nestor show how complex the tradition was that preceded Homer.[40] The individual heroes enjoy their own stores of legendary material, and the poet sometimes refers to stories and details about these heroes which have only incidental reference to the main narrative. Although we do not possess epics about Nestor or Diomedes (for example), we can certainly conceive that such heroic songs existed behind the brief Homeric references.

Another example is pertinent: the marriage of Eos and Tithonus is briefly mentioned at *Odyssey* 5.1-2, but the details of the story are not revealed by the poet. It is highly probable that Homer knew the details of the love-story, for we find it also in the *Homeric Hymn to Aphrodite* (218-38), Mimnermus (fr. 4 W, 1 G-P) and Sappho (fr. 55 V). But if the *Hymn to Aphrodite* or the fragments of Mimnermus or Sappho had not survived, some modern commentators might assume that the story of Eos and Tithonus in the *Odyssey* was a Homeric invention. The 'accidental' nature of the existence of these parallel accounts suggests that it is problematic to categorise certain stories as Homeric inventions purely because they lack parallel contemporary authority. Again, we must recognise how little we know of the vast range of pre-Homeric stories of gods and men.

A final example: the story of the binding of Zeus (*Il.* 1.399-406), which I examine in Chapter I, has been considered by many scholars to be a Homeric invention.[41] Although there may be no other reference to this account in Homer or later poets, it can hardly be said with any certainty that 'the gods had never presented a real threat to him'.[42] I will demonstrate that reminiscences of rebellion and challenge do exist in the *Iliad*; moreover, references to this divine strife are made at significant moments and with significant relevance to the central concerns of the epic.

By alluding to these stories in the form of digressions, the poet allows his audience to interact with his narrative: to imagine the extensive details and ramifications of the stories, to make comparisons, and to deepen their understanding of the present narrative. These digressions are sometimes very short and lacking in detail, but, however brief the reference, we must assume that the ancient audience would have enjoyed the dynamic resonance between the present narrative and the underlying allusion. It is these digressions which provide us with the imaginative background to the epic and make the narrative more impressive. From this perspective, the techniques of allusion and digression are powerful authorial devices which result in many of the epic's most attractive features. If we look at these stories simply as 'invention' and fail to recognise the vast wealth of pre-existing background material from the epic tradition, we lose much of the persuasive power of the stories and malign the composition's structural integrity. The ancients were only too well aware of this, as is demonstrated by Herodotus' comment on the various stories surrounding Helen and Paris:[43]

δοκέει δέ μοι καὶ ῞Ομηρος τὸν λόγον τοῦτον πυθέσθαι· ἀλλ᾽ οὐ γὰρ ὁμοίως ἐς τὴν ἐποιίην εὐπρεπὴς ἦν τῷ ἑτέρῳ τῷ περ ἐρχήσατο, μετῆκε αὐτόν, δηλώσας ὡς καὶ τοῦτον ἐπίσταιτο τὸν λόγον. δῆλον δέ, κατὰ παρεποίησε ἐν ᾽Ιλιάδι (καὶ οὐδαμῇ ἄλλῃ ἀνεπόδισε ἑωυτόν) πλάνην τὴν ᾽Αλεξάνδρου ...

I think Homer too knew this story; however he rejected it as less suitable for epic poetry than the one he actually used, showing that it was not unknown to him. This is clear from the passage in the *Iliad* (and he does not return to it elsewhere) when he relates the wanderings of Alexander ... (*Histories* 2.116)

*

For my translation of the texts cited, I owe much to the following published translations:

Martin Hammond, *Homer, the Iliad* (Penguin Books), 1987.
Richmond Lattimore, *The Iliad of Homer*, Chicago: University of Chicago Press, 1951.
Walter Shewring, *Homer: The Odyssey*, Oxford: Oxford University Press (Oxford World's Classics), 1980.
Richmond Lattimore, *The Odyssey of Homer* (Perennial Classics), 1967.
M.L. West, *Hesiod: Theogony and Works and Days*, Oxford: Oxford University Press (Oxford World's Classics), 1988.
Glenn W. Most, *Hesiod: Theogony, Works and Days, Testimonia*, Cambridge MA: Harvard University Press (Loeb Classical Library), 2006.
Apostolos N. Athanassakis, *The Homeric Hymns*, Baltimore: Johns Hopkins University Press, 1976.
M.L. West, *Homeric Hymns, Homeric Apocrypha, Lives of Homer*, Cambridge MA: Harvard University Press (Loeb Classical Library), 2003.
Jules Cashford, *The Homeric Hymns* (Penguin Books), 2003.

I

The Threat of Thetis

Book 1 of the *Iliad* presents a rich and complex mythic environment in which to examine the theme of a succession myth. When Achilles asks Thetis to go to Olympus to persuade Zeus, he suggests that she mentions her rescue of Zeus from his shackles (1.399-406). This story has puzzled readers since Zenodotus, who athetised 396-406. Modern scholars are also disposed to regard this story as the invention of the poet of the *Iliad*.[1] For example, Griffin writes that the poet of the *Iliad* even invents archaic-sounding myths of divine conflict in the olden days, such as the story which Achilles 'often heard Thetis tell', of the conspiracy against Zeus by Hera, Poseidon and Pallas Athena.[2] However, even if the poet invented or modified this episode to some extent, significant details of the passage can nevertheless be related to the mythological background that I characterise as 'challenges to the power of Zeus'.[3] Re-tracing this lost core story enables us to reclaim and restore the potential logic of this problematic reference for its surrounding narrative.

The importance of Thetis was first signalled by L.M. Slatkin.[4] It is necessary to cover some of the same ground – to take the reader over familiar material in order to lay the basis for Section 1, and to indicate points on which my interpretation goes further.

In spite of Achilles' suggestion that she should recount the story, Thetis does not actually do so when she makes her supplication to Zeus (1.503-10; 514-16). Although a multiplicity of possible explanations for this omission have been offered,[5] some new and additional ideas can be added: for example, Thetis' strategy is not to mention the story of Zeus' crisis in order to place increased emphasis on Achilles' mortality; moreover, Thetis' speech seems to imply some hidden relationship between herself and Zeus. As a consequence, a dynamic picture of the succession myth is subtly admitted into the narrative.

In her speech, the underlying image, which functions as a threat to Zeus, is the potential victory of the mightier son over his father. This notion, which is especially important in early Greek poetry (for instance, in the *Theogony*), is reflected not only in Book 1 but also in other parts of the *Iliad*, and in the *Odyssey*. The two-fold aim of this chapter is to discuss, first, how the mythological theme of the 'threat of the son' works in the scene between Zeus and Thetis (*Il.* 1.493-530); and, secondly, how the relationship between Achilles and Peleus can be construed within the ambit of a succession myth.

1. The supplication of Thetis

Thetis' supplication is of great significance in the *Iliad*, because its acceptance is the first step in the whole plot of the epic. The poem focuses on Achilles' destiny, and Zeus' decision is paramount in giving shape to the action. In narrative terms, Zeus' resolution becomes acceptable to the audience through the persuasiveness of Thetis.[6] Her supplication is a crucial intervention in the war,[7] and because of its significance we should not be surprised that her speech is so carefully worked out: as Kuch rightly notes, its structure is perfectly composed, a catalyst for the progression of the narrative.[8] The narrative strategy in this supplication is the key to understanding the power-relations between the characters of Zeus and Thetis. As we will see, Thetis' allusive words recall a past which offered a real threat to Zeus.

Thetis' address

The groundwork for Thetis' address is laid with deliberation. Let us consider the beginning of the scene when Achilles calls on Thetis for help. He begins with a remarkable definition of himself:

> μῆτερ, ἐπεί μ' ἔτεκές γε μινυνθάδιόν περ ἐόντα,
> τιμήν πέρ μοι ὄφελλεν Ὀλύμπιος ἐγγυαλίξαι
> Ζεὺς ὑψιβρεμέτης· νῦν δ' οὐδέ με τυτθὸν ἔτεισεν.

> Mother, since you bore me to be short-lived, surely honour at least should have been granted to me by Olympian Zeus of the loud thunder. But now he has paid me not even a little. (*Il.* 1.352-4)

Since it originated with Zeus, Achilles' destiny – a short life – is the explicit and legitimate rationale behind his appeal for fame:[9] if Thetis had not been compelled by Zeus to marry Peleus, her son would not have been 'short-lived';[10] therefore, had Zeus been his father, Achilles would have been immortal; moreover, by virtue of Thetis' potentiality, he would have been *mightier* than Zeus. Achilles is owed honour because he is the child of a goddess; but a further connotation is revealed by the special circumstances by which he is the child of *this* goddess. Finally, Achilles' opening words evoke the latent themes of generational strife and succession myth.

Thetis' reply echoes the first line of Achilles' speech and gains effect from being so placed, with the *linguistic* parallel reflecting the *thematic* parallel between the two speeches, and giving heavy emphasis to Achilles' short life and his inevitable destiny:

> ὤ μοι τέκνον ἐμόν, τί νύν σ' ἔτρεφον αἰνὰ τεκοῦσα;
> αἴθ' ὄφελες παρὰ νηυσὶν ἀδάκρυτος καὶ ἀπήμων
> ἧσθαι, ἐπεί νύ τοι αἶσα μίνυνθά περ, οὔ τι μάλα δήν·
> νῦν δ' ἅμα τ' ὠκύμορος καὶ ὀϊζυρὸς περὶ πάντων
> ἔπλεο·

14

I. The Threat of Thetis

Oh my child, why did I ever rear you, after the sorrow of your birth? If only you could sit beside the ships without tears or pain – because your fate is of short span, not very long at all. But now you are both short-lived and miserable as well, beyond all others. (*Il.* 1.414-17)

Thetis laments Achilles' destiny: αἰνὰ τεκοῦσα again alludes to her marriage with a human, giving birth to a child who is a mortal. She puts emphasis on his short life, wishing that he were now sitting by the ships, without grief and unharmed (415-16). She expresses two ideas (Kirk believes these to be contradictory[11]), and I conjecture that these are that Achilles could be free from the danger of battle, and live happily. The phrase 'παρὰ νηυσὶν ... ἦσθαι' (to sit by the ships, 415-16) implies, further, that Thetis regrets Achilles' involvement in the Trojan War. Although she accepts that his life *is* destined to be short (416), it seems that she would prefer him even for this short time to have 'an unharmed, griefless life' that is the preserve of the gods. Her lament once more concerns Achilles' mortality: her son could have been immortal, had she not been forced into marriage with a human. The complaints and laments of Thetis and Achilles are thus repeated and interrelated, as Kuch notes: the 'flashback' method ('das Mittel der Rückblende')[12] and repetition create a cumulative tension. Some arcane, close connection between Thetis, Achilles and Zeus is implied, and this gradually comes into focus as the theme of the succession myth is evoked.

Achilles' story: the binding of Zeus

In Achilles' account of how Thetis once freed Zeus from his shackles (1.396-406), Briareus or Aegaion is of central importance as Zeus' powerful supporter.[13] On one level, Achilles relates this episode in order to offer grounds for reciprocal benefaction. A more subtle reading exposes the recurrent theme of genealogical stasis:

ὃν Βριάρεων καλέουσι θεοί, ἄνδρες δέ τε πάντες
Αἰγαίων' – ὁ γὰρ αὖτε βίην οὗ πατρὸς ἀμείνων –

He is called Briareus by the gods, but Aegaion by all humans. For he is, in turn, mightier than his father (*Il.* 1.403-4)[14]

The ascription to Achilles of this particular reference emphasises the theme of succession. By mentioning Briareus/Aegaion, Achilles reminds Thetis of the possibility that he himself (as well as Briareus/Aegaion who is mightier than his father) could have been mightier than Zeus, if only she had been married to Zeus. Even viewed in the most general terms, this is a veiled threat to Zeus: just as Zeus was mightier than his own father Cronus, so too is Zeus always threatened with the possibility of having a son mightier than himself. In this

15

speech, Achilles implies that he is associated with the ongoing family history of Olympus.

Briareus is a typical supporter of Zeus, and is also particularly associated with binding which, as I will argue, is evocative of the succession myth theme.[15] In Hesiod's account, Briareus and his brothers Cottus and Gyes were bound and cast beneath the earth by Uranus, and later saved by Zeus and the other gods (*Theog.* 617-26). Zeus learns from Gaia that the side which persuades Briareus and his brothers to join it will be victorious (*Theog.* 627-8). In order to help Zeus, Briareus and his brothers bind Cronus and the other Titans, and cast them under the earth (*Theog.* 713-20). Thus, Achilles' mention of Briareus is highly allusive: just as Briareus is mightier than his father, so too could Achilles have been mightier than Zeus; just as Briareus helped Zeus to bind Cronus, so too could Briareus help Achilles; and just as Briareus saved Zeus at Thetis' request, so too could Briareus help Achilles at Thetis' request by binding Zeus, if ever she would make the request; of course this is a sort of moral blackmail, not an actual suggestion that Thetis can bring Briareus into play. That is, just as Briareus and his brothers were the guarantors or king-makers in the previous struggle for sovereignty, so too might they play a decisive role in *another* struggle.

Thetis' claim

In spite of Achilles' suggestion, Thetis does not repeat this story,[16] but simply remarks:

> Ζεῦ πάτερ, εἴ ποτε δή σε μετ᾽ ἀθανάτοισιν ὄνησα
> ἢ ἔπει ἢ ἔργῳ, τόδε μοι κρήηνον ἐέλδωρ·
> τίμησόν μοι υἱόν, ὃς ὠκυμορώτατος ἄλλων
> ἔπλετ᾽·

> Father Zeus, if ever I have done you service among the immortals by word or deed, grant me this wish, and show your favour to my son, who is short-lived beyond all other men. (*Il.* 1.503-6)

Thetis says surprisingly little, which, in itself, is significant: the effect of no mention of Achilles' story is to give emphasis to the word ὠκυμορώτατος (505).[17] Thetis secured Zeus' survival by giving birth to a mortal child. Therefore, by employing this word, she alludes to the *greatest* favour she has done Zeus: she did *not* activate her fatal power by giving birth to a child mightier than he. As Slatkin argues, Zeus' sovereignty is guaranteed at the cost of Achilles' mortality.[18] Because her request concerns Achilles' fame, it is much more effective for Thetis to mention his mortality than the story of Zeus' binding. Had the matter *only* concerned Zeus and Thetis, then Zeus' rescue would have provided sufficient reason for the return of a favour. However, the favour she asks is concerned with Achilles' glory.

I. The Threat of Thetis

As a hidden subtext, the story of the marriage between Thetis and Peleus becomes all the more powerful and significant as the justification for her supplication.

Achilles does not appeal to Zeus directly because *only* Thetis can make *this* particular appeal.[19] Having a decisive card to play, and being an immortal herself, it is Thetis who can translate the will of Achilles into the will of Zeus.[20] Moreover, only Thetis-the-mother can so forcefully relate the request to the uncertainty of succession – the ultimate threat to Zeus.

The groundwork which establishes Achilles' mortality is thus laid, and Thetis' supplication begins in earnest. The framework of supplication – invocation, reciprocal appeal, then precise request – is conventional. We notice exactly the same pattern occurring previously in the prayer of Chryses (1.37-42): invocation (37-9), reciprocal appeal (39-40), request (41-2). The parallel structure is pointed: just as Chryses' prayer is accepted by Apollo, so too should Thetis' prayer be accepted by Zeus. Chryses' prayer, as well as having its own significance, thus functions as a preparatory intertext which underscores Thetis' supplication: it offers a precedent for the successful conclusion of her appeal.

Zeus does not answer Thetis at once; there is, as Kirk puts it, 'a long and dramatic silence'.[21] This silence adds tension to the scene, capturing Zeus' hesitance to accept or reject her supplication. Then, Thetis offers her second speech:

νημερτὲς μὲν δή μοι ὑπόσχεο καὶ κατάνευσον,
ἢ ἀπόειπ᾽, ἐπεὶ οὔ τοι ἔπι δέος, ὄφρ᾽ ἐὺ εἰδέω
ὅσσον ἐγὼ μετὰ πᾶσιν ἀτιμοτάτη θεός εἰμι.

Promise me now without fail and nod your assent: or else refuse me, since you have nothing to fear, so that I shall know how far I am the most dishonoured goddess of them all. (*Il.* 1.514-16)

Again the address is brief: she does not cite any deeds beneficial to Zeus, nor give any explanation for her demand, but clings to Zeus' knees (ἐμπεφυυῖα,[22] 513). However, these brief words strike a chord with Zeus. First, ἐπεὶ οὔ τοι ἔπι δέος (515) is particularly significant. Kirk paraphrases the verse as 'since you can do as you like and need have no fear of anyone'.[23] I offer the following interpretation based on implications that we have already explored: Zeus knows that Thetis unbound him by summoning Briareus, and Thetis alone is credited with having had such power in the divine realm.[24] One might paraphrase , 'surely you are almighty, having no cause for fear ...?'[25] The subtext – 'but what I did once, I can do again', meaning that 'I can summon Briareus again, this time, for binding Zeus' – is latently threatening.[26] This is, again, moral blackmail: Zeus needs to remember how much he owes to Thetis and ought to show χάρις, even without any fears prompted by nebulous threats.

Secondly, Thetis' use of ἀτιμοτάτη (516) has a two-fold significance in temporal terms. This single word carries enormous weight: Thetis the mother is twice dishonoured, and her son will never have the power of an immortal. If her present supplication is rejected, dishonour will befall her, just as it did in the past when Zeus refused marriage with her. There is a further relevance: ἀτιμοτάτη also underscores the τιμή of Achilles, for which Thetis now pleads. She pleads for Achilles' honour as compensation for her own *dis*honour – her own lost τιμή.

Zeus confirms the underlying import of her threat when he replies by mentioning Hera:

> ἦ δὴ λοίγια ἔργ᾽ ὅ τέ μ᾽ ἐχθοδοπῆσαι ἐφήσεις
> Ἥρῃ, ὅτ᾽ ἄν μ᾽ ἐρέθῃσιν ὀνειδείοις ἐπέεσσιν·
> ἥ δὲ καὶ αὔτως μ᾽ αἰεὶ ἐν ἀθανάτοισι θεοῖσι   520
> νεικεῖ, καί τέ μέ φησι μάχῃ Τρώεσσιν ἀρήγειν.
> ἀλλὰ σὺ μὲν νῦν αὖτις ἀπόστιχε, μή τι νοήσῃ
> Ἥρη·

This is a grievous trouble – you will set me at odds with Hera, when she will provoke me to anger with her taunting words. Even without this she always accuses me before the immortal gods of helping the Trojans in battle. However, you must go back now, so that Hera does not see anything. (*Il.* 1.518-23)

Why, at this point, does Zeus mention that he is so afraid of Hera, who might *seem* irrelevant to Achilles' case? Hera would oppose a plan to help the Trojans, since she wishes for a Greek victory. However, this cannot be the only reason for Zeus' especial concern, because there are other gods as well who would oppose his plan. Rather, the problem seems to be a domestic one: Thetis' supplication relates to her abortive marriage to Zeus, as discussed above, and his fear of Hera is consequent to that. Hera's taunting words (540-3) confirm that the larger issues of victory and partisanship are not at stake. If we bear in mind the undercurrents noted above, we appreciate better the complex relationships between Zeus, Hera and Thetis which form a potent subtext to the Iliadic narrative.

It is the *Iliad*'s narrative strategy to accentuate this problem of generational strife. In this particular case, the strife manifests itself in the parallel, successful alliances of mother with son against father. The point of Thetis' claim is that Zeus could have been the father of Achilles: just as Gaia claimed her right to take revenge on the basis of Uranus' outrageous behaviour towards her children, so too does Thetis here claim her right on the basis of Zeus' outrageous decision about her marriage. Thetis offers a reminder to Zeus of Achilles' potentiality which was totally eliminated by Zeus' desire to retain cosmic power. In sum, Achilles and Thetis ask Zeus for compensation for their shared, dishonoured fates.

18

2. Phoenix as an example of generational strife in the *Iliad*

The story told by Phoenix (*Il*. 9.447-61) is a telling appearance of the motif of 'generational strife'. An intriguing aspect of this story is the mother's role. Phoenix enters into conflict with his father for the sake of his mother:

οἶον ὅτε πρῶτον λίπον Ἑλλάδα καλλιγύναικα,
φεύγων νείκεα πατρὸς Ἀμύντορος Ὀρμενίδαο,
ὅς μοι παλλακίδος περιχώσατο καλλικόμοιο,
τὴν αὐτὸς φιλέεσκεν, ἀτιμάζεσκε δ᾽ ἄκοιτιν,   450
μητέρ᾽ ἐμήν· ἡ δ᾽ αἰὲν ἐμέ λισσέσκετο γούνων
παλλακίδι προμιγῆναι, ἵν᾽ ἐχθήρειε γέροντα.
τῇ πιθόμην καὶ ἔρεξα· πατὴρ δ᾽ ἐμὸς αὐτίκ᾽ ὀϊσθεὶς
πολλὰ κατηρᾶτο, στυγερὰς δ᾽ ἐπεκέκλετ᾽ Ἐρινῦς,
μή ποτε γούνασιν οἷσιν ἐφέσσεσθαι φίλον υἱὸν   455
ἐξ ἐμέθεν γεγαῶτα· θεοὶ δ᾽ ἐτέλειον ἐπαράς,
Ζεύς τε καταχθόνιος καὶ ἐπαινὴ Περσεφόνεια.
τὸν μὲν ἐγὼ βούλευσα κατακτάμεν ὀξέϊ χαλκῷ·
ἀλλά τις ἀθανάτων παῦσεν χόλον,[27] ὅς ῥ᾽ ἐνὶ θυμῷ
δήμου θῆκε φάτιν καὶ ὀνείδεα πόλλ᾽ ἀνθρώπων,   460
ὡς μὴ πατροφόνος μετ᾽ Ἀχαιοῖσιν καλεοίμην.

... as I was when I first left Hellas, the land of lovely women, running away from the quarrel with my father Amyntor, son of Ormenos. He was enraged at me over his beautiful-haired concubine. He was giving his love to her without respect for his own wife, my mother, who constantly took me by the knees and entreated me to make love to this girl first, so that she would hate the old man. I agreed and did so. My father realised at once and wished many curses on me, calling up the hateful Erinyes, that he should never have to take a dear son born to me on his lap: and his curses were fulfilled by the gods, Zeus of the underworld and terrible Persephone. I planned to kill him with the sharp bronze. But one of the immortals stopped my fury, reminding me of the talk of my people and all the reproaches of men, so that I would not have the name of parricide among the Achaeans. (*Il*. 9.447-61)

The omission of explanatory details serves to render the narrative of this story rather inconsequential.[28] The main line of the story is this: Phoenix's father, Amyntor, brings home a concubine; Phoenix is persuaded by his mother to seduce the concubine; when his father finds out, he curses his son with childlessness;[29] as a result, Phoenix plans to kill him. The last part of this passage (9.458-61) is missing from the manuscripts and scholia, but it is hardly surprising that Phoenix planned to kill his father.[30] Multiple interpretations of the story have been proposed,[31] but I merely note two valuable points suggested by Alden: first, the story makes Achilles identify with Phoenix, for both have quarrelled with a superior about a woman; secondly, the story implies unpleasant consequences if Achilles persists with his quarrel.[32] However, I suggest that the story of

Phoenix has two further functions: first, it shows, on a broader scale, the story-pattern of generational strife in which mother and son co-operate in protest against husband and father; secondly, it offers a new perspective on Peleus (see Section 4 of this chapter). Phoenix contrived to help his mother and, at the same time, to overcome his father. Just as Gaia plays the decisive role in the major succession myth, here, too, another mother catalyses this generational strife: she knew what to do, she persuaded her son, and Phoenix followed her instructions. Mothers can be regarded as dangerous because they establish a close relationship with their sons, who, being young and vigorous, are capable of overcoming their fathers.[33] As the phrase ἵν᾽ ἐχθήρειε γέροντα (9.452) shows, Phoenix's mother foregrounds his youth and superior vigour. In spite of the fact that the problem was originally between husband and wife, once the son intervenes, it shifts to a conflict between father and son (and, there is no further mention of the mother after she successfully persuades Phoenix). The mother is dangerous, but the real threat to the father comes, eventually, from his own son.

3. Telemachus as an example of generational strife in the *Odyssey*

The bow-contest

The *Odyssey*, too, presents us with an example of the potential for conflict that may exist between a father and his son. The scene of the bow-contest in Book 21 offers interpreters some complex problems, among which I would single out two in particular: (1) why does Telemachus attempt to join the bow-contest (*Od.* 21.113) which aims primarily at deciding Penelope's new husband? (2) What do Telemachus' words (*Od.* 21.113-17) really mean? It has been thought that the stories about Telemachus in the *Odyssey* are based on 'the motif of seeking the father' or 'the motif of helping the father'. I suggest, however, that the narrative contains another motif, the conflict between fathers and sons, which also lies in the background behind the questions enumerated above. As I see it, the poet of the *Odyssey* has selected and rearranged aspects of this motif with deliberate intent, and that if we draw out the implications of this motif, the troublesome scene of Telemachus at the bow-contest becomes less abstruse.[34]

Telemachus' joining the bow-contest

First, let us examine the question of why Telemachus attempted to string the bow (*Od.* 21.113). This episode is problematic because there is no good reason for his taking part in the contest. As the rightful heir of the household, Telemachus might need to show here the authority and strength of character which he lacked in the assembly scene of Book

2.35-256.[35] However, it still seems strange that Telemachus, the son of Penelope, joined the contest which was designed to select a new husband for his mother. If, as Rutherford writes, he had wanted to demonstrate his authority, it would be difficult to explain why he stopped stringing the bow at Odysseus' nodding; Telemachus surely lost authority through this action.[36] Another prize of the bow-contest, although it is not narrated as such, might be the acquisition of royal power over the whole of Ithaca.[37] In this sense, Telemachus' joining the bow-contest might be considered an announcement that he too will be one of the candidates for succession to the throne. However, Telemachus knows already that his father has returned: thus any intent to gain the realm in this fashion certainly rests on faulty logic. What, then, is the significance of his joining the contest?

This question must be related to how Telemachus is presented in this epic. In the *Telemachia* (Books 1-4 of the *Odyssey*), it is emphasised that Telemachus is very much like his father: Mentes (Athena) notes that the shape of his head and his eyes are quite similar to those of his father (1.208-9); Nestor compares their like manner of speaking (3.124); Helen mentions his face (4.141-4); Menelaus notes his legs, hands, eyes, the shape of his head, and his hair (4.148-50). All of the people who meet Telemachus point out that he resembles his father in very many aspects of his appearance. It is natural, also, to focus solely on the physical similarity of father and son at this early stage of the narrative, when Telemachus, who is powerless against the suitors, can be seen to possess few of the qualities of the true hero, Odysseus.

However, we note on closer inspection that evidence is presented even at an early stage for the notion that Telemachus possesses the potential to become a great hero by taking revenge against the suitors (1.294-6). He is compared, for instance, to Orestes, that role-model for familial vengeance (1.298; 3.197-200). At 1.40-1, Zeus provides an ominous prefiguration of this potential for the young son to avenge the father and regain his property once he has grown up. Telemachus' potentiality is thus already implicitly foreshadowed at the beginning of the epic. Against this background of the son's growth towards heroic proportions, the scene of the bow-contest functions as the realisation of expectations about Telemachus. One might suggest that the reiterated comparisons of son to father have been steering us towards this climactic moment when the two appear together and of equal heroic stature.

καί νύ κε δή ῥ᾽ ἐτάνυσσε βίῃ τὸ τέταρτον ἀνέλκων,
ἀλλ᾽ Ὀδυσεὺς ἀνένευε καὶ ἔσχεθεν ἱέμενόν περ.

Now he [Telemachus] could have strung the bow when he tried with all his might for the fourth time, but Odysseus gave him a sign by nodding and stopped him, despite his eagerness. (21.128-9)

The unreal condition κε ... ἐτάνυσσε implies that Telemachus would have been successful in stringing his father's bow, thus providing the definitive proof that he had become a true hero, possessing the same capacity and power as his father.

The youthful Telemachus said, 'My mother certainly says that I am Odysseus' son, but I do not know' (1.215-16). However in the bow-scene, we see the moment where he becomes conscious that he is truly the son of Odysseus, as he almost strings his heroic father's bow. Odysseus, too, recognises and confirms that fact, as is signalled by his nodding to Telemachus. We might conclude, therefore, that Telemachus' attendance at the bow-contest is intended to confirm that he has grown up to become 'the son with similar power to his father'.

Telemachus' attempt at stringing the bow is, however, suddenly stopped by his father with a nod, as mentioned above. The nod was a secret and tacit sign that was not intended to be recognised as such by the suitors; if they had noticed the communication, it would surely have brought serious danger to Odysseus. This tacit sign, enabling father and son alone to recognise their blood bond, transforms the function of this scene further, becoming a sort of *anagnôrisis* between Odysseus and Telemachus, although the one who shows the proof is here reversed from the normal pattern.

The usual story pattern of the *anagnôrisis* in the *Odyssey* plays out by showing a definite proof of Odysseus' identity, such as his scar from the wild boar (19.392-3 to Eurycleia; 21.219 to Eumaeus and the cowherd; 24.331 to Laertes) or his knowledge of a secret that only the genuine Odysseus could know, such as that the bed was made from a living olive tree (23.188-202 to Penelope). These are the attractive 'recognitions' in which a touch of folklore remains. In the case of Telemachus no such *anagnôrisis* is offered: he simply believes Odysseus' words that this wanderer is his own father (16.202-14). The two kinds of *anagnôrisis* (the scar and the leg of the bed) perhaps belonged to 'the motif of homecoming of the wanderer' and that of 'choosing the husband by bow-contest'. Neither of these motifs has any particular link with a son (cf. n. 34), but one may presume that such powerful kinds of *anagnôrisis* created a demand for the story of the recognition of Telemachus. The demonstration that he possesses a power similar to that of his father may be regarded as a kind of *anagnôrisis* in the sense that there can be no more definite proof of the relationship of father and son than that Telemachus alone was his father's equal with the bow.[38] In that crucial, silently acknowledged moment, Telemachus is presented as being mighty enough to help his father.

Thus Telemachus' unexpected joining in the bow-contest functions first as the fulfilment of the potential presented at the very beginning of this epic, of Telemachus' fully grown character as 'the son who is like his father'; and, second, the scene allows an *anagnôrisis* between father and son. The moment of recognition – Odysseus' nod of warning and Telemachus' obedience – is decisive. By presenting a reversal of the motif of 'the defeat of the father by the mighty son' into the 'the mighty son who could help his father', the poet of the *Odyssey* has weakened the sense of menace that was presented by Telemachus' taking up the bow (that is, in order to usurp the kingship of his father).

Telemachus' speech

Secondly, let us examine the problematic speech of Telemachus in the scene of the bow-contest (*Od.* 21.113-17). I cite two published translations illustrating the different interpretations that the passage has suggested:

καὶ δέ κεν αὐτὸς ἐγὼ τοῦ τόξου πειρησαίμην·
εἰ δέ κεν ἐντανύσω διοϊστεύσω τε σιδήρου,
οὔ κέ μοι ἀχνυμένῳ τάδε δώματα πότνια μήτηρ   115
λείποι ἅμ᾿ ἄλλῳ ἰοῦσ᾿, ὅτ᾿ ἐγὼ κατόπισθε λιποίμην
οἷός τ᾿ ἤδη πατρὸς ἀέθλια κάλ᾿ ἀνελέσθαι.

And I myself should be glad to make trial of the bow. Perhaps I may string it and shoot clean through the iron; then I should not grieve to see my mother forsake this house in another's company, if I myself remained behind with prowess enough to take upon me such feats of mastery as my father's. (Tr. W. Shewring)

And I would like to try with this bow myself. If I tauten it and shoot through the iron, my lady mother would not, to my sorrow, leave this house, going with someone else, when I should be left behind already able to take off my father's fine prizes.[39] (Tr. R.D. Dawe)

When Telemachus offers the contest to the suitors, he announces that he would like to try the bow first. The phrase καὶ δέ κεν αὐτὸς ἐγὼ ('besides, I too', 21.113) suggests that he speaks as if a sudden thought has struck him;[40] but the role in which he casts himself seems ill-judged, occurring as it does in such a critical situation. The repeated mention of weeping and lament emphasises the moment's impact: when Penelope takes out the bow, she weeps aloud (κλαῖε μάλα λιγέως, 21.56); she laments with many tears (πολυδακρύτοιο γόοιο, 21.57); Eumaeus breaks down in tears (δακρύσας δ᾿ Εὔμαιος, 21.82), and the cowherd too begins to weep (κλαῖε δὲ βουκόλος, 21.83). All these phrases indicate that the time has finally come for Penelope to leave the house. In such a desperate situation, why has Telemachus taken it upon himself to act in this way? It appears as though Telemachus becomes one of the suitors in the contest for Penelope.

Much discussion has centred on the interpretation of the following difficult verses (21.115-17). Telemachus uses two optatives, λείποι and λιποίμην, at the beginning and end of line 116. The use of this mood stresses the uncertainty of the moment, and causes us to wonder about Telemachus' intentions. Interpretations of these verses follow two main lines of approach, depending on whether one takes οὔ (115) with μοι ἀχνυμένῳ in the same verse or with λείποι in 116: that is, (1) 'I would not be sorry if my mother were to leave, so long as I should remain here' (or 'while I were left behind', that is, if once Telemachus can prove he is as good as his father by using the bow, then he will not care if Penelope departs);[41] or, (2) 'she will not have to leave to my sorrow as long as I remain'; that is, by winning the contest he will retain his mother as the prize.[42] The choice between these two interpretations rests on one's rendering of ἀέθλια (117). Stanford shows a degree of uncertainty and comments that he 'diffidently' prefers the former.[43] Those who prefer the former interpretation take the word as 'the contests' (Monro)[44] or 'the weapons' (Hayman); Russo et al. offer no comment on ἀέθλια.

There is little doubt that the word ἄεθλον can designate Penelope, since it is announced by her that the prize in this contest is *herself*:

ἀλλ᾽ ἐμὲ ἱέμενοι γῆμαι θέσθαι τε γυναῖκα.
ἀλλ᾽ ἄγετε, μνηστῆρες, ἐπεὶ τόδε φαίνετ᾽ ἄεθλον·
θήσω γὰρ μέγα τόξον Ὀδυσσῆος θείοιο·

... but [you] always desire to marry me and make me your wife. So, come, suitors, since this is the prize shown before you. I shall now place the great bow of godlike Odysseus ... (*Od.* 21.72-4)

She describes herself as ἄεθλον, as R.D. Dawe translates, 'Come, suitors, now that the prize is here to be seen' (73). Telemachus repeats her use of ἄεθλον at 106, which is exactly the same as verse 73 above:

ἀλλ᾽ ἄγετε, μνηστῆρες, ἐπεὶ τόδε φαίνετ᾽ ἄεθλον,
οἵη νῦν οὐκ ἔστι γυνὴ κατ᾽ Ἀχαιΐδα γαῖαν,

But come, suitors, since this is the prize shown before you. Such a lady as she is not now to be found in the Achaean land ... (*Od.* 21.106-7)

Telemachus confirms that Penelope is the prize. Moreover, he admits that he is extraordinarily excited in this situation. His curious words (102-5) sharply reveal his emotion:

ὢ πόποι, ἦ μάλα με Ζεὺς ἄφρονα θῆκε Κρονίων·
μήτηρ μέν μοί φησι φίλη, πινυτή περ ἐοῦσα,
ἄλλῳ ἅμ᾽ ἕψεσθαι νοσφισσαμένη τόδε δῶμα·
αὐτὰρ ἐγὼ γελόω καὶ τέρπομαι ἄφρονι θυμῷ.

Oh, surely Zeus, the son of Cronus, has driven me out of my wits; my own beloved mother, sensible as she is, tells me that she will leave this house, following another man; while I am laughing and delighted in my witless heart. (*Od.* 21.102-5)

24

His words indicate some sort of 'play-acting' on his part. He is now enthusiastic to have the contest in order to determine who could obtain the prize, Penelope. Since Telemachus knows that Odysseus has already returned to his house, how should we interpret his words? It looks as if Telemachus is excited because he himself is hoping to get the prize, if he takes part in the contest.

In spite of admitting that Penelope is the prize, Telemachus uses at 117 a different word, ἀέθλια (the neuter plural, from the adjective ἀέθλιος), for what he hopes to accomplish. Interpretations of these words are, again, twofold: the first takes ἄεθλον (73, 106) and ἀέθλια (117) to convey a similar significance; the second reads them with different meanings. If the former holds true, one plausible reading of verse 117 is, 'I would (hereafter) be able to take up my father's glorious prize, Penelope.' This reading might offer a better understanding of Telemachus' conspicuous excitement during the efficient preparations which so amaze the suitors (118-23). Then, Telemachus declares that he will try the bow in order to remain in the house, to take Penelope and the kingship of Ithaca.[45]

If we follow the latter interpretation, the difference in meaning between the two words, ἄεθλον and ἀέθλια, has a significant effect on our perception of Telemachus' characterisation. Although both Penelope and Telemachus recognise that the prize of the bow-contest is Penelope, Telemachus now changes the word to ἀέθλια at 117 – implying that he will join the contest not for Penelope, but for the 'prizes'. By this change, his intention is made ambiguous (perhaps it would include ownership of the palace, or the kingship of Ithaca); and, significantly, the notion of incest is avoided. The Oedipus story is told in *Od.* 11.271-80, where the emphasis is on Epicasta's ignorance (and, by implication, the ignorance of Oedipus, 272-3), the ἄλγεα of Oedipus (275, 279), and the suicide of Epicaste (277-8). Although Oedipus' deed is not denounced explicitly, the *Odyssey* certainly casts incest in a negative light. Similarly, in the passage under discussion, Telemachus would not countenance marriage with his mother: for this reason the word ἀέθλια might be tendered in tactful exchange for ἄεθλον.

This latter interpretation suits Telemachus' 'decent' character. However, if we think about story patterns in more general terms, the motif of the son competing with his father – in this case, for his father's wife – could be applied also to this passage. That is, at the very least, we might suggest that the potential for competition between father and son (implied by the contest) is intensified by these ambiguous, contextual hints.

Of course, Telemachus fails even to string the bow. I will cite verses 21.128-9 again:

καί νύ κε δή ῥ' ἐτάνυσσε βίῃ τὸ τέταρτον ἀνέλκων,
ἀλλ' Ὀδυσεὺς ἀνένευε καὶ ἔσχεθεν ἱέμενόν περ.

Now he [Telemachus] could have strung the bow when he tried with all his might for the fourth time, but Odysseus gave him a sign by nodding and stopped him, despite his eagerness. (*Od.* 21.128-9)

Telemachus would have succeeded in stringing the bow had Odysseus not intervened with a nod of warning. It is significant that Odysseus does not stop Telemachus initially, and only intervenes when he almost succeeds. It could have been the suitors who stopped him: this would be more predictable in a situation where he is their competitor. After all, in this plot, Odysseus is only beggar and spectator. The suitors have good reason for stopping him, but, of course, so has Odysseus. Why, then, did he not stop Telemachus when he first announced that he would try the bow? What is at stake should Telemachus win? The delay serves a three-fold function: first, the narrative function of provoking suspense; second, the demonstration that Telemachus is deemed worthy enough by his father to pose a potential threat; finally, it could even presage an ironic situation in which Telemachus, as the successful son, wins for his prize Penelope, his own mother. However, of primary importance in this scene is an insidious growth of tension between father and son, and we see that the mounting crisis between the suitors and Odysseus is paralleled in a similar potential friction between son and father.

Reasons for introducing the motif of father-son conflict into the Odyssey

(a) The story of Odysseus' death

Why would the motif of 'the conflict between father and son', which looks irrelevant to the relation between Odysseus and Telemachus, intrude into this epic? This question is closely related, firstly, to the story of the death of Odysseus. According to the *Telegony*, Odysseus was unwittingly killed by his own son Telegonus. In the *Odyssey*, Teiresias foretells the death of Odysseus; 'gentle Death will come to you [Odysseus] out of the sea (ἐξ ἁλός)' (11.134-5). The phrase ἐξ ἁλός could be interpreted as either 'from the sea' or 'away from the sea'. The former may designate that Odysseus will be killed by Telegonus who will come over the sea (from the island Aiaie); the latter, that he will die in an inland place, away from the sea, not during his journey and adventures on the sea. Such a prophecy implies that the poet of the *Odyssey* knew the story of Odysseus' death which is told in the *Telegony*. Odysseus' death at the hands of Telegonus is attested not only by the *Telegony,* but also, for example, by Apollodorus (7.36), the scholia to *Od.* 11.134 and Hyginus (127).[46] Given that these texts considerably post-date the *Odyssey*, one might think that the poet of the *Odyssey* did not know that particular story. There is no doubt, however, that the unanimity of these later texts on Odysseus' death at Telegonus' hands suggests that the story belongs to an old tradition. There is no reason to assume that the poet of the *Odyssey* did not know the story that Odysseus was killed by his own son.[47]

I. The Threat of Thetis

For an audience who knew that Odysseus would be killed by Telegonus at some future time, Telemachus' ambiguous words (21.113-17) might serve to remind them of Odysseus' death at the hands of his own son. As their names suggest, some sort of parallel exists between Telemachus and Telegonus, but it is difficult to determine which son's story is rooted in the older tradition. If the story of Telegonus is older, one might suggest that this extra-narrative story-line is evoked in the background during that moment of crisis between Odysseus and Telemachus. Even if the Telemachean narrative was the only one current at the time, the challenge to the father which is avoided or mitigated in the *Odyssey* still lingers in the text through the audience's familiarity with such stories. The process of making epic from patterns of folk tale presented an ambiguity in the doubled theme of conflict between father and son(s) that the poet may well have recognised and manipulated.

(b) The interactions between the Trojan and Theban epic cycles

A second way in which the motif of conflict between father and son intrudes into the *Odyssey* may be seen in the interactions between the Trojan and Theban epic cycles. It is well known that they have a long history of exchange with each other. For example, Oedipus is mentioned both in the *Iliad* (23.679) and the *Odyssey* (11.271). The mention of Teiresias, the Theban prophet in the *Odyssey* (11.90ff.) who gives indispensable advice for Odysseus' return journey, suggests that the poet of the *Odyssey* must have been quite familiar with the Theban stories. The conflict between father and son which is the basic motif of the Oedipus story could thus have influenced the story of the fate of Odysseus, killed by Telegonus just as Laius was killed by Oedipus.

Thus, by eliminating the father, mothers and sons survive. Generational strife (son overcoming father) is a conspicuous theme in Greek myth; it is characterised by a father's fear of falling to his mightier son, and it constitutes a basic element in many Greek stories. The story of Odysseus, like that of Oedipus, is at the very heart of this tradition.

The rearrangement of the motif in the *Odyssey*, however, offers a revised and opposite significance: the new relationship of concord between father and son, as is categorically signalled by Telemachus' obedience to his father's nod. The crisis of their conflict is averted, and Telemachus is transformed into a help, not a threat, to his father.

The account of the two eagles

On the basis of this understanding of the father-son relation, the episode of the two eagles in flight after Telemachus' speech at the Assembly in Ithaca (*Od.* 2. 146-56), which has been somewhat resistant to satisfactory interpretation, is worth further exploration. Many scholars, and also the scholia (schol. E.H.Q.V. ad 2. 146), unanimously consider that the two

27

eagles which sail down wing to wing signify Odysseus and Telemachus. However, the passage depicting the behaviour of these two eagles is obscure:

> ἀλλ᾽ ὅτε δὴ μέσσην ἀγορὴν πολύφημον ἱκέσθην,
> ἔνθ᾽ ἐπιδινηθέντε τιναξάσθην πτερὰ πυκνά,
> ἐς δ᾽ ἱκέτην πάντων κεφαλάς, ὄσσοτο δ᾽ ὄλεθρον,
> δρυψαμένω δ᾽ ὀνύχεσσι παρειὰς ἀμφί τε δειρὰς
> δεξιὼ ἤϊξαν διὰ οἰκία καὶ πόλιν αὐτῶν.

> But when they were right above the assembly-place with the sound of voices, they wheeled about and shook their thick feathers, sweeping low over all those there, looking threateningly. Then with their talons they ripped at each other's cheeks and neck, and flew away to the right, over the houses and town. (*Od.* 2.150-4)

The two eagles' behaviour at v. 153 is understood in two different ways, either as signifying the vengeance on the suitors by Odysseus and Tele- machus, or as suggesting 'imagery interaction' by a human gesture of mourning.[48] However, both of these interpretations would be difficult: for the former interpretation, the active voice of the verb (δρύψαντε) would be needed, instead of the middle (δρυψαμένω); for the latter, a gesture of mourning would be unlikely for birds.[49] The reflexive word should be taken as implying mutual aggressiveness. But what is the significance of this?

These hostile eagles may be another allusion to the moment of potential crisis and conflict between Odysseus and Telemachus, as is implied in the scene of the stringing the bow by Telemachus. The departure of the eagles apparently in harmony may foretell the result of the crisis between Odysseus and Telemachus: the crisis passes and their conflict is averted. So, as suggested above, the motif of the conflict between father and son is deeply rooted in the *Odyssey* – latent in the episode of the two eagles as well as behind the scenes at the bow-contest.

4. Peleus and Achilles

Hera's upbringing of Thetis

When Hera mentions the marriage of Peleus and Thetis in book 24 of the *Iliad*, she says that she herself raised Thetis:

> αὐτὰρ Ἀχιλλεύς ἐστι θεᾶς γόνος, ἣν ἐγὼ αὐτὴ
> θρέψα τε καὶ ἀτίτηλα καὶ ἀνδρὶ πόρον παράκοιτιν.

> But Achilles is the son of a goddess, whom I myself brought up and reared and gave as wife to a man. (*Il.* 24.59-60)

Recalling Hera's suspicious attitude to Thetis in Book 1, Braswell suggests that the story of Hera's upbringing of Thetis is an invention for this occasion.[50] Braswell's interpretation is supported by Macleod, Willcock, Kirk and Richardson;[51] however, from the perspective of succession myth, Thetis' upbringing is of major significance to the narrative. As manifold episodes in the *Iliad* demonstrate, Hera is the goddess who persistently opposes the power of Zeus. Hera's favour towards Thetis is consonant with her interest in Thetis' potentiality, since she hoped that Thetis' son might overthrow the power of Zeus. Rather than being treated as an invention *per se*, the story of the upbringing of Thetis is better located in the echelons of succession myth on which I have elaborated.[52]

The phrase θρέψα τε καὶ ἀτίτηλα (24.60) is important. Following the scholia, Willcock notes that these words signify that Hera nursed Thetis as a small child:[53]

ἐξ ἀταλῆς ἐπεμελησάμην
I took care of her from when she was a tender child. (schol. T)

ἔτι ἀταλὴν ἤτοι νέαν καὶ ἁπαλὴν οὖσαν ἀνεθρεψάμην
I brought her up when she was still tender, that is, young and soft. (schol. b)

As both scholia explain, the connotation of ἀτίτηλα is not only to bring up but also to cherish the baby gently. This implies that Hera lavished special care and attention on Thetis. Moreover, the phrase has a particular interest, since the same two verbs recur in another passage, *Theogony* 480 (Gaia nourishes and raises Zeus):

Ζῆνα μέγαν· τὸν μέν οἱ ἐδέξατο Γαῖα πελώρη
Κρήτῃ ἐν εὐρείῃ τρεφέμεν ἀτιταλλέμεναί τε

... great Zeus. Mighty Earth accepted him from her [Rhea] to bring him up and rear in broad Crete. (*Theog.* 479-80)

In the *Theogony*, Gaia received Zeus from Rhea, nurturing him for the purpose of his ultimate de-throning of Cronus (468-74). I propose that, at *Theogony* 480, these two verbs signify the nurture of potential challengers to paternal sovereignty.[54] Therefore, in the context of *Iliad* 24, the subtext of Hera's raising of Thetis provides another marker of Hera's veiled intention: it also provides an important reference which ought to be added to our core of traditional material concerning succession myth.

The marriage of Zeus and Thetis

A fragment of the *Cypria*, paralleled in Hesiod (*Cyp.* fr. 2 *PEG* and Hes. fr. 151M=210 M-W), offers a truncated version of the story of the marriage of Thetis and Zeus:

ὁ δὲ τ]ὰ Κύπ[ρια ποιήσας ῞Η]ραι χαρ[ιζομένη]ν φεύγειν αὐ[τοῦ

29

τὸ]ν γάμον, Δ[ία δὲ ὀμ]όσαι χολω[θέντ]α διότι θνη[τῶι συ]νοικίσει·
κα[ὶ παρ᾽ Η]σιόδωι δὲ κε[ῖται τ]ὸ παραπλήσ[ιον.

The author of the *Cypria* says that Thetis, as a favour to Hera, refused marriage with Zeus; he was angry and swore that he would marry her to a mortal. A similar story is found in Hesiod. (*Cyp.* fr. 2 *PEG* and Hes. fr. 151 M = 210 M-W)

It is significant that this account makes no mention of Themis or Prometheus, but gives Ἥραι χαρ[ιζομένη]ν as the sole reason why Zeus' marriage with Thetis did not proceed. The 'favour to Hera' is supposed to allude to the story of Thetis' upbringing by Hera.[55]

This account raises several issues. First, *why* should the unwillingness of Thetis (because she wished to do Hera a favour) be the real reason why the marriage was prevented? Had Zeus truly desired to marry Thetis, would not her willingness or unwillingness have been irrelevant for the almighty Zeus?[56] Indeed, the circumstances surrounding the marriage of Peleus and Thetis demonstrate that her rejection of the marriage is not considered an issue, nor was it the reason why it was prevented.[57] Secondly, one might expect that it would be Hera who raised an objection to their marriage – for Hera's primary role in Greek myth is that of the 'jealous wife' harassing the unwilling lovers of Zeus.[58] On the contrary, Hera keeps silent, raising no objections.

Admittedly, this is a truncated version of the story, with few details: but to clarify the matter, let us turn to the version in Apollonius Rhodius (4.790-804), which supplies further illumination:

ἀλλά σε γὰρ δή   790
ἐξέτι νηπυτίης αὐτὴ τρέφον, ἠδ᾽ ἀγάπησα
ἔξοχον ἀλλάων αἵ τ᾽ εἰν ἁλὶ ναιετάουσιν,
οὕνεκεν οὐκ ἔτλης εὐνῇ Διὸς ἱεμένοιο
λέξασθαι (κείνῳ γὰρ ἀεὶ τάδε ἔργα μέμηλεν,
ἠὲ σὺν ἀθανάταις ἠὲ θνητῇσιν ἰαύειν),   795
ἀλλ᾽ ἐμέ γ᾽ αἰδομένη καὶ ἐνὶ φρεσὶ δειμαίνουσα
ἠλεύω· ὁ δ᾽ ἔπειτα πελώριον ὅρκον ὄμοσσε,
μήποτέ σ᾽ ἀθανάτοιο θεοῦ καλέεσθαι ἄκοιτιν.
ἔμπης δ᾽ οὐ μεθίεσκεν ὀπιπτεύων ἀέκουσαν,
εἰσότε οἱ πρέσβεια Θέμις κατέλεξεν ἅπαντα,   800
ὡς δή τοι πέπρωται ἀμείνονα πατρὸς ἑοῖο
παῖδα τεκεῖν· τῷ καί σε λιλαιόμενος μεθέηκεν
δείματι, μή τις ἑοῦ ἀντάξιος ἄλλος ἀνάσσοι
ἀθανάτων, ἀλλ᾽ αἰὲν ἑὸν κράτος εἰρύοιτο.

Now, I [Hera] have brought you [Thetis] up from infancy, and loved you more than any other goddesses who dwell in the sea, because you refused to lie in Zeus' bed though he longed for you – that is what he always desires, he wants to sleep with women, mortals or immortals – but out of respect for me and because you were scared, you kept away from him. He then swore a solemn oath that no immortal god would ever call you his wife. Yet despite your refusal, and though you were unwilling, he kept his eyes on you, until the venerable Themis told him in detail how you were destined to bear a son mightier than his father; though he still wanted you, he gave you up, being scared lest some rival should oust him as being king of the gods: he wished to keep his power for ever. (*Argonautica* 4.790-804)

Apollonius, too, narrates that Hera raised Thetis from a baby, and loved her (791). Two reasons are offered as to why the marriage between Zeus and Thetis did not occur: (a) Thetis first refused the marriage, as a favour to Hera (796); (b) Zeus, fearing that Thetis might bear a son mightier than himself, subsequently reneged because of Themis' prophecy (800-2). These two reasons are interrelated and, as such, highlight the same message – that of Thetis' potentiality: Thetis was favourably disposed towards Hera who had raised her; Hera, in the knowledge that Thetis could bear a son mightier than his father, reared her willingly. For this reason, Zeus refused the marriage. We discover that Hera's strategy was to create a god, since she herself was incapable of bearing a son mightier than Zeus: and even if this son was born from another goddess, he would at least be capable of usurping the Olympian.

In Apollonius' account, Hera's rhetoric is shrewd, as Hunter points out.[59] According to Hera, although Thetis refused marriage with Zeus, he did not stop attempting to seduce her against her will, until Themis announced the prophecy (799-800). Hera's speech makes clear that Themis' prophecy was the true reason for the marriage's prevention, seeing that Thetis' private emotions meant nothing to Zeus prior to it.[60]

Apollodorus (3.13.5) gives three explanations for the abortive marriage: (a) Zeus (and Poseidon) withdrew as a result of Themis' prophecy; (b) Prometheus declared that the son born to Zeus by Thetis would be lord of heaven; (c) Thetis would not marry Zeus because she had been brought up by Hera. We see that Apollodorus differs from Apollonius Rhodius only by adding Prometheus' prophecy:[61]

ἔνιοι δέ φασι, Διὸς ὁρμῶντος ἐπὶ τὴν ταύτης συνουσίαν, εἰρηκέναι Προμηθέα τὸν ἐκ ταύτης αὐτῷ γεννηθέντα οὐρανοῦ δυναστεύσειν.

But some say that when Zeus was eager to make love with her, Prometheus declared that the son borne to him by her would rule over heaven. (*Biblio.* 3.13.5)

These examples demonstrate that the story of Thetis' upbringing is associated with her potential marriage to Zeus; both accounts are closely related, and the common denominator is Hera's scheme to usurp Zeus' sovereignty: Hera's hatred of Zeus would lead her to raise Thetis in order that the sea-goddess might marry Zeus and have a son mightier than he.[62] Although the *Cypria*, Apollonius Rhodius and Apollodorus offer Thetis' objections as the reason why the marriage did not take place, another alternative lies in the prophecies of Themis or Prometheus.[63] Of course, Hera's plan for the marriage was ultimately unsuccessful, since Zeus was informed of the prophecy. However, had he not been informed, Thetis could have served Hera by marrying him. We may conclude, therefore, that although the *Cypria* and later writers suggest that Thetis refused to marry Zeus as a favour to Hera,[64] she might actually have *wanted* to marry him, *also* as a favour to Hera. This interpretation also helps to illuminate the question why Thetis tried to refuse Peleus' hand.

In the *Homeric Hymn to Apollo* (321), Hera mentions Thetis in a conspicuous way. After speaking of Hephaestus, whom she threw from heaven down to the ocean because he was lame, she suddenly speaks of Thetis:

καὶ νῦν νόσφιν ἐμεῖο τέκε γλαυκῶπιν Ἀθήνην,
ἣ πᾶσιν μακάρεσσι μεταπρέπει ἀθανάτοισιν·   315
αὐτὰρ ὅ γ᾽ ἠπεδανὸς γέγονεν μετὰ πᾶσι θεοῖσι
παῖς ἐμὸς Ἥφαιστος ῥικνὸς πόδας ὃν τέκον αὐτὴ
ῥίψ᾽ ἀνὰ χερσὶν ἑλοῦσα καὶ ἔμβαλον εὐρέϊ πόντῳ·
ἀλλά ἑ Νηρῆος θυγάτηρ Θέτις ἀργυρόπεζα
δέξατο καὶ μετὰ ᾗσι κασιγνήτῃσι κόμισσεν·   320
ὡς ὄφελ᾽ ἄλλο θεοῖσι χαρίσσασθαι μακάρεσσι.
σχέτλιε ποικιλομῆτα τί νῦν μητίσεαι ἄλλο;

... and now without me, he has given birth to bright-eyed Athena, who stands out among all the blessed immortals. But my son Hephaestus has grown to be weak-legged and lame among all the gods. I took him with my own hands, the one I myself produced, and threw him into the broad sea. But Thetis, the silver-footed daughter of Nereus, received him and looked after him together with her sisters. I wish she had done the blessed gods some other favour! O stubborn and cunning one! What else will you now devise? (*Hymn. Apol.* 314-22)

The disjointedness of the narrative is not without its problems: some editors assume a lacuna between 317 and 318.[65] In addition, Hera leaves the meaning of ἄλλο open, and does not specify what she would have preferred Thetis to do; immediately following this oblique comment, she changes the topic to Zeus and her fear of some new contrivance. It is clear that Thetis' act – saving Hephaestus in the ocean – was not what Hera wanted. In this sense, one interpretation of ἄλλο would be 'leaving Hephaestus to perish instead of saving him'. However this partial interpretation does not explain why destroying Hephaestus would be a favour for the gods (321).

I propose that Hera's words imply that her intention was cosmic in scale. What was it that could have been helpful not only for Hera herself, but also for the other gods? It is worth re-examining the context in detail: Zeus alone begat Athena, and she is most excellent by far among 'all the blessed gods' (314-15), whereas Hephaestus was born lame among 'all the gods' (316). The narrative concentrates on the production of offspring and its ramifications for the gods. Thus, when Hera wishes that Thetis had done something else 'to benefit the blessed gods' (θεοῖσι χαρίσσασθαι μακάρεσσι, 321), we may read this to denote, again, the potentiality that underscores Thetis' characterisation as a child-bearer in the *Iliad*: her potential ability to give birth to a son who is mightier than his father. In sum, had Thetis married Zeus, and her son overthrown him, *this* is what would have been beneficial to the blessed gods who are themselves subject to Zeus.

Since Hera's own son, Hephaestus, is handicapped, she would wish for a powerful child from Thetis. *If only* Thetis could have fulfilled her potentiality, and given birth to a child by Zeus, Hera could have avenged herself on her adversary. On this reading, Hera's ἄλλο would carry the implication, 'Instead of saving Hephaestus, if she had given birth to a child who was far mightier than Zeus.'[66] Any precise definition of ἄλλο remains open, but my hypothetical interpretation has the advantages of complementing both immediate and intertextual contexts. That is, we can certainly conjecture that an ancient audience, familiar with the stories surrounding Thetis, would have been reminded of other references to Thetis' essential potentiality by this pointed ἄλλο.

Antagonism between Zeus and Hera (with the other gods)

Hera is always conscious of the other gods and regards her situation not as a personal problem between divine husband and wife, but as a problem for the whole divine world.[67] Note, for instance, the clear antagonism in *Iliad* 15 between Zeus, on the one hand, and Hera and the rest of the gods, on the other. After quarrelling with Zeus (*Il.* 15.14-46), Hera returns to Olympus to join the gathering of the gods (ὁμηγερέεσσι δ' ἐπῆλθεν ἀθανάτοισι θεοῖσι, 84-5). In order to facilitate the involvement of the other gods in the quarrel, she emphasises her own inclusion among them (92-148); this explains why she uses the plural pronoun 'we' (not the singular 'I') when speaking of the quarrel, although it was, in fact, between her and Zeus: 'how foolish *we* are, thoughtless to storm against Zeus ...' (104). The word νήπιος is also significant. She appears to regret having resisted Zeus, but actually she is irritated by their past failure, and is still seeking a way to conspire against him. As Janko rightly remarks,[68] 'Hera overtly advises submission, but covertly stirs up revolt.' If Hera intervenes in the succession of the supreme god, the cosmic order will change – and inevitably all the gods will be involved. This is what Hera intends, and for this purpose we see, again, that Hera has a vested interest in the upbringing of Thetis.

To substantiate Hera's purpose, other remarks in the *Homeric Hymn to Apollo* are worth examining. Before the passage concerning Thetis, Hera speaks about Hephaestus in comparison with Athena at 314-22, as cited above. Hera is dissatisfied because her disabled Hephaestus cannot compare with Athena. She must have previously desired a powerful child. It is on this occasion that she speaks about Thetis' rescue of Hephaestus. Let us note, too, that the contrast between Athena's ability and Hephaestus' disability corresponds with Zeus' capability and Hera's incapacity. It is not surprising, therefore, that Hera is prompted to consider using the prophecy about Thetis as her revenge on Zeus.

It is also significant that Hera thinks of Zeus just after mentioning Thetis (322). The two epithets in this verse, σχέτλιε and ποικιλομῆτα, are appropriate expressions in this context for Hera to use of Zeus.[69] She is anxious that Zeus might contrive 'something else' (ἄλλο, 322). In order to compete with Zeus, Hera needs to contrive 'something else' (ἄλλο, 321), which might, as suggested above, be to procure a god (born from Thetis) who will be mightier than Zeus. There is a strong case for suggesting that Hera's hostility to Zeus underlies the passage describing her upbringing of Thetis (*Iliad* 24.59-60). This is supported by the *Homeric Hymn to Apollo* and later sources, such as Apollonius Rhodius and Apollodorus. After Hera has given birth to her crippled child Hephaestus, and rejected him, any hope for revenge must reside in her plan for Thetis.

The marriage of Peleus and Thetis

The marriage of Peleus and Thetis is twice mentioned by Achilles in the *Iliad* at 18.79-93 and 24.534-7. Let us consider the first passage: Achilles is bemoaning Patroclus' death, groaning deeply, βαρὺ στενάχων (18.78); here, especially at lines 84-7, Achilles explicitly says that it is a marriage with an unfortunate outcome:

μῆτερ ἐμή, τὰ μέν ἄρ μοι Ὀλύμπιος ἐξετέλεσσεν·
ἀλλὰ τί μοι τῶν ἦδος, ἐπεὶ φίλος ὤλεθ᾽ ἑταῖρος,   80
Πάτροκλος, τὸν ἐγὼ περὶ πάντων τῖον ἑταίρων,
ἶσον ἐμῇ κεφαλῇ· τὸν ἀπώλεσα, τεύχεα δ᾽ Ἕκτωρ
δηώσας ἀπέδυσε πελώρια, θαῦμα ἰδέσθαι,
καλά· τὰ μὲν Πηλῆϊ θεοὶ δόσαν ἀγλαὰ δῶρα
ἤματι τῷ ὅτε σε βροτοῦ ἀνέρος ἔμβαλον εὐνῇ.   85
αἴθ᾽ ὄφελες σὺ μὲν αὖθι μετ᾽ ἀθανάτης ἁλίῃσι
ναίειν, Πηλεὺς δὲ θνητὴν ἀγαγέσθαι ἄκοιτιν.
νῦν δ᾽ ἵνα καὶ σοὶ πένθος ἐνὶ φρεσὶ μυρίον εἴη
παιδὸς ἀποφθιμένοιο, τὸν οὐχ ὑποδέξεαι αὖτις
οἴκαδε νοστήσαντ᾽, ἐπεὶ οὐδ᾽ ἐμὲ θυμὸς ἄνωγε   90
ζώειν οὐδ᾽ ἄνδρεσσι μετέμμεναι, αἴ κε μὴ Ἕκτωρ
πρῶτος ἐμῷ ὑπὸ δουρὶ τυπεὶς ἀπὸ θυμὸν ὀλέσσῃ,
Πατρόκλοιο δ᾽ ἕλωρα Μενοιτιάδεω ἀποτείσῃ.

Mother, the Olympian has done all this for me. But what pleasure can I get from it, now that my dear friend is killed, Patroclus, a man I honoured above all my companions, as much as my own life? I have lost him, and Hector who killed him has stripped him of my huge armour, that lovely armour, marvellous to see, which the gods gave as a splendid gift to Peleus on the day when they brought you to a mortal man's bed. How I wish that you had stayed in your home with the immortal goddesses of the sea, and that Peleus had married a mortal wife! But in fact, you too would have immeasurable sorrow in your heart; you are going to lose your son, and will never welcome him coming back home again. For I have no wish to live or linger among men, unless, before all else, Hector is struck down by my spear and dies, paying me the price for killing Patroclus, son of Menoetius. (*Il.* 18.79-93)

Thetis had come out of the sea in order to ask Achilles why he was crying (18.65-77): he expresses profound grief at Patroclus' death (18.80-3), explaining its traumatic effect on him. However, his attention then shifts from the death of Patroclus to the marriage of his parents, with the divine armour functioning as the element which connects the two topics. At the news of Patroclus' death, Achilles immediately recognises his own identity and mortality, and thus his parents' marriage surfaces in his thought processes.

When Achilles says to Thetis that 'the gods brought (ἔμβαλον) you to the bed of a mortal man' (85), it is implied that the choice was not hers.[70] He bewails the fact that Thetis did not stay in her home with the immortal goddesses of the sea, leaving Peleus to marry a mortal wife (86-7). Despondent as he is over the circumstances of his parents' marriage, his words can be read as a protest against the will of Zeus who had arranged it in order to deprive Thetis of her potentiality. Achilles' lament, therefore, can be read on two levels: it is not only for the death of Patroclus, but also for himself, since Patroclus' death recalls his parents' fateful marriage, and subsequently his own birth.[71] His double lament is unified at last.

Achilles and Peleus

Although Achilles appears indifferent to his father in *this* passage, elsewhere he is very sympathetic to Peleus. Let us consider the second passage, from book 24, where Achilles' attitude toward Peleus seems much milder. Significantly, the *Iliad* ends with the reconciliation of Achilles and Priam, to whom Achilles compares his own father. The reconciliation is all the more surprising, since the war is not yet over; it is only a truce that Achilles has ordered (24.778-81). This scene is so familiar that a few specific comments will suffice in order to show the importance of Peleus. When Achilles first sees Priam, who has come to supplicate him with an enormous ransom, he is amazed. In this 'most dramatic moment in the whole of the *Iliad*,'[72] a significant simile is deployed – that of a homicide who goes into exile and seeks refuge in the home of a rich man:

ὡς δ' ὅτ' ἂν ἄνδρ' ἄτη πυκινὴ λάβῃ, ὅς τ' ἐνὶ πάτρῃ

φῶτα κατακτείνας ἄλλων ἐξίκετο δῆμον,
ἀνδρὸς ἐς ἀφνειοῦ, θάμβος δ᾽ ἔχει εἰσορόωντας,
ὣς Ἀχιλεὺς θάμβησεν ἰδὼν Πρίαμον θεοειδέα·

As when great folly takes hold of man, who murders someone in his own
country, and comes to another land, to a wealthy man's house, and amazement seizes all those who see his entry, so Achilles was amazed when he saw
godlike Priam. (*Il.* 24.480-3)

This simile could be interpreted as either expressing simple amazement
at the unexpectedness of Priam's arrival,[73] or representing the concept of
pollution which attends bloodshed.[74] These interpretations are valid, but
Richardson is surely correct to point out that the use of this particular
simile suggests that there is more at stake here than mere surprise or
curiosity.[75] Richardson does not specify what this might be, but I contend
that it functions as a subtle reminder of Peleus, since it is he who
frequently accepts suppliants in the *Iliad*, as mentioned below. Further,
this effective encapsulation of Peleus' past behaviour foreshadows Achilles' acceptance of Priam's supplication. Priam's speech, which inspires the
reconciliation, is an example of ring-composition, beginning and ending
with the mention of Peleus:[76]

μνῆσαι πατρὸς σοῖο, θεοῖς ἐπιείκελ᾽ Ἀχιλλεῦ,
τηλίκου ὥς περ ἐγών, ὀλοῷ ἐπὶ γήραος οὐδῷ·

Think of your own father, godlike Achilles, who is the same age as I am, at
the cruel threshold of old age. (*Il.* 24.486-7)

ἀλλ᾽ αἰδεῖο θεούς, Ἀχιλεῦ, αὐτόν τ᾽ ἐλέησον,
μνησάμενος σοῦ πατρός· ἐγὼ δ᾽ ἐλεεινότερός περ,

Fear the gods, then, Achilles, and have pity on me, remembering your own
father. But I am even more pitiable than he (*Il.* 24.503-6)

This appeal emphasises Peleus' vital importance to Priam's supplication
because it enables him to establish an empathetic bond with Achilles.[77] It
is worth considering why Peleus plays such a decisive role in the grand
finale of the epic.[78] As Edwards rightly notes,[79] on the level of narrative
structure, there is a long sequence of father-and-son relationships: Zeus'
loss of his son Sarpedon, and Patroclus' killing of Priam's sons, Lykaon and
Polydorus. In addition, Peleus is characterised as a respectable host, and
this, too, finds an echo in the simile of the rich man (24.480-2). Further to
these observations, I propose that, once again, a resonance of 'generational
myth' is operating, and here it prefigures Priam's successful supplication.

As I have discussed, because of Thetis' potentiality, Achilles might have
been mightier than Zeus. Achilles, however, never could intervene in the
succession myth,[80] and although elsewhere he displays affection for his

father, Peleus, his frustration with his own mortal inadequacy causes him to lament his parents' marriage and his own genealogy. We remember that, at the very beginning of the poem, when Achilles asks Thetis to supplicate Zeus, his rationale was that Zeus *could have been his father*,[81] and that this was also germane to Thetis' claim. Upon Patroclus' death, he expressed his antagonism to the marriage of his parents, protesting against the will of Zeus; but now, faced with the aged Priam, Achilles realises that this generational strife should be peacefully resolved. In this scene, Achilles is reconciled not only with the father of his most hated enemy, but also with his own father, his own genealogy, and his own mortality. His recognition of his own mortal destiny articulates for us a new appreciation of this age-old generational strife: in this case, the younger and mightier son will not overcome, but instead venerate, his father.

Achilles' attitude towards Peleus provides many depictions of an ideal relationship between father and son: Achilles asks Patroclus if there is any news from Phthia to indicate whether Peleus is alive (16.15); and he laments his father, who cannot welcome his son home (18.330-1), and who may no longer be alive or may be suffering the pain of old age (19.334-7). Peleus, too, is affectionate toward his son. His thoughtful farewell messages for Achilles on his departure to Troy are reported by Odysseus (9.252-8), Phoenix (9.438-43), and Achilles himself (23.144-9). Achilles even wishes to live 'in enjoyment of the wealth that old Peleus has won' (9.400). As well as this ideal relationship, the personality of Peleus is carefully depicted as an exemplar of hospitality in the *Iliad*. He welcomes as many as four people to his palace: Nestor (11.772-9), Phoenix (9.480-4), Epeigeus (16.571-4), and Patroclus (23.87-90). It is particularly significant that the last three all come to his house as suppliants, expelled from their own lands because of a homicide or some domestic trouble. There seems to be a very careful attempt to introduce Peleus as a respectful host towards the suppliants who seek refuge in his house.[82]

Note especially the story of Phoenix: Peleus gladly welcomes him, and loves him like a son:[83]

ἐς Πηλῆα ἄναχθ'· ὁ δέ με πρόφρων ὑπέδεκτο,
καί μ' ἐφίλησ' ὡς εἴ τε πατὴρ ὃν παῖδα φιλήσῃ
μοῦνον τηλύγετον πολλοῖσιν ἐπὶ κτεάτεσσι.

... to king Peleus' house. He welcomed me gladly, and loved me as a father loves his only son who is late-born, the heir to a great estate. (*Il.* 9.480-3)

Phoenix is cherished and protected by this substitute-father, Peleus. This characterisation of Peleus as a good father foreshadows the reconciliation of Achilles and Priam. Looking at Priam, Achilles thinks of Peleus: in this sense, Priam is a substitute for Achilles' father. It seems that the stories of Peleus' welcome to suppliants are narrated in preparation for the final scene of the epic – the presentation of a new father-son relationship.[84]

While repeated *rejection* of supplication or prayer is conspicuous throughout the *Iliad*,[85] it is significant that the poem is framed by two *acceptances* of supplication: that of Thetis to Zeus, and Priam to Achilles. Slatkin observes that 'cosmic equilibrium is bought at the cost of human mortality'; 'the alternative would mean perpetual evolution, perpetual violent succession, perpetual disorder ...'; she concludes that 'the wrath of Thetis ... becomes absorbed in the actual wrath of her son.'[86] I would support this interpretation, but I further submit that the characterisation of Peleus is the key to resolving some problems: on the cosmic level, his marriage with Thetis secures Zeus' sovereignty; and on the human level, Achilles' anger evaporates at the recollection of him. Consequently, the suffering of Achilles and the sympathy which he feels for Priam can be more fully understood by recognising the significance of Peleus in the succession myth.[87]

A new reception of the generational strife in Iliad 24

The myth of generational strife resonates throughout the *Iliad*, and it has a profound effect on the poem. There was perhaps an early, lost myth in which Zeus had to fight not only Gigantes and monsters but also his own son,[88] possibly born of Thetis. From the very beginning of the *Iliad*, the motif of 'the son mightier than his father' is clearly recognisable through Achilles' own words, and the poem ends not with the defeat of Hector or the death of Achilles, but, in the most ingenious way, with a (temporarily) peaceful reconciliation between Achilles and Priam, which achieves a completely new understanding of this generational strife. The extraordinarily wrought narrative of the wrath of Achilles progresses from initial desire for heroic τιμή against Agamemnon and Hector, to a realisation of himself and his own mortality. Thus the Διὸς βουλή will be fulfilled: Zeus has now successfully escaped the danger of Thetis' potentiality.[89] As Lynn-George notes,[90] the imperfect verb (Διὸς δ᾽ ἐτελείετο βουλή, 1.5) intimates that Zeus' plan is a process without end and, at the same time, without beginning; certainly, we are not informed when the plan was conceived and when it was fulfilled. Among a multiplicity of possible interpretations of the plan, the reduction of the population of the earth is but one,[91] and in this chapter I have suggested that, in addition, the theme of 'overcoming the threat of a mightier son' must surely be recognised as a deep and subtle undercurrent running through the *Iliad*.

II

The Golden Chain of Hera

The Κόλασις Ἥρας (*Il.* 15.18-33), the story of the binding of Hera with the golden chain, is unique in the *Iliad*: the highest goddess of Olympus is humiliated, bound and hung up by her husband. Its uniqueness might explain why Zenodotus athetised the passage (15.18-31). However, Hera's punishment has a deeper significance in the story than might first appear, and in this chapter I view this passage from the perspective of cosmic strife.[1] The story appears to derive from an earlier tradition of the battle of the gods. Behind Hera's punishment one can detect the vestiges of her challenge to Zeus. Throughout the *Iliad* there are suggestions of threats of rebellion in which Hera acts as a ringleader, and among these accounts, the story of her binding deserves special attention.

Hera's role in the *Iliad* is rather comical. Even when she becomes angry, her behaviour provokes laughter from the audience: for example, when she is jealous of Zeus and Thetis (1.531-67), or when she is furious at being scolded by Zeus (8.432-68). These scenes are amusing because the gods do not behave as one would expect them to, as Xenophanes points out:[2] instead, they are involved in seemingly ordinary domestic troubles.[3] It is understandable, in this respect, that Heracles should state of the gods in Euripides' *Heracles* (1341-4) 'I do not think, have never believed, and will never be convinced that the gods have illicit love affairs or bind each other with chains, or that one can be master of another'. By depicting Hera's story in terms of a punishment by a husband within a family, and by telling it as a story of the remote past, the strategy of the poet of the *Iliad* seems to be to make the story laughable. However, as I will argue, behind the comic features of this story lies a dangerous tension between the gods, and one can trace a grim subtext of punishment as a consequence of divine conflict.

Hera, after all, is a significant and complex figure in the *Iliad*, as a recurrent obstacle to Zeus' plans, as O'Brien emphasises,[4] even if she is ultimately unable to thwart him. She has great power among the Olympians and has many supporters, both overt and covert. Starting with the connotations of δεσμός, I discuss the rebellion of Hera, her influence upon the other gods (especially Poseidon), and the role of Heracles in the rebellion, all of which are implied and hinted at in the *Iliad*.

1. The δεσμός of the gods in the *Iliad*

When Zeus awakes at Hera's side and finds the Trojans fleeing in confusion (*Il.* 15.4-8), he furiously threatens Hera, reminding her of a previous punishment which he inflicted, namely hanging her in the sky from her chained hands with anvils on her feet (15.18-20). This scene is often discussed in tandem with a similar story, that of the suspension of the Olympians in their tug-of-war with Zeus (8.19-27).[5] Zeus, hanging a gold cord from heaven, boasts that all the gods and goddesses could not pull him down. Moreover, he proclaims that he will fasten the cord round a peak of Olympus, so that everything and everyone – earth, sea, and the gods – would be suspended in mid-air. Certainly, these stories have similarities: both contain the motif of hanging in the air; the material used for the hanging is gold; and Zeus himself tells both stories for the purpose of asserting his overwhelming power. There is, however, a significant difference, often neglected, between the two stories, namely, the instrument for the hanging: the golden chain for Hera (δεσμὸς χρύσεος, 15.19-20), and the golden cord for the tug-of-war (σειρὴ χρυσείη, 8.19; 8.25). The difference is significant because these two words convey the characteristic tone of these two stories. On the one hand, the cord signifies a mere sport, as the light-hearted tone of Zeus' jesting offer demonstrates: 'Come, try it, gods' (εἰ δ᾽ ἄγε πειρήσασθε, 8.18). On the other hand, the chain signifies severe punishment. I suggest that the poet of the *Iliad* makes a precise distinction between σειρή and δεσμός: the grievous connotation of δεσμός effectively emphasises the great disgrace involved in this harshest of punishments suffered by Hera.[6]

The word δεσμός is used infrequently and with care in the *Iliad*. It occurs nine times, always with reference either to the Trojans or the gods, but never to the Greeks. When the word is applied to the Trojans (four times), it is a general term for 'fastening' with no implication of punishment: it signifies 'halter' in the two identical similes which denote Paris and Hector (6.507 = 15.264); it also refers to the binding of Dolon (10.443) and the hair-band (δέσματα) of Andromache (22.468). Although the use of the word in these accounts has interesting features,[7] our concern at the moment is for its use in reference to the gods.

In the divine context, a δεσμός carries a more or less dangerous connotation, since binding is the supreme penalty for the gods who, by definition, can never die. Moreover, the motif of binding on Olympus evokes the succession myth.[8] For example, the binding of the Cyclopes (*Theog.* 501-2) and that of the Hecatoncheires (*Theog.* 617-18) are mentioned in the context of the struggle for sovereignty between the old gods and the new power under Zeus' control.[9] In the *Theogony*, the theme of binding is thus an integral part of the myth about sovereignty. In the *Iliad*, however, the connotations of δεσμός have a wider range. There are five examples of divine δεσμός (four gods involved): Zeus bound (1.401); the

40

fastenings (rivets) of Hephaestus (in the plural, 18.379); Ares bound (5.386, 391); and the golden chain of Hera (15.19). I will here discuss the last four examples, as I mentioned the story of Zeus' binding in the previous chapter.

Hephaestus

Hephaestus was forging the fastenings (δεσμούς, 18.379) for his twenty tripods when Thetis came to his house, asking him to make Achilles' shield (18.369-79). The theme and diction of this account are telling, although it is the enjoyable side of this story which is usually emphasised; for example, Edwards comments that 'this scene comes as a relief after the sorrows [of the death of Patroclus]';[10] Austin suggests that the five speeches between Thetis, Charis and Hephaestus repeat the theme of hospitality and past indebtedness, while slowly advancing toward the present need;[11] a scholiast notes the sense of joy surrounding the half-finished work (schol. bT ad 18.379). I agree that part of the attraction of the story lies in its enjoyable aspect. However, I think that we can read further, behind the narrative, as is largely suggested by the weighty word δεσμούς. It is worth examining the account of the tripods:

τρίποδας γὰρ ἐείκοσι πάντας ἔτευχεν
ἑστάμεναι περὶ τοῖχον ἐϋσταθέος μεγάροιο,
χρύσεα δέ σφ' ὑπὸ κύκλα ἑκάστῳ πυθμένι θῆκεν,   375
ὄφρα οἱ αὐτόματοι θεῖον δυσαίατ' ἀγῶνα
ἠδ' αὖτις πρὸς δῶμα νεοίατο, θαῦμα ἰδέσθαι.
οἱ δ' ἤτοι τόσσον μὲν ἔχον τέλος, οὔατα δ' οὔ πω
δαιδάλεα προσέκειτο· τά ῥ' ἤρτυε, κόπτε δὲ δεσμούς.

He was making a set of twenty tripods to stand around the wall of his well-built house. He had fitted golden wheels to all their legs, so he could have them moving of their own accord, running by themselves to where the gods were gathered and then returning again to his house, marvellous to see. They were so far finished, but he had still to put on the worked handles. He was fitting these, and cutting the rivets. (Il. 18.373-9)

What is remarkable about this story is that Hephaestus has not finished the tripods, but is still at work forging the fastenings (δεσμοί). It is a *topos* that when a person arrives, he interrupts some ongoing activity: for example, Achilles is singing when Phoenix, Odysseus and Ajax visit him (Il. 9.189); Calypso is singing and working at the loom when Hermes visits her (Od. 5.61-2). However, in the case of Thetis' visiting Hephaestus, let us note that the work which is interrupted is specifically mentioned as forging δεσμοί.[12] The significance of the unfinished work is that it reveals the δεσμοί before they are fitted to the tripod. The passage thus characterises Hephaestus as the god who would naturally forge δεσμοί.[13] Abundant fastenings are now prepared for the tripods, and this functions to emphasise Hephaestus' role in forging δεσμοί for the gods.

Further, let us examine the two speeches of Zeus and Hera (354-67) preceding the tripod-making, which emphasise the danger of the situation :

> Ζεὺς δ᾽ Ἥρην προσέειπε κασιγνήτην ἄλοχόν τε·
> " ἔπρηξας καὶ ἔπειτα, βοῶπις πότνια Ἥρη,
> ἀνστήσασ᾽ Ἀχιλῆα πόδας ταχύν· ἦ ῥά νυ σεῖο
> ἐξ αὐτῆς ἐγένοντο κάρη κομόωντες Ἀχαιοί."
>   Τὸν δ᾽ ἠμείβετ᾽ ἔπειτα βοῶπις πότνια Ἥρη·   360
> "αἰνότατε Κρονίδη, ποῖον τὸν μῦθον ἔειπες.
> καὶ μὲν δή πού τις μέλλει βροτὸς ἀνδρὶ τελέσσαι,
> ὅς περ θνητός τ᾽ ἐστὶ καὶ οὐ τόσα μήδεα οἶδε·
> πῶς δὴ ἔγωγ᾽, ἥ φημι θεάων ἔμμεν ἀρίστη,
> ἀμφότερον, γενεῇ τε καὶ οὔνεκα σὴ παράκοιτις   365
> κέκλημαι, σὺ δὲ πᾶσι μετ᾽ ἀθανάτοισιν ἀνάσσεις,
> οὐκ ὄφελον Τρώεσσι κοτεσσαμένη κακὰ ῥάψαι; "

And Zeus spoke to Hera, his sister and wife: 'So you have achieved it in the end, ox-eyed queen Hera – you have roused swift-footed Achilles. It must be then that the long-haired Achaeans were children of your own.' Then the ox-eyed queen Hera replied: 'Dread son of Cronus, what a thing to say! Even a man, a mortal not equipped with such knowledge as ours, will achieve his purposes for other men. How then could I, who claim to be the greatest of goddesses, both by birth and because I am your acknowledged wife, and you are king of all the gods, how could I not make trouble for the Trojans, when they have angered me?' (*Il.* 18.356-67)

This short quarrel strikingly breaks off the lament for Patroclus and the work of washing, anointing and clothing his corpse (343-55). The sudden change from a detailed description of laying out a dead human being to a divine conversation is dramatic and surprising, and Hera's dignified proclamation that 'I claim to be the greatest of the goddesses' (364) intensifies the perilous tension between the two gods. The antagonism in this scene, coupled with the immediate switch of setting to Hephaestus' forge where he is working on chains, provides a subtextual echo of the gods' quarrel – and Zeus' threat to Hera of the golden chains – in Book 15. We see that the reference to Hephaestus' forging of chains is therefore particularly apt.

In the second song of Demodocus (*Od.* 8.266-366), Hephaestus' famous trap for catching Aphrodite and Ares is also called δεσμοί:

> ἐν δ᾽ ἔθετ᾽ ἀκμοθέτῳ μέγαν ἄκμονα, κόπτε δὲ δεσμοὺς
> ἀρρήκτους ἀλύτους, ὄφρ᾽ ἔμπεδον αὖθι μένοιεν.

He laid his great anvil on its base and forged the bonds that could neither be broken nor torn asunder, so as to keep them staying in place. (*Od.* 8.274-5)

> ἀμφὶ δ᾽ ἄρ᾽ ἑρμῖσιν χέε δέσματα κύκλῳ ἀπάντῃ·

II. The Golden Chain of Hera

All round the bed-posts he threw the bonds. (*Od.* 8.278)

τὼ δ᾽ ἐς δέμνια βάντε κατέδραθον· ἀμφὶ δὲ δεσμοὶ
τεχνήεντες ἔχυντο πολύφρονος Ἡφαίστοιο

So they went to the bed and lay down to sleep, but the cunning bonds of crafty Hephaestus fell around them. (*Od.* 8.296-7)

ἀλλά σφωε δόλος καὶ δεσμὸς ἐρύξει,
εἰς ὅ κέ μοι μάλα πάντα πατὴρ ἀποδῷσιν ἔεδνα

... but my cunning bonds shall hold them both fast until her father Zeus pays me back all the betrothal gifts (*Od.* 8.317-18)

His cunning contrivance is characterised by his bindings (or chains). We see, therefore, that Hephaestus is the god who forges impressive chains in both the *Iliad* and the *Odyssey*.

Ares

The binding of Ares (*Il.* 5.386 and 5.391) is one of three stories exemplifying gods who are damaged by mortals: Ares by Otus and Ephialtes (5.385-91), Hera by Heracles (5.392-4), and Hades (Aides) by Heracles (5.395-402). Together with the main narrative of Aphrodite wounded by Diomedes (5.330-40),[14] Book 5 contains four similar types of stories, but the story of Ares, in particular, exhibits distinctively different features.[15] In the other three stories, the gods are wounded by a spear (Aphrodite) or an arrow (Hera and Hades), and they feel similar pain. Thus Aphrodite says λίην ἄχθομαι, 361; in Hera's case, μιν ἀνήκεστον λάβεν ἄλγος, 394; and Hades is κῆρ ἀχέων, 399. Despite the narration of their pains, they receive only grazes and soon recover. Bound by chains, however, Ares' suffering is quite different from theirs: his affliction is far more serious than 'pain'.

The battle between Ares and the twin Aloadae, Otus and Ephialtes, is presented at *Odyssey* 11.305-20. Although this story was athetised by Aristarchus, modern critics are disposed to accept it as genuine.[16] It is significant that the scene bears some relation to the chaining of Hera. Otus and Ephialtes try to pile Pelion and Ossa on Olympus, threatening to attack the gods in the sky, but are killed by Apollo before they accomplish their endeavour. The twins are of monstrous size: about four metres across the shoulders (ἐννεαπήχεες), they are sixteen metres tall (ἐννεόργυιοι) when nine years of age (*Od.* 11.311-12). They might well be called 'Gigantes', though the poet of the *Odyssey* does not specify this. Like Typhon, to whom Earth gave birth (*Theog.* 821), the twins were brought up by the fruitful land (οὓς δὴ μηκίστους θρέψε ζείδωρος ἄρουρα, *Od.* 11.309). Although it is sometimes suggested that Otus and Ephialtes are equivalent to Typhon and the Titans,[17] they are similar only in their size and chthonic nature.

43

In contrast with Typhon, a dreadful dragon with a dark, flickering tongue (*Theog.* 825-6), they are characterised as the most beautiful by far after Orion (*Od.* 11.310). These features fit well with many vase-paintings of archaic and classical date, which depict the Gigantes as fully human.[18]

The twins attempt to make a stairway to heaven, and in so doing they threaten revolution against the gods:

οἵ ῥα καὶ ἀθανάτοισιν ἀπειλήτην ἐν Ὀλύμπῳ
φυλόπιδα στήσειν πολυάϊκος πολέμοιο.
Ὄσσαν ἐπ᾽ Οὐλύμπῳ μέμασαν θέμεν, αὐτὰρ ἐπ᾽ Ὄσσῃ
Πήλιον εἰνοσίφυλλον, ἵν᾽ οὐρανὸς ἀμβατὸς εἴη.

They threatened to raise the din of furious war even against the immortals in Olympus. They desired to pile Mount Ossa on Olympus, and on Ossa, Pelion with trembling leaves, in order to make a stairway up to heaven. (*Od.* 11.313-16)

Their purpose in ascending to heaven is, of course, to occupy it, taking the place of the Olympian gods. Thus their threats (313-14) portend furious war against Zeus' sovereignty. It is tempting to guess that Otus and Ephialtes' unsuccessful assault would have featured as one of the scenes in the war of the Gigantes. This war receives only one mention in the *Odyssey*, at 7.59:

ὁπλοτάτη θυγάτηρ μεγαλήτορος Εὐρυμέδοντος,
ὅς ποθ᾽ ὑπερθύμοισι Γιγάντεσσιν βασίλευεν.
ἀλλ᾽ ὁ μὲν ὤλεσε λαὸν ἀτάσθαλον, ὤλετο δ᾽ αὐτός

... the youngest daughter [Periboia]of great-hearted Eurymedon, who once was king of the insolent Gigantes, but then he brought destruction to his reckless people, and was himself destroyed. (*Od.* 7.58-60)

Eurymedon, king of the Gigantes, is defeated and killed in the war. There are several reasons for arguing for a combination of these two accounts, namely the threat to the gods from the Gigantic twins Otus and Ephialtes (*Od.* 11.305-20) and the defeat of the Gigantes led by king Eurymedon (*Od.* 7.58-60).[19] Although some sources treat these two events separately,[20] if we could suppose that they are in some sense related to each other, the verses introductory to the story of the binding of Ares are worth looking at:

πολλοὶ γὰρ δὴ τλῆμεν Ὀλύμπια δώματ᾽ ἔχοντες
ἐξ ἀνδρῶν, χαλέπ᾽ ἄλγε᾽ ἐπ᾽ ἀλλήλοισι τιθέντες.

Many of us who have dwellings on Olympus have suffered at the hands of men, in the grievous pain that we bring on each other. (*Il.* 5.383-4)

Dione makes this remark to Aphrodite in order to illustrate the general

44

point that gods get into difficulties by involving themselves in mortal affairs. But the phrase ἐπ' ἀλλήλοισι (384) may indicate that the war in which Ares was involved was not simply between Gigantes and gods; rather, the gods themselves fought against each other as well.[21] As a scholion (bT) elucidates, the gods injured each other and suffered cruel pain.[22] The passage above implies for sure that when Ares was bound by Otus and Ephialtes, he was involved in some quarrel that divided gods as well as men. This may or may not be the Gigantomachy, but at least we could say that it is this dangerous tension between the gods which, I suggest, is the key to understanding the myth of the golden chain of Hera.

2. The golden chain of Hera

The anvils

When Zeus awakens (*Il.* 15.4), he reasserts his invincible power. Hera's punishment is sometimes termed as that of 'a cosmic slave'.[23] The use of the two anvils (ἄκμονας ... δύω, 15.19), tied to Hera's feet, surely in order to increase her pain, has intriguing implications: why is an *anvil* specified in this punishment? The anvil is an instrument for forging, from which we conclude that it must have belonged to Hephaestus.[24] Moreover, when an anvil is mentioned, it is usually in conjunction with a chain, the two being considered as a set or a pair. For example, in the *Theogony* we find δεσμοῖσιν (718) with ἄκμων (722); in the house of Hephaestus in the *Iliad* we read δεσμούς (18.379) with ἀκμοθέτοιο (18.410), ἀκμοθέτῳ (476) and ἄκμονα (476). We should not be surprised to find that, when a chain is used by Zeus to punish Hera, an anvil is present as well.

As chains on Olympus are exclusively manufactured by Hephaestus, the golden chain of Hera would also have been forged by him. Zeus could easily get a set of chains and anvil from the house of Hephaestus, even though Hephaestus might have forged them for another purpose. I suggest, then, that Hera was tied and suspended by a chain made by her own son. Also, the chain for binding Zeus (*Il.* 1.399) would have been forged by Hephaestus, as no other god could do it. Zeus had hurled Hephaestus from heaven when Hephaestus tried to help Hera (*Il.* 1.590-1). The *Iliad* does not specify what kind of help Hephaestus offered; however, it is tempting to speculate that he was forging a chain for binding Zeus.[25] If Zeus, instead, took that chain and bound Hera by it, fastening the anvils which lay beside the chain to add extra weight, this would certainly be both the most severe *and* most appropriate punishment for mother and son.

Reciprocity

When gods are released from binding, which was contrived by Cronus, it is their custom to present Zeus with valuable gifts. The Cyclopes showed their gratitude by presenting Zeus with the thunderbolt (*Theog.* 501-5) which became the indispensable instrument for his victory. The Hecatoncheires offered to fight against the Titans, rendering powerful assistance to Zeus (*Theog.* 649-63). Prometheus, in return for his liberty, revealed the secret of Thetis' son (Aesch. *P.V.* 209-10).[26] These rewards were crucial for ensuring Zeus' sovereignty.

According to Libanius (as quoted by Voigt at Alc. Fr. 349e), even Hera offered rewards. When she was trapped in the chair with hidden bonds inside it, sent by Hephaestus, Dionysus successfully brought Hephaestus to release her.[27] In gratitude, Hera persuaded the other gods to admit Dionysus to Olympus as one of the Twelve. Hyginus (*Fab.* 166) records the tale that, for releasing Hera, Zeus awarded Hephaestus the hand of Athena.[28]

A new restoration of the fragment of the *Homeric Hymn to Dionysus*[29] has lately been proposed by M.L. West.[30] This fragment narrates the story of Hera's release from Hephaestus' chair. According to West's restoration, all 25 lines of the papyrus form a single speech, addressed by Zeus to the immobilised Hera.[31] Lines 18-22 are as follows:

δοιοὶ] γὰρ πάρεασι τεοῖς [καμάτοισιν ἀρωγοί
υἱέες] ἡμέτεροι πινυτόφ[ρονες· ἔστι μὲν Ἄρης,
ὃς θοὸ]ν ἔγχος ἀνέσχε τα[λαύρινος πολεμιστής
      ]ην ἰδέε[ιν] καὶ παλ[
ἔστι δὲ] καὶ Διόνυσος᾽ ε.[

for two helpers are at hand for your trouble,[32] sons of mine, who are wise in mind; one is Ares who held up his swift spear, being a warrior, and bears a shield of bull's hide [. . . . . .] to see; there is also Dionysus (*P.Oxy.* 670, ll. 18-22)

West suggests that πάρεασι (18) refers to Ares and Dionysus as available helpers for Hera in her suffering, and Zeus encourages Hera, intimating that there are two able young gods at hand.[33] This fragment corroborates Zeus' intervention in rewarding the release of Hera from Hephaestus' chair.

The *Iliad* does not explicitly mention the release of Hera from the golden chain, nor does it describe rewards for this deed. However, immediately following the account of the golden chain, the main narrative does hint at these events. I refer to Poseidon's obedience to Zeus:

εἰ μὲν δὴ σύ γ᾽ ἔπειτα, βοῶπις πότνια Ἥρη,
ἶσον ἐμοὶ φρονέουσα μετ᾽ ἀθανάτοισι καθίζοις,
τῷ κε Ποσειδάων γε, καὶ εἰ μάλα βούλεται ἄλλῃ,
αἶψα μεταστρέψειε νόον μετὰ σὸν καὶ ἐμὸν κῆρ.

Well, if from now on, ox-eyed queen Hera, you take your seat among the immortals with your thoughts in harmony with mine [Zeus], then Poseidon, however contrary his wish might be, would quickly bend his mind to follow your heart and mine. (*Il.* 15.49-52)

This passage fits well with the context, because Poseidon's intervention to help the Achaeans was prominent from Book 13 onwards. If we look at the construction of the two narratives of the occasions when Zeus slept, in Books 14 and 15, we see that this passage functions as the conclusion for both accounts:

(a) The story told by Hypnus (14.242-62) and by Zeus (15.18-28) runs as follows:
1. The conquest of Troy by Heracles (14.250-1; also 5.638-42);
2. Zeus' sleep (14.252-3);
3. Hera's contrivance to drive Heracles to Cos (14.253-6; 15.26-8);
4. Zeus' punishment of the gods (14.256-7) and of Hera (15.18-20).
(b) The main narrative from Book 14 onwards is:
1. The defeat of the Greeks (14.1-152);
2. Zeus' sleep (14.346-51);
3. Hera's contrivance to defeat the Trojans (14.378-507);
4. Zeus' threat to Hera (15.14-33);
5. Hera's assurance to Zeus that she would advise Poseidon to be loyal in future (15.34-52).

Since the two stories (a) and (b) run quite similarly from 1 to 4, the final part 5 can be read as the conclusion following the logic, not only of the main narrative (b), but also of the past story (a).

It is worth noting Hera's extremely solemn language at 36-40 in this final part (5):

ἴστω νῦν τόδε Γαῖα καὶ Οὐρανὸς εὐρὺς ὕπερθε
καὶ τὸ κατειβόμενον Στυγὸς ὕδωρ, ὅς τε μέγιστος
ὅρκος δεινότατός τε πέλει μακάρεσσι θεοῖσι,
σή θ᾽ ἱερὴ κεφαλὴ καὶ νωΐτερον λέχος αὐτῶν
κουρίδιον, τὸ μὲν οὐκ ἂν ἐγώ ποτε μὰψ ὀμόσαιμι·

May now Earth and the wide Heaven above be my witness, and the flowing water of Styx, which is the greatest and most awesome oath for the blessed gods, and also your sacred head and the bed of our own marriage, by which I would never swear falsely. (*Il.* 15.36-40)

This line-up of as many as five witnesses including Styx lays great emphasis on the significance of her oath, showing how critical her situation is at this moment. Her oath then leads up to her claim that she has had nothing to do with Poseidon's behaviour towards the Trojans. If this claim by Hera accords with the logic of both the stories mentioned above, one might argue that in return for being released from the chain, Hera swore obedience to Zeus and, by her authority, made Poseidon loyal to Zeus. It would mean a great deal to Zeus to obtain Poseidon's loyalty – a direct clash with Poseidon would be perilous to Zeus' sovereignty.

The binding as a deterrent

The unique nature of Hera's binding is also worth noting. Zeus usually punishes gods by hurling them from Olympus: so Hephaestus (1.590-1), Hypnus (by implication: 14.258), an undefined number of gods (15.22-4), and Ate (19.130). Or, if Zeus had wanted to destroy Hera completely, he could have struck her with his thunderbolt and thrown her into Tartarus, as he did to Typhon (*Theog.* 853-68). Hera's binding is different from these types of punishment. Hurling from Olympus is a momentary event (even if the fall might take a whole day because of Olympus' great height, as at *Il.* 1.592), whereas hanging in the sky persists over time: it exposes the miserable figure to the other gods for a considerable time. As often happened in the Middle Ages, public hanging acts as a deterrent by presenting the punishment to the watchers. This is Zeus' intention: to punish Hera and, at the same time, to threaten the other gods who see her suffer. Thus does he demonstrate his overwhelming power to all those who might attempt to challenge him.

The first target of Zeus' threat is, again, Poseidon. While Zeus sleeps, Poseidon intervenes in the war with extraordinary eagerness (14.361ff.). When Poseidon first receives from Hypnus the news of Hera's success, the narrative tells us,

> αὐτίκα δ᾿ ἐν πρώτοισι μέγα προθορὼν ἐκέλευσεν·
> " Ἀργεῖοι, καὶ δὴ αὖτε μεθίεμεν Ἕκτορι νίκην
> Πριαμίδῃ, ἵνα νῆας ἕλῃ καὶ κῦδος ἄρηται; ..."

Immediately he leapt forward among the front-fighters and called loud to them: 'Argives, are we once more to leave the victory to Hector, son of Priam, so he can take our ships and win his glory? ...' (*Il.* 14.363-5)

The word αὐτίκα at the beginning of line 363 effectively presents the excitement of Poseidon. He knows that his leadership in the war will not last long – only, as Hypnus suggested, 'for a little while' (μίνυνθά περ, 358)[34] – but he energetically continues to encourage the Achaeans until the end of Book 14. Furthermore, Hera and Poseidon collaborate closely.

So it is quite natural that Zeus at once sees Poseidon when he awakens from sleep (15.8). After mentioning the golden chain, the next thing that Zeus says concerns Poseidon, as quoted above:

> τῷ κε Ποσειδάων γε, καὶ εἰ μάλα βούλεται ἄλλῃ,
> αἶψα μεταστρέψειε νόον μετὰ σὸν καὶ ἐμὸν κῆρ.

then Poseidon, however contrary his wish might be, would quickly bend his mind to follow your heart and mine. (*Il.* 15.51-2)

Since Zeus is well aware that Poseidon is working against him (καὶ εἰ μάλα βούλεται ἄλλῃ, 51), he is careful to avoid a direct clash with him.[35] By threatening Hera with the reminder of the golden chain, Zeus successfully manoeuvres her into appeasing Poseidon.

This dangerous tension between Zeus and Poseidon has been present in the narrative from the beginning of Book 13. The juxtaposition of Zeus' perspective from Mount Ida (13.1-9) with that of Poseidon from the peak of Samos (13.10-16) brings into focus the serious tension between the two.[36] Poseidon's frustrated inferiority is well represented:

> ἤχθετο γάρ ῥα
> Τρωσὶν δαμναμένους, Διὶ δὲ κρατερῶς ἐνεμέσσα.
> ἦ μὰν ἀμφοτέροισιν ὁμὸν γένος ἠδ᾽ ἴα πάτρη,
> ἀλλὰ Ζεὺς πρότερος γεγόνει καὶ πλείονα ᾔδη.   355
> τῶ ῥα καὶ ἀμφαδίην μὲν ἀλεξέμεναι ἀλέεινε,
> λάθρῃ δ᾽ αἰὲν ἔγειρε κατὰ στρατόν, ἀνδρὶ ἐοικώς.

... it distressed him [Poseidon] to see them beaten by the Trojans, and he was furious with Zeus. The two gods were of the same descent and parentage, but Zeus was the older and had wider knowledge. For this reason, Poseidon avoided giving open help to the Argives, but secretly kept on urging them up and down the ranks, in the shape of a man. (*Il.* 13.352-7)

Although Poseidon is inferior to Zeus in age[37] and knowledge (13.355), nevertheless, if he collaborates with Hera, he could cause serious problems for Zeus. Zeus' reference to the golden chain, therefore, effectively diminishes the threat offered by Hera and Poseidon.

The *Iliad* confines the antagonism between Zeus and Poseidon to the issue of which side they support in the human battle. However, this antagonism reflects a cosmic tension on a wider scale. Similarly, the golden chain of Hera, mentioned in order to check Hera's support for the Achaeans, reflects the broader cosmic struggle between the gods.

3. Heracles: the motive for the golden chain

The Meropis; *Heracles' expedition to Cos*

We are told that Hera's punishment with the golden chain was provoked by the discovery that it was she who had contrived to send Heracles to Cos (14.249-56; 15.18-30). According to later writers (Apollod. 2.7.1 and Plu. *Mor.* 304c-d), the story runs as follows: having sacked Troy, Heracles encountered a storm sent by Hera; driven to Cos, he was attacked, wounded and almost killed by the people there. From this crisis he escaped either because he was rescued by Zeus (Apollodorus), or because he hid in the house of a Thracian woman, in whose clothes he dressed himself and fled (Plutarch). Then, summoned by Athena, he went to Phlegra to fight against the Gigantes.

The Catalogue of Ships (*Il.* 2.676-9) records that Cos was the city of Euryalus. The fleet from Cos and the surrounding islands was led by Pheidippus and Antiphus, the sons of Thessalus, son of Heracles.[38] In the *Homeric Hymn to Apollo* (42), Cos is described as the city of the people called Meropes. So, by the fifth century, the Meropes were regarded as the early inhabitants of Cos. The main settlement in the Mycenaean period was on the east coast of the island.[39]

A recently discovered papyrus fragment of the epic poem called the *Meropis*[40] has revealed more about Heracles' expedition to Cos. The papyrus, from the first century BC, contains 24 lines of a local heroic epic with a commentary by the Hellenistic writer Apollodorus of Athens, the follower of Aristarchus, *c.* 150-125 BC. A Hellenistic date has been suggested for the epic,[41] but it seems more likely to date from the seventh or sixth century BC.[42]

In this poem, Heracles is nearly killed by Asterus, one of the Meropes (vv. 1-7); Apollodorus explains in his commentary that Asterus is invulnerable (ἄτρωτος, 25). However, Athena comes to Heracles' aid and kills Asterus with her spear (vv. 8-17) and, after stripping and drying it, uses Asterus' strong skin for her aegis (vv. 18-24). According to Apollodorus, she considers that the skin will be useful for other dangerous situations (35).

As is suggested by the episode in which Asterus' skin forms Athena's aegis, the Meropes are not ordinary humans but are Gigantes.[43] Philostratus (*Heroicus* 8.14) writes of the Meropes that ἐννεόργυιοι ἀτεχνῶς ἐγένοντο – the same height as Otus and Ephialtes (*Od.* 11.311-12). Fragment 637 of Aristotle (schol. to Aristides *Panathenaicus* 189.4) records that Asterius – as he is referred to here – was a giant who was killed by Athena.[44]

The salient part of the *Meropis* fragment, for us, is its mention of Athena's intervention:

> κ[αί νύ] κεν Ἡρακλεῖα κατέκτ[ανεν], εἰ μὴ Ἀθήνη
> λαβρὸν [ἐπεβρόν]τησε διὲγ νεφέων κα[ταβᾶ]σα
> πληξαμενήιθε.[   ] δ' ἁπαλὸν χρόα πρόσθ[ε φάαν]θη

he would have killed Heracles, if Athena had not thundered furiously, coming down through the clouds, and struck [   ] tender skin ... she appeared in front. (*SH* 903 vv. 8-10)

Lloyd-Jones compares *Il.* 8.130-4, where Zeus helps the Trojans:[45]

> ἔνθα κε λοιγὸς ἔην καὶ ἀμήχανα ἔργα γένοντο,
> καί νύ κε σήκασθεν κατὰ Ἴλιον ἠΰτε ἄρνες,
> εἰ μὴ ἄρ' ὀξὺ νόησε πατὴρ ἀνδρῶν τε θεῶν τε·
> βροντήσας δ' ἄρα δεινὸν ἀφῆκ' ἀργῆτα κεραυνόν,
> κὰδ δὲ πρόσθ' ἵππων Διομήδεος ἧκε χαμᾶζε·

50

II. The Golden Chain of Hera

Then there would have been ruin and deeds beyond all remedy, and the Trojans would have been penned back in Ilion like lambs, if the father of men and gods had not quickly seen it. He thundered terribly, and let fly his white lightning-bolt, and hurled it to the ground in front of Diomedes' horses. (*Il.* 8.130-4)

As Kirk points out, this passage is one example of an abrupt change of direction, characterised by vivid expression.[46] The effect of this sophisticated narrative technique is to heighten a present moment and to shift the course of the narrative immediately.[47] Similarly, the *Meropis* passage is impressive: Athena's fierce and dynamic movement is effectively depicted. Such an emphatic description seems to indicate that her intervention is the indispensable factor in this epic, just as is that of Zeus (*Il.* 8.130-4) and Aphrodite (*Il.* 5.311-17) in the *Iliad*. Athena intervenes in order to save Heracles and to gain her own fame in the war.

Heracles' expedition to Phlegra

Heracles' subsequent expedition to Phlegra is not narrated in the extant fragment of the *Meropis*, but a fragment of the *Catalogue of Women* (fr. 43a M-W) offers further information. After narrating the genealogy of the rulers of Cos from Poseidon to Antagoras (55-60), the fragment states that Heracles sacked the city of Antagoras on his way home from Troy, and that he killed the arrogant Gigantes at Phlegra:

τῶι δὲ καὶ ἐξ ἀρχῆς ὀλίγης Διὸς ἄλκιμος υἱὸς
ἔπραθεν ἱμερόεντα πόλιν, κε[ρ]άϊξε δὲ κώμας
εὐθὺ[ς ἐπ]εὶ Τροίηθεν ἀνέ[πλε]ε νηυσ[ὶ] θ[οῆσιν
..[......]λαιων ἕνε[χ᾽ ἵπ]πων Λαομέδοντος.
ἐν Φλέγρηι δ]⁴⁸ὲ Γίγαντας ὑπερφιάλους κατέπεφ[νε.

so from a small beginning the brave son of Zeus destroyed the lovely city, and ravaged the villages straight after he sailed away from Troy in his swift ships [.....] for the sake of the horses of Laomedon. In Phlegra he killed the overbearing Gigantes. (Hes. fr. 43a M-W, vv. 61-5)

If verse 65 is genuine,[49] it provides us with important information. After his exploits on Cos, Heracles went to Phlegra to fight against the Gigantes. This explains why Athena intervened in the war with the Meropes: she (and the other gods) needed Heracles in the war against the Gigantes, so she had to save him when he was nearly defeated.

Pindar mentions Heracles' battle against the Gigantes several times, and in *Nemean* 4.25-7 and *Isthmian* 6.30-3, he mentions Heracles' role, in the same order, in his sack of Troy, his battle against the Meropes of Cos, and against the giant Alcyoneus:[50]

σὺν ᾧ ποτε Τροΐαν κραταιὸς Τελαμὼν
πόρθησε καὶ Μέροπας
καὶ τὸν μέγαν πολεμιστὰν ἔκπαγλον Ἀλκυονῆ

With him [Heracles], mighty Telamon once destroyed Troy and the Meropes,
and the huge warrior, horrible Alkyoneus (*Nem.* 4.25-7)

εἶλε δὲ Περγαμίαν, πέφνεν δὲ σὺν κείνῳ Μερόπων
ἔθνεα καὶ τὸν βουβόταν οὔρεϊ ἶσον
Φλέγραισιν εὑρὼν Ἀλκυονῆ

He [Heracles] took Pergamus' city, and with him [Telamon] killed the tribes
of the Meropes, and the ox-herd like a mountain, Alcyoneus, whom he found
at Phlegrai (*Isth.* 6.31-4)

Nemean 4.25-7 does not mention the location of Heracles' battle with
Alcyoneus; but *Isthmian* 6.31 explicitly states that the hero met Alcyoneus at Phlegra. Furthermore, *Nemean* 1.67-9 offers the information
that the Gigantomachy in which Heracles joined with the gods was at
Phlegra:

καὶ γὰρ ὅταν θεοὶ ἐν πεδίῳ Φλέ-
    γρας Γιγάντεσσιν μάχαν
ἀντιάζωσιν, βελέων ὑπὸ ῥι-
    παῖσι κείνου φαιδίμαν γαίᾳ πεφύρσεσθαι κόμαν
ἔνεπεν·

For when the gods meet the Gigantes in battle on Phlegra's plain, he
[Teiresias] told that bright hair shall be fouled in the dust beneath the rush
of arrows of him [Heracles]. (*Nem.* 1.67-9)

Such repetition of the same information, in the same sequence by Pindar
– Heracles' expeditions to Troy, to Cos, and then to Phlegra – proves that
these events were a well-established part of Heracles' legend.

Apollodorus offers a similar story in the final part of his account of
Heracles' campaign on Cos (*Bibl.* 2.7.1): Heracles came to Phlegra, where
he fought with the gods against the Gigantes. These accounts offer us the
outline of the story of Heracles on Cos and after Cos: he was sent to Cos
by Hera, where he fought the Meropes; almost defeated, but saved by
Athena, he went to Phlegra to fight the Gigantes.

The role of Heracles in the Gigantomachy

We must now recall the curious role of Heracles in the war against the
Gigantes. A scholion to Pindar's *Nemean* 1.101 informs us of his contribu-
tion to the war:

Φλέγρα τόπος ἐν Θράκῃ καὶ κώμη, ἔνθα οἱ Γίγαντες ἀνῃρέθησαν ὑπὸ θεῶν. τῶν δὲ ἐχόντων τὴν μάχην πρὸς τοὺς Γίγαντας καὶ μὴ περιγινομένων τῆς μάχης, φασὶν εἰρηκέναι τὴν Γῆν μὴ ἄλλως ἁλῶναι τούτους, εἰ μὴ συμμαχήσειαν αὐτοῖς δύο τῶν ἡμιθέων· Ἡρακλέους τοίνυν καὶ Διονύσου συνελθόντων ἐκράτησαν οἱ θεοὶ τῶν Γιγάντων.

Phlegra is a place and a village in Thrace, where the Gigantes were defeated by the gods. When the gods were engaged in battle with them, and could not prevail over the Gigantes, they say that Gaia told that the Gigantes would not be defeated unless two of the demi-gods should fight as the gods' allies. When Heracles and Dionysus joined the battle, the gods triumphed over the Gigantes. (schol. Pind. *Nem.* 1.101)

Apollodorus (*Bibl.* 1.6.1) offers a similar story: the gods received an oracle stating that none of the Gigantes could perish at the hands of the gods, but they would be destroyed with the help of a mortal. So, Zeus summoned Heracles by means of Athena:

τοῖς δὲ θεοῖς λόγιον ἦν ὑπὸ θεῶν μὲν μηδένα τῶν Γιγάντων ἀπολέσθαι δύνασθαι, συμμαχοῦντος δὲ θνητοῦ τινος τελευτήσειν. αἰσθομένη δὲ Γῆ τοῦτο ἐζήτει φάρμακον, ἵνα μηδ᾽ ὑπὸ θνητοῦ δυνηθῶσιν ἀπολέσθαι. Ζεὺς δ᾽ ἀπειπὼν φαίνειν Ἠοῖ τε καὶ Σελήνῃ καὶ Ἡλίῳ τὸ μὲν φάρμακον αὐτὸς ἔτεμε φθάσας, Ἡρακλέα δὲ σύμμαχον δι᾽ Ἀθηνᾶς ἐπεκαλέσατο.

Now an oracle was given to the gods that none of the Gigantes could be destroyed by them, but if a mortal should fight as their ally, they could overcome them. Learning of this, Earth sought for a medicinal plant to prevent the Gigantes from being destroyed even by a mortal. But Zeus, on the one hand forbade Dawn and the Moon and the Sun to shine, and he cut off the medicinal plant himself, before anybody else could get it, and on the other hand, by means of Athena, he summoned Heracles to fight as his ally. (*Bibl.* 1.6.1)

It is clear from these accounts that Heracles' intervention in the war against the Gigantes was crucial. This is why he was helped by Athena on Cos, and was taken to the battle against the Gigantes. This explains why it was to Cos that Hera sent Heracles: Hera attempted to render him unable to join the war.[52] According to the traditional story pattern, Hera persecuted Heracles out of jealousy; but another version can perhaps be seen behind Hera's hostility to Heracles, if we read this story in the light of the Gigantomachy. Had her plan been successful, Zeus would have been defeated by the Gigantes,[52] and it could be for this treachery that Zeus punished her by binding her with the golden chain.

The *Iliad* states that Hera's plot against Heracles resulted in the harsh punishment of binding. Heracles' status as the beloved son of Zeus is offered as a reason for the severity of the punishment. We can, however, suggest a further cause for a punishment which appears overly stringent merely for diverting a mortal off his course – even though Zeus' punishments were sometimes disproportionate to the crimes. I suggest that this harsh punishment would be appropriate for an attempt to overthrow Zeus' sovereignty. Therefore, I conclude that Hera's dispatch of Heracles to Cos could have been intended to hinder him from joining the Gigantomachy, which, had it been successful, would have seriously endangered the sovereignty of Zeus. This is why Hera received that most grave and shameful punishment.

In the light of the generational strife, where mothers (Gaia and Rhea) play the decisive roles in affecting their sons (Cronus and Zeus) against their fathers (Uranus and Cronus), Hera, step-mother of Heracles, failed to make him (covertly) challenge his father, Zeus. Although Heracles was by no means stronger than his father, his help was at least essential for Zeus' sovereignty. The motif of the son who is mightier than his father might be thus transferred in the Heracles story.[53]

Hera and the Gigantes

Gaia gives birth to the Gigantes because of her anger over the treatment of the Titans (Apollod. *Bibl.* 1.6.1). When we think about the relationship between Hera and Gaia, we conclude that Hera would favour the side of Gaia and the Gigantes in the war. The close link between Hera and the Gigantes is confirmed by a scholion:

> ἔνιοι δέ φασι παρθένον οὖσαν Ἥραν ἐρασθῆναι Εὐρυμέδοντος, ἑνὸς τῶν Γιγάντων, καὶ ἐξ αὐτοῦ τεκεῖν τὸν Προμηθέα· Δία δὲ ἐγνωκότα τὸν μὲν ταρταρῶσαι, τὸν δὲ Προμηθέα προφάσει τοῦ πυρὸς σταυρῶσαι.

> Some say that Hera, when she was a maiden, fell in love with Eurymedon, one of the Gigantes, and by him bore Prometheus. Zeus, knowing this, hurled Eurymedon into Tartarus, and on the pretext of the stolen fire, chained up Prometheus. (schol. T ad *Il.* 14.296)

It is true that a variant version makes Eurymedon a rapist,[54] but we cannot be certain that the virgin Hera would be a maidenly victim in the manner of human virgins. We see that Hera has three reasons for supporting the Gigantes: (a) the Gigantes originate from Gaia, with whom Hera is closely linked; (b) one of the Gigantes was Hera's lover in one version of the myth; and (c) the Gigantes could overthrow Zeus if only Heracles were prevented from joining the war. Hence Hera, aware of the future role of Heracles in the war, attempted her unsuccessful plot against him.

The chthonic nature of Poseidon

Apollodorus (*Bibl.* 1.6.2) gives a list of the gods who fight against the Gigantes; for example, Ephialtes is killed by Apollo, Eurytus by Dionysus, and Clytius by Hecate. Poseidon is mentioned close to the end of the list, where he is said to chase Polybotes through the sea to Cos, and then to throw a massive piece of the island onto him, which became another island, Nisyrus.[55] There is no account of the Gigantomachy that makes him fight against the gods. However, in view of what seems to have been a long history of his rivalry with Zeus, he would not have been an implausible accomplice of Hera.

One episode in the *Iliad* shows that Poseidon is an ambiguous figure. In spite of his frequent support of the Achaeans, we recall that he once built the walls of Troy (*Il.* 7.452-3; *Il.* 21.441-57).[56] The *Iliad* gives no reason for this ambiguity, but a scholion reports that Poseidon was forced to build the Trojan wall as a punishment from Zeus:

"θητεύσαμεν": ἠθέλησαν γὰρ συνδῆσαι τὸν Δία Ποσειδάων καὶ Φοῖβος Ἀπόλλων" (Α 400). οἱ δὲ ἐπὶ τῷ πειρᾶσαι τὴν ὕβριν Λαομέδοντος· "καί τε θεοὶ ξείνοισιν ἐοικότες" (ρ 485). ὡς ἀποθανόντος οὖν τοῦ αἰτίου, τιμώμενος νῦν ἐν Ἰλίῳ, Κίλλῃ, Χρύσῃ, Τενέδῳ, βοηθεῖ αὐτοῖς. οἱ δὲ δύο φασὶν ἐργασαμένους ἀμισθὶ ἀναθεῖναι Ἀπόλλωνι καὶ Ποσειδῶνι. οἱ δε ὅτι ἀπὸ τῶν ἱερατικῶν χρημάτων ᾠκοδόμησεν αὐτά.

'We laboured': for 'Poseidon and Phoebus Apollo' (*Il.* 1.400) wanted to bind Zeus, but some say, [they laboured] in order to test the insolence of Laomedon; 'and gods pretending to be strangers' (*Od.* 17.485). As the guilty party was dead, Apollo, now being honoured in Ilion, Cilla, Chryse and Tenedos, helps them. Some say that 'two working without pay' refers to Apollo and Poseidon, but others say that [Laomedon] built these [walls] from sacred funds. (schol. T ad *Il.* 21.444)

The scholiast, who gives no source, explains Poseidon's work by reference to the story of Zeus' binding at *Iliad* 1.400, where Poseidon is one of the three gods who tries to bind him. Although the attempt to bind Zeus was unsuccessful, the reference provides important evidence of Poseidon's antagonism toward him.

The chthonic nature of Poseidon's offspring in the *Theogony*, the *Homeric Hymns* and the scholia to the *Iliad* may also assist in explaining his antagonistic attitude to Zeus. According to the *Theogony*, Poseidon married Medusa, who bore him two sons Pegasus and Chrysaor (278-81). The scholia offer the story of Poseidon's mating, in the form of a horse, with a Harpy (schol. T ad *Il.* 23.347) or with an Erinys (schol. Ab ad *Il.* 23.346 and schol. T ad *Il.* 23.347). The Erinys is named Tilphossa or Telphusa,[57] whose spring is buried beneath stones by Apollo in the *Hymn to Apollo* (375-87).[58] The fleet horse Areion is born from the spring Telphusa – so the myth of Poseidon-Telphusa-Areion repeats the myth of Poseidon-Medusa-Pegasus.[59] The *Hymn to Apollo* (231-8) and the *Hymn to Hermes* (186) mention Poseidon's sanctuary at Onchestus, which had a specific association with horses.[60] Polyphemus is his son by Thoösa (*Od.* 1.68-73), and Otus and Ephialtes are his sons by Iphimedeia. Poseidon, who has such chthonic offspring, has another reason for opposing the power of Zeus.[61]

A hypothetical outline of the Gigantomachy

The story of the golden chain of Hera (15.18-24) and that of Hephaestus' hurling from Olympus (1.590-3) clearly describe the same incident.[62] If we take this incident together with the war when Ares was bound by the monstrous twins (Otus and Ephialtes), we can construct a hypothetical outline of the Gigantomachy.[63] The war takes place at Phlegra, Eurymedon being the king of the Gigantes (*Od.* 7.58-9). Otus and Ephialtes bind Ares (*Il.* 5.385), and almost succeed in ascending to Olympus (*Od.* 11.313-16). Hera, knowing Gaia's prophecy about Heracles' role in the fighting (schol. P. *Nem.* 1.101), sends him to Cos in order to prevent him from joining the war (*Il.* 14.249-56, 15.18-30). On Cos, Athena saves him when he is nearly killed by the Meropes (*Meropis* vv. 8-9) and takes him to Phlegra (Hes. fr. 43a M-W, l. 65). With the decisive help of Heracles, the gods win the war and Eurymedon and the Gigantes are destroyed (*Od.* 7.60). As a punishment for her dispatch of Heracles, Zeus binds and hangs Hera (*Il.* 15.16-28), probably with the chain that Hephaestus forged, and hurls Hephaestus from Olympus (*Il.* 1.590-3).

Some scholars doubt whether Homer knew the legend of the battle of the Gigantes against the gods, and claim that the whole tale of the Gigantomachy was invented.[64] However, the poet's mentions of the war, scattered and scanty as they are, undoubtedly indicate that the legend was pre-Homeric and known to the poet. Moreover, the consistency of these accounts clearly shows that they belong to a lost work of the epic tradition, the Gigantomachy; as Janko remarked, 'the poet in fact draws on an early gigantomachy or *Heracleid*'.[65]

The existence of such a story is attested by two early witnesses. The first is *Theogony* 50-2:

αὖτις δ' ἀνθρώπων τε γένος κρατερῶν τε Γιγάντων
ὑμνεῦσαι τέρπουσι Διὸς νόον ἐντὸς Ὀλύμπου
Μοῦσαι Ὀλυμπιάδες, κοῦραι Διὸς αἰγιόχοιο.

And again, singing of the race of men and of the powerful Gigantes, they delight the heart of Zeus within Olympus, the Olympian Muses, daughters of Zeus the aegis-holder. (*Theog.* 50-2)

The second is fragment 1 of Xenophanes:

ἀνδρῶν δ' αἰνεῖν τοῦτον, ὃς ἐσθλὰ πιὼν ἀναφαίνῃ,
    ὥς οἱ μνημοσύνη καὶ πόνος ἀμφ' ἀρετῆς·
οὔτε μάχας διέπει Τιτήνων οὔτε Γιγάντων

Among the people, praise the man who, when he drinks, sets forth noble deeds, as his memory and a striving for virtue enable him. He deals neither with the battles of Titans nor of Gigantes (Xenophanes 1.19-21 W)

II. The Golden Chain of Hera

The verses in the proem to the *Theogony* tell us that the Muses delight the mind of Zeus by singing of the race of men and the powerful Gigantes. This could be taken to suggest that such an epic did exist.[66] In the fragment of Xenophanes, the poet includes the battle of the Gigantes as one of the topics which a noble man should avoid. This suggests that there was some sort of poem in existence at least by the time of Xenophanes in the latter half of the sixth century BC. The discovery of the fragment of the *Meropis* also confirms that such poems existed.

There was another epic about Heracles, called the *Oechaliae Halosis*.[67] This epic probably offered themes of suffering and labour.[68] Nagy discusses a parallel between this epic and the *Iliad*, namely the emphasis on mortality.[69] If we did not know of the existence of the epics about Heracles – the *Gigantomachy* as well as the *Meropis* and the *Oechaliae Halosis*, or the earlier versions of these epics – the expressive potential of Achilleus' words 'even Heracles could not escape death' (*Il.* 18.117) would hardly be understandable. If this famous phrase could console the speaker as well as the listener,[70] it seems that these Heraclean epics not only existed but also enjoyed wide currency in the Homeric period.

To conclude, behind the account of the golden chain of Hera lies, I have argued, the battle against the Gigantes. Heracles secured Zeus' sovereignty, and Hera was punished for her role as the ringleader of Zeus' challengers, among whom might have been Poseidon, as he is always a potential rival of Zeus, given the history of the division of domains between them.[71] Having suppressed the story of Zeus's crisis in the Gigantomachy, the *Iliad*, instead, presents the story of the golden chain of Hera as a comic punishment for mischief. However, if Hera's treachery had succeeded, it would have posed a real threat to Zeus, as the grievous punishment of binding proves.

In failing, Hera falls under the control of Zeus, and he upholds the cosmic equilibrium. As O'Brien remarks, from a Panhellenic point of view, the *Iliad* has more need of her than of others, since Panhellenism was not conceivable without subordination and hierarchy.[72] Through this process, Hera has been degraded, and so too has the impact of her rebellion. After the *Iliad*, we see Hera much less frequently.[73] However, as I have demonstrated, the *Iliad* nevertheless preserves traces which suggest that Hera had once been a truly powerful goddess, and of course her importance in cult continued to be very significant in later times.

III

The Reordering of the Universe

This chapter offers a conceivable reconstruction of events which are, I suggest, merely glossed in the *Iliad*. My interpretation is only one among the plethora of alternatives that a close reading of such a complex work could entail. But my exploration will demonstrate that there is an undercurrent beneath the narrative of human battle which seems to suggest one particular version of cosmic mythological interrelations. By studying the literary technique of the analogous presentation of the gods and men, I suggest that a reading of cosmic strife underlying the text would lead to a fuller appreciation of the poet's subtle intertextualities.

Throughout the battles against the Titans (674-720) and Typhoeus (820-68) in the *Theogony*, the image of cosmic disorder is emphasised. These battles are put to an end by the power of Zeus' thunderbolt, and his victory, therefore, symbolises a reordering of the universe. In the *Iliad*, by contrast, Zeus' rule seems unassailable. However, the antagonism between the gods still resurfaces occasionally, intimating the rebellion which had existed in the recent past.

In the *Iliad*, hostility between the gods is characteristically expressed through the motif of protection: in the Achaean and Trojan armies, their various favourites act as their surrogates as they vie with each other on behalf of their benefactors.[1] It is sometimes held that the myths of the battles between the gods serve as background to the human battle. Certainly the divine battles function as exemplars – cautionary or rallying – for their human counterparts.[2] Also, the antagonism between Zeus and Poseidon strongly contributes to the ominous atmosphere, which is appropriate for the development of the human battle. While, importantly, these battles of gods are self-contained and recounted for their own sake, the partisanship and characterisation of the gods are surprisingly consistent.

It must be true that the poet is free to introduce new episodes or details, and as Andersen puts it, 'the past is more or less an open field, to be exploited as it is most fruitful'.[3] Certainly the details of the stories of the gods are sometimes inconsistent, but it is also true that, as Andersen comments, 'innovations and reconstructions do not set it apart from tradition'.[4] This suggests that the poet of the *Iliad* uses the traditional material to create his own work in which he presents a consistent characterisation not only of heroes but also of gods.[5] It is worth noting that such consistency implies that the poet has a general picture of the gods' past conflicts, and sometimes may perhaps refer to a particular rebellion such as the Gigantomachy.

Following the narration of the attempt to bind Zeus (*Il.* 1.396ff.), tension between him and the other gods becomes conspicuous, although it is sometimes set forth comically. In this chapter, I sketch the antagonism between Zeus and the other gods, which can be observed behind the scenes of the human battlefield. Among the divine oppositions to Zeus, the alliance of Hera and Poseidon is the most often addressed (as I discussed in Chapter II). As Poseidon is the only male deity who explicitly challenges the power of Zeus in the *Iliad*,[6] I will focus on him as the ring-leader in attempted coups against Zeus, and also as the last obstacle to Zeus' reordering of the universe.

1. The tug-of-war between Zeus and Poseidon (*Il.* 13.1-360)

In Book 13 of the *Iliad*, Zeus and Poseidon stretch the tug-of-war rope and pull on it alternately:

τοὶ δ' ἔριδος κρατερῆς καὶ ὁμοιΐου πτολέμοιο
πεῖραρ ἐπαλλάξαντες ἐπ' ἀμφοτέροισι τάνυσσαν,
ἄρρηκτόν τ' ἄλυτόν τε, τὸ πολλῶν γούνατ' ἔλυσεν.

So those gods knotted and tied the rope of hard strife and levelling war, and stretched it taut over both armies. The rope was not to be or broken or undone, but it broke the knees of many men. (*Il.* 13.358-60)

This rope metaphor symbolises that the human battle, as well as that of the two gods, is locked in stalemate.[7] The peculiar aspect of this episode is that Zeus and Poseidon tested each other's physical strength in 'single combat'. Since binding represents the ultimate defeat for a god, who by definition does not die, this 'crossing and tying the ropes' carries great significance. I argue that this tug-of-war summons up a previous battle between these gods, and is not necessarily to be read merely as an entertainment for the human audience. An examination of the structure of the first half of Book 13 of the *Iliad* will demonstrate the plausibility of this hypothesis.

The presentation of Poseidon

The beginning of Book 13 emphasises the increasing tension between Zeus and Poseidon. The two gods sit on opposite mountain-tops; Zeus looks far over the countries of the Thracians, the Mysians, the Hippemolgoi and the Abioi (13.4-6), and Poseidon watches the whole of Ida, the battlefield of Troy, and the ships of the Achaeans from the highest peak of Samos (Samothrace) (13.12-14). Their mutual, exclusive loftiness suggests a dangerous pressure between them. Zeus looks away from the battlefield, but Poseidon maintains an intense interest in the battle (οὐδ' ἀλαοσκοπιὴν εἶχε, 13.10), particularly emphasised by the double negative in this phrase. We read, too, that he is motivated by fierce anger toward Zeus (Διὶ δὲ κρατερῶς ἐνεμέσσα, 16). The narrative suggests that Poseidon will surely – stealthily and behind Zeus' back – join the war, which would provoke a direct clash. Although Zeus looks far over the land of the Thracians and other people, as if he has no suspicion that any of the gods would intervene in the human battle (3-9), still, attention is emphatically twice drawn to his shining eyes (ὄσσε φαεινώ, 3 and 7). This repeated reference to his 'shining eyes' within a short interval implies that, beneath his seemingly indifferent attitude toward human battlefield, Zeus, too, does feel the danger and anticipates a clash.[8] Significantly, these hints of antagonism between the two big gods cast ominous shadows over the beginning of Book 13.

When Poseidon pities the Achaeans, he departs from his mountain-top on Samos to arm at Aegae *at once*: αὐτίκα δ' ἐξ ὄρεος κατεβήσετο παιπαλόεντος (13.17, 'at once he came down from the rocky mountain'). The expression reminds us of the speed with which he races to encourage the Achaeans while Hera seduces Zeus: αὐτίκα δ' ἐν πρώτοισι μέγα προθορὼν ἐκέλευσεν (14.363, 'at once he [Poseidon] called loud among the front fighters'). The use of the word αὐτίκα effectively characterises Poseidon's position toward Zeus. Whenever he desires to carry out his own plans, his time is short and limited, as he can work only while Zeus looks away from the battlefield.[9] This is because he knows that he is no match for Zeus, whose superior strength is repeatedly emphasised by Poseidon's own words (8.210-11), and by Zeus (15.164-6).

> οὐκ ἂν ἔγωγ' ἐθέλοιμι Διὶ Κρονίωνι μάχεσθαι
> ἡμέας τοὺς ἄλλους, ἐπεὶ ἦ πολὺ φέρτερός ἐστιν.

I [Poseidon] would not want the rest of us to fight against Zeus, son of Cronus, since he is by far greater than us. (*Il*. 8.210-11)

> μή μ' οὐδὲ κρατερός περ ἐὼν ἐπιόντα ταλάσσῃ
> μεῖναι, ἐπεί ἕο φημὶ βίῃ πολὺ φέρτερος εἶναι
> καὶ γενεῇ πρότερος·

even if he [Poseidon] is mightier, he may not be able to stand my attack, since I [Zeus] say that I am far superior to him in strength and senior by birth. (*Il*. 15.164-6)

What is significant is that, in spite of this recognition, Poseidon – like Hera – does not yield but persists in his attempts to challenge Zeus.

The following passages describe Poseidon's prodigious journey (13.17-22) and his majestic horse (23-4), armour (25) and whip (25-6).[10] The same arming combination is repeated later, in Achilles' preparation for joining the war: armour (19.369-91), horse (19.392-5), whip (19.395-6).[11] The elaborate description of Achilles' arming precisely fits the context: his rejoining the war is the point on which the whole plot of the *Iliad* turns, and it naturally demands careful treatment. On the other hand, the overt grandiloquence which describes Poseidon's impressive arming appears ironic, since Poseidon does not actually fight in the war, but only encourages the Achaeans with words (to the two Aeantes at 13.47-58; and to Teucer and others at 13.95-124). We might thus suspect that Poseidon's grand equipment would be more suitable for merely an individual battle against Zeus than for encouraging the human battle. Reinhardt is correct to suggest that Poseidon arms like a hero for his *aristeia*.[12]

It is worth noting how carefully Poseidon is presented in Book 13, especially in his speeches. Poseidon's speeches to the Achaeans are constructed in such a way that, while they are aware of their own inferiority, they are nevertheless encouraged to fight and overthrow their enemy who has the advantage. His message is, of course, appropriate to the Achaeans' desperate situation, but it is also remarkably analogous to Poseidon's own circumstances:[13] that is, while he admits his inferiority to Zeus, he still does not give up his challenge. Let us examine Poseidon's words to Teucer and others:

αἰδώς, Ἀργεῖοι, κοῦροι νέοι· ὕμμιν ἔγωγε   95
μαρναμένοισι πέποιθα σαωσέμεναι νέας ἁμάς·
εἰ δ' ὑμεῖς πολέμοιο μεθήσετε λευγαλέοιο,
νῦν δὴ εἴδεται ἦμαρ ὑπὸ Τρώεσσι δαμῆναι.
ὢ πόποι, ἦ μέγα θαῦμα τόδ' ὀφθαλμοῖσι ὁρῶμαι,
δεινόν, ὃ οὔ ποτ' ἔγωγε τελευτήσεσθαι ἔφασκον,   100
Τρῶας ἐφ' ἡμετέρας ἰέναι νέας

Shame, you Argives, mere young boys! I trusted in your fighting to save our ships. But if you hang back from the grievous war, then the day is now to be seen, when we are beaten down by the Trojans. Oh, what a great marvel I see with my own eyes, a dreadful thing that I thought never could happen: the Trojans are coming against our ships. (*Il.* 13.95-101)

Encouragement to the younger Achaeans (κοῦροι νέοι, 95) would be appropriate for Poseidon himself to use in addressing the younger gods if a new divine conflict were to break out, as he is considered to be a senior deity among the Olympians:

ἄρχε· σὺ γὰρ γενεῆφι νεώτερος· οὐ γὰρ ἔμοιγε
καλόν, ἐπεὶ πρότερος γενόμην καὶ πλείονα οἶδα.

Begin, then, since you [Apollo] are the younger; it would not be well for me [Poseidon] to start, as I was born before you, and have more knowledge. (*Il.* 21.439-40)

Poseidon's next exhortation is likewise noteworthy: ἀλλ' ἀκεώμεθα θᾶσσον· ἀκεσταί τοι φρένες ἐσθλῶν (13.115, 'Let us set things right immediately: the minds of noble men can be easily be put right'). The word ἀκεώμεθα can be understood as 'let us correct our slackness'[14] or, by implication, 'let us forget our dissatisfaction with Agamemnon and fight hard for the common cause.'[15] 'Correction' or 'change' is especially appropriate to Poseidon's character, since he is the deity who challenges the stability of Zeus' sovereignty, by undermining his rule. So, the latter half of verse 115 – 'the minds of noble men can be healed' – could be understood, again, not only as a palliative addressed to the distressed Achaeans, but also to himself. By implication, although Poseidon may have been defeated once by his mightier brother Zeus, he neverthless tries to soothe his own mind and to set out for another duel with Zeus.

A comparable reference to Poseidon's vacillation occurs in 15.203, where he is asked by Iris to retreat: ἦ τι μεταστρέψεις; στρεπταὶ μέν τε φρένες ἐσθλῶν (15.203, 'Will you change your mind? There can be change in the minds of noble men'). Taking this phrase from Poseidon's own words at 13.115, mentioned above, Iris is persuasive and tactful. But this time, his change of mind is negative: he must retreat and yield to Zeus. Poseidon's 'changing mind' is, thus, a notable part of his characterisation in the *Iliad*, and can be seen as a reminder of his tragic destiny – to be second best among the gods.

Poseidon's next speech to Idomeneus (13.237-8) sounds rather curious, but can be explained if we view Poseidon as always being relegated to 'second best'. Poseidon talks in the disguise of Thoas:

συμφερτὴ δ' ἀρετὴ πέλει ἀνδρῶν καὶ μάλα λυγρῶν
νῶϊ δὲ καί κ' ἀγαθοῖσιν ἐπισταίμεσθα μάχεσθαι.

When they stand side by side, even the poorest turn into brave men; if two of us fight together, we [Idomeneus and Thoas] could fight even against good warriors. (*Il.* 13.237-8)

What Poseidon means is that 'even if we are poor fighters, two of us together can fight the brave'. This might be a pre-fabricated maxim,[16] and it fits Thoas, whose guise Poseidon has assumed, but strikingly it fits Poseidon himself, who must rely on an alliance with the other gods in order to overcome Zeus.[17]

The reply of Idomeneus concludes the discourse between Poseidon and the Achaeans, and occurs just before the tug-of-war image. It is significant that Idomeneus compares Ajax with Achilles:

οὐδ' ἂν Ἀχιλλῆϊ ῥηξήνορι χωρήσειεν
ἔν γ' αὐτοσταδίῃ· ποσὶ δ' οὔ πως ἔστιν ἐρίζειν.
νῶϊν δ' ὧδ' ἐπ' ἀριστέρ' ἔχε στρατοῦ, ὄφρα τάχιστα
εἴδομεν ἠέ τῳ εὖχος ὀρέξομεν, ἠέ τις ἡμῖν.

III. The Reordering of the Universe

He [Ajax] would not even give way to Achilles, who breaks men in battle, in a close combat; but for speed of feet, no one can compare with Achilles. So keep on as we are to the left of the army, so that we shall soon see whether we shall give triumph to some other, or he will give it to us. (*Il.* 13.324-7)

The word αὐτοσταδίη (325), used only once in the *Iliad*, means 'standing in the same place'; that is, in close combat.[18] When the Achaeans are reluctant to respond to Hector's challenges in Book 7, it is Ajax who is recognised as the second best of the Achaeans (after Achilles) when he fights with Hector (7.181-99). Given that the chief point of Idomeneus' speech is the anticipation of Ajax's victory, it is pertinent to note the mention of Ajax's *disadvantage* in open fighting. Ajax – second best – is appropriately analogous to Poseidon: although Ajax is not mightier than Achilles, there is at least some hope of victory in close combat. Consequently, this passage could be interpreted as underscoring the tug-of-war metaphor which we take to represent a duel of sorts between Zeus and Poseidon. It is apt that, immediately after Idomeneus' speech, Poseidon attempts a tug-of-war with Zeus (13.345-60) – an αὐτοσταδίη, in fact, with none of the thunderbolts or lightning which typify divine open-air combat.

The tug-of-war

The opening of the tug-of-war passage focuses attention back on the two gods:

τὼ δ᾽ ἀμφὶς φρονέοντε δύω Κρόνου υἷε κραταιὼ
ἀνδράσιν ἡρώεσσιν ἐτεύχετον ἄλγεα λυγρά.

And the two powerful sons of Cronus, their thought divided against each other, brought bitter agonies to fighting warriors. (*Il.* 13.345-6)

The tension operates on two levels: on the surface, the passage alludes to the human battle and the sides to which the two gods lend their support; Ζεὺς μέν ῥα Τρώεσσι (347, 'Zeus for the Trojans'), Ἀργείους δὲ Ποσειδάων (351, 'Poseidon for the Greeks'). The sub-text, however, is the serious conflict between Zeus and Poseidon themselves, as the sentence construction clearly denotes. The narrative then offers an intensely focused account of Poseidon's subordination in 13. 352-60, already quoted in Section 2 of Chapter II (13.352-7), and in this Section above (13.358-60).

The repetition of the two gods' mutual antagonism (ἐνεμέσσα, 353; ἔριδος, 358) reveals that there is more at stake here than merely a playful allusion to the humans' war; rather, the passage raises the spectre of cosmic war. Just as Ajax is subordinate to Achilles, so is Poseidon to Zeus (355): Poseidon is younger in age[19] and inferior in knowledge. The scholiast condemns Poseidon's tactics as lacking in dignity (schol. bT) – but what alternative does he have if he is to persist in challenging the mightier Zeus?

As the *Iliad* narrates it, the result of the human battle depends on the outcome of this combat between the two gods. While we cannot know for certain the outcome of the *Ur*-battle between the gods, we can postulate that their combat might have settled the cosmic war. In terms of military strategy, the duel would occur in the early stage of the conflict:[20] a duel being preferable to a clash of entire armies. For instance, when Paris agrees to fight a duel with Menelaus, both armies are delighted (3.111), expecting that the war will then come to an end, in accordance with the outcome of the duel. After this duel is unsuccessful – inconclusive in settling the war – another is suggested, this time between Hector and Ajax (7.206-302). Likewise, in the divine sphere, we might expect that the gods would rejoice at the opportunity for a timely duel between Zeus and Poseidon, thus putting an end to their conflict.

The tug-of-war image in 13.358-60 is appropriate for such a duel. The apparently too grand arming of Poseidon (13.23-6), discussed above, is best viewed from this perspective, for now his arming becomes neither superfluous nor grandiose, but fitting for the preparation for a duel of such magnitude and significance. Thus Poseidon, as the mightiest among his followers, represents his entire faction. In *Iliad* 13.1-360, I suggest that we can trace an earlier stage in the battle of the gods which begins with the increasing tension between Poseidon and Zeus, and culminates in a duel between the two leaders.

The result of the tug-of-war contest remains ambiguous: it appears to be a tie. However, if we link this episode with the tug-of-war in 8.19-27, where Zeus boasts that all of the gods and goddesses could not pull him down,[21] Zeus must emerge victorious. Zeus' boastful proclamation in Book 8 – τόσσον ἐγὼ περί τ᾽ εἰμὶ θεῶν περί τ᾽ εἴμ᾽ ἀνθρώπων (8.27, 'this is how superior I am to gods and men') – could thus be interpreted as a triumphant declaration of his comprehensive victory over all his opponents.

2. The parallel presentation of wrath (15.47-235)

The disastrous wrath of Achilles is the dominant theme of the *Iliad*, evinced by the poet's commencement of the epic with the word μῆνις.[22] The narrative technique of Book 15 correlates Achilles' wrath with firstly that of Zeus, and secondly that of Poseidon. Poseidon's wrath in particular receives sympathetic treatment, and appears most analogous to that of Achilles.

The wrath of Zeus, and his antagonism against the other gods

While Poseidon is the focus of Book 13, Book 15 commences with a description of Zeus. Following Hera's deception in Book 14, Zeus' fury is emphasised in Book 15. He scowls terrifyingly at Hera (δεινὰ δ᾽ ὑπόδρα ἰδὼν

Ἥρην, 15.13),[23] and his wrath, χόλος, is mentioned in 15.72 and 15.122 in significant contexts.

First, in 15.72, his wrath is associated with that of Achilles; that is, Zeus' wrath will subside when Achilles renounces his own:

> τοῦ δὲ χολωσάμενος κτενεῖ Ἕκτορα δῖος Ἀχιλλεύς.
> ἐκ τοῦ δ' ἄν τοι ἔπειτα παλίωξιν παρὰ νηῶν
> αἰὲν ἐγὼ τεύχοιμι διαμπερές, εἰς ὅ κ' Ἀχαιοὶ   70
> Ἴλιον αἰπὺ ἕλοιεν Ἀθηναίης διὰ βουλάς.
> τὸ πρὶν δ' οὔτ' ἄρ' ἐγὼ παύω χόλον οὔτε τιν' ἄλλον
> ἀθανάτων Δαναοῖσιν ἀμυνέμεν ἐνθάδ' ἐάσω,
> πρίν γε τὸ Πηλεΐδαο τελευτηθῆναι ἐέλδωρ

In anger for him [Patroclus], godlike Achilles will kill Hector. And from that time on I [Zeus] will drive the fighting constantly back from the ships, until the Achaeans capture steep Ilion through the designs of Athena. But before then, I shall not cease my anger or allow any other of the immortals to give help to the Danaans, until the desire of the son of Peleus has been fulfilled. (*Il.* 15.68-74)

Achilles' wrath against Agamemnon, and then Hector, is parallel with that of Zeus against Hera, Poseidon and other gods.[24] The wrath of the two mightiest of the gods and the heroes is amalgamated into one, and functions as the major motivation for the plot.

Secondly, Zeus' χόλος, already roused by Hera's deception in Book 14 and amplified in the tense aftermath, is renewed in 15.122 by Ares' challenge to Zeus' will through his desire to avenge the death of his son Ascalaphus (115-18). This time, Athena checks Ares' recklessness:

> ἔνθα κ' ἔτι μείζων τε καὶ ἀργαλεώτερος ἄλλος
> πὰρ Διὸς ἀθανάτοισι χόλος καὶ μῆνις ἐτύχθη,
> εἰ μὴ Ἀθήνη πᾶσι περιδείσασα θεοῖσιν
> ὦρτο διὲκ προθύρου, λίπε δὲ θρόνον ἔνθα θάασσε,
> τοῦ δ' ἀπὸ μὲν κεφαλῆς κόρυθ' εἵλετο καὶ σάκος ὤμων,   125
> ἔγχος δ' ἔστησε στιβαρῆς ἀπὸ χειρὸς ἑλοῦσα
> χάλκεον·

And now there would have been wrought another greater and more dangerous anger and fury from Zeus among the immortals, if Athena, in her fear for the sake of all the gods, had not left the chair where she was sitting and gone out after him [Ares] through the forecourt, and taken the helmet off from his head and the shield from his shoulders, and seized the bronze spear out of his massive hand and put it away. (*Il.* 15.121-7)

The ponderous phrase χόλος καὶ μῆνις (122, 'wrath and fury') is further emphasised by the unreal conditional sentence.[25] What is also notable is that Zeus' wrath is directed not only toward Ares but also toward the other gods (ἀθανάτοισι, 122). This antagonism between Zeus and a divine alliance is heightened by Zeus' position of emphatic aloofness. Zeus is now on top of Mount Ida (15.5), whereas Hera goes back to Olympus where the gods gather together in Zeus' house (ὁμηγερέεσσι δ᾽ ἐπῆλθεν / ἀθανάτοισι θεοῖσι Διὸς δόμῳ, 84-5). She speaks with the gods, making clear her irritable mood (ὣς εἰποῦσα καθέζετο πότνια Ἥρη, / ὄχθησαν δ᾽ ἀνὰ δῶμα Διὸς θεοί, 100-1, 'so speaking, queen Hera sat down, and there was anger among the gods in Zeus' house'), whereas Zeus remains alone (ὁ δ᾽ ἀφήμενος, 106). Zeus' isolation from the other gods is also implied in the conversation between Hera and Poseidon in book 8.207-11. Hera urges Poseidon to help the Achaeans, wishing that 'Zeus would be annoyed, all alone on Ida' (αὐτοῦ κ᾽ ἔνθ᾽ ἀκάχοιτο καθήμενος οἶος ἐν Ἴδῃ, 207). However, Poseidon is not persuaded:

> τὴν δὲ μέγ᾽ ὀχθήσας προσέφη κρείων ἐνοσίχθων·
> " Ἥρη ἀπτοεπές, ποῖον τὸν μῦθον ἔειπες.
> οὐκ ἂν ἔγωγ᾽ ἐθέλοιμι Διὶ Κρονίωνι μάχεσθαι
> ἡμέας τοὺς ἄλλους, ἐπεὶ ἦ πολὺ φέρτερός ἐστιν."

The powerful shaker of the earth answered her, deeply troubled: 'Hera, what a thing to say! This is reckless talk. I would not want the rest of us to fight against Zeus, son of Cronus, since he is by far greater than us.' (*Il.* 8.208-11)

Poseidon's answer redirects the focus of Hera's question: although her request is directed to him, he understands it as a problem for all the gods, himself included (ἡμέας τοὺς ἄλλους, 211); surely he knows that if he protests against Zeus it will involve the other gods. The stress placed on the unique word ἀπτοεπές (209)[26] anticipates the grave situation that would arise if the gods really went to war against Zeus.

In Book 15, the narrative reveals an increased tension between Zeus and the other gods. Zeus asserts that he is the best of the immortal gods:

> φησὶν γὰρ ἐν ἀθανάτοισι θεοῖσι
> κάρτεΐ τε σθένεΐ τε διακριδὸν εἶναι ἄριστος.

... he [Zeus] asserts that among the immortal gods he is pre-eminently the greatest in power and strength. (*Il.* 15.107-8)

Athena predicts that challenging such a powerful figure will bring catastrophe:

> αὐτίκα γὰρ Τρῶας μὲν ὑπερθύμους καὶ Ἀχαιοὺς
> λείψει, ὁ δ᾽ ἡμέας εἶσι κυδοιμήσων ἐς Ὄλυμπον,
> μάρψει δ᾽ ἐξείης ὅς τ᾽ αἴτιος ὅς τε καὶ οὐκί.

Because he [Zeus] will immediately leave the high-hearted Trojans and the Achaeans, and come back to Olympus to beat us about, and he will lay hold each of us in turn, guilty and innocent alike. (*Il.* 15.135-7)

III. The Reordering of the Universe

Ares and Poseidon are the only gods who venture to protest against Zeus, and once Ares is persuaded to renounce his fight to the death (he acknowledges that he will be destroyed by Zeus' thunderbolt, 15.117-18), Poseidon remains the final contender to challenge the lordship of Zeus.

A direct clash is ingeniously avoided by Zeus' employment of the messenger, Iris. Significantly, her function mirrors that of Athena when the latter intervenes in the quarrel between Agamemnon and Achilles in the very beginning of the *Iliad* (1.194-214). When Iris speaks to Poseidon, she repeats Zeus' words, but adds a further threat of her own devising:

> εἰ δέ οἱ οὐκ ἐπέεσσ' ἐπιπείσεαι, ἀλλ' ἀλογήσεις,
> ἠπείλει καὶ κεῖνος ἐναντίβιον πολεμίξων[27]
> ἐνθάδ' ἐλεύσεσθαι·

And if you [Poseidon] will not obey his [Zeus] words but intend to ignore them, he threatens to come here himself to fight against you face to face. (*Il.* 15.178-80)

Zeus did not mention that he would 'fight face to face' (ἐναντίβιον πολεμίξων, 179) in his speech to Iris (15.158-67). The implication of a duel is extremely effective because, as discussed above, Zeus' superiority in strength has already been emphasised, just before Iris' message (15.165-6), and Poseidon admits it (8.211), as mentioned above:

> ἐπεί ἐο φημὶ βίῃ πολὺ φέρτερος εἶναι
> καὶ γενεῇ πρότερος·

... since I [Zeus] assert that I am far mightier in strength than he is, and elder by birth. (*Il.* 15.165-6)

Of the two aspects of superiority which Zeus claims – strength and greater age – Poseidon challenges Zeus only on the issue of birth.[28]

A doublet of Poseidon and Achilles

As another example of parallel presentation, the dangers of the rivalry between Zeus and Poseidon are echoed in the quarrel between Agamemnon and Achilles. In a much-cited passage, Achilles, robbed of a prize and dishonoured by Agamemnon, appeals to Thetis, as quoted in Chapter I, Section 1 above:

> μῆτερ, ἐπεί μ' ἔτεκές γε μινυνθάδιόν περ ἐόντα,
> τιμήν πέρ μοι ὄφελλεν Ὀλύμπιος ἐγγυαλίξαι
> Ζεὺς ὑψιβρεμέτης· νῦν δ' οὐδέ με τυτθὸν ἔτεισεν·

Mother, since you bore me to be short-lived, surely honour at least should have been granted to me by Olympian Zeus of the loud thunder. But now he has paid me not even a little. (*Il.* 1.352-4)

The claim for τιμή encapsulated in Achilles' appeal is also thematically central to the poem as a whole. Achilles asserts that honour is due to him on the basis of his birth as a man destined to be short-lived (μινυνθάδιόν περ ἐόντα, 1.352).[29]

Poseidon, too, being 'sorely angered' (ὀχθήσας, 15.184), claims τιμή on the basis of his birth. His appeal for the equal division of the universe (187-95)[30] is assured by his birthright as one of the three children of Cronus. The division of the universe involved the sharing of τιμή 'honour' (ἔκαστος δ᾽ ἔμμορε τιμῆς, 15.189), the notion of which is closely connected with the strife surrounding cosmic sovereignty.[31] Poseidon also asserts in 15.209 that he and Zeus hold equal shares and were granted the same lot (ἰσόμορον καὶ ὁμῇ πεπρωμένον αἴσῃ, 15.209). Poseidon's bid for the equal division of portion or honour directly confronts the notion of a hierarchical order.[32] Since possessions are inseparable from honour, Poseidon could duly demand equal honour with Zeus – and deny the supreme domination of Zeus. Thus, an extraordinarily similar logic (insult → wrath → claim of τιμή on the basis of birth) is used in both cases, of Achilles and of Poseidon.[33] They each claim a proper portion of honour, and, as the Homeric concept of sharing already inculcates the idea of limit and justice,[34] they are angry at the unjust treatment they receive from their respective rulers, Agamemnon and Zeus, and, similarly, protest against the legitimacy of their rulers' sovereign rights.

On the basis of these similarities, it is significant that Poseidon levels a reproach at Agamemnon for his behaviour toward Achilles:

> ἀλλ᾽ εἰ δὴ καὶ πάμπαν ἐτήτυμον αἴτιός ἐστιν
> ἥρως Ἀτρεΐδης, εὐρὺ κρείων Ἀγαμέμνων,
> οὕνεκ᾽ ἀπητίμησε ποδώκεα Πηλεΐωνα,
> ἡμέας γ᾽ οὔ πως ἔστι μεθιέμεναι πολέμοιο.

> But even if all the blame truly belongs to the son of Atreus, wide-ruling Agamemnon, for his dishonour to the swift-footed son of Peleus, yet we cannot possibly hold back from fighting. (*Il.* 13.111-14)

Although Poseidon supports the Achaeans, this reproach is severe: he even speaks of the fault of the leader (ἡγεμόνος κακότητι, 108). Such a vehement accusation is appropriately expressed by Poseidon, because he and Achilles are counterparts in sharing a common wrath against their leaders.

These two, Poseidon and Achilles, share another trait: both must finally yield to superior power. Through Iris' persuasion, Poseidon finally decides to yield to Zeus:

> Ἶρι θεά, μάλα τοῦτο ἔπος κατὰ μοῖραν ἔειπες·
> ἐσθλὸν καὶ τὸ τέτυκται, ὅτ᾽ ἄγγελος αἴσιμα εἰδῇ.
> ἀλλὰ τόδ᾽ αἰνὸν ἄχος κραδίην καὶ θυμὸν ἱκάνει,
> ὁππότ᾽ ἂν ἰσόμορον καὶ ὁμῇ πεπρωμένον αἴσῃ

νεικείειν ἐθέλῃσι χολωτοῖσιν ἐπέεσσιν.　210
ἀλλ᾽ ἤτοι νῦν μέν γε[35] νεμεσσηθεὶς ὑποείξω·
ἄλλο δέ τοι ἐρέω, καὶ ἀπειλήσω τό γε θυμῷ·
αἴ κεν ἄνευ ἐμέθεν καὶ Ἀθηναίης ἀγελείης,
Ἥρης Ἑρμείω τε καὶ Ἡφαίστοιο ἄνακτος,
Ἰλίου αἰπεινῆς πεφιδήσεται, οὐδ᾽ ἐθελήσει　215
ἐκπέρσαι, δοῦναι δὲ μέγα κράτος Ἀργείοισιν,
ἴστω τοῦθ᾽, ὅτι νῶϊν ἀνήκεστος χόλος ἔσται.

Divine Iris, what you have said is quite right and true. It is a good thing when a messenger is possessed of right sense. But this comes as a bitter sorrow to my heart and spirit, when Zeus tries to abuse with angry words one who has an equal share with him and has the same portion assigned to him. Still, for this time I will hold myself back and give in to him. But I tell you something else, a threat I make in my heart. If ever, against my will and that of Athena, goddess of spoil, and Hera and Hermes and Lord Hephaestus, Zeus spares steep Ilios, and will not sack it and grant a great victory to the Argives, let him be sure of this, that there will be no more healing of anger between us. (*Il.* 15.206-17)

Janko notes the similarity between this speech of Poseidon and that of Achilles in 16.49-63:[36] that is, (1) acknowledgement of what was said (15.206-7/16.49-51); (2) restating the grievance (15.208-10/16.52-9); and (3) yielding with a threat (15.211-17/16.60-3). The sorrow of Poseidon overshadows that of Achilles, and the two speeches are similar in diction. Verses 15.208 cited above and 16.52 are exactly the same, and the following verses (15.209-10 and 16.53-4) express similar wrath against the ruler.

ἀλλὰ τόδ᾽ αἰνὸν ἄχος κραδίην καὶ θυμὸν ἱκάνει,
ὁππότε δὴ τὸν ὁμοῖον ἀνὴρ ἐθέλῃσιν ἀμέρσαι
καὶ γέρας ἂψ ἀφελέσθαι, ὅ τε κράτεϊ προβεβήκῃ·

But such a bitter sorrow comes to my [Achilles] heart and spirit, whenever a man is willing to do down his equal and take back a prize of honour, as he is superior in his power. (*Il.* 16.52-4)

Both Poseidon and Achilles share 'bitter sorrow' (αἰνὸν ἄχος, 15.208 and 16.52),[37] and both think that they should be treated on equal terms with their rulers. Both of them must yield: as Achilles recognises Agamemnon's greater power (16.54), so, too, must Poseidon admit Zeus' power and seniority in age (15.165-6).

If Poseidon had not yielded, a great war might have erupted; note Zeus' words:

οἴχεται εἰς ἅλα δῖαν, ἀλευάμενος χόλον αἰπὺν
ἡμέτερον· μάλα γάρ τε[38] μάχης ἐπύθοντο καὶ ἄλλοι,
οἵ περ ἐνέρτεροί εἰσι θεοί, Κρόνον ἀμφὶς ἐόντες.

69

> He [Poseidon] has left and gone into the holy sea, to avoid the stark fury that would have been ours. Truly even other lower gods, who gather round Cronus, have experienced battle (against me). (*Il.* 15.223-5)

Zeus knows that a divine conflict would involve *all* the gods, even the Titans ('lower gods', 225), and that his lordship is secured by undermining Poseidon. The moment when Poseidon decides to retreat, therefore, is pivotal to Zeus' sovereignty. The critical significance of this moment is akin to that in which Athena caught Achilles by his hair (1.197): Achilles then goes to his own huts (1.305-6) and retreats from the war. Similarly, we see that, after his withdrawal from the burgeoning conflict, Poseidon also retreats physically, going down into the sea (*Il.* 15.223).

Surrender of Poseidon

Poseidon's final threat as he yields (*Il.* 15.211-17) is a reflection of his self-respect or pride and desire for honour. Iliadic heroes are also motivated to risk their lives to defend their pride. For instance, Sarpedon, facing his inevitable death, says, 'if we were to live forever, ageless and immortal, I would not be fighting in the front ranks' (*Il.* 12.322-4). Unlike Sarpedon, Poseidon is immortal, but his pride remains of great significance, and he cannot tolerate humiliation. As Nilsson notes, the anthropomorphism of the Iliadic gods shows their human traits; and gods, too, must be measured by the same moral standards as mankind.[39] Just as the heroes in the *Iliad* are not morally unfettered princes or supermen, so too the gods, especially Poseidon, are constrained; Poseidon's life is not easy: he yields and suffers.[40]

Gods are said to be 'blessed' and to 'live at ease'. Achilles tells Priam that humans live in misery but 'gods are free from care' (*Il.* 24.526). Indeed, the delightful circumstances of the gods are often emphasised.[41] However, Homeric gods are not uncomplicated; they are not infallible, and even the heroes recognise that there are limits on divine power. For example, Nature goes her own way (*Il.* 6.146-8), and the gods cannot protect their favourites against death.[42] As Odysseus says, even Poseidon cannot restore the Cyclops' eye (*Od.* 9.525).

One's portion is one's due and regular share, and the final inevitable portion for humans is death. If death for humans signifies the change from the brightness of life to the dark and meaningless existence of death,[43] exactly the same picture is offered to those gods hurled into Tartarus. According to Détienne and Vernant,[44] to strike a god with Zeus' thunderbolt is to deprive him of the vital force that previously animated him, and to relegate him, forever paralysed, to the limits of the world, far from the dwelling of the gods where he formerly exercised power. The thunderbolt is the ultimate source of Zeus' authority, as we see from the fates of the Titans and Typhoeus – defeated, banished to a meaningless existence, never to emerge. Even gods abhor the dark place beneath (*Il.* 20.65). Thus although by definition there is no death for gods, Zeus' threat of a duel with Poseidon (15.179) implies that, in defeat, Poseidon too would suffer the fate of descending into this dark and meaningless existence. Before he yields, Poseidon faces a crisis equal to that of human death. When he yields, however, he still clings to the shreds of his pride and self-respect.

We have noted that the characterisation of Poseidon is remarkably analogous to that of Achilles. In the light of my suggestion that the poet of the *Iliad* drew inspiration from an earlier story of the battle of the gods, we might propose that his focus on Achilles' heroic wrath and striving for honour is patterned on this stratum of material. The poem is built around attitudes which reflect fundamental questions of heroic wrath, heroic shame, and the acceptance of death.[45] Both human characters and Poseidon are delineated through their responses to these questions. As the fate of Achilles is tragic, so, in a sense, is that of Poseidon. By using the motif of Poseidon's wrath as another integral element in his poem, the poet makes the dispute surrounding Achilles' wrath clearer and more profound. Thus the motifs of wrath – of Zeus and Achilles, Poseidon and Achilles – work together to develop a more coherent artistic product.

3. The reordering of the universe
(*Iliad* 20.54-74; 21.385-520)

In the opening scene of Book 20, the gods make preparations for the fight, suggesting a conflict on a cosmic scale (20.54-74). The combat pairing of the gods is listed (20.67-74) and the actual fighting is described (21.385-520). Overall, the gods are divided into two camps, and those who favour the Greeks stand on the Greek side with Poseidon. This sub-plot is so well integrated that it seems a natural consequence for the gods to join the human war. But why, as Apollo complains at 21.462-3, do the gods fight with each other on behalf of humans? I suggest that reading an earlier cosmic battle underlying this text makes possible a fuller appreciation of the poet's subtle intertextualities. On such an interpretation, in some pre-Iliadic stories, the gods could have been antagonistic to each other; and in this text they may retain their original spirit of partisanship, which operates aside from the human battle.[46] That is, the human battle does not motivate the gods to fight in partisan formation; rather, they fight in the human battle *because* of their original, partisan nature. This might explain their apparent preoccupation with fighting and shouting at each other (21.385-6).

Some scholars criticise the imbalance of the two accounts of the Theomachy: the solemn proclamation (20.54-74), then the 'anticlimax' of this major divine battle (21.385-520) in which some gods are reluctant to fight.[47] I will focus on the passages concerning Poseidon and Zeus to determine the interrelation of these two apparently imbalanced accounts, and to consider why some change of mood occurs.

The battle of the gods

When Zeus calls the gods to assembly at the beginning of Book 20 (1-12), the only conversation cited is between Poseidon and Zeus (13-30). Poseidon sits in the middle of the gods (ἷζε δ' ἄρ' ἐν μέσσοισι, 15), and as the senior of the assembled gods, he speaks first to Zeus, asking the reason for the assembly (16-18). This should remind us of how Achilles opens the debate in 1.59-67. Zeus answers, 'you know, Earth-shaker, the decision in my mind' (20.20). The tension between the two is overt *and* double-edged, for this discourse seems to function as a declaration of war.

In terms of the structure of battle, we have already recognised the preliminary stage, namely the duel between the mightiest of the two sides – as we interpreted the tug-of-war incident between Zeus and Poseidon (13.358-60). Now, we see the meeting of the leaders of both sides, and anticipate that the war will soon be fought. Although Zeus says that he will stay on Olympus to see the human battles (20.22-3), he thunders terribly in response to the other gods (20.56). The description of the shaking, from above and below, of the valleys and mountains (20.54-74) sets the scene for a huge conflict, and is highly appropriate to a war on the cosmic scale:[48]

> ὣς τοὺς ἀμφοτέρους μάκαρες θεοὶ ὀτρύνοντες
> σύμβαλον, ἐν δ' αὐτοῖς ἔριδα ῥήγνυντο βαρεῖαν·
> δεινὸν δὲ βρόντησε πατὴρ ἀνδρῶν τε θεῶν τε
> ὑψόθεν· αὐτὰρ νέρθε Ποσειδάων ἐτίναξε
> γαῖαν ἀπειρεσίην ὀρέων τ' αἰπεινὰ κάρηνα.

> So the blessed gods stirring on both sides, brought them to the clash: and they broke out bitter conflict among themselves. The father of men and gods thundered terribly from high above, while beneath them Poseidon shook the limitless earth and the high peaks of the mountains. (*Il.* 20.54-8)

The tension which was foreshadowed in 13.1-16 is now reaching its climax. As is proper procedure, the leaders of both sides, Zeus and Poseidon, are honoured with introductions. It appears that a fierce clash will now begin. However, the situation has suddenly changed, as Zeus steps aside of the war:

> ἄϊε δὲ Ζεὺς
> ἥμενος Οὐλύμπῳ· ἐγέλασσε δέ οἱ φίλον ἦτορ
> γηθοσύνῃ, ὅθ' ὁρᾶτο θεοὺς ἔριδι ξυνιόντας.

> Zeus heard it where he sat on Olympus, and his heart laughed for joy in his heart, when he watched the gods joining in conflict. (*Il.* 21.388-90)

III. The Reordering of the Universe

These passages – Zeus' prediction and his action – make it clear that the Theomachy is suddenly put on for Zeus' amusement. No one knows whether the earlier myth of the battle of the gods is recalled in this passage or not. What we are now given is essentially mock fighting, and Zeus is a superior bystander and no longer a participant. This change of direction away from the anticipated, serious Theomachy is a sharp deviation by the poet which completes – and demonstrates the completion of – the reordering of the universe by Zeus.

The laughter of Zeus (21.389) can be compared with the delight of Agamemnon (*Od.* 8.78), who rejoices at a quarrel between Odysseus and Achilles.[49] But I would also suggest that Zeus' laughter here is analogous to that in the *Hymn to Hermes* (389) which decisively – and mysteriously – settles the dispute between Apollo and Hermes.[50] In the Theomachy, Zeus is not the leader of a combatant side, but the judge who respects the claims of all parties.

As the result of this change, his attitude to the battle of the gods becomes similar to his attitude to the human battle. In contrast to Book 13, Zeus now watches the battles of gods as well as humans. Like Achilles at the funeral games for Patroclus (*Il.* 23.262-897), Zeus is in charge and no longer merely a participant. Although he stirs up the battle (πόλεμον δ' ἀλίαστον ἔγειρε, 20.31), he will not be involved in the fighting between the gods. His involvement might have caused cosmic disorder, but his supremacy will remain secure.

The end of the battle of the gods

In the episode where Apollo refuses to fight against Poseidon (21.462-7), Artemis' accusation about Apollo's refusal (21.472-7) implies that there had been antagonism between Poseidon and Apollo even before this incident:[51]

νηπύτιε, τί νυ τόξον ἔχεις ἀνεμώλιον αὕτως;
μή σευ νῦν ἔτι πατρὸς ἐνὶ μεγάροισιν ἀκούσω
εὐχομένου, ὡς τὸ πρὶν ἐν ἀθανάτοισι θεοῖσιν,
ἄντα Ποσειδάωνος ἐναντίβιον πολεμίξειν.

You [Apollo] fool, why then do you carry a bow which is nothing more than wind? Let me [Artemis] not hear you boasting in our father's house among the immortal gods, as you did before, that you could fight face to face against Poseidon. (*Il.* 21.474-7)

Artemis' specific mention of previous occasions when Apollo declared his boastful decision to defeat Poseidon is significant: these occurred in their father's house, among the immortal gods (475-6). That is, Apollo made his boastful claim in front of Zeus, in assemblies of the gods. Were these assemblies similar to the one to which Zeus called the gods in 20.4-5 (that

73

is, preceding the outbreak of war)? On such an occasion the young Apollo might have uttered, perhaps with Zeus' favour,[52] such an appropriately threatening proclamation against the leader of the 'enemy'.

Hera's response to Artemis' reproach calls for attention. Hera perceives Artemis' condemnation as hostile toward herself:

πῶς δὲ σὺ νῦν μέμονας, κύον ἀδεές, ἀντί᾽ ἐμεῖο
στήσεσθαι;

How do you [Artemis] dare now, you shameless bitch, to stand against me?
(*Il.* 21.481-2)

For Hera, an insult to Poseidon is an insult to herself; the alliance between Hera and Poseidon is thus consistent throughout the epic.

The story of Apollo's ceding victory to Poseidon without a fight finds a parallel in the episode of the spear-throwing contest in which Achilles awards Agamemnon the prize without a contest (23.884-97). The nobility of Achilles is particularly marked in the funeral games in Book 23, because it differs so greatly from his cruel treatment of Hector's body in the preceding account. Achilles' behaviour is now perfectly under control in the games, and he renders fair judgement to all. His decision with regard to Agamemnon – admitting that Agamemnon is 'supreme in power' (23.891) – marks their final reconciliation. Likewise, Poseidon's victory without a battle implies a peaceful close to the battle of the gods.

Just as Achilles watches and presides over the funeral games, so too does Zeus preside at the battle of the gods. The centripetal progress of Zeus in this scene is conspicuous in several ways. First, it is because of respect for Zeus that Apollo and Hermes refuse to fight: Apollo avoids the fight against his uncle out of respect (21.468); Hermes says it is dangerous to fight against the wives of Zeus (498-9). Second, all of the gods gather round Zeus after their fight: Artemis comes to Olympus and sits in tears on Zeus' lap (505-6), and the other gods also take their seats beside him (520).[53]

Verses 518-20 function as the closing section of the Theomachy, symbolising that all disputes and conflicts are settled, and Zeus has achieved his supremacy over the Olympian cosmos:

οἱ δ᾽ ἄλλοι πρὸς Ὄλυμπον ἴσαν θεοὶ αἰὲν ἐόντες,
οἱ μὲν χωόμενοι, οἱ δὲ μέγα κυδιόωντες·
κὰδ δ᾽ ἷζον παρὰ πατρὶ κελαινεφεῖ·

But the rest of the gods, who live forever, went back to Olympus, some in anger and others greatly exulting, and they sat down beside their father, the lord of the dark clouds. (*Il.* 21.518-20)

Even those who are angry (οἱ μὲν χωόμενοι, 519) come to sit beside Zeus. A problematic aspect of the Olympians' interrelationship has been settled and they seem to become systematised into an ordered divine community. Two prominent deities are described, emphatically, as 'brother of Zeus' (Poseidon, 469) or 'the wife of Zeus' (Hera, 479, 499).[54] This is quite a different picture from the stories of Uranus or Cronus, where the father seems to be 'a stranger who is nothing to do with the mother and the children'.[55] In Zeus' cosmos, the family now enjoy a relationship with him. The existence of challengers implied disorder, but with their defeat the Olympian regime has been set on a new footing.

In the last analysis, the plan of Zeus is a mystery.[56] We do not know exactly how Zeus finally subdued Poseidon and his alliance. But, in the poet's hands, under the plan of Zeus, not only humans but also gods suffer or rejoice. As Penelope says (*Od.* 1.338), both gods and men accomplish mighty deeds that will become epic song. Griffin's words about the humans – 'from suffering comes song, and song gives pleasure'[57] – are applicable even to the gods. The function of the Homeric gods is sometimes relegated to that of mere background to human deeds, but the stories of the gods not only have their own internal logic and consistency, but also they function as foreshadowing and echoing the human behaviour. As I have suggested, by tracing the parallel presentation of Zeus and Achilles, and of Poseidon and Achilles in this chapter, the stories of the gods play much more integral parts of the construction of the epic than is usually perceived.

It is generally admitted that, even if Homer created an original poem, he drew upon a rich earlier epic tradition. I believe that the poet of the *Iliad* composed his poem by exploiting and repeatedly referring to an earlier epic of the battle of the gods, probably the *Gigantomachy*. The consistency in the portrayal of the characters of the *Iliadic* gods thus reflects the *aristeia* of the gods of the distant past.

The Birth of Athena

Hesiod's *Theogony* celebrates, thematically and structurally, the supremacy of Zeus. Hesiod's grand theme is Zeus' sovereignty and its meaning: in spite of the various challenges to his power, Zeus obtains both dominance and the means to secure it. Although some scholars claim that it did not occur to Hesiod to question why Zeus' sovereignty would survive,[1] I assume that one of the main purposes of the *Theogony* is to clarify the reasons for Zeus' success and ultimate victory. My interpretation is that the stories of Uranus and Cronus' generational strife are intended as *lessons* for Zeus – aids to his own survival – which influence Zeus' ingenious way of eliminating this perpetual cycle of internecine conflict by giving birth to Athena. To demonstrate this, I will start with Near Eastern influences on Hesiod's succession myth.[2]

1. Near Eastern succession myth and Hesiod's *Theogony*

Hurrian myth

Archaeological evidence demonstrates that the representation of the thunderbolt, usually conceived as a typically *Greek* image of Zeus, is clearly dependent on an eastern model.[3] In the realm of epic, too, Oriental myths undoubtedly provided Hesiod with raw material which he arranged in new patterns. It is widely accepted that the succession of Greek heavenly rulers, Uranus, Cronus and Zeus, has an obvious parallel in Hurrian myth.[4] Alalu, the first king, is defeated by Anu (the Sky-god), and goes down to the dark earth. Anu takes the throne, but nine years later is castrated by Kumarbi, who swallows Anu's sexual organs. Kumarbi is impregnated and spits out three 'dreadful' gods: the Storm-god, the river Aranzahas, and Tasmisus. Anu advises the Storm-god, while he is still inside Kumarbi, of the places from which the Storm-god may emerge from Kumarbi; he also plots to destroy Kumarbi with the help of the Storm-god. The Storm-god defeats Kumarbi and takes over the kingship in heaven. The succession is as follows:

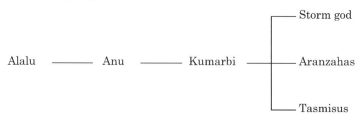

Alalu ——— Anu ——— Kumarbi ——— Storm god / Aranzahas / Tasmisus

Burkert posits the correspondence of the Storm-god to Zeus.[5] Certainly, several features of their succession myths are analogous: first, the motif of swallowing; second, Kumarbi (identifiable with Cronus) castrates the previous ruler Anu (identifiable with Uranus); third, the Storm-god (= Zeus) is one of three brothers; and, fourth, Anu helps the Storm-god against Kumarbi by giving advice even before the Storm-god is born – just as Uranus (with Gaia) ensures Zeus' survival by giving advice to Rhea before Zeus' birth (*Theog.* 474-6).

There are also differences, not only in detail but also in the main structure of the plot.[6] The most conspicuous is that Zeus (the third god) halts the cycle of sovereign strife; in the Hurrian myth the Storm-god (the fourth god) does not seek to stop the cycle of strife, nor to rule over Heaven eternally. Although the detail of the story that follows the victory of the Storm-god is unclear, the Hurrian myth seems to emphasise continuous change of sovereignty; in contrast, the significant element of the *Theogony* is Zeus' final victory. Clearly Hesiod puts great emphasis on the *cessation* of generational strife that resulted from Zeus' triumph.

The myths also differ in that, in the Hurrian myth, succession to sovereignty is effected by violence in battle – *not* as a consequence of a blood relationship between father and son. These battles are repeated between Alalu and Anu, Anu and Kumarbi, and Kumarbi and the Storm-god, and in each case we see that the previous ruler is overcome by the physical strength of his successor. The simplest principle works here: the strongest wins and rules the universe. In Hesiod's *Theogony*, physical strength is less of a *motivating* force in succession than is generational strife, in the sense that a female figure, either a wife or a mother, always interferes in the process of succession. Although the physical strength of Zeus is often mentioned in the *Theogony*,[7] in fact it is Gaia who is the dominant figure in plotting the succession and who plays the decisive, i.e. motivating, role. In terms of succession myth, we will see that the *Theogony* puts into the foreground the inter-generational problems between father(s) and son(s), which, as I discuss, are narrated in terms of the theme of the mightier son who overcomes his own father.

The Hesiodic theogony can be thus characterised, and differentiated from its Hurrian ancestor, by two basic distinctions: (a) Zeus, the third god, stops the cycle of succession; and, (b) succession is the outcome of generational strife. The reasons for these divergences cannot easily be determined,[8] but I will view these differences, and the concepts embodied in them, as significant in themselves for examining the *Theogony*. The *Theogony* constructs a different mythological pattern from that presented in Hurrian myth, in order to aid the author's own teleology: that is, in order to demonstrate how and why Zeus could act preventatively to overcome the foreseeable crisis of constant generational strife by halting the perpetual process of violent succession.

Babylonian myth

Hesiod's divergence from traditional mythic structures is also in evidence when we compare his *Theogony* with the Babylonian myth presented in the *Enuma Elish,* composed around 1000 BC at the latest,[9] and based on Sumerian cosmology.[10] The dominant figure is the god Marduk.[11] Tiâmat prepared an assault against Ea who had killed her husband Apsu. Ea was frightened and sought aid from her grandfather Anshar. Anshar planned first to send Anu to Tiâmat, but Anu returned in terror; then he ordered Marduk to go into battle. The battle between the gods ended with the victory of Marduk, who divided Tiâmat's body into two parts to create the universe.[12] Thus the succession is:

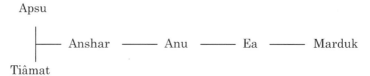

The chief object of this epic seems to be to honour Marduk as the champion of the gods and creator of heaven (Tablets VI-VII), offering cosmological reasons for his supremacy.[13] The design of this story is quite similar to that of the *Theogony*:[14] the battles for sovereignty take place between gods who are related by blood, and one of the battles by which Marduk obtains supreme regal power is analogous to the Titanomachy of the *Theogony*. Some details correspond remarkably well: before the battle, sweet wine is served at the Court of Assembly of the gods, then their spirit is exalted (Tablet III, ll. 136-7); this reminds us of *Theogony* 639-41, where Zeus gives *nectar* and *ambrosia* to the Hecatoncheires before the Titanomachy; then their courage is also exalted:

> ἀλλ' ὅτε δὴ κείνοισι παρέσχεθεν ἄρμενα πάντα,
> νέκταρ τ' ἀμβροσίην τε, τά περ θεοὶ αὐτοὶ ἔδουσι,
> πάντων <τ'> ἐν στήθεσσιν ἀέξετο θυμὸς ἀγήνωρ
> [ὡς νέκταρ τ' ἐπάσαντο καὶ ἀμβροσίην ἐρατεινήν,]
> δὴ τότε τοῖς μετέειπε πατὴρ ἀνδρῶν τε θεῶν τε·

But when Zeus provided them with everything appropriate, nectar and ambrosia, which the gods themselves eat, and the heroic spirit grew in all their hearts, [once they received nectar and lovely ambrosia] then, the father of men and gods spoke among them. (*Theog.* 639-43)

Again, however, there are conspicuous differences between the *Enuma Elish* and the *Theogony*. Most notably, the succession in the *Enuma Elish* is not as straightforward as that of the *Theogony* (i.e. grandfather – father – son); in the *Enuma Elish* Tiâmat is the opponent of the final conqueror

Marduk. She is the female ocean god, and four generations older than Marduk. The antagonism presented in the *Enuma Elish* exists between the first generation of gods (Apsu and Tiâmat) and an alliance of gods of the second, third and fourth generations: that is, the *Enuma Elish* does not present a picture of generational strife in which, as in the *Theogony*, a son overcomes his father.

We see that Hesiod's *Theogony*, for all its similarities to Near Eastern myth, offers elements unique to its own narrative. As Solmsen points out,[15] there are passages which, while neither wholly traditional nor wholly original, nevertheless exhibit an old mythical manifestation in a new light, with a new interpretation. As Herodotus says, Hesiod systematised the [Greek] gods (2.53.2). The narrative structures of his epic highlight the value systems of his own society: to paraphrase Nagy, Hesiod, like Homer, recreates for his listeners the inherited values that serve as the foundation for their society.[16]

By emphasising how Hesiod's arrangement of traditional elements differs from that of the Near Eastern sources which influenced him or his predecessors, I suggest that it is these unique features – the differences – which indicate Hesiod's specific purpose. A brief comparison between Hesiod's account and the Hurrian myth and the Babylonian *Enuma Elish* clarifies the two main, unique, characteristics of the *Theogony*: (a) succession occurs through 'generational strife' – specifically, that between son and father, in which the son overcomes the father; and (b) Zeus, a god of the third generation, halts the cycle of strife. I would suggest that these thematic differences reveal Hesiod's ultimate objective: to show the ascent of Zeus to permanent sovereignty in the world as an inevitable and unchallengeable fact.

2. The Hesiodic account: the route to Zeus' victory

In order to investigate Hesiod's logic, let us look closely at some passages in the *Theogony*. Hesiod presents us with several determinants which effect Zeus' final victory, such as his conspicuous physical power and wisdom. In these passages, the utmost significance is given to the method by which he rids himself of the challenge of usurpation by a son mightier than himself. The fates of his predecessors, Uranus and Cronus, can be read as lessons from which Zeus derives his strategy.

Uranus

According to the text, Uranus conceals his children in a hiding place within Gaia[17] because he hates them:

ὅσσοι γὰρ Γαίης τε καὶ Οὐρανοῦ ἐξεγένοντο,
δεινότατοι παίδων, σφετέρῳ δ᾽ ἤχθοντο τοκῆι   155

ἐξ ἀρχῆς· καὶ τῶν μὲν ὅπως τις πρῶτα γένοιτο,
πάντας ἀποκρύπτασκε, καὶ ἐς φάος οὐκ ἀνίεσκε,
Γαίης ἐν κευθμῶνι, κακῷ δ᾽ ἐπετέρπετο ἔργῳ
Οὐρανός·

For all those who were born of Earth and Heaven were the most terrible of
their children; they were hated by their own father from the beginning. As
soon as any of them was born, Heaven hid them all away in a hollow of Earth,
and did not let them come up into the light, and he rejoiced in his wicked
work. (*Theog.* 154-9)

It looks as if Uranus' violence is to be read as a malicious act *per se* (κακῷ
... ἔργῳ, 158), but the description of his children offers a tangible reason for
his hatred: Uranus fears them because they are dreadful and strong. The
Cyclopes have insolent hearts (ὑπέρβιον ἦτορ ἔχοντας, 139), and the Hecatoncheires are presumptuous children, not to be touched (ὑπερήφανα τέκνα,
149; ἄπλαστοι, 151). In particular, Cronus is most dreadful of all – and he
also hates his father:

τοὺς δὲ μέθ᾽ ὁπλότατος γένετο Κρόνος ἀγκυλομήτης,
δεινότατος παίδων, θαλερὸν δ᾽ ἤχθηρε τοκῆα.

After them the youngest was born, crooked-counselled Cronus, most terrible
of children; and he hated his lusty father. (*Theog.* 137-8)

The connotation of these passages is that Uranus feels threatened by his
sons' presumptive power. Significantly, this is almost the same implication we receive from the prophecies given to Cronus and Zeus. Unlike
them, Uranus does not receive an *explicit* prophecy that he will be dis-
placed by his own son, but the reasoning underlying the actions by which
Cronus and Zeus avoid *their* children can be extended, by implication, to
their predecessor: the threat of defeat at the hands of one's offspring.[18]

Uranus' precaution is unsuccessful; he is defeated by Gaia's contrivance
(δολίην δὲ κακὴν, 160) and the courage of Cronus (θαρσήσας δὲ μέγας Κρόνος,
168). By this example, Hesiod offers a first lesson, demonstrating that
imprisoning children in the mother's hiding place is of no use – and it is
contrivance and courage with physical power which become the decisive
factors for securing sovereignty.

Cronus

Gaia's oracle forewarns Cronus that he will be overcome by his own son.
From this point, Gaia's knowledge functions as a force driving the succession story:

πεύθετο γὰρ Γαίης τε καὶ Οὐρανοῦ ἀστερόεντος
οὕνεκά οἱ πέπρωτο ἑῷ ὑπὸ παιδὶ δαμῆναι,

80

καὶ κρατερῷ περ ἐόντι, Διὸς μεγάλου διὰ βουλάς.   465
τῷ ὅ γ᾽ ἄρ᾽ οὐκ ἀλαοσκοπιὴν ἔχεν᾽ ἀλλὰ δοκεύων
παῖδας ἑοὺς κατέπινε· Ῥέην δ᾽ ἔχε πένθος ἄλαστον.

For he learned from Earth and starry Heaven that he was destined to be
defeated by his own child, powerful though he was, through the plans of great
Zeus. For this reason, he never kept careless watch, but observed and swallowed
his children; then Rhea suffered unforgettable grief. (*Theog.* 463-7)

It is not surprising that Gaia has an oracular capacity – she is said to have
been the first occupant of the Delphic oracular seat.[19] Hence, at the very
beginning of Aeschylus' *Eumenides*, Gaia is honoured as the first prophet
at Delphi:

Πρῶτον μὲν εὐχῇ τῇδε πρεσβεύω θεῶν
τὴν πρωτόμαντιν Γαῖαν·

First among the gods in this prayer I honour Earth, as the first prophet.
(Aesch. *Eum.* 1-2)[20]

The oracle given to Cronus does not, however, specify the *name* of the child
who will overthrow him[21] and, as a consequence, although the threat (from
a child) is less opaque than in Uranus' case, Cronus still cannot identify
his real enemy with certainty. Both Cronus and Zeus know that it is their
destiny to be dethroned by one of their own sons, and both are faced with
having to avert the decree of destiny by trickery. However, since Cronus
does not know his *actual* opponent, his precautions have to be extended to
all of his children – and, as a result, he misses the most important one.

Cronus has learned from the fate of Uranus that he should hide his
children on his own, without his wife's involvement, because his wife could
choose to support her children against her husband. As Caldwell remarks,
Cronus understands that it is the mother as much as the son who is his
enemy.[22] His children must be separated from their mother, but, despite
this knowledge, Cronus still cannot avoid the inevitable alliance between
mother (Rhea) and son (Zeus).

There are several formulaic correspondences between the story of Cronus' attempt to swallow Zeus, and Zeus' swallowing of Metis.[23]

Cronus:

καὶ τοὺς μὲν κατέπινε μέγας Κρόνος, ὥς τις ἕκαστος
νηδύος ἐξ ἱερῆς μητρὸς πρὸς γούναθ᾽ ἵκοιτο,   460
τὰ φρονέων, ἵνα μή τις ἀγαυῶν Οὐρανιώνων
ἄλλος ἐν ἀθανάτοισιν ἔχοι <u>βασιληίδα τιμήν</u>.
πεύθετο γὰρ Γαίης τε καὶ Οὐρανοῦ ἀστερόεντος
οὕνεκά οἱ πέπρωτο ἑῷ ὑπὸ παιδὶ δαμῆναι,
καὶ κρατερῷ περ ἐόντι, Διὸς μεγάλου διὰ βουλάς.   465

Great Cronus swallowed them, when each of them came from their mother's holy womb to her knees. He had this in mind, that no other gods of the noble children of Heaven, than he, should have the honour of kingship among the immortals. For he learned from Earth and starry Heaven that he was destined to be defeated by his own child, powerful though he was, through the plans of great Zeus. (*Theog.* 459-65)

τῷ δὲ σπαργανίσασα μέγαν λίθον ἐγγυάλιξεν
Οὐρανίδῃ μέγ᾽ ἄνακτι, θεῶν προτέρων βασιλῆι·
τὸν τόθ᾽ ἑλὼν χείρεσσιν ἑὴν ἐσκάτθετο νηδύν

Then she [Gaia] wrapped a large stone in swaddling-clothes and put int the hands of the son of Heaven, the great lord, king of the former gods. Seizing it in his hands, he put it away in his belly. (*Theog.* 485-7)

Zeus:

ἀλλ᾽ ὅτε δὴ ἄρ᾽ ἔμελλε θεὰν γλαυκῶπιν Ἀθήνην
τέξεσθαι, τότ᾽ ἔπειτα δόλῳ φρένας ἐξαπατήσας
αἱμυλίοισι λόγοισιν ἑὴν ἐσκάτθετο νηδύν,   890
Γαίης φραδμοσύνῃσι καὶ Οὐρανοῦ ἀστερόεντος·
τὼς γάρ οἱ φρασάτην, ἵνα μὴ βασιληίδα τιμὴν
ἄλλος ἔχοι Διὸς ἀντὶ θεῶν αἰειγενετάων.
ἐκ γὰρ τῆς εἵμαρτο περίφρονα τέκνα γενέσθαι·
πρώτην μὲν κούρην γλαυκώπιδα Τριτογένειαν,   895
ἶσον ἔχουσαν πατρὶ μένος καὶ ἐπίφρονα βουλήν,
αὐτὰρ ἔπειτ᾽ ἄρα παῖδα θεῶν βασιλῆα καὶ ἀνδρῶν
ἤμελλεν τέξασθαι, ὑπέρβιον ἦτορ ἔχοντα·

But when she [Metis] was about to give birth to the bright-eyed goddess Athena, he [Zeus] deceived her mind by cunning words, and put her away in his belly on the shrewd advice of Earth and starry Heaven. They advised him in this way, so that no other gods than Zeus should have the honour of kingship among the eternally-living gods. For it was destined that exceedingly wise children should be born from Metis: first a bright-eyed daughter, Tritogeneia, possessing strength and clever counsel equal to her father's, and then she was to bear a son, king of gods and men, possessing a violent heart. (*Theog.* 888-98)

First, in both cases Uranus and Gaia represent their kingship through the same phrase (βασιληίδα τιμήν, 462 and 892). Iliadic uses of this phrase demonstrate that it conveys not only the idea of sovereignty in the abstract, but also the concrete meaning of 'estate': δῶκε δέ οἱ τιμῆς βασιληΐδος ἥμισυ πάσης (*Il.* 6.193). Iobates, king of Lycia, decides to give half of his estate to Bellerophontes as reward for Bellerophontes' heroic exploits in killing the Chimaera (6.173-83), defeating the Solymoi (6.184-5), destroying the Amazons (6. 186) and, finally, fighting against the best warriors of Lycia (6.188-90). Like Bellerophontes' fame, Uranus' kingship is primarily based on his physical strength, as the phrase καὶ κρατερῷ περ ἐόντι (465) clearly states.

Second, the act of swallowing is expressed by the same phrase: 'put it/her in his belly' (ἑὴν ἐσκάτθετο νηδύν, 487 and 890) – that is, Cronus and Zeus carry out exactly the same action in order to solve their problem. I propose, however, that the duplicate phrasing effectively emphasises the *difference* in what follows: Cronus spares the mother (leaving her free to aid her son), while Zeus eliminates the threat of the mother for good and at the same time appropriates her intelligence.[24]

In the account of Zeus' swallowing of Metis, a decisive factor in his success is deceit. Consecutive words of cunning connotation (δόλῳ φρένας ἐξαπατήσας / αἱμυλίοισι λόγοισιν, 889-90) signify that it is, in particular, Zeus' wily nature which will enable his successful acquisition (and main-tenance) of power. Of course, Cronus too is characterised as cunning, receiving the epithet ἀγκυλομήτης (168, 473, 495). But it is Zeus who receives the epithet μητιόεις (the counsellor, 457). With these two epithets, Hesiod differentiates the nature of Cronus, and Zeus' intelligence.[25] The difference is, apparently, not based on moral grounds: as far as the account of the swallowing of Metis is concerned, Zeus' *metis* has nothing to do with any ethical idea such as justice.[26] The significance is that Zeus' cunning is realised in an innovation which escaped Cronus; namely, producing a child by parthenogenesis. But the swallowing of Metis gives him the scope to create stability and order, as is discussed later in this section.

Gaia

Throughout the *Theogony*, Gaia is the figure predominantly characterised by cunning and *metis*. Against Uranus, she contrives deceitful and evil chicanery (δολίην δε κακὴν τ᾽ ἐφράσσατο τέχνην, 160), which she reveals to Cronus (δόλον δ᾽ ὑπεθήκατο πάντα, 175). Against Cronus, Gaia again re-veals her μῆτις, this time to Rhea (μῆτιν συμφράσσασθαι, 471). Her advice to Zeus is termed 'shrewdness' (φραδμοσύνῃσι, 891). Gaia is undoubtedly a king-maker, but her actions do not extend beyond words: the recipient needs the courage and cunning required to carry the deeds through. Interpreting her words and finding the means to overcome the difficulty involved in putting them into action are decisive factors in obtaining sovereignty,[27] since the prophecy given to Zeus (888-98, cited above) is somewhat ambiguous. The precise implication of what Gaia and Uranus said to Zeus is unclear; was it about swallowing Metis, or deceiving Metis in order to swallow her, or about a son of Metis who is going to be a king of gods and men, or perhaps, all of these?

We remember that Zeus is not necessarily Gaia's choice for eternal king of heaven. After Zeus destroys the Titans, Gaia gives birth to Typhoeus, her youngest child in the Hesiodic version (821).[28] We note that the youngest son is always the greatest threat to paternal sovereignty, as in the case of Uranus and Cronus. Thus, Typhoeus should have continued the chain of succession by overthrowing Zeus' rule. As the promoter of succession (and attempts to change the world order), this particular succession could be read as Gaia's original plan. Indeed, Hesiod mentions the possibility of Typhoeus' overthrowing Zeus – though it is narrated in an unreal conditional sentence:

καί νύ κεν ἔπλετο ἔργον ἀμήχανον ἤματι κείνῳ,
καί κεν ὅ γε θνητοῖσι καὶ ἀθανάτοισιν ἄναξεν,
εἰ μὴ ἄρ᾽ ὀξὺ νόησε πατὴρ ἀνδρῶν τε θεῶν τε·

On that day an intractable deed might have been accomplished, and he [Typhoeus] might have become king of mortals and immortals, if the father of gods and men had not taken sharp notice. (*Theog.* 836-8)

This further reference to a son overthrowing his father and ruling over gods and men (837) emphasises the Hesiodic logic of succession, and the phrase ἤματι κείνῳ (836) makes palpable the crisis facing Zeus. The long account of Typhoeus' strength (823-35) and his battle with Zeus (839-68) emphasises how strong an enemy Typhoeus is for Zeus. Typhoeus' lack of success in a battle based purely on violence and physical power also anticipates the introduction of the motif of successful *intellectual* deception.

After Zeus' strength and courage are proved in the battles against Typhoeus and the Titans, Gaia tests another of Zeus' abilities.[29] In the passage about Metis, which immediately follows the battles (886-900), Gaia examines whether Zeus is as well qualified in cunning and deceit as he is in physical strength.[30] As the example of Uranus shows – destroyed by the contrivance of Gaia (160) and the courage of Cronus (168) – Zeus must prove himself wily enough to avert the next danger that Gaia sends.

Gaia sets tests and Zeus takes the most resourceful decisions in the light of the advice given him, which implies that he is in danger of becoming the father of a son who will be 'proud of heart'. Gaia reveals the future to Zeus, just as she did to Cronus, then observes how Zeus reacts. She judges Zeus' cunning: how will he deal with this exigency?

Zeus passes the test, and Hesiod shows that Zeus, unlike his predecessors, possesses all the assets needed for successful sovereignty. He has learned the lesson/s from his predecessors' failures: from Uranus' case he learns that the son must be separated from his mother, and from Cronus' case he learns that separation is not enough – the existence of the mother herself is also dangerous. It is no solution to put his dangerous children inside either his wife's body or his own; rather, as his wife is the more dangerous enemy, he has no choice but to swallow his wife.

IV. The Birth of Athena

The prophecies

In spite of conspicuous similarities between the prophecies given to Zeus and Cronus, a slight but explicit difference in phrasing is noticeable, as quoted above. I will cite the verses again:

To Cronus:

> τὰ φρονέων, ἵνα μή τις ἀγαυῶν Οὐρανιώνων
> ἄλλος ἐν ἀθανάτοισιν ἔχοι βασιληίδα τιμήν.

He [Cronus] had this in his mind, that no other gods of the noble children of Heaven than he should have the honour of kingship among the immortals. (*Theog.* 461-2)

To Zeus:

> τὼς γάρ οἱ φρασάτην, ἵνα μὴ βασιληίδα τιμὴν
> ἄλλος ἔχοι Διὸς ἀντὶ θεῶν αἰειγενετάτων.

They [Gaia and Uranus] advised him in this way, so that no other gods than Zeus should have the honour of kingship among the eternally-living gods. (*Theog.* 892-3)

In Cronus' case, the threat that someone might usurp his kingship is narrated as Cronus' own notion; but in Zeus' case, it is the concern of Gaia and Uranus. The phrasing suggests that Zeus's security is now Gaia's care: but why has Gaia changed her policy? We remember that the overthrow of the kingship was motivated by revenge. Gaia proclaims that they will avenge the outrage of the father (πατρός κε κακὴν τεισαίμεθα λώβην, 165); and Rhea seeks the means for her vengeance (τείσαιτο δ᾽ ἐρινῦς πατρὸς ἑοῖο / παίδων, 472-3). The act is always expressed in terms of the son's vengeance against the father, not the wife's vengeance against her husband/father; this implies that, although vengeance is primarily motivated by the mother, she needs her son to realise it. Having lost her last son (Typhoeus) in battle, Gaia has no other son to challenge Zeus' power. Thus she begins to change her attitude toward Zeus, and he responds properly to her prophecy.

Once a mighty child was born,[31] Zeus would meet the same fate as Uranus and Cronus. The stories of Uranus and Cronus are intended to focus attention on Zeus' victory *against the odds*. Zeus obliterates Metis, the potential architect of his downfall, by swallowing her and putting her inside his *own* body. In swallowing Metis, Zeus takes over Metis' function as a mother, and, as Austin suggests,[32] takes control of the reproductive process. Zeus proves himself the superior god by devising this plan and carrying it through by beguiling 'intelligent' Metis with his deceitful words

(889-90).[33] The myth of Metis narrates the final resolution of the age-old struggle between the father and an alliance of mother and son: Zeus' success signifies that the cosmic evolutionary process *and* the Hesiodic narrative process are reaching their similar goals.

3. The birth of Athena

The authenticity of *Theogony* 886-900, the passage about the swallowing of Metis and the birth of Athena, has been doubted by many scholars.[34] But there is much support for judging the passage as genuine.[35] I suggest that the passage is genuine because it touches on one of the most important themes of the poem, namely, the threat from a son who is mightier than his father, and Zeus' avoidance of this threat. My close reading of this passage aims to demonstrate that this theme runs through, and weaves together, the structure of the poem as a whole.[36]

Metis and Thetis

Integral to this unity[37] is the narration of the delivery of Athena. Structurally, we notice a tripartite ring composition:

- (a) swallowing of Metis; mention of the birth of Athena (888-91);
- (b) prophecy surrounding Metis; mention of the birth of a mighty son (892-4);
- (a) swallowing of Metis, mention of the birth of Athena and a son (895-900).

The prophecy – that is, the warning of the birth of a mighty son from Metis – forms the core of this ring composition. Significantly, we note that Athena is not mentioned in the prophecy; rather, the prophecy emphasises – a central idea – the *potentiality* of Metis, who can bear a child stronger than Zeus. The purpose of swallowing Metis is, primarily, to get rid of this unnamed potential son.[38]

In myth, Zeus overcomes two similar threats to his power – the birth of sons from Thetis *and* from Metis. The existence of duplicate oracles in the mythic material indicates the seriousness and significance of the apparently inescapable danger facing Zeus. Hesiod truncates the potentiality of Thetis, mentioning only briefly that she gives birth to Achilles (1006-7); but there are conspicuous similarities between Metis and Thetis: both goddesses are sea-powers; both change their shapes; both are destined to bear a son who will overcome his father; and, in both cases, this danger is averted by an oracular warning and divine guile. It is intriguing that, while Hesiod places the story of Metis at the centre of his poem and ignores Thetis' potentiality, Homer, on the other hand, remains silent about Metis' potentiality *and* the birth of Athena from Zeus' head. This does not appear simply coincidental. As I argue, it is the choices – the variations in treatment of their material – which the poets make that are significant for a teleological understanding of their poems.[39] That is, Homer and Hesiod adapt this material to fit their themes and structures, so that, in the case of the epic, Homer develops the potentiality of Thetis because his theme is the heroic destiny of Achilles; similarly, Hesiod puts in the foreground the story of Metis in order to connect it with the birth of Athena – an important thematic focus.

The variant form of the story cited by Chrysippus Fr. 908 (quoted by Galen, *On the Opinions of Hippocrates and Plato* 3.8.11-14 = Hes. fr. dub. 294 Most [343 M-W], *Theogony* lines 929a-t in Evelyn-White's edition) is generally deemed inauthentic.[40] The purpose of Chrysippus' citation is to discuss the place of wisdom, and, although the variant may not be genuine, it does provide us with some interesting, supplementary, information:

ἐκ ταύτης ἔριδος ἣ μὲν τέκε φαίδιμον υἱὸν
Ἥφαιστον τέχνῃσιν ἄνευ Διὸς αἰγιόχοιο
ἐκ πάντων παλάμῃσι κεκασμένον Οὐρανιώνων·
αὐτὰρ ὅ γ᾽ Ὠκεανοῦ καὶ Τηθύος ἠυκόμοιο
κούρῃ νόσφ᾽ Ἥρης παρελέξατο καλλιπαρήου   5
ἐξαπαφὼν Μῆτιν καίπερ πολύιδριν ἐοῦσαν·
συμμάρψας δ᾽ ὅ γε χερσὶν ἑὴν ἐγκάτθετο νηδύν,
δείσας μὴ τέξῃ κρατερώτερον ἄλλο κεραυνοῦ·
τούνεκά μιν Κρονίδης ὑψίζυγος αἰθέρι ναίων
κάππιεν ἐξαπίνης. ἣ δ᾽ αὐτίκα Παλλάδ᾽ Ἀθήνην   10
κύσατο· τὴν μὲν ἔτικτε πατὴρ ἀνδρῶν τε θεῶν τε
πὰρ κορυφήν, Τρίτωνος ἐπ᾽ ὄχθῃσιν ποταμοῖο.
Μῆτις δ᾽ αὖτε Ζηνὸς ὑπὸ σπλάγχνοις λελαθυῖα
ἧστο, Ἀθηναίης μήτηρ, τέκταινα δικαίων,
πλεῖστα θεῶν εἰδυῖα καταθνητῶν τ᾽ ἀνθρώπων.   15
†ἔνθα θεὰ παρέδεκτο ὅθεν†[41] παλάμαις περὶ πάντων
ἀθανάτων ἐκέκασθ᾽ οἳ Ὀλύμπια δώματ᾽ ἔχουσιν,
αἰγίδα ποιήσασα φοβέστρατον ἔντος Ἀθήνης·
σὺν τῇ ἐγείνατό μιν, πολεμήϊα τεύχε᾽ ἔχουσαν.

Out of this strife she [Hera] bore a glorious son by her devices, without Zeus who holds the aegis, Hephaestus, who excelled all the sons of Heaven with his skilled hands. But he [Zeus] lay with the daughter of Ocean and beautiful-haired Tethys, apart from fair-cheeked Hera, deceiving Metis, shrewd though she was. But he seized her with his hands and put her down into his belly, fearing that she might bring forth something stronger than his thunderbolt: for this reason, the son of Cronus, who sits on high and dwells in the aether, swallowed her down suddenly. But she at once conceived Pallas Athena: and the father of men and gods gave her birth by way of his head on the banks of the river Triton. Then, Metis was sitting concealed in Zeus' entrails; she is Athena's mother, who builds up works of righteousness and knows the most among gods and mortal men. The goddess [Athena] then received that [the aegis] by which she surpassed in her skilled hands all the immortals who dwell in Olympus. She [Metis] made the aegis, Athena's host-scaring equipment.

Together with it [the aegis], he [Zeus] gave birth to her [Athena],who was wearing warlike armour. (Hes. fr. 294 Most [343 M-W] vv. 1-19)

Kauer, who attempts a close comparison of this fragment with the *Theogony*, concludes that Chrysippus' quotation is a fragment of a lost epic poem on the theme of Metis and the birth of Athena, and that it has parallels with Hesiod's work, but can be viewed as independent from it.[42]

Kauer is correct to emphasise that Hesiod innovates in the order of Hephaestus and Athena's births.[43] Although it is difficult to say which text (the *Theogony* or the fragment) is older,[44] the fragment seems to draw on an older tradition, namely the narration of events in the following order: (a) the quarrel between Zeus and Hera;[45] (b) the birth of Hephaestus; (c) the birth of Athena. In the *Theogony*, the birth of Hephaestus (927-8) is the result of the quarrel between Zeus and Hera, but the birth of Athena (924-6) is treated as a separate event, which is narrated before the birth of Hephaestus. Kauer is surely right to juxtapose the similar qualities of Hephaestus and Athena, for they present complementary features: the former is a son born from the mother without a father, the latter is a daughter born from the father without a mother. What is distinctive about fr. 294 is that it juxtaposes their births, and links Athena's birth with the prophecy about Metis.

The prophecy surrounding Metis is mentioned in the fragment, but is not integrated with the birth of Athena. Two reasons are given for Athena's birth – the quarrel with Hera (v. 5) and the prophecy of Metis (v. 8) – but the latter appears to be additional and less important. The significance of Hesiod's account is that it involves separating the birth of Hephaestus from that of Athena: he strips away other material to place emphasis on the prophecy about Metis' potentiality, the swallowing of Metis, and the birth of Athena.[46]

By contrast, in the *Homeric Hymn to Apollo* the quarrel between Zeus and Hera receives a different emphasis (307-30): Hera gives birth to Hephaestus, and then Typhon, because Zeus produced Athena:

κaì νῦν νόσφιν ἐμεῖο τέκε γλαυκῶπιν Ἀθήνην,
ἣ πᾶσιν μακάρεσσι μεταπρέπει ἀθανάτοισιν·
αὐτὰρ ὅ γ' ἠπεδανὸς γέγονεν μετὰ πᾶσι θεοῖσι
παῖς ἐμὸς Ἥφαιστος, ῥικνὸς πόδας, ὃν τέκον αὐτὴ

And now apart from me, he has given birth to bright-eyed Athena, who stands out among all the blessed immortals. But my son, Hephaestus, whom I myself give birth to, has grown to be weakly and lame among all the gods. (*Hymn. Apol.* 314-17)

κaì νῦν μέν τοι ἐγὼ τεχνήσομαι ὥς κε γένηται
παῖς ἐμός, ὅς κε θεοῖσι μεταπρέποι ἀθανάτοισιν,
οὔτε σὸν αἰσχύνασ' ἱερὸν λέχος οὔτ' ἐμὸν αὐτῆς.

And now I will contrive to have my child [Typhon], who will stand out among the immortal gods, and I will not bring shame to your holy bed or to my own.(*Hymn. Apol.* 326-8)

In this version there is no mention of Metis' potentiality; rather, anger is the main motif.[47] Comparison with these two stories (Chrysippus' fragment and the *Hymn to Apollo*) demonstrates that the Hesiodic account is designed to focus – structurally and thematically – on the significance of the prophecy about Metis, to the exclusion of other mythic variants which might lessen the impact and centrality of his theme.

According to a scholion (bT ad *Il.* 8.39) of unknown data and origin, Metis is already pregnant with Athena by the Cyclops Brontes when Zeus swallows her:

Μῆτιν τὴν Ὠκεανοῦ ἀμείβουσαν εἰς πολλὰ τὴν μορφὴν Ζεὺς βουλόμενος παρ' ἑαυτῷ ἔχειν κατέπιεν ἔγκυον οὖσαν ὑπὸ Βρόντου τοῦ Κύκλωπος.

Zeus, wishing to keep her by himself, swallowed Metis, daughter of Oceanus, who changed into various shapes, and who was pregnant by the Cyclops Brontes. (schol. bT ad *Il.* 8.39)

Brontes is one of the three Cyclopes, the children of Uranus and Gaia (*Theog.* 140), who gave thunder and the thunderbolt to Zeus (*Theog.* 141). Brontes is particularly associated with thunder (ἡ βροντή), as his name indicates. If we link this account with verse 8 of the variant cited by Chrysippus, a remarkable analogy between Thetis and Metis becomes overt, and clarifies the ambiguous accounts of Hesiod about Metis. Verse 8 states,

δείσας μὴ τέξῃ κρατερώτερον ἄλλο κεραυνοῦ

fearing that she might give birth to something stronger than the thunderbolt (Hes. fr. 294 Most [343 M-W], 8)

Zeus fears that Metis will give birth to someone mightier than the thunderbolt. So, Metis, as well as Thetis, has the potential to bear a son mightier than his father.

In Thetis' case, Zeus avoids the danger of begetting a son mightier than himself by making Peleus, a human, her husband. But in Metis' case, her impregnator is a Cyclops who provided Zeus with his strongest weapon, the thunderbolt. Once Metis gives birth to a son who is mightier than his father (that is, mightier than the thunderbolt), Zeus will surely be defeated. Therefore he must swallow Metis, and thereby swallow the thunderbolt, too, with which his supremacy might otherwise have been challenged.

This explains the ambiguities in the Hesiodic account of Metis. First, the father of the unnamed son of Metis is not apparent in Hesiod. Although Hesiod seems to imply (at *Theogony* 897-8) that the father is Zeus, a more subtle reading which draws on variants in the mythic corpus, could imply that Brontes – Thunder – is the father of this unnamed son. Second, it is unclear in Hesiod how mighty the son is. Hesiod says that the son is to have an overwhelming spirit (ὑπέρβιον ἦτορ ἔχοντα, 898), and he is to be a king of gods and men (897). Is he to be mightier than Zeus?

Hesiod's primary concern is his intention to emphasise the birth of Athena and the importance of the relationship between Athena and Zeus. That is, if he had mentioned that Brontes was the father of the unnamed mighty son, this would weaken the link between Athena and Zeus. Athena's genealogy is the indispensable factor for Hesiod,[48] and the blood connection between Zeus and Athena is of primary, vital significance for Zeus' solution to the problem of generational strife.[49]

As Brown suggests,[50] if Athena had been born from her mother in the normal way, she, as well as her (potential) brother, would have represented a threat to Zeus' sovereignty. Since it is crucial for Zeus to subordinate his children to himself, his cunning contrivance to give birth to her *himself* provides the precise response that will safeguard his supremacy.[51] In this way, Zeus eliminates Athena's connection with her (potentially dangerous) mother Metis, and recruits her to his cause. The image of the unnatural birth of Athena reflects the ambivalent nature of the relationship between Zeus (now father and mother?) and his daughter.

The swallowing of Metis, and her advice from inside Zeus, justifies Zeus' epithet μητιόεις: Zeus is, quite literally, filled with *metis*. As Caldwell writes,[52] we are aware of Hesiod's progressive endeavour to elevate Zeus from god of brute force to a deity of wisdom. One way in which this essential aspect of Zeus' rule is conveyed can be seen in Hesiod's choice of names for Zeus' wives and children: the Muses and Horae, Dike and Eirene characterise Zeus' new world order. Metis, we see, is likewise meaningful on various levels: in the apparently crude myth of the swallowing of Metis-the-mother, we see Zeus acquiring *metis*-intelligence.[53]

Athena and an unnamed son

The logic can be traced back, once again, to the prophecy in which Hesiod elucidates why the swallowing of Metis renders Zeus' rule invincible:

πρώτην μὲν κούρην γλαυκῶπιδα Τριτογένειαν,
ἶσον ἔχουσαν πατρὶ μένος καὶ ἐπίφρονα βουλήν,
αὐτὰρ ἔπειτ' ἄρα παῖδα θεῶν βασιλῆα καὶ ἀνδρῶν
ἤμελλεν τέξεσθαι, ὑπέρβιον ἦτορ ἔχοντα·

first a bright-eyed daughter, Tritogeneia, with strength and wise counsel equal to her father's, and then she was to bear a son, a king of gods and of men, possessing a very proud heart. (*Theog.* 895-8)

IV. The Birth of Athena

The birth of an unnamed son who would be mightier than Zeus is transformed into 'the birth of a daughter equal to her father in power and wisdom' (895-6). The juxtaposition of Athena and an unnamed son is pivotal for expressing the mechanics of this decisive transformation of the threat of generational strife: the repeated threat from a mighty son has been thwarted, and a new relationship between father and daughter has begun. As Arthur points out,[54] the father-daughter unity of Zeus' rule presents a moment of dynamic stasis. Zeus cuts the old, original bond between mother and child, and constructs a new bond between father and daughter. To put it another way, Zeus averts the danger of a mighty but combative son by producing a daughter equal to him in ability *and loyalty*. This is the ultimate reason for Zeus' success.[55]

In this new relationship the mother – catalyst of previous usurpations – is excluded. Athena, born without a mother, is deprived of her own potential motherhood – her female nature – and will never bear a child. In addition, she has to be a virgin, and we note that she is listed in the *Homeric Hymn to Aphrodite* as the first of three goddesses whom Aphrodite's power of love cannot affect (7-8).[56] Athena's sterility through virginity is vital because it frees Zeus from the cycle of usurpation.

The motherless goddess Athena is more like a man than a woman; or, as Harrison suggested, she is rather a sexless thing, neither man nor woman.[57] She appears as an equal to Zeus, and shares several qualities with him, including intelligence. The most telling, and curious, correlation is their sharing of the aegis.[58] The phrase 'aegis-bearing' (αἰγίοχος) is one of Zeus' most common epithets, and the aegis itself is made by Hephaestus for Zeus in the *Iliad* (15.308-10). However, Zeus' use of the aegis is mentioned only twice in the *Iliad*: when he frightens the Achaeans (17.593-6); and in the reference to its use as foretold on the day of Troy's destruction (4.166-8).

Yet in the Chrysippus fragment cited above (Hes. fr. 294 Most [343 M-W] 18-19), Metis makes the aegis *for Athena*:

αἰγίδα ποιήσασα φοβέστρατον ἔντος Ἀθήνης·
σὺν τῇ ἐγείνατό μιν, πολεμήϊα τεύχε᾽ ἔχουσαν.

She [Metis] made the aegis, Athena's host-scaring equipment. Together with it [the aegis], he [Zeus] gave birth to her [Athena], who was wearing warlike armour. (Hes. fr. 294 Most [343 M-W], 18-19)

The aegis is prepared for Athena even before her birth. In the fragment of the *Meropis* discussed in Chapter II, the aegis is made by Athena herself from the skin of the Giant Asterus whom she killed in the Gigantomachy.

In the *Odyssey*, there is one reference to the word (22.297-8): Athena holds up the aegis to terrify the suitors. In the *Iliad*, Athena wears the aegis to encourage the Achaeans (2.446-9; 5.738-42) and to fight with Ares

(21.400-14); she also casts it over Achilles' shoulder (18.203-4).[59] Two of these passages, 5.738-42 and 21.400-14, in particular merit our attention for their connection with Zeus.

In the first passage, Athena prepares to join the war, to fight against Ares in order to prevent his support for the Trojans:

> αὐτὰρ Ἀθηναίη, κούρη Διὸς αἰγιόχοιο,
> πέπλον μὲν κατέχευεν ἑανὸν πατρὸς ἐπ᾽ οὔδει
> ποικίλον, ὅν ῥ᾽ αὐτὴ ποιήσατο καὶ κάμε χερσίν·   735
> ἡ δὲ χιτῶν᾽ ἐνδῦσα Διὸς νεφεληγερέταο
> τεύχεσιν ἐς πόλεμον θωρήσσετο δακρυόεντα.
> ἀμφὶ δ᾽ ἄρ᾽ ὤμοισιν βάλετ᾽ αἰγίδα θυσσανόεσσαν
> δεινήν, ἣν περὶ μὲν πάντη Φόβος ἐστεφάνωται,
> ἐν δ᾽ Ἔρις, ἐν δ᾽ Ἀλκή, ἐν δὲ κρυόεσσα Ἰωκή,   740
> ἐν δέ τε Γοργείη κεφαλὴ δεινοῖο πελώρου,
> δεινή τε σμερδνή τε, Διὸς τέρας αἰγιόχοιο.

And Athena, daughter of Zeus who holds the aegis, let slip off to the floor of her father's house her embroidered dress, which she herself had made and worked with her hands. And she put on the tunic of Zeus, who gathers the clouds, then dressed in her armour for the war that causes tears. Round her shoulders she hung the tasselled, terrible aegis, all round which Fear is set in a circle: and on it there is Hatred, Strength, and chilling Rout, and set there too is the head of the fearful monster Gorgon, a thing of fright and terror, a portent of Zeus who holds the aegis. (*Il.* 5.733-42)

Athena takes off her embroidered robe – a reference which, of course, emphasises the feminine nature of the clothing – and puts on, surprisingly, Zeus' tunic in Zeus' house (5.734-6).[60] Then she hangs the aegis round her shoulders (5.738). It is no coincidence that the phrase Διὸς αἰγιόχοιο is used twice in this passage (5.733 and 742): it effectively signifies that Zeus owns the aegis, and that all of Athena's arms are furnished from Zeus' property. Athena, going out to war, is emphatically identified with Zeus.

In the scene following Athena's arming, Hera asks Zeus' permission to defeat Ares. Zeus answers,

> ἄγρει μάν οἱ ἔπορσον Ἀθηναίην ἀγελείην
> ἥ ἑ μάλιστ᾽ εἴωθε κακῆς ὀδύνῃσι πελάζειν.

To your work, then. Launch Athena against him, the goddess of spoil, she is the one who most often brings cruel pain upon him. (*Il.* 5.765-6)

As Ares destroys many Greek warriors on the battlefield, this is a good reason for opposing Ares in the context. But as for the subtext, some different features may emerge. In the light of the importance given to the motif of generational strife, it is significant that Athena's target is Ares, the son of Zeus and Hera, and, as such, a potential candidate for the role of father-usurper. In the *Iliad*, Zeus' supremacy looks secure, but the motif of the threat of a son may be present in this passage; it gives Zeus reason to dislike Ares. Zeus might be expected to be wary of his sons lest he should experience the same calamity as Uranus and Cronus, even after he attained sovereignty. Ares is not actually challenging the power of Zeus, but his insubordinate role in the *Iliad* seems to reflect the motif of potential father-usurper as a subtext. In this context, it is understandable that Zeus consents to Ares' defeat at Athena's hands.[61] The symbolism is profound: it is as if Zeus himself defeats Ares when he sends forth Athena – born from Zeus, armed by Zeus, dressed in Zeus' tunic, and equipped with Zeus' aegis.

At 21.400-14, Athena, wearing the aegis, fights Ares:

ὣς εἰπὼν οὔτησε κατ' αἰγίδα θυσσανόεσσαν   400
σμερδαλέην, ἣν οὐδὲ Διὸς δάμνησι κεραυνός·
τῇ μιν Ἄρης οὔτησε μιαιφόνος ἔγχεϊ μακρῷ.
ἡ δ' ἀναχασσαμένη λίθον εἵλετο χειρὶ παχείῃ
κείμενον ἐν πεδίῳ μέλανα, τρηχύν τε μέγαν τε,
τόν ῥ' ἄνδρες πρότεροι θέσαν ἔμμεναι οὖρον ἀρούρης·   405
τῷ βάλε θοῦρον Ἄρηα κατ' αὐχένα, λῦσε δὲ γυῖα.
ἑπτὰ δ' ἐπέσχε πέλεθρα πεσών, ἐκόνισε δὲ χαίτας,
τεύχεά τ' ἀμφαράβησε· γέλασσε δὲ Παλλὰς Ἀθήνη,
καί οἱ ἐπευχομένη ἔπεα πτερόεντα προσηύδα·
"νηπύτι', οὐδέ νύ πώ περ ἐπεφράσω ὅσσον ἀρείων   410
εὔχομ' ἐγὼν ἔμεναι, ὅτι μοι μένος ἰσοφαρίζεις.
οὕτω κεν τῆς μητρὸς ἐρινύας ἐξαποτίνοις,
ἥ τοι χωομένη κακὰ μήδεται, οὕνεκ' Ἀχαιοὺς
κάλλιπες, αὐτὰρ Τρωσὶν ὑπερφιάλοισιν ἀμύνεις."

So speaking he [Ares] stabbed against the tasselled fearful aegis, which not even Zeus' thunderbolt can break: and bloody Ares struck there with his long spear. She [Athena] stepped back and picked up a stone in her massive hand. The stone was lying on the plain, black, rugged and huge, and men of an earlier time had set it there to mark the boundary of a field. With this she hit furious Ares on the neck, and loosed his limbs. He fell to the ground, covering seven acres, his hair sullied in the dust, and his armour clashed about him. Pallas Athena laughed aloud, and spoke winged words of triumph over him: 'Foolish child, not even yet have you learned how much mightier I can claim to be than you, if you try to match your power against me. So this can be payment for your mother's furies; she is angry and wishes you ill, because you abandon the Achaeans and give your aid to the reckless Trojans.' (*Il.* 21.400-14)

Even Zeus' thunderbolt cannot break the aegis (401): this indicates its extraordinary power, since Zeus' thunderbolt is his ultimate weapon, used to destroy his most dreadful enemy, Typhoeus (*Theog.* 853-5). Ares tries to strike at the aegis with his long spear (*Il.* 21.400-2): this could be interpreted as symbolising Ares' challenge to Zeus, even though it is worn by Athena at that moment. If Ares succeeded in piercing the aegis, he could overwhelm even Zeus' thunderbolt, and could conquer the defenceless Zeus.

However, Ares' challenge is quite easily beaten off by Athena, and we note her words after she strikes him with a large, rough black stone (404):[62] 'you have not yet realised how much stronger I am' (410-11). The triumphant claim reminds us, again, of the theme of (inter-)generational strife, as Athena reiterates – backed up by Zeus' aegis – that the son cannot defeat his father.

Zeus' strategy is to 'divide and rule'. By giving birth to Athena, he acquires a counterpart who fights on his side and as his deputy, defeating his son who might prove a challenger to his power. When Athena claims her victory, she laughs (γέλασσε, 408); only nineteen verses earlier, Zeus, too, laughed with joy (ἐγέλασσε, 389) to see the gods joined, separately, in conflict, while he maintained his supremacy. This reminds us of Zeus' delight at the appearance of Athena in the *Homeric Hymn to Athena* (γήθησε δὲ μητίετα Ζεύς, *Hymn. Ath.* XXVIII, 16).

It is a marker of Athena's functional affinity to Zeus that, as Zeus becomes more remote from human beings, she eventually replaces him as the chief guardian of the state and people.[63] In the *Iliad*, Zeus cares for particular mortals (for example, Sarpedon: 16. 433) and Διὶ φίλος is a frequent epithet applied to these mortals.[64] Even people's intelligence is compared to Zeus' (Διὶ μῆτιν ἀτάλαντος),[65] but none of these phrases appear in the *Odyssey* – instead, Athena becomes the dominant figure.

When Athena emerges from the head of Zeus in the *Theogony*, she is purely a warrior and guardian of the state:

αὐτὸς δ᾽ ἐκ κεφαλῆς γλαυκώπιδα γείνατ᾽ Ἀθήνην,
δεινὴν ἐγρεκύδοιμον ἀγέστρατον ἀτρυτώνην,
πότνιαν, ᾗ κέλαδοί τε ἅδον πόλεμοί τε μάχαι τε·

He gave birth to bright-eyed Athena from his head; she is the terrible rouser of the battle, leader of armies, the unwearied queen, and delights in din, wars and battles. (*Theog.* 924-6)

In Hesiod, there is no mention of her patronage of craftsmanship. She is a new leader, but will not displace her father; rather, she will carry out his will as his deputy. In the *Iliad*, Athena is expected to participate in war (5.430), which contrasts with Aphrodite's stated domains of marriage and love. Zeus tells Aphrodite to leave fighting to Ares and Athena:

οὔ τοι, τέκνον ἐμόν, δέδοται πολεμήϊα ἔργα,
ἀλλὰ σύ γ᾽ ἱμερόεντα μετέρχεο ἔργα γάμοιο,
ταῦτα δ᾽ Ἄρηϊ θοῷ καὶ Ἀθήνῃ πάντα μελήσει.

No, my child, the works of warfare are not for you, rather, concern yourself with sweet work of love and marriage, while all this will be dealt with by quick Ares and Athena (*Il.* 5.428-30)

94

IV. The Birth of Athena

For human beings, the gender division is clearer, as in Hector's words to Andromache:

πόλεμος δ᾽ ἄνδρεσσι μελήσει
πᾶσι, μάλιστα δ᾽ ἐμοί, τοὶ Ἰλίῳ ἐγγεγάασιν.

War will be the concern of all the men, and mine above all – we the men who were born in Ilios. (*Il.* 6.492-3)

These passages imply that the *goddess* Athena functions like a male god. A deity *could* do everything, but in the case of Athena, the boundary between male and female remains ambiguous. The creation of such a deity, a weaker doublet of Zeus himself, is the ultimate resolution to the internecine conflict, and it is in this creation that we view the culmination of Hesiod's logic. The inevitable replacement of father by son – elder generation by younger – is bypassed with the creation of this co-operative daughter. Athena is the symbolic representation of the rule of Zeus; as Brown comments, she is the symbol of a new kind of state, or of the cultural renewal of Zeus' world.[66]

In classical times, Athena becomes a champion of human skill and intelligence.[67] In Plato's discussion of Athenian education, boys and girls are encouraged to imitate Athena (*Laws* 796c).[68] The relation between Zeus and Athena is even intensified; thus in Aeschylus' *Eumenides* (738), Athena says κάρτα δ᾽ εἰμὶ τοῦ πατρός (I am very much of my father).[69] Athena knows the will of Zeus, and effects it as he wishes.[70]

In both Homer and Hesiod Athena is a daughter of Zeus, younger and subordinate. However, it is generally acknowledged that Athena had a long history of her own, probably as a pre-Greek goddess.[71] Pausanias reports a tale of Athena's origin which differs from that of Homer and Hesiod: she is the daughter of Poseidon and Lake Tritonis (1.14.6).[72] We note Campbell's point that, at the earliest stages of Greek civilisation, 'wherever the Greeks came, in every valley, every isle and every cave, there was a local manifestation of the mother-goddess of the world whom Zeus, as the great god of the patriarchal order, had to master in a patriarchal way'.[73] The story of Athena's motherless birth from Zeus' head is a product of this context.

Through marriage Zeus overcomes and integrates the problems posed by many of these goddesses.[74] Athena, however, is chosen to be his daughter, perhaps because she is too strong and dangerous to be a wife. By making Athena a *maiden* daughter, he not only succeeds in removing the threat of a potentially powerful son as challenger, but also establishes a new, protective and preventative relationship between father and daughter. Uranus and Cronus were doomed by the cyclic predictability of the father-to-son relationship; Zeus, however, ensures his survival by transforming the relationship into one of father-to-daughter.

A daughter, however strong, will never usurp her father. For the ancient Greeks, the fundamental perception of the state is as the 'father-land' (πάτρα, πατρίς).[75] The state is a family and the image of the ruler is one of a 'father'. Such ideology leaves no place for the daughter as sovereign heir; the daughter cannot be a threat.[76] In Hesiod, Zeus' innovation is to construct a new relationship which will not displace him.[77] The creation of a new type of deity – feminine but akin to masculine – is the greatest factor actuating Zeus' success.

This idea was undoubtedly developed by Hesiod in response to the cultural and social conditions of his age. Greek culture was emerging from the Dark Age into a period of historical awareness and maturity. It is a time of pan-Hellenisation: strong centralising forces are present in all aspects of Greek life. Local and regional myths and rites were transformed by the Panhellenic poets, Homer and Hesiod, who created a Panhellenic Olympian religion.[78] In response to this trend, Hesiod represents the powerful, unchallengeable sovereignty of Zeus in his *Theogony*. The concept of a strong alliance between Zeus and Athena fits perfectly both with Panhellenic ideals *and* Greek societal and moral norms, thus ensuring the continued popularity and success of Homer and Hesiod.

V

Prometheus, God of Forethought

Prometheus is the only god in the *Theogony* who challenges the deceptive intelligence of Zeus. This fascinating myth has been the subject of much speculation, and a great many attempts have been made to find solutions to the many puzzles posed by the myth and its presentation. I will concentrate particularly on aspects of, and problems raised by, the design and inner logic of the myth as presented by Hesiod.

The myth of Prometheus in the *Theogony* (507-616) is often viewed as incoherent, or artificially conflated, or even arbitrary.[1] Since the content of the *Theogony* is basically genealogical, it has been suggested that genealogies and narrative myth offered conflicting principles of organisation, and that admittedly it was difficult to devise a completely satisfactory scheme for them.[2] However, the sequence of the three elements of the story (the division of the sacrifice, the stolen fire and the creation of the first woman) does appear to be integrated into Hesiod's design of a coherent scheme. And I would suggest, a major thrust of this design is to present a powerful and compelling myth on the theme of the pursuit of sovereignty.[3]

In the *Theogony,* which recounts the creation of the universe through the birth of the gods, the essential aim of the epic is, as Zeitlin puts it, 'to establish Zeus' claim to supreme power over the universe and to chart the steps that lead to the eventual consolidation of his reign'.[4] What, then, is Hesiod's intention in introducing the myth of Prometheus into this epic? An aetiological purpose would be the most obvious answer. There is no doubt that the myth follows a basically aetiological pattern, since Hesiod adds concluding lines typical of aetiology at the end of the myth (556-7).[5] Or one could suggest that Hesiod uses this story in order to give the reason for Zeus' concealment of fire. As Zeus is the god not only of might but also of justice, Prometheus must do something wrong first, so that Zeus can defeat him. I would contend, however, that Hesiod does not tell the story merely for its aetiological value, but in connection with the challenge to Zeus' sovereignty.

It is widely accepted that, for the majority of later Greeks, the *Theogony* became the 'true story' of how the world and the gods began. However, it is also likely that the *Theogony* was not the only poem to narrate the history of the world and of the gods; it seems certain that other theogonies existed, not only at the time of Hesiod's composition of the *Theogony*, as Caldwell suggests,[6] but also before this time. As Graf reminds us, Hesiod stood in a poetic tradition as one of the bards,[7] and we should think of him as handling his narrative just as the poets of the *Iliad* and the *Odyssey*, working in a long tradition of oral epic, handled their compositions. Hesiod selected, modified and arranged the traditional myths, including even Oriental myths,[8] and, of course, he often invented new stories to suit his own purposes. Through such processes as selection, modification, arrangement and invention, I would argue that Hesiod presents the Prometheus myth as a unique variation on the story of the challenger of Zeus who fights against Zeus by using his intelligence. For this purpose, I examine the logic of the story and interpret the design which promulgates Hesiod's intentions. As J. Griffin remarks, 'myths are not just stories but stories of guaranteed importance, and those who appear in myths illustrate and explain something about the order of the world and the relationship of gods and men'.[9] What message, then, does the Prometheus myth offer us? What is the significance of Zeus' victory over Prometheus? And, what are the ramifications of this victory for the mythic relationship between gods and men?

1. The myth of Prometheus in the *Theogony*

Mankind in the Theogony

Since the *Theogony* deals not only with the birth of the gods but also interprets the present universal order, mankind too is given its own specific position within the Hesiodic framework. When examining the Prometheus myth it is particularly important to understand how mankind is presented in the world ruled over by Zeus. In the *Theogony*, Zeus comes down to the human world at Mecone (now Sicyon) to settle the issue of the sacrifice. He does so because, as Hesiod believes, it is Zeus' determination to be 'the father of gods *and men*'. This defining attribute of Zeus is often mentioned: he is πατὴρ ἀνδρῶν τε θεῶν τε (542, 643, 838). Variants include θεῶν πατέρ' ἠδὲ καὶ ἀνδρῶν (47) and ὅ γε θνητοῖσι καὶ ἀθανάτοισιν ἄναξεν (837). These phrases indicate that Zeus needs to be master not only of gods but also of human beings in order to enjoy the full benefit of his power, and to be worshipped as their father. Humans are, undoubtedly, necessary members of the world of Zeus, even though there are stories of his threatening to destroy them. Considering their significance, it is all the more remarkable that the myth of Prometheus is the only story in the *Theogony* to involve human beings.

Fire, one of the central elements of the myth, is particularly connected with human beings. As Zeitlin remarks, Zeus' control over the cosmic fire later determines his victories in the cosmos, first over the Titans, and then over Typhoeus.[10] And fire, of course, stands for the material basis of civilisation in the human world. Prometheus may have been understood first and foremost as a fire god.[11] However, what is striking to us is that the Prometheus of the *Theogony* does not fight against Zeus with fire. If he were the god of fire, he could have overcome Zeus with his fire. Nor does he offer fire to Zeus as his gift; there is no reciprocity between them, as mentioned below, p. 109. This role is performed by the Cyclopes, who present Zeus with a sort of fire, namely thunder and the thunderbolt (140-1, 504). It is significant that Prometheus' fire is exclusively connected with human beings and used as his gift to them, not to Zeus. This aspect of the story – that Prometheus is a benefactor of mankind – is particularly emphasised as the main feature of his myth.

Hesiod's description and explanation of the origins of mankind are somewhat ambiguous. The creation of man is not narrated in the *Theogony* but, rather, the narrative assumes that human beings are already present. Let us consider how Hesiod deals with men in his poem.

The first mention of human beings is the poet himself (22) and the shepherds (26), among whom Hesiod is included. The shepherds are called 'mere bellies'[12] (γαστέρες οἶον, 26) by the Muses. It should be noted that the first woman is compared to a drone and the belly analogy reappears in this comparison:[13]

ποιμένες ἄγραυλοι, κάκ᾽ ἐλέγχεα, γαστέρες οἶον

Shepherds who dwell in the field, wretched and cowardly, mere bellies (*Theog.* 26)

οἱ δ᾽ ἔντοσθε μένοντες ἐπηρεφέας κατὰ σίμβλους
ἀλλότριον κάματον σφετέρην ἐς γαστέρ᾽ ἀμῶνται·
ὣς δ᾽ αὔτως ἄνδρεσσι κακὸν θνητοῖσι γυναῖκας
Ζεὺς ὑψιβρεμέτης θῆκε, ξυνήονας ἔργων

but the drones remain inside in the covered beehives and gather the toil of others into their own bellies. In just the same way, high thundering Zeus set up woman as evil for mortal men (*Theog.* 598-601)

The Muses' addressing of the shepherds with the word 'belly' (26) effectively evokes their hard life, and is echoed by their hard work in 598-601. Their hardship is further emphasised by Hesiod's repeated mention of poverty (593) and labour (596-7).

Like other epic poets, Hesiod quite often uses the word βροτός for men, instead of ἄνθρωπος. The word ἄνθρωπος is a more generic term; βροτός designates a mortal man, as opposed to ἀθάνατος or θεός, one enjoying eternal life. Sometimes the adjectives θνητός (223; 500) or καταθνητός (903) are added in order to intensify the connotation of βροτός as 'ephemeral' or 'wretched'. The effect of Hesiod's use of the word βροτός is to impress upon the audience the degree of differentiation that exists between the state of men and that of the blessed gods: this is the Hesiodic attitude towards men. Consider some examples of this use of βροτός: 'mortal men are given both evil and good at their birth by fate' (218-19); 'deadly Night gave birth to Nemesis as a calamity for <u>mortal men</u>' (223-4); 'it is hard for a <u>mortal man</u> to tell all the names of the rivers' (369); 'Zeus set the stone, which Cronus vomited in Pytho to be a sign thereafter and a marvel to <u>mortal men</u>' (497-500); 'Horae, Eunomia, Dike and Eirene take care of the works of <u>mortal men</u>' (901-3); 'mighty Heracles killed Geryones, who was the strongest of all <u>mortal men</u>' (981-2). Although these can also be viewed as instances of conventional or formulaic expression, the cumulative effect is to emphasise what short-lived and feeble creatures men are.

In contrast, when Hesiod talks about kings (βασιλῆες) in the proem, the descriptions used are very different, although the kings too are, of course, human: the kings are 'respected' (αἰδοίοισιν, 80), 'brought up by Zeus' (διοτρεφέων, 82), 'wise in heart' (ἐχέφρονες, 88), 'happy, being loved by the Muses' (ὄλβιος, ὄντινα Μοῦσαι φίλωνται, 96-7). Both the kings and the exceptional Heracles[14] occupy a special position in Hesiod's scheme, and are differentiated from ordinary 'wretched mortal men'. These exceptions apart, for Hesiod human beings in general are apparently feeble and powerless.

Surprisingly, human beings are juxtaposed with the Gigantes:

αὖτις δ᾽ ἀνθρώπων τε γένος κρατερῶν τε Γιγάντων
ὑμνεῦσαι τέρπουσι Διὸς νόον ἐντὸς Ὀλύμπου
Μοῦσαι Ὀλυμπιάδες, κοῦραι Διὸς αἰγιόχοιο.

and again, the Olympian Muses, the daughters of Zeus the aegis-holder, by singing of the race of human beings and of the mighty Gigantes, give pleasure to Zeus' mind within Olympus. (*Theog.* 50-2)

M.L. West offers some explanations for this juxtaposition of men and Gigantes: the Gigantes were thought by the people of the fifth century BC to be men; or, perhaps, Hesiod is thinking of his own myth of Ages, where the bronze generation has some of the characteristics of the Gigantes.[15]

The relationship between men and Gigantes is unclear. J.S. Clay develops a novel idea that 'human beings are descended from the union of the Giants and the Melian Nymphs and ... the origin of the human race is the casual by-product of a violent cosmic drama', and she maintains that 'the *Theogony* depicts human beings as closely related to gigantic warriors, creatures perhaps even capable of challenging Zeus, ... so Zeus intended to bring about the separation of gods and men ... so that they can never pose a serious threat to his reign.'[16] Her argument is certainly intriguing, particularly since she is at pains to set the myth of Prometheus into the framework of Zeus' establishing his rule over the universe. Her idea would be more convincing if she could offer evidence strong enough to bolster the assertion about 'the violent nature of powerful men' in the *Theogony*. On the contrary, as I have noted above, Hesiod's choice of descriptive terms for men more clearly illustrates the idea that they are rather feeble and miserable beings. They do not appear to be similar to the Gigantes nor do they possess the potential to threaten the power of Zeus. I also note that, if men had been so ferocious that they could compete with Zeus' power, Zeus would at once have defeated them, instead of leaving them as they are.

One might compare the Gigantes in the *Theogony* (147-51) with the twin Aloadae, Otus and Ephialtes, whose story is narrated in the *Odyssey* 11.305-20 (as discussed in Chapter II, Section 1). They might well be Gigantes, though the poet of the *Odyssey* is not specific. Otus and Ephialtes are children of Poseidon, but according to the account in the *Odyssey* they do not look like the 'proper' gods, because they are 'short-lived':

> ἣ δὴ φάσκε Ποσειδάωνι μιγῆναι,
> καί ῥ᾽ ἔτεκεν δύο παῖδε, μινυνθαδίω δὲ γενέσθην,
> Ὦτόν τ᾽ ἀντίθεον τηλεκλειτόν τ᾽ Ἐφιάλτην,
> οὓς δὴ μηκίστους θρέψε ζείδωρος ἄρουρα
> καὶ πολὺ καλλίστους μετά γε κλυτὸν Ὠρίωνα·

She [Iphimedeia] told me that she had mingled in love with Poseidon and given birth to two children, though they were short-lived, godlike Otus and far-famed Ephialtes, who were the tallest that the fertile earth has brought up, and the most handsome by far after famous Orion. (*Od.* 11.306-10)

Perhaps they are some sort of intermediate being.[17] The myth of the Gigantomachy would thus presuppose that there was once such a tribe as the Gigantes, and that their antagonism towards the Olympian gods had caused the war. However, the point here is that Hesiod's view of men presents them as radically different from the Gigantes. It is possible that the juxtaposition of Gigantes and men should not be taken to suggest that they are one and the same race, but rather that they are two mortal races who are under Zeus' control.

The myth of Prometheus relates to mankind in every aspect of the story: the ox divided between Zeus and men; fire stolen for men; and Woman fabricated as the 'reward' for fire stolen for men. Yet men themselves remain curiously behind the scenes in all of these stories. There is no mention of men's reaction to each episode; no joy is depicted when they obtain fire, no gratitude is expressed to Prometheus, and no sorrow is shown for Zeus' binding of the latter. Hesiod does not seem to have any interest in recounting the details of mankind's behaviour in the *Theogony*. Men just keep silent, unable to do anything without Prometheus' help. Although one can agree that 'men are integral to all parts of the story'[18] – in the sense that all of the stories about Prometheus are connected with men – their presentation nevertheless remains problematic. Importantly, men are always mentioned whenever Prometheus is centre-stage on the one hand; on the other, they themselves never play the central role in the story. I suggest that the purpose of this treatment of men is to emphasise that the main concern of this myth is the conflict between Zeus and

101

Prometheus, and that men appear only because of their necessary but secondary attachment to the myth of Prometheus.

The son of Iapetus

In Hesiod's genealogy, Prometheus is the son of Iapetus. Iapetus occupies a significant position in the *Theogony*: he is mentioned as early as verse 18 in the proem and he gains further importance from the juxtaposition of his name with that of Cronus:

Λητώ τ᾽ Ἰαπετόν τε ἰδὲ Κρόνον ἀγκυλομήτην

[The Muses praise] Leto, Iapetus and Cronus crooked of counsel (*Theog.* 18)

The praise of the Olympian gods starts with Zeus at verse 11, continues with the major Olympian gods (Hera, Athena, Apollo, Artemis, Poseidon, Aphrodite, Hebe, Dione, Leto), and then Iapetus and Cronus follow. In spite of this seemingly honourable position, the myth of Iapetus differs from those of the other Olympian gods, as it is totally unknown – as is his relation to Cronus.

Iapetus and Cronus are, as West comments,[19] the only two of the Titans who will become, later in the *Theogony*, a serious danger to Zeus. In the *Theogony*, the story of Iapetus is not narrated; instead it is only the stories of his sons Prometheus, Menoetius and Atlas which are recounted. One can argue that the reason for Hesiod's prominent placement of Iapetus' name here is to prepare the audience for a narrative about his sons – and, above all, Prometheus. The mention of Iapetus foreshadows events to come and focuses attention on the myth of Prometheus. The positioning of Iapetus with the other prominent families of Greek theogonic myth thus indicates the importance placed by Hesiod on his family, and hints that the defeat of Prometheus will be critical for Zeus' reign. In addition, the mention of Iapetus along with Cronus is meant to make the audience aware that the clash with Prometheus will be of similar importance for Zeus to that of Zeus with Cronus.

It is worth noticing that Iapetus is mentioned only once in the *Iliad* (8.479) in the speech of Zeus, remarkably with Cronus in the same order with the *Theogony*:

οὐδ᾽ εἴ κε τὰ νείατα πείραθ᾽ ἵκηαι
γαίης καὶ πόντοιο, ἵν᾽ Ἰαπετός τε Κρόνος τε
ἥμενοι οὔτ᾽ αὐγῆς Ὑπερίονος Ἠελίοιο
τέρπoντ᾽ οὔτ᾽ ἀνέμοισι, βαθὺς δέ τε Τάρταρος ἀμφίς·

... not even if you would reach the utmost boundary of earth and sea, where Iapetus and Cronus sit, and enjoy neither the rays of the Sun Hyperion nor winds, but deep Tartarus all around. (*Il.* 8.478-81)

V. Prometheus, God of Forethought

The *Iliad* reveals that Iapetus and Cronus are now in Tartarus, expelled far from mortal and immortal climes. The context of this passage in the *Iliad* is significant: Zeus says in his speech to Hera that he does not mind how furiously angry with him she is, and then reminds her of the Titanomachy. As was discussed in Chapter II, Section 2 above, the antagonism between Zeus and Hera is always depicted comically in the *Iliad*, but behind the scenes there are signs of a dangerous clash among the Olympian gods. Then, in this present passage, Zeus mentions Iapetus and Cronus as the two strong figures who stood against him. Neither Homer nor Hesiod recounts the story of Iapetus, but the mention of the same two gods in the same order in both the *Iliad* and the *Theogony* strongly suggests that this is an established formulaic expression, and that the audience would have been familiar with the story of the Titanomachy. In the *Theogony*, Hesiod seems to use the phrase not only to allude to the Titanomachy but also to foreshadow the fact that the son of Iapetus will be a dangerous divine opponent for Zeus.[20] Leaving the role of Iapetus in the Titanomachy unexplained, Hesiod's focus thus falls on Prometheus.

As Cronus is the last son of Uranus and Gaia (134-8), Iapetus is an older brother of Cronus. It is often pointed out that Aeschylus introduces Prometheus as belonging to the older generation, treating him as a Titan.[21] This arrangement is, of course, devised by Aeschylus for the sake of the plot of his play.[22] In Hesiod's genealogy, however, Prometheus is not a Titan but the son of a Titan, being a cousin of Zeus; thus he belongs to the same generation as Zeus. Therefore Prometheus ought not to have joined the Titanomachy, which was basically a generational war between the Titans and the Olympian gods.

We tend to class the Olympian gods who belong to the same generation as Zeus as more or less his supporters against the older generation. However, we should recognise that not all of the Olympian gods support Zeus, and some gods apparently oppose him, just as the sons of Iapetus do. It is necessary for Zeus to subjugate, in some way or other, those gods of his own generation who are unwilling to live under his control. In this situation, Zeus has to take suitable measures not only against ferocious gods like Typhoeus, but also against those who are just dissatisfied with his rule and may possibly cause trouble in future.

This is the same picture as that which is depicted and implied in Books 14 and 15 of the *Iliad*, where the apparently serious conflicts between Zeus and Hera, and Zeus and Poseidon are highlighted as forming the background of war in the human world. It was shown in Chapters II and III that these stories allude to the clash between Zeus and other Olympian gods: it seems that even after the establishment of Zeus' reign, there are some who remain antagonistic. In the *Theogony*, too, it is implied that the conflict between Zeus and the gods of his own generation becomes a serious problem for Zeus.

It is important to recognise also that Zeus adopts different strategies against his enemies from the older generation and against those of his own. With regard to the former, he destroys them instantly – either by hurling his thunderbolt against them or throwing them into Tartarus straightway; against the latter group, however, he may punish them in a way that enables them to function as a warning to other gods. Examples of this cautionary type of punishment are Zeus' ordering Atlas to hold up the heavens, and the bondage of Prometheus in chains.

This type of punishment has been discussed in Chapter II, Section 2, where we saw that Hera was hung from heaven by Zeus (*Il.* 15.18-24). In that case, Zeus punished Hera as a sort of warning to the other Olympian gods, especially Poseidon. In the *Theogony*, too, Zeus seems to contrive the same type of punishment. He binds the dangerous challenger Prometheus and, by doing so, tries to control the other gods. Prometheus' binding can therefore be regarded as a cunning strategy devised by Zeus in order to subjugate, before the event, any other potential challengers.

The context of the myth of Prometheus in the Theogony

Hesiod has placed the myth of Prometheus during the Titanomachy, after Zeus' deposition of Cronus. As critics have noted, the myth strikingly breaks the expected temporal sequence.[23] Obviously Hesiod inserted the myth of Prometheus in this present place for some significant reason. Hesiod's device for the coherent introduction of this out-of-place story is to smoothe out and highlight the transition by framing it with thematically relevant passages slightly before and after the myth of Prometheus. Both of these stories recount the liberation of the earlier gods from binding:

λῦσε δὲ πατροκασιγνήτους ὀλοῶν ὑπὸ δεσμῶν,
Οὐρανίδας, οὓς δῆσε πατὴρ ἀεσιφροσύνῃσιν·

And he freed from their deadly bonds the brothers of his father, sons of Heaven, whom their father had bound in his foolishness. (*Theog.* 501-2)

μνησάμενοι φιλότητος ἐνηέος, ὅσσα παθόντες
ἐς φάος ἂψ ἀφίκεσθε δυσηλεγέος ὑπὸ δεσμοῦ
ἡμετέρας διὰ βουλὰς ὑπὸ ζόφου ἠερόεντος.

remembering our faithful friendship, and how much you suffered before you came back to the light from your cruel bondage under misty gloom through our plans. (*Theog.* 651-3)

These two passages, which depict the same moment in the Titanomachy, operate as the frame for the Prometheus myth. After the myth of Prometheus, the audience (and we, the readers) are naturally guided back to the Titanomachy by the same event being narrated as a sort of a marker.[24] The reciprocity engendered by this event (liberation of the gods as a gift, and then their helping Zeus in exchange) is decisive for Zeus, because the aid of the older gods is indispensable for victory over the Titans. What is the function and the significance of the insertion of the myth of Prometheus at this point, instead of continuing with the consequences of the gods' liberation? I suggest that the arrangement (Titanomachy – Prometheus – Titanomachy) is intended to highlight important parallels between the myths and to demonstrate that Zeus' victory over Prometheus has a significance similar to his victory over the Titans.

Immediately before Hesiod turns to the story of Prometheus, we find that Zeus has just banished the old ruler, Cronus, in the Titanomachy. Now Zeus has become the champion of a new order, although his rule is still insecure. His victory over Cronus is of momentous import, as his victory in this generational strife is cardinal for his sovereignty. Then, in order to commemorate this moment, Zeus places the stone, which had been disguised as a baby Zeus, on Parnassus.

πρῶτον δ᾽ ἐξήμησε λίθον, πύματον καταπίνων·
τὸν μὲν Ζεὺς στήριξε κατὰ χθονὸς εὐρυοδείης
Πυθοῖ ἐν ἠγαθέῃ, γυάλοις ὕπο Παρνησσοῖο,
σῆμ᾽ ἔμεν ἐξοπίσω, θαῦμα θνητοῖσι βροτοῖσι.

... he [Cronus] vomited up first the stone which he had swallowed last. And Zeus set it fast in the wide-pathed earth at holy Pytho in the glens of Parnassos, to be a sign thereafter and a marvel for mortal men. (*Theog.* 497-500)

Zeus fixes the stone as a σῆμα, a sign of the resolution of the father-son struggle. By this act, he proclaims that his sovereignty is to be established not only in the divine realm, but also in the human world (it is explicitly said that the stone was fixed in the human world, on Parnassus).[25]

After the setting of the stone, Hesiod begins narrating the myth of Prometheus. Now that Zeus has put an end to Cronus' control, it is imperative that he consolidate his rule. In order to become the ruler of mortals and immortals (506), he needs, first, to punish Prometheus, his strong opponent among the gods of Zeus' generation and, second, to force mortals to become subordinate to him. Thus it is that Prometheus becomes the first challenger of Zeus to be defeated after the proclamation of Zeus as a new ruler.

The narrative of the myth of Prometheus in Theogony 521-616

Hesiod begins the narrative about Prometheus with a sort of summary of the story (521-34). In this summary, he starts with the end: Prometheus is now bound by Zeus (521-2).[26] This way of presenting the end point at the beginning is characteristic of Hesiod's narrative; for example, this is demonstrated, as Hamilton shows, in the Proem of the poem.[27] The reason for Prometheus' binding is given in the last verses of the summary at 534, before the details of the story are recounted (535-616):

οὕνεκ᾽ ἐρίζετο βουλὰς ὑπερμενέι Κρονίωνι.

because he [Prometheus] challenged the very mighty son of Cronus in his own plans (*Theog.* 534)

The word βουλὰς (line 534) deserves further comment: it has been translated as 'Prometheus matched in wit with the almighty son of Cronus' (Evelyn-White); 'because Prometheus had contended in counsels with Cronus' very strong son' (G.W. Most); or, 'he pitted his wits against the son of Cronus' (M.L. West in his 1988 translation). As these translations illustrate, this verse is usually understood to define the significant feature of this conflict: it is not one of physical power, but of contrivance. As West has explained, however, the word βουλή should perhaps not be taken specifically as 'cunning device', but rather interpreted more generally as 'design', 'will', or 'plan'.[28] This verse can thus be interpreted as implying that the conflict between Zeus and Prometheus is caused by a difference in their plans or designs. This should remind us of the well-known phrase in the proem of the *Iliad* 1.5, Διὸς δ᾽ ἐτελείετο βουλή ('thus, the will/plan of Zeus was going to be accomplished'). So, in the *Theogony*, βουλαί could be read as will/plans, and line 534 of the *Theogony* interpreted as Prometheus' challenging of Zeus in his plans or designs.[29]

What, then, were the βουλαί of Prometheus? Interpretations of the Διὸς βουλή of the *Iliad* are twofold: either, as Aristarchus comments, it implies Zeus' promise to Thetis to avenge the slight on Achilles by favouring the Trojans (schol. bT); or that Zeus' plan is to lighten the over-burdened earth by means of heavy casualties at Troy (schol. D). The latter interpretation might throw light on the plans of Prometheus here, as the former is exclusively applied to the plot of the *Iliad*. If the plan of Zeus in the *Iliad* is to diminish the human population, the plan of Prometheus in the *Theogony* could be, on the contrary, to enable human beings to flourish – with himself as their patron. This would certainly create a clash between Zeus and Prometheus. Furthermore, on this reading Prometheus is transformed – no longer simply a trickster (as is often understood[30]), he is revealed as a formidable figure with determined plans for mankind in mind.

In the opening verses of the sacrifice scene, Prometheus' attitude is clearly drawn:

καὶ γὰρ ὅτ᾽ ἐκρίνοντο θεοὶ θνητοί τ᾽ ἄνθρωποι
Μηκώνῃ, τότ᾽ ἔπειτα μέγαν βοῦν πρόφρονι θυμῷ
δασσάμενος προύθηκε, Διὸς νόον ἐξαπαφίσκων.

106

V. Prometheus, God of Forethought

For when the gods and mortal men had a dispute at Mecone, then Prometheus of his own free will cut up a big ox and served it in such a way as to mislead Zeus. (*Theog.* 535-7)

The verb ἐκρίνοντο (535) has been understood to mean that 'men and gods were separated'; but, as F.C. Philip rightly comments, it is basically a legal word referring to some sort of settlement of an issue.[31] They were going to reach an agreement about the apportioning of the ox, and then Prometheus cut it πρόφρονι θυμῷ (willingly; of his own free will, 536). The phrase πρόφρονι θυμῷ, with its pointed focus on the mind of Prometheus, suggests that he now willingly challenges Zeus by intervening in this 'settlement' between gods and men.

After cutting the big ox, Prometheus puts the two portions before Zeus; one is meat and entrails covered in ox's stomach, the other is bones covered in glistening fat (538-41). Then begins the conversation between Zeus and Prometheus. The first lines of the exchange between Zeus and Prometheus, in which each calls to the other, attract our attention because of the similarity and dissimilarity of their formulation:

(by Zeus)
Ἰαπετιονίδη, πάντων ἀριδείκετ' ἀνάκτων
Son of Iapetus, renowned among all rulers (*Theog.* 543)

(by Prometheus)
Ζεῦ κύδιστε μέγιστε θεῶν αἰειγενετάων
Zeus, most glorious and greatest of the everlasting gods (*Theog.* 548)

Both speak with extravagant praise, and surely here in sarcasm, which helps to emphasise their antagonistic characters. K. Stoddard draws attention to the ironic and ambiguous tone of Zeus (543), because the word ἄναξ has two meanings, 'god' or 'mortal king'.[32] So, Zeus is either calling Prometheus 'most renowned of all the gods' or 'most renowned of all mortal kings'. The former would be hyperbole, the latter insult. The word ἀριδείκετε (543) is also ambiguous. This adjective can have a negative connotation, because it is used for Kratos (Power) and Bia (Violence) as the 'renowned children' to whom Styx gave birth (Κράτος ἠδὲ Βίην ἀριδείκετα γείνατο τέκνα, 385). Zeus takes advantage of the ambiguity, then Prometheus answers with exaggerated praise. Since Prometheus, it seems, grasps the irony of ἄναξ as meaning mortal king, he adds the adjective αἰειγενετάων (548), putting the emphasis on the everlastingness of the gods. The battle is totally one of the mind here, and Hesiod successfully focuses our attention on their antagonistic characters and their preferred choice of weapons.

After Zeus chose the portion of the ox that only appeared to be better, he became angry:

χώσατο δὲ φρένας ἀμφί, χόλος δέ μιν ἵκετο θυμόν
He became enraged in his heart, and wrath came upon his spirit. (*Theog.*
554)

The repeated mention of his anger (χώσατο, χόλος) seems to suggest that
Zeus has been thoroughly deceived by Prometheus. Yet Hesiod goes on to
emphasise that Zeus *deliberately* made the wrong choice, as part of his evil
design against mortals (550-2). The text explicitly says that Zeus knew of
the deception (550-1).[33] There is, however, a more subtle meaning to be
found in this passage. Certainly, the story cannot continue unless Zeus
takes up the wrong share. Perhaps Zeus has no real choice between the
two portions, because he could not lose face by taking the one covered with
the ox's stomach, as he is provoked by Prometheus' addressing him as 'the
most glorious and greatest of the everlasting gods' (548). Zeus was, in a
sense, induced to take the seemingly better one. So, Prometheus' action is
not simply one of trickery, or an illustration of the theme of outward
appearance versus reality, but rather hints at a deeper issue – that of the
problem of having no real choice.[34]

One word in Zeus' speech seems very strange. It might allude to
Prometheus' past:

ὦ πέπον, οὐκ ἄρα πω δολίης ἐπελήθεο τέχνης.
So you did not yet forget your deceptive craft. (*Theog.* 560)

The word πω here means 'yet' or 'even now',[35] implying that he deceived
Zeus before. Hesiod says nothing further about this; it is possible that he
alludes here to a story well-known to the audience – something which took
place before the deception at Mecone. He has suppressed the reasons
underlying Prometheus' beneficence to mankind, so we cannot specify a
particular event to which the word πω alludes. Given the close attachment
between Prometheus and men (all the stories of Prometheus narrated in
the *Theogony* have something to do with men), the past event alluded to
here would most likely also be related to men, and it is tempting to
speculate that it could be the story about mankind's origin.

What motivates Zeus' binding of Prometheus? In the *Theogony*, the
theme of binding is an integral part of the myth-narrative about sovereignty. However, the trick at Mecone and the theft of fire have, as such,
nothing to do with the theme of sovereignty. If Prometheus is a real threat
to Zeus, comparable with Cronus and Typhoeus (as shown by the juxtaposition of their stories), the motivation for binding should be more serious
than these two tricks alone, and, importantly, it should relate to an
endangerment of Zeus' sovereignty. If the event alluded to by the word πω
is the creation of men by Prometheus, this would be a threat to the
sovereignty of Zeus, since it is Zeus' aim to become 'the father of gods and
men'. On a more practical level, one reason to suppress the story of human

creation is that if it was not the work of Zeus but of Prometheus, this story simply would not fit with Hesiod's overall design for the poem.

I understand, as many commentators do, that even after Heracles' coming Prometheus remained under bondage (which is explicitly pointed out in the closing verses 615-16).[36] The logic of the story does not allow for the release of Prometheus since, unlike the Cyclopes and Hecatoncheires, Prometheus has nothing to offer Zeus in return for his release. As the mythic parallels suggest, without reconciliation between Zeus and Prometheus in the form of this reciprocity, Prometheus can never be released.[37] The killing of the eagle becomes just an episode through which Heracles adds another achievement to his own glorious career.

Thus was Prometheus defeated. Prometheus is an ambiguous figure, as is his status in the divine world. By defeating him, what did Zeus obtain? Unlike the cases of the defeat of Cronus or Typhoeus, the answer is not clear-cut. One peculiarity of the Prometheus myth is the two-fold nature of the punishments now given: binding for Prometheus; a woman for mankind. Why is mankind to be punished as well? The connection between Prometheus and men is, again, the key to this problem: if men were created by Prometheus, Zeus would naturally abhor them, and would dole out punishment to them as well as to their creator.

2. The defeat of Prometheus

The name of Prometheus

The story of Prometheus is not told in the Homeric epics, nor is it mentioned in extant choral lyric. We do not know how far his name goes back in the past. P. Chantraine suggests that the second half of the name, '-metheus', is from the neutral form *μῆθος, which belongs to the same family as μανθάνω, μαθεῖν, and that Προμηθής was formed in analogy to μῆτις.[38] H. Frisk, giving the form προμήθεια (Vorsicht), explains the meaning of προμηθής as 'vorbedacht, vorsichtig'.[39] So far, the meaning of the name Prometheus appears to be clear, and possesses a distinctive etymological explanation. However, if the connotation of the name of the god is clear, that very fact is itself peculiar.

J. Chadwick remarks that, among the Olympian deities, Zeus is the only god whose name can be claimed to be etymologically Indo-European in origin, being reconstructed as *dyêus in Indo-European (conceived as the god of clear sky).[40] According to Chadwick, many Olympian deities can, despite their non-Greek origin, be explained by their alleged etymologies, as is the case for Poseidon, Demeter, Hermes, Athena and, of course, Aphrodite,[41] and he continues that, 'any account of a god which begins from an explanation of the meaning of his name ought to be treated with grave suspicion'.[42] If he is right, the name Prometheus seems to be extraordinary in that the connotation and etymology of his name is too obvious.

K. Bapp's suggestion in Roscher's Lexicon, old as it is, remains noteworthy: Bapp posits that 'Prometheus' would be 'ein Beiname' (epithet), like 'Phoebos' for Apollon.[43] The adjectival form of the word, προμηθής, is used by later writers, such as Thucydides (3.82.4) and Plato (in the comparative form, *Laches* 188B). As an epithet, it is attached to Zeus (Ζεὺς Προμανθεύς, Lycophr. 537). If the word 'Prometheus' was originally an epithet, it is fully understandable that it possesses a readily discernible and distinctive meaning. In turn, it appears that the true name of the god who possesses this epithet remains hidden. We might even infer that the true name of Prometheus (if ever he had one) remains unknown for some specific reasons: one possibility is that this god was originally so mighty and dreadful that even to mention his true name was taboo – as in the case of the Erinyes-Eumenides.[44]

W. Burkert offers the story of a Sumerian hero Ninurta or Ningirsu in a hymn by Gudea, which offers some notable similarities with the myth of Prometheus. It is 'the liberation of the Sun-God from his Mountain-grave', that deity whom a bird of prey is about to attack.[45] If we draw out the parallels between this story and that related of Prometheus, it would appear that fire, one of the main elements associated with Prometheus, was originally possessed not by Zeus but by the sun.[46] If 'Prometheus' is the epithet of the god who brought fire to mankind, then the real name of the god could either have something to do with the sun, and/or be of non-Greek origin.

His brother Epimetheus, 'Afterthought', is regarded as a fabricated figure by many commentators; perhaps, and as M.L. West puts it, he was specially created for the role, just to become the receiver of Pandora.[47] If Epimetheus is a double of Prometheus, Prometheus was, then, 'caught in the trap which he himself set'.[48] It becomes evident that Prometheus, in spite of his name (or of his epithet), could not see the future. Indeed, he was unable to foresee the result of both his trickery at Mecone and his theft of fire. Prometheus was supposed to have 'forethought', but Zeus categorically demonstrated that he did not. He is, then, in fact, 'Epimetheus'.

Prometheus proved not to be the benefactor of mankind, although he may have imagined himself thus: his intervention in human affairs brought evil consequences. That is, while in appearance his acts appeared beneficial to men, in point of fact, as Hesiod demonstrates, the result was the opposite.[49]

Prometheus and mankind

There are other figures in Greek myth who are punished by Zeus for their deception. For example, Tantalus' trickery is sometimes compared with that of Prometheus: Tantalus stole ambrosia, deceiving the gods with a meal with hidden contents.[50] It would seem that Hesiod could have chosen other myths in order to demonstrate that Zeus holds sway both in intelligence and physical strength. We return, therefore, to the reason for the selection of the Prometheus story. It possesses a unique significance because, unlike the other stories, it is exclusively connected with human beings.

Iapetus and his descendants are closely linked with mankind. Among the several versions of the genealogy of his family, the *Theogony* demonstrates that Epimetheus received the first woman (513-14) and, by implication, that Epimetheus became the ancestor of the human race. According to a scholion on Apollonius Rhodius (3.1086), Hesiod says in the *Ehoiai* that Deucalion was the son of Prometheus and Pandora; and Hellen, of whom the Hellenes and Hellas are the descendants, was the son of Prometheus (or Deucalion) and Pyrrha (Hes. fr. 3 Most [Comm. on 2.1 H; 2 M-W]). This genealogy is set out in the following diagram:

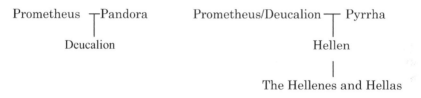

In another genealogy, Deucalion is a son of Prometheus and Clymene/Prynoe (Hes. fr. 5 Most [4 M-W], in *Schol. Hom. Od.* 10.2). Although the flood is not mentioned in the *Theogony*, Pindar says that after Zeus caused the water to recede, Deucalion and Pyrrha came down from Parnassus and created people out of stones (*Ol.* 9.42-6).[51] In the Hes. fr. 251 Most [234 M-W], Zeus gave to Deucalion 'pebble-people' (λαοί) gathered from the earth. Pindar perhaps might have got his idea from this. As varied as these genealogies are, one feature peculiar to this family is its close connection with human beings. The strength of the tie probably lies in a member of this family having been the ancestor of mankind: Prometheus, Epimetheus or Deucalion.

In later Greek literature there are many references which claim that Prometheus is the creator of men, or related to human creation. The first Greek reference to the belief that the human race was formed from either earth or clay by god(s) is Aristophanes' *Birds* 686 (πλάσματα πηλοῦ). In the *Protagoras* (320D), Plato says that the gods moulded the forms of men by mixing earth and fire: Epimetheus was ordered by the gods to equip men with proper faculties, and Prometheus, after examining Epimetheus' work, gave men wisdom and fire. The first attribution of man's creation to Prometheus is that of Philemon, the New Comedy poet of the fourth century BC:

ὁ Προμηθεύς, ὃν λέγουσ᾿ ἡμᾶς πλάσαι
καὶ τἆλλα πάντα ζῷα ...

Prometheus, who they say, moulded us and all other animals ... (Philem. fr. 93, vv. 1-2 K-A, in Stobaeus III 2.26)

Apollodorus (1.7.1) writes that Prometheus moulded men out of water and earth and gave them fire, hiding it in a stalk of fennel. In a later period the idea that Prometheus is the creator of mankind seems to have become well established, since we have more references for the story.[52] Plentiful references indicate that there was a strong tradition of belief that Prometheus was a creator of men. It is uncertain how far we can trace back the origin of the story, and as Dunbar comments,[53] the idea of Prometheus as a creator of men is likely to be much older than the time of Philemon in the fourth century BC. It is uncertain whether the legend goes back to Hesiod's time: either he did not know the story, or perhaps he ignored it. Whatever the case may be, it is remarkable that Prometheus and his family are exclusively connected to human creation; either Prometheus created men, or his progeny became the ancestors of men.

In the Five Ages of Men of the *Works and Days*, the Races of Gold and Silver were made by 'the immortals who live in the mansions on Olympus' (110; 128). From the Third Race on, men were made by Zeus (143; 158; 173d). This narrative seems to indicate that the first and second races were created by gods other than Zeus, although Hesiod does not specify who they were. There is no doubt that there remains a persistent ambiguity about the creation of men/ancestry of mankind in Hesiod, but at the very least it is possible to infer that Iapetus' family, or Prometheus himself, were somehow involved. As Philips remarks, the basic plot of the story of Prometheus might be Prometheus' theft of fire for the men he had created, and his subsequent punishment.[54] It appears that Zeus extinguishes the real name of Prometheus from the history of human creation, so that Zeus can become, in the true sense of the words, 'the father of gods and men'.

3. Elpis

The creation of a woman is introduced as the outcome of the strife between Zeus and Prometheus, which, then, becomes a part of the larger struggle for power.[55] The episode recounted in *Works and Days* of ἐλπίς, which remained in the jar, can be seen as relating closely to the intrinsic quality possessed by Prometheus.

When Pandora opened the lid of the jar, evils came out and spread among men (100):

μούνη δ' αὐτόθι Ἐλπὶς ἐν ἀρρήκτοισι δόμοισιν
ἔνδον ἔμεινε πίθου ὑπὸ χείλεσιν οὐδὲ θύραζε
ἐξέπτη· πρόσθεν γὰρ ἐπέμβαλε πῶμα πίθοιο
αἰγιόχου βουλῇσι Διὸς νεφεληγερέταο.
ἄλλα δὲ μυρία λυγρὰ κατ' ἀνθρώπους ἀλάληται·   100

Only Elpis remained there in the impregnable dwelling inside, under the rim of the jar, and did not fly out from the door; because, before that, she [the Woman] put on the lid of the jar, by the plans of aegis-holding Zeus who gathers clouds. But other millions of miseries roam about among mankind. (*Works and Days* 96-100)

There have been many discussions of the confusion raised by the episode of Pandora's jar in the *Works and Days* – such as whether Elpis is good or bad, or whether the jar contained both good and evil or only evil.[56] The story of ἐλπίς remaining in the jar is usually taken to mean that at least we have hope in this world which is now full of evils.[57] This interpretation is problematic: according to the logic of the story, the jar had a lid which prevented its contents from coming out; thus ἐλπίς, which remained in the jar, is also prevented from coming out. The narrative is explicit: the jar, where ἐλπίς remained, is like a house never to be broken into (96); and ἐλπίς can never go out of the door (97). In this context, Hesiod clearly pronounces that ἐλπίς is now concealed, and that it never is in this world.[58]

The main problem here is how ἐλπίς should be interpreted. As Verdenius writes, the original meaning of the verb ἔλπομαι is not 'to hope' but 'to anticipate'.[59] In later Christian texts, ἐλπίς always denotes hope, particularly the hope of salvation. So, problems are caused by the persistent idea that ἐλπίς means 'hope': that is, hope, as it might naturally be understood, of good things. In classical Greek, however, ἐλπίς is not only 'good hope' but also 'anxious thought about the future' (LSJ). So, ἐλπίς means both good and bad expectation or anticipation.[60] The *Iliad* offers a very good example of both meanings of the related verb, ἔλπομαι:

τό μιν οὔ ποτε ἔλπετο θυμῷ
τεθνάμεν, ἀλλὰ ζωὸν ἐνιχριμφθέντα πύλῃσιν
ἂψ ἀπονοστήσειν, ἐπεὶ οὐδὲ τὸ ἔλπετο πάμπαν,
ἐκπέρσειν πτολίεθρον ἄνευ ἕθεν, οὐδὲ σὺν αὐτῷ·

So, he [Achilles] never anticipated in his heart that he [Patroclus] had died, but that he would return alive after reaching the gate, since he never anticipated that Patroclus would destroy the city without him, or even with him. (*Il.* 17.404-7)

The word ἔλπετο in 404 is undoubtedly 'bad anticipation' or 'anxious thought about the future', because Achilles is thinking of Patroclus' death. But in 406, it is 'good anticipation', because Achilles hopes for Patroclus' victory over Troy, although he negates the possibility.[61] Compare other writers' examples of such usage: Aeschylus has φόβου ... ἐλπίς, 'anticipation of fear' (*Ag.* 1434); and Plato defines ἐλπίς as δόξα μελλόντων, 'opinion about the future' (*Laws* 644C). Thus ἐλπίς does not simply mean good hope, but rather the expectation of something good *and* bad in the future. Therefore, if we disregard the prejudicial, later connotation of the word, ἐλπίς means not only 'hope' but also 'anticipation' or 'foresight' in its most neutral sense .

To be more precise, which, of 'anticipation' and 'foresight', should we take as the meaning of the Hesiodic ἐλπίς? The distinction between these two meanings of the word is not clear in the *Iliad*, as the passage cited above (17.404-7) shows.[62] But it is significant to compare how Aeschylus understood the account of ἐλπίς remaining in the jar, and how he used it in his tragedy *Prometheus Bound*. Although Aeschylus altered the story substantially, he accurately reflected the critical sense of the concealment of ἐλπίς in the jar – which he takes to represent man's deprivation of foresight:

> Πρ. θνητούς γ᾽ ἔπαυσα μὴ προδέρκεσθαι μόρον.
> Χο. τὸ ποῖον εὑρὼν τῆσδε φάρμακον νόσου;
> Πρ. τυφλὰς ἐν αὐτοῖς ἐλπίδας κατῴκισα.

> Pr. I made mortals no longer foresee their fate.
> Ch. What kind of remedy did you find for this anguish?
> Pr. I put blind hopes into their minds. (*P.V.* 248-50)

Aeschylus communicates the idea that one of the important messages of the myth of Prometheus is that foresight is forever concealed from men. In the tragedy, Aeschylus made Prometheus, instead of Zeus, play the major role in this concealment, and Prometheus did this as a benefit for men. From these verses, it is clear that Aeschylus does not take ἐλπίς as 'good hope' in our sense. Moreover, he offers a clear distinction in meaning to the Hesiodic usage of the word: 'foresight' (προδέρκεσθαι, *P.V.* 248), and 'anticipation' (τυφλὰς ἐλπίδας, *P.V.* 250). So, according to Aeschylus, man is, on the one hand, unable to see his future fate but, on the other hand, allowed blind hope (anticipation).

The phrase τυφλὰς ἐλπίδας makes clear how uncertain and arbitrary is the 'anticipation' of mankind. As Griffith comments, hopes are blind because they make mankind 'act without constantly being aware of the exact limits on their aspiration'.[63] In Hesiod ἐλπίς is also seen in a similar context. Hesiod mentions this word only three times, all of which are found in the *Works and Days*. Apart from the instance under discussion, the word appears at 498 and 500 – κενὴν ... ἐλπίδα (unreliable anticipation, *W.D.* 498); ἐλπὶς δ᾽ οὐκ ἀγαθὴ κεχρημένον ἄνδρα κομίζειν (ἐλπίς is not any good at caring for a needy man, *W.D.* 500). We see, therefore, that Hesiod is aware of the two connotations attached to the word ἐλπίς. As Aeschylus rightly suggests, anticipation is something that certainly exists among men, whereas, as is explained by Pandora's story, foresight, clear knowledge of the future, does not. It is, thus, not beyond the bounds of possibility that lines 248-50 of this tragedy offer a relic of the original mythic message and suggest that the loss of foresight is paradigmatic to the Prometheus story.

V. Prometheus, God of Forethought

According to the *Works and Days*, Hesiod emphasises that it is by the plan of Zeus (βουλῆσι Διός) that men are prohibited from possessing foresight (99).[64] Thus, when the god of 'Forethought' is defeated by Zeus, men are also forbidden to have ἐλπίς, 'foresight'. It is evidently not a coincidence that a cognate type of punishment was given to Prometheus *and* men by Zeus; it is the punishment concerning the power to see the future for both of them. Through his binding of Prometheus, Zeus interrupted the relation between men and their patron god. It is now Zeus himself who steps forth to assume the mantle of world supremacy.

The victory over Prometheus has been variously elaborated by scholars: for example, Zeus establishes his rule not only through might and violence but also through intelligence and justice; 'Prometheus' forethought and cleverness are 'short-sighted', no match for Zeus' wisdom';[65] or, 'the sovereign power of Zeus combines all the forms of power which existed in the preceding generation'.[66] As was discussed earlier in this chapter, the most striking feature of the myth concerning the struggle for sovereignty is that Zeus defeated Prometheus by depriving him of his power of forethought and, perhaps, even of his real name. Zeus takes action to prevent men from possessing the power of forethought and from benefitting from Prometheus' beneficence. So, Hesiod claims in the *Theogony* that it is only with the removal of Prometheus, the benefactor and likely creator of mankind, that Zeus can finally and definitively proclaim himself as 'the father of gods and men', and thus ensure his permanent dominion over the universe.

The outcome of the story of Prometheus is reminiscent of that of Iasion as told both in the *Odyssey* (5.125-8) and the *Theogony* (969-72). It is generally thought that Iasion was an annual god in origin – one who undergoes death and resurrection (representing the yearly cycle of vegetation) – who functions as a consort of the Mother Goddess.[67] However, both in the *Odyssey* and the *Theogony*, he is already transformed into a mortal lover of Demeter, and has been deprived of his cardinal power of resurrection. This story too, then, reflects a familiar feature of the reign of Zeus: in order to become the ruler of the world and to maintain the stability of the universe, it is indispensable for him to deprive his challengers of their most important powers. Prometheus, as the god of forethought and, perhaps a creator of men, must be deprived totally of his primeval power.

It is of great interest to try to interpret and recapture the universe that Hesiod imagined in the shape of the *Theogony*. Even before Hesiod's manipulations, the Prometheus myth would have had a long history and have passed through repeated re-adaptations. Naturally it is difficult fully to comprehend the nuances of a myth which has had such a long and varied history, and these gaps in our knowledge add to the difficulty of grasping completely the motivations underlying Hesiod's design and his own reinterpretation of the stories. My reading has drawn out some hitherto unexplored aspects of Hesiod's reworking of the Prometheus myth, high-lighting apparent inconsistencies and demonstrating how Hesiod's use of the myth can be more coherently viewed within his overall mythic pro-gramme. The history of myth can indeed be baffling – 'continuously reinterpreted and adapted to new developments in the process of which it is a symbol'[68] – but, as this investigation has sought to demonstrate, while Hesiod's Prometheus myth may well be artificial in construction, it is by no means arbitrary.

VI

Typhon, Son of Hera

The composition and unity of the *Hymn to Apollo* are controversial problems. Since David Ruhnken suggested that the *Hymn to Apollo* consists of
two originally independent poems, most scholars have divided the hymn
into a 'Delian' and a 'Pythian' part.[1] Recent scholarly work, however, tends
to harmonise the differing views, admitting, on the one hand, the separate
authorship of the Delian and Pythian sections, but recognising, on the
other hand, a certain unity between the two.[2]

I align myself with these recent scholars: although differences in outlook, style, language and metrical technique cannot be ignored, I contend
that the combination is not accidental. I do not, however, take the purely
Unitarian view of Penglase, who writes that 'the unity of construction by
one poet seems to be the only reasonable conclusion'.[3] Rather, as many
scholars point out, the differences between the two parts are readily
observable. Nevertheless, they are also connected by many similarities,
and the whole poem seems to have a coherent design. The comic poet
Aristophanes probably knew the hymn as a unity, since he seems to quote
from both the Delian and the Pythian parts.[4] With this rationale in mind,
I shall treat the text that we have before us as one composition.

The digression of the Typhon episode (305-55) has often been regarded
as an interpolation. Some even hold that the hymn has been pieced
together from three different sources: the Delian, Pythian and Typhon
episodes.[5] The main reason for regarding the Typhon episode as an interpolation is that its connection to the main narrative seems awkwardly
contrived.[6] However, the details of connection are worth investigating
more closely: how does the linkage – if any – work? I suggest that there *is*
a design in the arrangement of the motifs, and that this design contributes
logically to the structural and thematic effectiveness and persuasiveness
of this digression. It is the aim of this chapter, therefore, to examine the
details of the digression of the Typhon story and, on the basis of this
examination, to elucidate the logical connection between the digression
and the narrative as a whole. One significant consequence of my analysis is the demonstration that increased emphasis ought to be placed on
the issue of cosmic strife – in this case, between Typhon and Zeus, and
also between Apollo and Zeus – as an important constructional motif in
the hymn.

117

1. The arrangement of the motifs

Telphousa

The digression has manifold effects, among which is undoubtedly the accumulation of similar motifs that emphasise the importance of the female dragon.[7] Thus three episodes about monsters are presented: Typhon, the dragon (Python), and Telphousa.[8] Let us now consider the Telphousa episode in relation to that of Typhon-Python.

In the story of Telphousa and that of the Typhon-Python, there are obvious similarities, and yet conspicuous contrasts as well. Remarkably, the beautiful spring is attributed to both Telphousa and the dragon. The fair-flowing (καλλίρροος) water of the spring of Telphousa is thrice mentioned (376, 380, 385), just as the abode of the dragon is also near it (κρήνη καλλίρροος, 300).[9] As another similarity, both in Telphousa's and Hera's minds, anger motivates their rivalry. Telphousa becomes angry at Apollo (ἐχολώσατο, 256) when Apollo begins to build his temple. As is mentioned below at p. 126, in the digression of the Typhon-Python episode Hera is also characterised as being angry at Zeus.

Differences between the motifs are noteworthy in several ways: Telphousa seems to have been on good terms with humankind, since humans water horses and mules there (263); however, the dragon and Typhon are both baneful to men (304, 306, 352). Telphousa recognises that Apollo is stronger and mightier than herself (267), but the dragon and Typhon boast of their overweening power and violence. In the light of their opposing characters, it is significant that Telphousa uses the power of persuasion against Apollo, unlike the violence we see in the dragon and Typhon. In her arguments, she gives sufficient reasons for denying Apollo's offer (262-6), and suggests an alternative that would suit Apollo's intent (267-71). She speaks positively and decisively to Apollo:

ἔπος τί τοι ἐν φρεσὶ θήσω
I am going to say something to put in your heart (257)

ἀλλ᾽ ἔκ τοι ἐρέω, σὺ δ᾽ ἐνὶ φρεσὶ βάλλεο σῇσι
But I will speak out, then you should take it in your heart (261)

Yet she diplomatically degrades herself as well:

σὺ δὲ κρείσσων καὶ ἀρείων
ἐσσὶ ἄναξ ἐμέθεν
You are mightier and stronger than I, Lord (267-8)

In spite of the fact that she does not recommend violence, her speech is somewhat forceful and deceptive. Her persuasion is effective enough, then, to succeed in changing Apollo's mind for a time. As a result of her deceit,

118

she is punished by Apollo (379-81); however, she is not utterly destroyed, as she and Apollo eventually share the resulting fame:[10]

ἐνθάδε δὴ καὶ ἐμὸν κλέος ἔσσεται, οὐδὲ σὸν οἴης
The fame of this place shall be mine [Apollo], not yours [Telphousa's]
alone (381)

In this way, the most conspicuous feature of the Telphousa episode is that words are directly exchanged by Telphousa and Apollo. Apollo proclaims his intentions for building his sanctuary to Telphousa and Crisa using similar words (247-53 ~ 287-93), but only Telphousa answers verbally (257-74), as she, unlike Crisa, is personified. Therefore, when Apollo discovers that he has been deceived, and returns in anger to punish Telphousa, he still talks with her (379-81). In the hymn, this Telphousa episode obviously casts light on Apollo as the master of λόγος. Therefore, however mighty he may be, he gives oracles in verbal form – in clear contrast with the oracles of Zeus.[11] Thus Apollo's dual nature – his mental and physical aspects – enables him to overwhelm both types of opponents. By giving these two extreme examples, the hymn further suggests the full range of Apollo's powers.[12]

The female dragon

I now turn to the episode of the female dragon, essential because it functions as the framework of the digression. With his strong arrow, Apollo kills the female dragon who lives by the fair-flowing spring (300-1). The digression of the Typhon episode begins five lines after the killing of this dragon. Both the story of the dragon and the digression itself begin very abruptly (300ff.). At line 282, Apollo comes to Crisa and peacefully builds his temple there (285-93). Apollo speaks to Crisa with words similar to those that he employed towards Telphousa, quoted above, but the narrative then differs sharply: no objection is raised in Crisa, nor is there any mention of the existence either of the dragon or of anything that might become an obstacle to his building a temple. Then, immediately, the killing of the female dragon is narrated. The only word linking Crisa and the dragon is ἀγχοῦ (300); the location of the dragon is 'near' the 'fair-flowing stream', with which Crisa herself is identified.

ἀγχοῦ δὲ κρήνη καλλίρροος, ἔνθα δράκαιναν
κτεῖνεν ἄναξ Διὸς υἱὸς ἀπὸ κρατεροῖο βιοῖο
ζατρεφέα μεγάλην, τέρας ἄγριον, ἢ κακὰ πολλὰ
ἀνθρώπους ἔρδεσκεν ἐπὶ χθονί, πολλὰ μὲν αὐτοὺς
πολλὰ δὲ μῆλα ταναύποδ᾽, ἐπεὶ πέλε πῆμα δαφοινόν.

Nearby is the fair-flowing spring, and there the lord, the son of Zeus, killed the female dragon with his mighty bow, a great fat creature, a wild monster,

who practised many evils on the people of the earth, many to themselves,
and many to their sheep with slender feet, for she was a savage affliction
(300-4)

There are no sinister words from the dragon, nor any direct speech
between Apollo and the dragon; unexpectedly, the first mention of the
dragon is its killing (301). In the next three lines we note effective word
play and alliteration: κακά and πολλά (302), πολλά (303), πολλά (304), ἐπεὶ
πέλε πῆμα (304). With these imposing words, the awesome character of the
dragon is emphatically expressed. Notably, they can also be interpreted as
providing Apollo with a motive for slaying her.

The epithet which introduces Apollo in this episode should also be
noted: he is called ἄναξ Διὸς υἱὸς (301) – the lord, the son of Zeus. It is
crucial that the relationship between Apollo and Zeus is emphasised. As
discussed at pp. 129-31 below, not only in the digression, but also throughout the entire hymn, Apollo's strong kinship with Zeus is the leitmotif
which pervades the narrative.

The episode which tells the story of Hera's generation of Typhon is
introduced as abruptly as that of the killing of the dragon. The phrase καί
ποτε (305) starts the digression, and in this unexpected way 'the past
intrudes into the present'.[13] In the parallel created between the dragon and
Typhon, it is curious that only the *birth* of Typhon and the *death* of the
dragon are narrated. It seems that there is some reason advantageous to
the composer for this arrangement, and some significant motive for omit-
ting mention (a) of a detailed account of the dragon, and (b) of the death of
Typhon. In order to trace the design of the digression, let me begin by
postulating why there is no detailed account of the dragon.

Had the story of the dragon's birth been part of the narrative, we might
expect it to have mentioned the place (Delphi) that she occupied: however,
this would then imply that oracles had been given there before the advent
of Apollo. Certainly, there are other versions of the myth in which either
Themis or Gaia give oracles, and the dragon is the protector of that place.[14]
However, the hymn declares that Apollo's oracle is a new foundation: this,
therefore, would strongly resist any notion of his having a predecessor.
The defeat of the monster would obviously signify the usurpation of the
ancient shrine by a new god, yet the narrative is carefully designed to
avoid any mention of this.[15] That is, the poet's strategy is to conceal any
detailed account of the dragon, in order to stress that Apollo's first oracular installation was without precedent.

Folk etymology suggests another reason why any detail of the dragon is
suppressed. Although Simonides, quoted in a letter of the Emperor Julian,
gives the name of the dragon as Python (fr. 573 Page; Jul. *Ep.* 24. 395D),
this is not mentioned in the hymn.[16] Had a detailed account of the dragon
been offered, one might reasonably expect it to have been named. Therefore, the names of both the dragon and the location must be carefully

concealed before it is killed, since the hymn insists that the place-name is derived from the rotting of the corpse (Πυθὼ, 372);[17] logically, the location could not have a name before Apollo came, because it was uninhabited (only after Apollo built his sanctuary did he start to consider what kind of people should be brought in, 388-90). When the account of Apollo's advent is narrated, the place is very carefully called 'Crisa, under snowy Parnassus' (269), suggesting the poet's attempt to avoid calling it Delphi or Pytho. Thus, for encomiastic purposes, it is of great importance that Apollo should found his oracular temple in a place previously unoccupied. It is this special concern for etymology and for the sacred identification of the place with Apollo which provides us with a second reason – namely, the aetiological design of this hymn – why the dragon is unnamed and its birth and life remain untold.[18]

A third reason why the dragon's story is curtailed is to afford a connection with Typhon. One of the few bits of information given about the dragon in this hymn is that it is female. This differs from other versions, where the dragon is male.[19] This one detail has great significance: being female, the dragon is able to become nurse to Typhon. According to the text (354, cited below), it is the only factor which connects the dragon with Typhon. Since few particulars of the dragon are given, and her other attributes remain mysterious, the revelation of her gender becomes all the more pointed and deliberate.

2. The digression of the Typhon episode

Typhon

The treatment of Typhon in this hymn is unique. He is introduced in connection with the dragon, yet he is not the central figure of the digression. Only his birth is narrated: there is no mention of his appearance, his fight with Zeus, or his death. The parallel between Typhon and the female dragon is clear: Typhon is 'affliction to mortals' (πῆμα βροτοῖσιν, 306), and the dragon is 'savage affliction' (πῆμα δαφοινόν, 304). The characterisation of the monsters at the start of the digression is echoed by the same words in line 354, φέρουσα κακῷ κακόν, bringing evil to evil. This cannot be random: Typhon and the dragon are thus consciously paralleled as 'kindred spirits'.[20]

The poet's deliberate choice of these two episodes – the female dragon as Apollo's opponent, and the Typhon episode as a digression – is worth noting, since, in myth, the dragon is not the only enemy whom Apollo fought. Indeed scholars have suggested that the dragon and Typhon are variants of the same monster in combat myth; moreover, the names Typhon and Python are possibly variants of a single name.[21]

The only reference to Typhon in the *Iliad* occurs in the explanation of earthquakes:

γαῖα δ᾽ ὑπεστενάχιζε Διὶ ὣς τερπικεραύῳ
χωομένῳ ὅτε τ᾽ ἀμφὶ Τυφωέϊ γαῖαν ἱμάσσῃ
εἰν Ἀρίμοις, ὅθι φασὶ Τυφωέος ἔμμεναι εὐνάς·

The earth groaned under them as if Zeus were angry, who delights in thunder, when he lashes the ground over Typhon, in the land of Arimoi, where they say Typhon makes his bed. (*Il.* 2.781-3)

The myth of Typhon who lives underground at (or among the) Arimoi was already known,[22] but a detailed account of the fight between Zeus and Typhon is suppressed in the *Iliad*. However, the details – the thunderbolt and the anger of Zeus (Διὶ τερπικεραύνῳ / χωομένῳ, 2.781-2), and his smiting the ground over Typhoeus (ἀμφὶ Τυφωέϊ γαῖαν ἱμάσσῃ, 2.782) – indicate that the myth of their combat was known to the composer of the *Iliad*.

According to the *Theogony* (820-68), Typhon is the last threat to Zeus' power.[23] The Hesiodic account of Typhon's attributes (character and appearance) and power is precise and detailed. The fight with Zeus is vividly described: the land, sea, heaven, rivers, and even the underground regions are affected. These details emphasise both Typhon's awesome strength *and* the superior might of Zeus who must destroy him. On the other hand, in the hymn, all these stories are suppressed, although the composer seems to be well acquainted with the Hesiodic version.[24] The only reference to Typhon's character is that he is not like humans or gods (351), and that he is baneful to humans (352). This is a remarkably compact version of his 'history'.

Interestingly, similar descriptions to that of Typhon in the hymn are given (a) to Echidna in the *Theogony* (295-6), who resembles neither gods nor men, and (b) to the Nemean Lion, who is baneful to humans (329). In their genealogy, too, these two monsters are closely related to Typhon: Echidna is the wife of Typhon, and the Nemean Lion is his grandson. Moreover, the Nemean Lion is reared by Hera (328) and killed by Heracles, the son of Zeus (332).

There is another monster in the *Theogony* who has strong links with the hymnic Typhon: the serpentine Hydra of Lerna, who is the daughter of Typhon. She is reared by Hera out of malice towards Heracles (314-15) and subsequently destroyed by him (316). The genealogy of those creatures is as following:

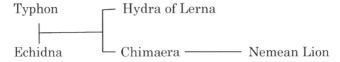

Our hymnic Typhon is closely connected with Typhon in Hesiodic genealogy; all of his family members, except the Chimaera, either have a similar nature to the hymnic Typhon or show Hera's strong influence. Thus the description of Typhon in the hymn reminds us of the many other monsters antagonistic towards Zeus in the Hesiodic version, and the shadow of Hera's rivalry with Zeus is never far in the background.

The most significant reason for the omission of Typhon's full history is that he is not, in fact, treated as the main figure of the digression. The second reason is thematic: this is a hymn to Apollo, not to Zeus, and therefore the encomiastic purpose of the hymn would be distorted and weakened if full details of Typhon and his fight with Zeus were given.[25] A third reason is that the hymn seems to presuppose the audience's knowledge of the Typhon myth, so a brief summary can suffice.

At the start of the digression, the identity of the central figure is ambiguous – in the first line (305), Hera is mentioned but, in the second line, so is Typhon:

καί ποτε δεξαμένη χρυσοθρόνου ἔτρεφεν Ἥρης
δεινόν τ᾿ ἀργαλέον τε Τυφάονα πῆμα βροτοῖσιν,
ὅν ποτ᾿ ἄρ᾿ Ἥρη ἔτικτε χολωσαμένη Διὶ πατρὶ
ἡνίκ᾿ ἄρα Κρονίδης ἐρικυδέα γείνατ᾿ Ἀθήνην
ἐν κορυφῇ·

And once she [the female dragon] received from Hera, who sits on a golden throne, and nurtured dreadful and terrible Typhon, to be a calamity to mortals, Hera once gave birth to him, being angry at father Zeus, when indeed the son of Cronus gave birth to glorious Athena out of his head. (*Hymn. Apol.* 305-9)

One might think that the central figure in the digression will be Typhon, given the connection with the dragon, and given that Typhon's birth is narrated immediately (307-8). However, it is noticeable that the emphasis gradually begins shifting to Hera, and when her speech starts (311), it becomes clear that it is she who plays the most important role in the digression.[26] In the *Theogony*, Typhon's death, and not his birth, is narrated in detail, because it emphasises Zeus' victory over Typhon: here the hymn narrates only Typhon's birth in order to focus on Hera who gave birth to him.

Instead of the myth of combat with Zeus, the hymn illustrates a different aspect of Typhon which can be paralleled with Hephaestus (316-21, cited below). By contrast with the Hesiodic version, Hephaestus here is the son of Zeus and Hera.[27] Hera's anger at Hephaestus' deformity, coupled with her rage at the birth of Athena, brings about her creation of Typhon.[28] The similarity of Hephaestus to Typhon is conspicuous: both are not the favourites of their mother, Hera,[29] and both are protected by nurses (Hephaestus by Thetis, and Typhon by the dragon). In addition, I propose another parallel: their imminent crisis. The *Iliad* gives two versions of the fall of Hephaestus: at 1.590 he is thrown from heaven by Zeus; at 18.395 this is carried out by Hera – this latter version being followed in the hymn. The former version, however, would indicate that there existed a myth concerning Hephaestus' insubordination against Zeus and his subsequent punishment.[30] Thus, both Typhon and Hephaestus share the same function as possible challengers of Zeus' power. The coincidence cannot be accidental: in this context, the mere mentioning of their names together is significant, although the threat to Zeus is never fully delineated.

Hera

Hera's major function in the digression is suggested by the mention of her name in the first line (305). The composer's preference for the version in which Hera is the mother of Typhon is relevant. In the *Theogony*, Typhon is a son of Gaia and Tartarus (821-2); but in this presentation in the hymn, Hera becomes the central figure in the Typhon episode, and her speech constitutes the main part of the digression.

An elaborate example of the technique of ring-composition is observed in the hymn:

300-304 (A1) the killing of the female dragon by Apollo
305-310 (B1) Typhon who is reared by the female dragon
311-315 (C1) Hera's speech – Athena's birth
316-321 (D) Hera's speech – Hephaestus' birth
322-325a (C2) Hera's speech – reproach to Zeus for Athena's birth
326-355 (B2) Hera's speech – her resolve to bear Typhon
356-362 (A2) the death of the female dragon

The earlier part of the Typhon story (B1), that of the nurse-baby relationship, functions as the link between the female dragon and Typhon; the latter part (B2) narrates the detailed story of Typhon's birth. The birth is contrived by Hera as a challenge to Zeus, while Athena's birth is Zeus' contrivance to secure his own power in Olympus. In this neatly structured composition, Hephaestus' birth is, literally and metaphorically, surrounded by contrivances and by challenges between Zeus and Hera. This arrangement, with his birth in the centre of the ring,[31] emphasises the significance of Hephaestus' birth as a challenge to Zeus. In other words, the detailed story of Typhon's birth, on the one hand, reveals Hera's contrivance against Zeus, and, on the other, significantly contributes to the background of rivalry that underlies the episode of Hephaestus' birth.

A similarly grounded motif at the heart of this ring composition is Hera's sudden lament over Thetis' actions: this lacks preliminaries or any detailed explanation[32]:

αὐτὰρ ὅ γ᾽ ἠπεδανὸς γέγονεν μετὰ πᾶσι θεοῖσι
παῖς ἐμὸς Ἥφαιστος ῥικνὸς πόδας ὃν τέκον αὐτὴ
ῥῖψ᾽ ἀνὰ χερσὶν ἑλοῦσα καὶ ἔμβαλον εὐρέϊ πόντῳ·
ἀλλά ἑ Νηρῆος θυγάτηρ Θέτις ἀργυρόπεζα
δέξατο καὶ μετὰ ᾗσι κασιγνήτῃσι κόμισσεν·   320

124

ὡς ὄφελ᾽ ἄλλο θεοῖσι χαρίσσασθαι μακάρεσσι.

But my son, Hephastus, whom I myself gave birth to has grown to be a weakling and lame among all the gods. I picked him up with my own hands and threw him into the broad sea. But Thetis, the silver-footed daughter of Nereus, received him and took care of him with her sisters. I wish she had done some other favour to the blessed gods. (316-21)

What does Hera mean by saying that 'I wish she had done the blessed gods some other favour' (ἄλλο, 321)? The word ἄλλο is pregnant with possibility, as she does not specify her meaning. I propose that it refers to Thetis' power to bear a child mightier than his father.[33] That is, Hera is referring to Thetis' potential: she regrets that Thetis has not realised this, thus missing a rare chance to usurp Zeus' throne. Since Hera's own son, Hephaestus, is incapable of challenging the power of Zeus, perhaps the reminder of Thetis, well known in another story as the potential parent of a child who would usurp the sovereignty of the universe, prompts Hera to form her plans to bear a mighty child herself (325a-28). The core of the ring composition, therefore, is Hera's ultimate desire for a mighty child, one capable of defeating Zeus. Being deprived of any hope of activating Thetis' potentiality, Hera gave birth to Hephaestus, but he was not mighty enough to usurp Zeus' power. When she strikes the ground with her hand (χειρὶ καταπρηνεῖ δ᾽ ἔλασε χθόνα, 333), she resolves once more to have a child, this time with the aid of the chthonic power of Gaia.

The narration gives full details of Hera's generation of a child, and this presents a clear contrast with Leto's maternal experiences. In the account in the *Hymn to Apollo* concerning Leto, even though she has to search for a place where she can give birth, there is great emphasis on her happiness as a mother:

> χαίρει δέ τε πότνια Λητώ,
> οὕνεκα τοξοφόρον καὶ καρτερὸν υἱὸν ἔτικτεν.
> χαῖρε μάκαιρ᾽ ὦ Λητοῖ ἐπεὶ τέκες ἀγλαὰ τέκνα
> Ἀπόλλωνά τ᾽ ἄνακτα καὶ Ἄρτεμιν ἰοχέαιραν

... queen Leto rejoices, because she gave birth to a strong son who carries the bow. I salute you, O blessed Leto, because you gave birth to glorious children, the lord Apollo and Artemis, who delights in arrows (12-15)

> ἦ ὥς σε πρῶτον Λητὼ τέκε χάρμα βροτοῖσι

Shall I sing how first Leto gave birth to you, a joy to mortals (25)

> χαῖρε δὲ Λητὼ
> οὕνεκα τοξοφόρον καὶ καρτερὸν υἱὸν ἔτικτεν.

Leto rejoiced because she gave birth to a strong son who carries the bow. (125-6)

οἱ δ' ἐπιτέρπονται θυμὸν μέγαν εἰσορόωντες
Λητώ τε χρυσοπλόκαμος καὶ μητίετα Ζεὺς
υἷα φίλον παίζοντα μετ' ἀθανάτοισι θεοῖσι.

Golden-haired Leto and wise Zeus are delighted in their great hearts as they
watch their dear son playing among the immortal gods. (204-6)

In lines 204-6, Leto shares her happiness with Zeus: many gods gather,
singing and dancing (188-201), and Apollo plays the lyre among them
(201-3) while Zeus and Leto rejoice to look at him.

In contrast, Hera is angry and solitary. Her anger and resentment are
emphatically repeated: she gives birth to Typhon, being angry (χολωσαμένη)
at Zeus (307); she became angry (χολώσατο) when Zeus gave birth to
Athena from his head (309); she remained aloof from the gods, being angry
(χωομένη, 331); and she contrived to have a child while apart from Zeus
(ἀπὸ σεῖο / τηλόθεν, 329-30; νόσφι Διός, 338). Hera's unhappy situation is
emphasised further by the contrast between their sons: the outstanding
Apollo on the one hand, and the crippled Hephaestus or monstrous Typhon
on the other. Moreover, it serves to echo the jealous rivalry that inspired
Hera to keep Eileithuia away from Leto (99-101); similarly, it is designed
to show that she is condemned and punished for her malice concerning
Leto's travail.[34] Finally, her rebellion against Zeus is accentuated: Hera is
now going to retaliate. In response to Zeus' contrivance (μητίσεαι, 322),
she, too, will engineer something (μητίσομαι, 325a, τεχνήσομαι, 326). Her
wish is to have a child who is stronger than Zeus in proportion to the
strength that Zeus has over Cronus (339).[35] So far as the narrative of the
hymn reveals, the result is uncertain:

ἀλλ' ὅτε δὴ μῆνές τε καὶ ἡμέραι ἐξετελεῦντο
ἂψ περιτελλομένου ἔτεος καὶ ἐπήλυθον ὧραι,   350
ἡ δ' ἔτεκ' οὔτε θεοῖς ἐναλίγκιον οὔτε βροτοῖσι
δεινόν τ' ἀργαλέον τε Τυφάονα, πῆμα βροτοῖσιν.
αὐτίκα τόνδε λαβοῦσα βοῶπις πότνια Ἥρη
δῶκεν ἔπειτα φέρουσα κακῷ κακόν, ἡ δ' ὑπέδεκτο·
ὅς[36] κακὰ πόλλ' ἔρδεσκε κατὰ κλυτὰ φῦλ' ἀνθρώπων.   355

But when the months and the days were fulfilled as the year came round
again and the seasons came, she gave birth to dreadful and terrible Typhon,
to be a calamity to mortals, who resembled neither gods nor mortals. At once,
cow-eyed queen Hera took him and gave him to her [the dragon], bringing
evil to evil, and she [the dragon] accepted him. He worked many evils on the
famous races of men. (349-55)

It is emphatically reiterated that Typhon's advent is a calamity for human
beings (352, 355); but to what extent is he also harmful towards the gods?
It is curious that Typhon's threat to the gods is not mentioned at all,
whereas the consequences of his nature for humans are stressed in the

hymn, which is not mentioned in the Hesiodic version. Although the details are ambiguous, we may read this intricate treatment of the motif as implying that Hera is contriving something sinister for Zeus, and that her only intention is to have a child who is mightier than Zeus (338). When she prayed, smiting the ground with her hands,[37] she rejoiced (τέρπετο, 342). While she was staying in her temple, she rejoiced (τέρπετο, 348). If we take the word ἀλλ' in 349 in the context of the narrative, τέρπετο – τέρπετο – ἀλλ', the result is disappointment for Hera: her child does not fulfil her expectations after all.[38] When the baby was born, Hera at once gave him to the dragon (353-4). Although it was customary for the children of good families to be reared by nurses, and Hera could simply be handing her child over to a nurse, something more can be inferred at line 353-4; αὐτίκα (at once) is stressed through its emphatic position as the first word of the line[39] and it can support several interpretations here. First, the nature of the creature is so alarming – since it is not like gods or humans (351)[40] – that Hera is prompted to hand the creature over *at once*; secondly, Typhon should *at once* be protected and shielded from attack by Zeus, just as Zeus himself was shielded in the cave on Mount Ida in Crete; thirdly, the child might not be the one she expected. Since nothing more is said about Typhon, the exact consequences of Hera's contrivance are equivocal: but the implication is that the 'dreadful' child might do, at least, something 'dreadful'. To this I would add that his dreadful nature is further heightened by the nature of the nurse, as the phrase κακῷ κακόν (354) shows.

The passage that narrates the birth of Typhon forms the last part of the digression, after which (from 356 onward) the hymn returns to the main narrative. The transition is as abrupt as the initial switch at the beginning of the digression:

δῶκεν ἔπειτα φέρουσα κακῷ κακόν, ἡ δ᾽ ὑπέδεκτο·
ὃς κακὰ πόλλ᾽ ἔρδεσκε κατὰ κλυτὰ φῦλ᾽ ἀνθρώπων.   355
ὃς τῇ γ᾽ ἀντιάσειε, φέρεσκέ μιν αἴσιμον ἦμαρ
πρίν γέ οἱ ἰὸν ἐφῆκεν ἄναξ ἑκάεργος Ἀπόλλων
καρτερόν·

Hera gave him [Typhon] to her [dragon], bringing evil to evil, and she accepted him. He worked many evils on the famous races of men. Whoever might meet *her* [dragon], the day of doom would carry him away until far-shooting lord Apollo shot her with a strong arrow; (354-8)

The main narrative begins with ὅς at 356, then we have ὅς twice in the same position in the two consecutive lines. Curiously enough, however, these denote two different objects: the former ὅς (355) is Typhon, the latter (356) is somebody unspecified (whoever);[41] and the subject changes in the apodosis ('Whoever might meet her, the day of doom would carry him away'). οἱ (357) refers to τῇ (356), and this τῇ refers to ἡ (354). These pronouns denote the dragon, and are straightforward, but, at the same time, they give the impression that something linguistically intricate is happening. This repetition of pronouns would be an effective device to give significant emphasis to the dragon.[42] Moreover, the abrupt transition caused by the asyndeton at 356 also attracts our attention. The cumulative effect of these unusual narrative features is twofold: (a) a sudden switch for dramatic effect on the audience;[43] (b) a style of narrative which might also be identified with oracular diction. The Delphic oracle was renowned, as we are informed by Heraclitus,[44] for its ambiguous utterances. Those messages were sometimes astonishingly compact and abrupt (and could lack both explanation and understandable context), and are thus analogous to the abruptness of this hymn. Omission of the subject or object in the oracles, which led to the terrible mistakes, for example, of Croesus (Herod. 1.53, 71), and of Nero (Suet. *Nero* 38),[45] clearly recalls this hymn's narrative technique. The use of such a conspicuous style in the final part of the digression would seem to communicate some unexpressed, or inexpressible, message. Since this hymn is in honour of Apollo, it would not be appropriate for the digression to give a comprehensive account of Hera's role.

Typhon's challenge to Zeus

Typhon plays an important role in other mythic versions as a challenger to Zeus. According to Apollodorus (1.6.3), Typhon overpowered Zeus and rendered him impotent by removing his sinews. He hid the sinews in the Corycian cave, where they were guarded by the δράκαινα Delphyne.[46] In the *Theogony*, the defeat of Zeus is omitted (naturally, in view of the purpose of the poem), but his great difficulty in achieving victory is implied. Only after endless clamour and fearful fighting does Zeus raise himself up to destroy him (*Theog.* 851-3).[47] These versions may imply that Typhon was almost as strong as Hera wished, and that Zeus was actually in danger of being overthrown.[48]

In the hymn, despite his brief mention, Typhon *is* a threat to the maintenance of Zeus' power. Since Gaia has ceased to challenge Zeus, Hera may now attempt to destroy Zeus' order by initiating a cycle of succession made possible by her son Typhon's rebellion.[49] Indeed it may be Apollo's connection with the tradition about Typhon that motivates the inclusion of the digression here. If we consider the killing of the dragon in the context of a succession myth, the close association between Apollo and Typhon becomes clear.

It is crucial in the hymn that the dragon is the nurse of Typhon. In the succession myth, Gaia is the nurse of Zeus, who is entrusted to her by Rhea. It is possible to regard the relationship between Gaia and the dragon as analogous; in this case, Typhon is the figure who might have overthrown Zeus, helped by the dragon, just as Zeus overthrew Cronus, aided by Gaia.[50] Without Gaia's contrivance (*Theog.* 485-6, 494), Cronus would have continued to control the universe. Thus, Gaia, the nurse, played the decisive role in the succession myth. A new significance, therefore, can be given to the killing of the dragon by Apollo. The dragon (the nurse), by helping Typhon, could have played the decisive role in the usurpation of Zeus' power, if Apollo had not killed her. Indeed, Typhon is explicitly said to be the presumptive king over mortals and immortals (*Theog.* 857), and as the examples of the succession myths suggest, the linkage between the usurpers and their mother/nurse is the decisive factor for their purpose. By killing the dragon, Apollo thus totally extinguishes the assistance of the nurse, and this inflicts the ultimate injury on Typhon. The killing of the dragon is, therefore, not merely one of the elements of Apollo's *aristeia*, but importantly, it contributes a much deeper significance: Apollo intervenes in the succession myth, alleviating a potential crisis for Zeus.

Hera might have accomplished her purpose if Apollo had not come to the aid of Zeus by killing the dragon – this seems to be the implication of the hymn. According to Fontenrose, following Otto Gruppe, a story of Apollo's victory lies behind the hymn.[51] While Apollo's assistance to Zeus is not explicitly narrated, we may read the opening scene of the hymn as the celebration of this victory.[52]

3. The opening scene of the *Hymn to Apollo*

In this opening scene, an assembly of gods is held at the palace of Zeus (2). Apollo, the young heroic god, enters the palace, and when he approaches, bending his shining bow (2-4), the gods tremble and stand up from their seats. The impact is startling: the hymn begins with a scene that appears to imply a potential threat to Zeus' sovereignty. Does it suggest that Apollo has just returned from the battle with the dragon, and is demonstrating his authority among the gods? The next nine lines are significant:

Λητὼ δ' οἴη μίμνε πατρὶ Διὶ τερπικεραύνῳ,   5
ἥ ῥα βιόν τ' ἐχάλασσε καὶ ἐκλήϊσε φαρέτρην,
καί οἱ ἀπ' ἰφθίμων ὤμων χείρεσσιν ἑλοῦσα
τόξον ἀνεκρέμασε πρὸς κίονα πατρὸς ἑοῖο
πασσάλου ἐκ χρυσέου· τὸν δ' εἰς θρόνον εἷσεν ἄγουσα.
τῷ δ' ἄρα νέκταρ ἔδωκε πατὴρ δέπαϊ χρυσείῳ   10
δεικνύμενος φίλον υἱόν, ἔπειτα δὲ δαίμονες ἄλλοι
ἔνθα καθίζουσιν· χαίρει δέ τε πότνια Λητώ,
οὕνεκα τοξοφόρον καὶ καρτερὸν υἱὸν ἔτικτεν.

Leto alone remained beside Zeus who delighted in thunder, she unstrings Apollo's bow and closes the quiver, taking the bow with her hands from his strong shoulders, she hangs it up on a golden peg on a pillar in his father's house, and after that she leads him to a seat. Then his father offers him nectar in a golden goblet, and drinks a toast to his dear son; and after that the other gods sit down; then queen Leto rejoices, because she gave birth to a strong son who carries the bow. (5-13)

When Leto puts the bow down and closes Apollo's quiver (6), she indicates that she welcomes Apollo's return; she also makes clear to him that the battle has finished and that these gods are not his enemies. It is she herself who disarms Apollo, taking the bow from his shoulder with her own hands, and hanging it up on the golden peg on the pillar (7-9).[53] This elaborate narrative effectively presents Apollo's might, and emphasises the importance of his disarming, which is intensified by Leto's careful handling of his arms. The place where the bow is hung is also meaningful: it is the pillar of Zeus' house. This has three implications: first, that Apollo cannot use the bow without the consent of Zeus (thus Apollo is subject to his power); second, that great honour is given to Apollo's bow (and to Apollo himself); third, that the pillar symbolises Zeus' power and, therefore, implies that his house stands firm. This may also signify that Apollo is a pillar of strength to his father. Next, Leto takes him to his seat (9), signifying that no more fighting should be done. By her action, she instructs Apollo that he should surrender to Zeus.

Zeus welcomes his son and himself offers him nectar in a golden cup (10-11). This may be read as a celebration of Apollo's victory over the female dragon at Delphi, which is going to be narrated later in this hymn, – but it is also a demonstration of Zeus' gratitude to Apollo, a recognition of his dignity, and also a celebration of an overall peace between the two of them. Only after this (ἔπειτα ... ἔνθα, 11-12) do the other gods take their seats with relief, and Leto rejoices that she has borne a bow-bearing mighty son (12-13). Significantly, it is Leto who organises all these events. There is a marked contrast between her and Hera: Hera attempts (albeit temporarily) to overthrow Zeus by using Typhon; in contrast, Leto assists Zeus, and acts as a king-maker by influencing Apollo: significantly, Hera is absent from the assembly of gods in the opening scene. The opening scene of this hymn and the digression of the Typhon episode are thus remarkably interrelated, and illustrative of the wider struggle for cosmic power.

In my analysis and argument so far, I have dealt with some characteristics which are peculiar to the digression in this hymn. To sum up, the digression about the dragon demonstrates the compositional technique of a 'story-within-a-story', and this technique increases the importance of the dragon. The abrupt transition back to the main narrative emphasises the doublet of the dragon and Typhon, and also functions as a deliberate device which develops the broader perspective, but leaves the exact linkage inexplicit.

The repetition of motifs is another aspect of the digression. The retelling of these two similar stories of violent creatures gives the effect of emphasising their aggressive natures: if Typhon is powerful and harmful, the dragon should also be powerful and harmful. The motif of Telphousa also functions to emphasise the dragon's violence.

The repetition of motifs is a constant not only in the digression, but also in the whole composition of this hymn. The travels of Leto in search of a favourable place (30-50) are repeated by the similar travels of Apollo (216-28), and the motif of the assembly of gods recurs as well (2-4, 187-206).[54] The latter assembly of gods is also juxtaposed with the assembly of the Ionian people at Delos (146-64): the people sing about the gods (158-9), and the divine Muses sing of the sufferings of men (190-3). The songs of the Delian girls can be cited as a further example of this embedding technique, the story-within-a-story, since they are singing the hymn to Apollo, Leto, and Artemis (158-9) within the *Hymn to Apollo* itself. Structurally and thematically the hymn can indeed be described as a unity, the digression about the dragon being linked to the narrative by the devices of repetition and nesting or embedding.

One of the poet's main purposes in selecting the story of the dragon and Typhon was to sing about Hera. By means of Hera's entrance into the narrative, the encomiastic aim of this hymn is fully achieved. Apollo degrades Hera by destroying the dragon, and the end result is the winning of great esteem, not only for himself, but also for Leto. The killing of the dragon is, consequently, the most critical moment in the process of establishing Apollo's dignity and position on Olympus, because of his achievement, which is indispensable for the security of Zeus' sovereignty. The comment of Austin on the digressions of Homer can be aptly applied to this hymn: 'where the drama is most intense, the digressions are the longest and the details the fullest'.[55] The digression of the dragon, then, achieves its greatest effect through the development and colouring of the motifs and their arrangement within the structure of the embedded narrative.

The Bitter Sorrow of Aphrodite

The *Hymn to Aphrodite* portrays the problems of love and death caused by excessive intimacy between gods and mortals. The love of Aphrodite and Anchises is mentioned in both the *Iliad* (2.819-21) and the *Theogony* (1008-10), but without any detail. The *Hymn to Aphrodite* develops the theme most ingeniously and dramatically, illustrating the sombre gulf between mortality and immortality.

The date of the hymn would seem to be around the seventh century,[1] although other dating opinions range from the time of Homer to the Hellenistic period.[2] It is widely believed that this hymn was composed in honour of noble patrons in the Troad who claimed descent from Aeneas.[3] As regards the characteristics of this hymn's diction, the use of frequent repetition might be understood as the product of oral composition,[4] but the possibility of a written composition cannot be totally excluded.[5] Also detectable are a number of modifications to the verses which are thought to represent a later stage of development in epic diction relative to that of Homer;[6] the numerous similarities with the *Hymn to Demeter* are also noteworthy.[7]

The theme of this hymn – the love affair between a goddess and a mortal – is romantically appealing, and indeed the hymn starts in a happy mood. Some have argued that the dominant tone of this hymn is humorous.[8] I submit, however, that, while there are some elements of humour, there is nevertheless a poignant recognition of mortality which resonates throughout the whole hymn.[9] Rutherford's comment on Sophoclean tragedies is appropriate to this hymn: the optimistic tone signalled at the beginning creates a clear contrast with the result of the affair which follows.[10] In the case of this hymn, the dramatic function of the opening 'joy' seems deliberately designed to emphasise the pessimistic outcome of its latter half.

At the end of the hymn there is a passage praising the nymphs (259-72), which does offer some joy and consolation, but the predominant tone is tragic, since even the nymphs die eventually (269-72). Unlike other hymns, which end with the triumph of the gods, Aphrodite is here defeated by Zeus.[11] It seems that the poet's strategy is to subordinate Aphrodite to Zeus' power, and that this occurs as a response to generational strife. I develop the idea that the tragic message of this hymn operates on two levels: on the one hand, through the recognition of human limitation, effectively emphasised by the perceptible use of ironical or ambiguous words; on the other hand, through the recognition of the limitation of

132

VII. The Bitter Sorrow of Aphrodite

Aphrodite's power, which is explicitly and implicitly evident in her subjection to Zeus. I discuss these two levels, emphasising their relation to the encomiastic purpose of the hymn, and in particular, to the sovereignty of Zeus on Olympus. I also suggest that the phrase 'bitter sorrow' (αἰνὸν ἄχος, 198-9) which characterises this hymn, serves to unify the two levels of its message.

1. The irony of human limitation

When the poet narrates the love affair between Aphrodite and Anchises (53-167), he uses ironic and paradoxical words. Such diction fits well with the hymn's cautionary tone: dangerous consequences are inevitable if the distinction between mortal and immortal is blurred. In the deceptive speech of Aphrodite, the boundary between truth and falsehood is also equivocal, and the ironical words effectively emphasise the fluctuation of this boundary.

The opening scene of their encounter is sharply marked by the prominent mention of Anchises in 53, and τότε in 54 draws attention to his way of life and physical beauty at that time when he was tending his father's cattle:

Ἀγχίσεω δ᾽ ἄρα οἱ γλυκὺν ἵμερον ἔμβαλε θυμῷ
ὃς τότ᾽ ἐν ἀκροπόλοις ὄρεσιν πολυπιδάκου Ἴδης
βουκολέεσκεν βοῦς δέμας ἀθανάτοισιν ἐοικώς.

So he [Zeus] cast sweet longing for Anchises in her heart, who at that time on the mountain heights of Ida with many springs tended cattle, in looks like an immortal. (53-5)

After their love affair, when the narrative returns to the mundane world with a description of Anchises' fellow herdsmen, we read:

ἦμος δ᾽ ἂψ εἰς αὖλιν ἀποκλίνουσι[12] νομῆες
βοῦς τε καὶ ἴφια μῆλα νομῶν ἐξ ἀνθεμοέντων

And at the time when herdsmen turn their oxen and fat sheep back to the stables from the flowering meadows (168-9)

By encircling the narrative with the two words for time, τότε (54) and ἦμος (168), the poet intensifies the singularity of this encounter between goddess and mortal.

Anchises is described as 'like an immortal' (55). His appearance is mentioned in this hymn only twice: here at 55, and in 77. In both verses he is compared to an immortal; in 77, fitting well with his noble birth, a descendant of Zeus, his beauty is said to derive from the gods, θεῶν ἄπο κάλλος ἔχοντα. It is worth noting that this meagre description is in distinct

133

contrast to the attention given to Aphrodite's appearance, which is described in detail: for example, her cosmetics, costume and accessories (61-5, 86-90, 162-4), her beautiful cheeks (174), and her neck and eyes (181). In comparison, Anchises' appearance remains impressively unelaborate. It is ironic how the simplicity of description – he is a human who looks like a god – works to emphasise how dangerously close he stands to the boundary between human and divine.

When Aphrodite appears before him, she is described as follows:

στῆ δ᾽ αὐτοῦ προπάροιθε Διὸς θυγάτηρ Ἀφροδίτη
παρθένῳ ἀδμήτῃ μέγεθος καὶ εἶδος ὁμοίη,
μή μιν ταρβήσειεν ἐν ὀφθαλμοῖσι νοήσας.

And Aphrodite, the daughter of Zeus, stood before him, in stature and form like an unmarried maiden, so that he should not be afraid when he saw her. (81-3)

She, too, stands at the point of boundary: a god pretending to be a human, she is divine yet looks human.[13] Yet she does not try to conceal her true identity; indeed, as Smith suggests, 'she wants to show herself unmistakably a goddess'.[14] Since the Graces, who symbolise the embodiment of beauty, bathe and anoint her with immortal oil (61-2), Aphrodite shines more than ever.[15]

We note how peculiarly ineffective this disguise is, particularly in light of general opinions held about the disguises of the gods: 'their disguises are alien to their true nature'.[16] For example, Demeter, in the *Hymn to Demeter*, disguises herself as an old woman in such a way that no one knows who she is (94-5). In the *Hymn to Aphrodite*, however, it is Aphrodite herself who stands in front of Anchises. Although she disguises herself as a Phrygian girl, her beauty in fact possesses – retains – a superhuman quality, emphasising, again, the peculiar use of irony in this text: this is not a 'disguise' in the true sense at all.[17]

Gods cannot appear as themselves when they desire to mate with humans: this provides us with another explanation for Aphrodite's disguise. Thus Zeus comes to Ganymede as an eagle, or to Io as a bull. Also, when Semele asked Zeus to come to her in his true divinity, this meant that she was destroyed by his thunderbolt. Even if gods were susceptible to mortal charms in the same way as mortals, what they express must be differentiated from human 'love'. As gods are invulnerable to death and are constrained to leave dying mortals,[18] so too must their attitude to love – and the beloved – differ.

The exceptional difference in their situation – the unimaginably beautiful Aphrodite and the apprehensive Anchises – is deliberately expressed in their first words. Anchises asks the identity of Aphrodite, offering the names of five goddesses, the Graces and the Nymphs:

VII. The Bitter Sorrow of Aphrodite

Χαῖρε ἄνασσ', ἥ τις μακάρων τάδε δώμαθ' ἱκάνεις,
Ἄρτεμις ἢ Λητὼ ἠὲ χρυσέη Ἀφροδίτη
ἢ Θέμις ἠϋγενὴς ἠὲ γλαυκῶπις Ἀθήνη

Greetings Lady, welcome to this house, whoever of the blessed gods you are,
whether you are Artemis, or Leto, or golden Aphrodite, or well-born Themis,
or bright-eyed Athena (92-4)

This long list of goddesses shows both how apprehensive he is and how
eagerly he desires to know her identity.[19] Anchises does not know anything
about this beautiful girl who suddenly appears before him, so he can only
wonder at and admire her form and height (84-5). His words may also be
a standard Greek 'pick-up line': a manner of speech to use for every
passing girl.[20] The obvious irony here is that she really is a goddess.

Aphrodite, however, calls Anchises by name without adding any title:

τὸν δ' ἠμείβετ' ἔπειτα Διὸς θυγάτηρ Ἀφροδίτη·
Ἀγχίση, κύδιστε χαμαιγενέων ἀνθρώπων,
οὔ τίς τοι θεός εἰμι· τί μ' ἀθανάτῃσιν ἐΐσκεις;

And then Aphrodite, the daughter of Zeus, answered him: Anchises, most
glorious of men born from the earth, I surely am no goddess; why do you
compare me with the immortals? (107-9)

Her speech is ironically coloured from the very beginning. Aphrodite
knows his name, though she has just met him, and does not address him
by his patronymic. The vocative Ἀγχίση, significantly the first word of the
line *and* the first word of her first speech, is forceful enough to overwhelm
him. It is a startling beginning to a speech by one who describes herself as
a modest maiden (παρθένος ἀδμής, 82); her authority and assurance unmistakably denote that she is beyond human, and the overt nature of these
qualities can be read as the verbal counterparts to her disguise.[21]

This initial ironic tone governs the tenor of her whole speech. After
addressing Anchises by name, she calls him 'most glorious of men who are
born from the earth' (108). The word χαμαιγενής, used only once each in
the *Theogony* and the *Hymn to Demeter*, has connotations of the humble,
emphasising the negative and weak side of human beings:

ἔργ' ἐρατὰ φθείρουσι χαμαιγενέων ἀνθρώπων
[winds] spoil the lovely fields of men who are born from the earth (*Theog.*
879)

φθῖσαι φῦλ' ἀμενηνὰ χαμαιγενέων ἀνθρώπων
in order to destroy the feeble human race who are born from the earth[22]
(*Hymn. Dem.* 352)

It is worth noticing that both of these verses contain words for destruction,

135

which strengthens the negative connotation of χαμαιγενής. Given that the meaning and the connotations of this word are far from noble or honourable, its juxtaposition with κύδιστε is itself highly ironical. Moreover, as the phrase χαμαιγενέων ἀνθρώπων is metrically equivalent to καταθνητῶν ἀνθρώπων, which breaches the epic principle of economy formulated by Parry,[23] we can suggest that the hymn-poet intentionally chooses the former.[24] Anchises is a prince, fifth generation after Dardanus, a descendant of Zeus (Dardanus is a son of Zeus); but in spite of his noble birth, Aphrodite uses the humble word χαμαιγενής in order to give emphasis to Anchises' mortality.

Aphrodite, on the other hand, is introduced in the preceding verse as a daughter of Zeus (Διὸς θυγάτηρ, 107), which is, again, metrically equivalent to Aphrodite's other epithet, φιλομμειδής.[25] As a choice between these two epithets is possible, Διὸς θυγάτηρ in 107 is used specifically to highlight Aphrodite's superior origin, in direct contrast with χαμαιγενής.

The scene of this encounter has been likened by some critics to that of the meeting of Odysseus and Nausicaa, as the first words of Odysseus are similar to those of Anchises.[26] However, in the *Odyssey*, Nausicaa, in the modest manner appropriate to a princess speaking to a stranger, never asks Odysseus' name, and in her first words addresses Odysseus as ξεῖνε (*Od.* 6.187). In the *Hymn*, on the other hand, the manner of Aphrodite's address to Anchises sounds exactly like the speech of a goddess, not of a mortal princess; but the irony is particularly apparent in the next two lines when she strongly *denies* that she is a goddess (109-10).

After Aphrodite's fervent denial of her true identity, she begins the false story by which she introduces herself. She offers a highly rationalised explanation, anticipating Anchises' questions; first, how she is able to speak the Trojan language:

> γλῶσσαν δ᾽ ὑμετέρην καὶ ἡμετέρην <u>σάφα οἶδα</u>·
> Τρωὰς γὰρ μεγάρῳ με τροφὸς τρέφεν, ἡ δὲ διὰ πρὸ
> σμικρὴν παῖδ᾽ ἀτίταλλε φίλης παρὰ μητρὸς ἑλοῦσα.
> ὣς δή τοι γλῶσσάν γε καὶ ὑμετέρην <u>εὖ οἶδα</u>.

> But I know your language very well and ours too, because a Trojan nurse brought me up in my house; she took me from my dear mother and cared for me throughout my childhood. For this reason indeed I know your language, too. (113-16)

The repetition of σάφα οἶδα (113) and εὖ οἶδα (116) gives prominence to Aphrodite's knowledge of language; at the same time, she insinuates (again, ironically?) Anchises' own ignorance. Aphrodite knows not only Anchises' language, but also his identity, and even what is to happen next. Anchises, on the other hand, does not (we presume) know *her* language (Phrygian?), her identity, or, least of all, what she is going to do. The more emphatically the poet repeats the idea *that Aphrodite knows something*, the more clearly the audience become aware of the corresponding implication: *Anchises knows nothing.* This passage, too, reinforces for the audience the notion that Anchises is only mortal and has only the limited knowledge permitted to a mortal man.

Her second explanation, in the next fourteen lines, accounts for how she comes to be there (117-30). The story that she was abducted by Hermes is equivocal and duplicitous, being underscored by a complex irony: the disguised Aphrodite, who tries now to seduce Anchises, describes her own abduction by Hermes. Who is the real seducer, and who is really seduced? As a seductress, Aphrodite takes the initiative and holds overwhelming power; but as a maidenly abductee, she blatantly places herself in a position of complete – and mortal – weakness.[27]

Aphrodite pretends to be confident of persuading Anchises, and the unusual situation (the sudden appearance of the abducted princess) itself contributes to the mysterious aura that surrounds her. Anchises is kept uncertain about her identity right up to the middle of the *Hymn*, and this account of Hermes' abduction only serves to make him *more* hesitant about the true identity of this girl. So, while her speech appears persuasive enough to make him decide on pursuing a seduction, it seems that he might still be considering whether she is, in fact, a goddess. For example, Anchises says εἰ μὲν θνητή τ' ἐσσί, γυνὴ δέ σε γείνατο μήτηρ (145 'if you are a mortal and the mother who gave you birth is a mortal woman ...'). In this conditional sentence, he is very careful about his words, especially in using the indicative (ἐσσί).[28] He tries not to include any sense of doubt, leaving it as a simple conditional, but the apodosis of the long conditional is rather curious if he is going to make love to a mortal woman:

οὔ τις ἔπειτα θεῶν οὔτε θνητῶν ἀνθρώπων
ἐνθάδε με σχήσει πρὶν σῇ φιλότητι μιγῆναι
αὐτίκα νῦν.

neither god nor mortal man will restrain me from making love to you, right now. (149-51)

On the surface, it appears that this is simply a negative statement to indicate that nothing will stop him. However, the strong negative sentence with οὔ in the initial position may also illustrate his doubt and fear: he anticipates that something – divine or mortal – might intervene in their love to prevent it. That is to say, this strong denial paradoxically suggests that he still feels some uncertainty. By expressing his feeling in this way about the possibility of divine or human intervention, he might be trying to push aside his fear. So, possibly, he is still uncertain about her identity.

Is Anchises finally persuaded or deceived by Aphrodite's speech? It appears that the hymn-poet deliberately suggests an ambiguous non-resolution:

ὁ δ᾽ ἔπειτα θεῶν ἰότητι καὶ αἴσῃ
ἀθανάτῃ παρέλεκτο θεᾷ βρότος, οὐ σάφα εἰδώς.

Then by the will of the gods and destiny, he, a mortal, lay beside an immortal goddess, not knowing the truth. (166-7)

The poet says that Anchises has no clear knowledge.[29] One may assume that Anchises believes her false story and does not know her true identity,[30] since he is quite aware of the danger of making love to a goddess. However, the phrase οὐ σάφα εἰδώς ingeniously implies that he has not completely abandoned the suspicion. Who else, other than a goddess, could be so beautiful? Who else could appear suddenly on the top of the mountain? And who else could speak with such dignity? Anchises dares to leave her identity in doubt, οὐ σάφα εἰδώς, because if she is exposed as a goddess, he also knows that he will be unable to make love to her. The situation presents us with what we might call 'self-deception' on the part of Anchises, which forms an ironic counterpart, again, to the flagrant deception wrought by Aphrodite.

The juxtaposition of θεᾷ βρότος (167) is striking as well as ironic. Although this phrase could be derived from the *Iliad* (2.821)[31] or from a traditional formula, the poet of the hymn grants it a use remarkably dramatic and impressive, denoting the perilous blurring of the boundary. Indeed, a major theme of the hymn is symbolised in this phrase.

The final part of Anchises' answer helps to confirm the view that he still thinks that she may be a goddess:

βουλοίμην κεν ἔπειτα, γύναι εἰκυῖα θεῇσι,
σῆς εὐνῆς ἐπιβὰς δῦναι δόμον Ἄϊδος εἴσω.

O woman like a goddess, willingly would I go down to the house of Hades, once I have climbed into your bed. (153-4)

Another intentional juxtaposition – that of γύναι and θεῇσι (153) – builds on the ironic momentum of the moment, since γύναι is used only of human women.[32] Yet this is *exactly* Aphrodite's role: pretending to be human while remaining, intrinsically, a goddess. Anchises was, therefore, quite right in his suspicion of her identity as well as her deception; and now he, too, implies that he believes her speech. The diction of verse 154 is also effective: the line of hissing sigmatism culminates in 'Hades'. More death imagery is given by the playful 'up to your bed' and 'down to Hades'. But even if it were right to suppose that he knows she is a goddess and is joking with her and playing along, the image is a dark one nevertheless: the reference to Hades prefigures Anchises' own mortality, and also, men have indeed died for less than this, such as Actaeon who was punished by Artemis.

The bitter sorrow

The scene after their love-making evokes a dismal mood. In spite of the fact that Aphrodite accomplishes her desire, she feels bitter sorrow. At this moment she should proclaim her victory: she is, after all, the radiant conqueror who has taken the initiative throughout their encounter and achieved all that she wanted. However, her first words after she awakens Anchises are far from the sweet words of lovers; she is now humiliated by her own act:

τῷ δὲ καὶ Αἰνείας ὄνομ᾽ ἔσσεται οὕνεκά μ᾽ αἰνὸν;
ἔσχεν ἄχος, ἕνεκα βροτοῦ ἀνέρος ἔμπεσον εὐνῇ.

Aineias shall be his name, because I was seized by bitter sorrow for falling into a mortal man's bed. (198-9)

The phrase αἰνὸν ἄχος is spoken in relation to the name Aeneas – a kind of pseudo-etymology of which the Greeks were especially fond, yet the phrase has a significance that goes far beyond the simple presentation of an aetiology.[33] In structural terms, Aphrodite's emotion marks a turning point in the structure of the hymn. Before this stage, everything goes exactly as she wishes, and she appears to be happy and confident in her plans. But, from this point on and throughout the second half of the *Hymn*, Aphrodite and Anchises are dogged by deep depression. For example, to denote the same action, earlier Anchises says 'σῆς εὐνῆς ἐπιβὰς' ('climbing/going up to your bed', 154, cited above), while here Aphrodite laments by saying 'ἔμπεσον εὐνῇ' ('I fell into the bed', 199). Thematically, the *sorrow* of 'the *blessed* goddess' forms the centre of all the ironical expressions built up within the hymn. The effect is further heightened by the poet's ingenious device of placing additional thematic emphasis on the name 'Aeneas', by linking it overtly with the αἰνὸν ἄχος of Aphrodite.

As the text shows, her bitter sorrow is primarily caused by the fact that she has slept with a mortal, but a further reason may come from the way in which her immortality is compromised by her disguise as a human. Although Aphrodite assumes mortal stature,[34] she does not disguise herself completely – if 'disguise' means to become something *different* from one's own self. She becomes even more beautiful than usual, as was discussed above. Had she met Anchises under a guise completely different from that of her normal self, and succeeded in making love to Anchises because of it, she would have been amused by her own deceitful technique – it would be something done for entertainment, like Odysseus' deception at *Odyssey* 13.256-86.[35] But in the hymn, even in disguise, Aphrodite is too

serious and betrays a demeanour appropriate to her 'mortal' role. Seriousness is not an appropriate attribute for gods, who are immortal without
any sorrow.[36] Here, although she still has great power as a goddess,
Aphrodite conceives and grieves like a human. We see that, not only for
Anchises but for Aphrodite as well, 'the boundary between divinity and
mortality is perilous and usually catastrophic'.[37] Aphrodite laments her
own blurring of this boundary, which will bring about the birth of a mortal
child to a goddess.

Stories of Ganymede and Tithonus

Aphrodite promises Anchises, who pleads for mercy (187-90), a future
lineage of fertile offspring down the generations, and then recounts to him
the stories of Ganymede, who is given eternal youth (202-17), and
Tithonus, granted eternal life but not eternal youth (218-38).[38] In this long
address, the main concern remains mortality and immortality. In telling
these stories, Aphrodite presents Anchises with her decision. However, we
note that, after the stories are told, there is no comment by Aphrodite, and
no mention of any response by Anchises – interpretation is apparently left
to the audience. My understanding is that both stories are warning
examples, illustrating the consequences of mortal transgression, and that
Aphrodite, after narrating the fates of Tithonus and Ganymede, which are
both inapplicable to Anchises, offers him a third and better choice.

The story of the aged Tithonus is unanimously accepted as a negative
example:[39] he becomes hated by the goddess who enjoys everlasting youth
and, even though he escapes death, he is miserable and has no place
among mortals or immortals. The story of Ganymede is more problematic.
Those who read the fate of Ganymede in sharp opposition to the wretch-
edness of Tithonus think that Aphrodite wanted to give Anchises immortality
and everlasting youth – as Ganymede had – but she could not.[40]

Immortality, which Ganymede is offered, might be intrinsically attractive for humans. However, Greek texts are ambivalent on the subject of
immortality. For example, when Odysseus is offered immortality by Calypso (*Od.* 5.203-13), he rejects her offer. He admits Calypso's youth,
beauty and divine nature, but he willingly chooses Penelope and mortality
(*Od.* 5.215-20). His rejection delineates a significant message: to live as a
mortal, however painful, is better than to possess immortality, however
happy. I offer a further example: Achilles speaks of human destiny,
declaring that mortals live in misery, but gods have no sorrow (*Il.* 24.525-
6). He appears to desire the sorrowless life of gods; however, he never
wishes explicitly to live like them. He acknowledges that there is no choice
for humans but to live a sorrowful life, willingly accepting their destiny:
immortality is both unattainable and undesirable for a human, however
attractive it might appear.[41]

It seems to be more logical to read both stories (Tithonus and

Ganymede) as examples of warning for Anchises. Eternal youth is not accessible for him, and eternal life without agelessness is not desirable, so Aphrodite proposes a third, most desirable choice, by concluding that he (too) will be enfolded by merciless old age:

νῦν δέ σε μὲν τάχα γῆρας ὁμοίιον ἀμφικαλύψει
νηλειές, τό τ᾽ ἔπειτα παρίσταται ἀνθρώποισιν,
οὐλόμενον καματηρόν, ὅ τε στυγέουσιν θεοί περ.

But now old age will soon enfold you, as equally for everyone, merciless, which one day stands beside human beings, baneful, wearisome, and abhorred even by the gods. (244-6)

The message is that life is not eternal, and mortality must be accepted.[42] Even the favourites of the gods must struggle and die.[43] Therefore, the myths of Tithonus and Ganymede are used to explore, as Smith points out,[44] the value of mortality, and it is through their juxtaposition with the story of Anchises[45] that we see their complementary, warning aspects.

The best that Aphrodite can do for Anchises is thus to get the nymphs to take special care of the child she will give birth to, then bring him to Anchises, and he will take pleasure in seeing his son (γηθήσεις ὁρόων, 279). And Aphrodite has already made clear what his future and that of his descendants will be (196-7, 200-1).

Aphrodite refers again to her sorrow in 243, when she laments for Anchises:

ἀλλ᾽ εἰ μὲν τοιοῦτος ἐὼν εἶδός τε δέμας τε
ζώοις, ἡμέτερός τε πόσις κεκλημένος εἴης,
οὐκ ἂν ἔπειτά μ᾽ ἄχος πυκινὰς φρένας <u>ἀμφικαλύπτοι·</u>
νῦν δέ σε μὲν τάχα γῆρας ὁμοίιον <u>ἀμφικαλύψει</u>

But if you would live on such as you are now in appearance and body and be called my husband, then sorrow would never enfold my prudent heart. But now old age will soon enfold you, as equally for everyone (241-4)

The striking repetition of the verb ἀμφικαλύπτω (243-4) seems to be a deliberate device employed to express Aphrodite's sympathy towards Anchises.[46] These verses can be paraphrased as: 'Anchises will soon be enfolded by old age; then Aphrodite will be enfolded by sorrow.' Aphrodite and Anchises share the same metaphor, in the same space, at the ends of adjoining verses.

However, despite the extent to which Aphrodite sympathises with and pities Anchises, she *can* turn away from him. Although both are 'enfolded' – Anchises by old age and Aphrodite by ἄχος – the difference between them is evident. Old age inevitably leads Anchises to death, as is emphasised by νῦν δέ (244), which denotes the actual state of affairs. In contrast, Aphrodite's ἄχος is merely a touching sorrow for her.

141

The overwhelmingly dignified manner of Aphrodite's speech makes Anchises listen and obey; and after restoring order and foretelling the future, Aphrodite departs in a dramatic fashion which again asserts her divinity and shows her superiority – an exit remarkably reminiscent of the *deus ex machina* of later Euripidean tragedies. Leaving Anchises, Aphrodite retires (or, rather, soars off) from the realm of human suffering into the realm of the gods' blessedness. Men learn, then, that they must go modestly, because 'human endeavour which exceeds the limit is bound to drive them to sorrow and ruin'.[47]

After Aphrodite's journey from Cyprus to Ida near the beginning of the hymn, she observes and rejoices in the coupling of wild animals (68-74). This scene presents the joyfulness of sexual union, and serves as a prelude to the human experience immediately to follow.[48] Yet, in the passage describing Anchises' bed (158-60), the *skins* of these same animals are strewn on it:

αὐτὰρ ὕπερθεν
ἄρκτων δέρματ᾽ ἔκειτο βαρυφθόγγων τε λεόντων,
τοὺς αὐτὸς κατέπεφνεν ἐν οὔρεσιν ὑψηλοῖσιν.

... besides, skin of bears and deep-roaring lions were laid on it, which he himself had killed on the high mountains (158-60)

The animal skins on Anchises' bed provide, literally, another reinforcement to the theme of the temporary nature of love and life. The animals, which are looked at by Aphrodite as joyfully uniting, share with human beings the same destiny of death.[49]

In the first half of the *Hymn*, Aphrodite's appearance is godlike despite her disguise as a human; in the latter half, her feelings are human-like in spite of the fact that she speaks as a goddess. The immortals, even the goddess of love, are involved in the natural cycle of mortal birth and death. This elaborately devised paradox is central to my understanding of the *Hymn* – and Aphrodite's emotion of αἰνὸν ἄχος symbolises this paradoxical irony.

2. The Sorrow of Aphrodite

The origin of Aphrodite

In order to explore the deeper significance of the story of Aphrodite in the hymn, it is worth looking briefly at the origin of the goddess. Aphrodite's origin is much disputed. There are two perspectives to the question, and each of these offers two further subdivisions: (a) from the view-point of the history of religion (whether Near Eastern or Indo-European); (b) from the view-point of epic tradition (whether she is born from Uranus or from Zeus). However, in spite of such complexities in her origin, Aphrodite's role as love goddess is always predominant in Greek epic.

142

VII. The Bitter Sorrow of Aphrodite

Since Herodotus (1.105, 131), Aphrodite's Near Eastern origin has been widely admitted.[50] Among scholars, Rose offered the most extreme perspective, suggesting that, 'Aphrodite is, of course, no Greek goddess at all',[51] and proposed the earliest date of Minoan-Mycenaean times for the original story of Aphrodite and Anchises. Although Rose's opinion is not wholly convincing, many elements of Aphrodite's mythographic construction seem to have been inherited from Near Eastern tradition.

One of the conspicuous features of the Near Eastern Mother Goddess is that her name has changed from time to time, from place to place, while her type has remained constant.[52] She is Inanna in Sumerian hymns around 3000-2100 BC, Ishtar in Babylonia and Assyria around 1800-600 BC, and Astarte among the Phoenicians of 1000-700 BC.[53] These figures are characterised as goddess of love, Queen of Heaven, and, also, as warrior goddess.[54]

Even before Inanna, as far back as the Palaeolithic Age, one finds a nameless goddess universally worshipped around the Mediterranean as the Mighty Mother.[55] According to Vermaseren,[56] she is the all-creating Earth Mother; she provides food and drink, being identified with the fertile furrow after ploughing was invented (c. 3000 BC), and even creates gods and goddesses who rule their own domains and perform their own tasks under her control; sometimes she is identified with mountains, or escorted by animals. Behind the figure of Aphrodite there clearly stand these ancient mother goddesses.[57]

In the Greek Bronze Age, the name of Aphrodite is not found on any of the extant Linear B tablets. The Pylos tablet Tn 316, which lists the names of fourteen or fifteen deities, does not mention Aphrodite.[58] The possibilities are: (a) the Mycenaeans did not know Aphrodite; (b) the Mycenaeans knew Aphrodite, but her name happens not to be on the tablets; (c) 'the goddess *potnia*' (*potinija*)[59] is the Mycenaean name of Aphrodite. It is difficult to determine the correct answer, but if we consider the Near Eastern origin of this goddess, and the extent of Near Eastern influence in the eighth century, it appears that possibility (a) – that Aphrodite had not been introduced into Greece by the Mycenaean period – might be the most likely solution.

Burkert provides a persuasive discussion of the significance of oriental influence around the eighth century BC.[60] As he says, if, in this period, Greek representational style underwent basic modifications by taking up, imitating and transforming the motifs of eastern art,[61] then myth would also have been subject to oriental influence.[62]

Boedeker suggests an Indo-European origin for Aphrodite[63] and regards iconographical similarities between Aphrodite and the Great Goddess as overestimated and misinterpreted; she points out the independent but parallel developments of similar features, and suggests that Aphrodite's entry into Greek epic is an extension of expressions originally formulated for the Dawn-goddess.[64] However, Boedeker's position is difficult to sustain. First, she admits the resemblance between Aphrodite and the Great Goddess, and especially between Aphrodite and Astarte.[65] However, it is improbable to think of 'independent parallel development' when Greece and the Eastern countries had, as has been demonstrated, so many interrelations.[66] Second, if Aphrodite, like Zeus, is Indo-European in origin, her name should be etymologically explicable in some other Indo-European language(s), and have a cognate even in Sanskrit (like the name of Zeus).[67] Thus Friedrich finds it necessary to integrate the two opinions, suggesting that Aphrodite is indeed Indo-European in origin, but admitting, too, an oriental influence on her.[68]

Contrary to Friedrich, I trace Aphrodite's origin primarily to the Near East, but see some kind of assimilation to other goddesses, including the Dawn-goddess, after her advent in Greece.[69] Of course, the problem is that, by the time of the composition of the Homeric and Hesiodic epics, Aphrodite had lost much of the all-embracing power of the Great Mother Goddess.[70] Deprived, notably, of her power in war and politics, she is transformed into the beautiful and refined love-goddess; and Homer himself did much to reduce her power and even to ridicule her.[71]

Aphrodite in the Greek epics

The Hesiodic story of Aphrodite's birth (*Theog.* 188-206) stands in opposition to her Homeric genealogy, since both in the *Iliad* and the *Odyssey* she is always a daughter of Zeus.[72] Her birth from the sea-foam and the seed of Uranus in the *Theogony* has a crude, early look,[73] and this is a good indication of her Near Eastern origin.[74] In Hesiod, it is emphasised that Aphrodite is a goddess of fertility, with her role in the universe conceived as one of enrichment.[75] For my particular theme, however, the most important aspect of this story is her birth as a result of generational strife between Uranus and Cronus.[76] Aphrodite was born at a crucial moment when Uranus, the first cosmic sovereign, was supplanted by the second, in a period not very long after the first cosmic differentiation – the separation of heaven and earth. Her power of love is thus of a primordial nature, and fundamental to the whole universe. She is the first anthropomorphic deity in the *Theogony*, and, naturally, is older than all the Olympian gods, including Zeus. Moreover, unlike Cronus' children who were saved by Zeus, Aphrodite owes nothing to him. Her cult title Οὐρανία preserves, as West suggests,[77] the remains of her link with Uranus.

In Homer, Aphrodite's parentage is well established: she is the daughter of Zeus and her mother is Dione (*Il.* 5.370-1). Only here is Dione recorded as the mother of Aphrodite; and we note that the name 'Dione' is a feminised form of 'Zeus'.[78] The frequent use in epic of the phrase Διὸς θυγάτηρ is, obviously, something more than the repetition of a formulaic expression. It not only emphasises Aphrodite's kinship with Zeus, but also, importantly, her *subordination* to Zeus,[79] which seems to be Homer's strategy. Whether or not the poet of the *Hymn to Aphrodite* was acquainted with the *Theogony*, he nevertheless adapts the Homeric version of Aphrodite's birth, and, following this, tries to place Aphrodite under the control of Zeus.

A demoted Aphrodite in Homer

This Homeric demotion of Aphrodite is evident not only in her epithet, but also in other passages. For instance, in the famous scene in the *Iliad* when Aphrodite goes to the battlefield to rescue Aeneas (5.311-430), she is defeated by Diomedes:

> ὁ δὲ Κύπριν ἐπῴχετο νηλέϊ χαλκῷ,
> γιγνώσκων ὅ τ᾽ ἄναλκις ἔην θεός, οὐδὲ θεάων
> τάων αἵ τ᾽ ἀνδρῶν πόλεμον κάτα κοιρανέουσιν,
> οὔτ᾽ ἄρ᾽ Ἀθηναίη οὔτε πτολίπορθος Ἐνυώ.

He [Diomedes] was moving on to attack the Cyprian goddess with the pitiless bronze, knowing that she was a feeble goddess, and not one of the goddesses who are the masters of men's battles, not Athene or Enyo, the sacker of cities. (*Il.* 5.330-3)

> εἶκε, Διὸς θύγατερ, πολέμου καὶ δηϊοτῆτος·
> ἦ οὐχ ἅλις ὅττι γυναῖκας ἀνάλκιδας ἠπεροπεύεις;
> εἰ δὲ σύ γ᾽ ἐς πόλεμον πωλήσεαι, ἦ τέ σ᾽ ὀΐω
> ῥιγήσειν πόλεμόν γε καὶ εἴ χ᾽ ἑτέρωθι πύθηαι.

Give way, daughter of Zeus, from battle and fighting. Is it not enough for you to seduce the wits of soft women? If you frequently come to the battle-field, then I [Diomedes] think you will come to shudder at war, even hearing of it somewhere else. (*Il.* 5.348-51)

The mortal Diomedes – not a god – knows that she is an ἄναλκις θεός (5.331), a feeble goddess.[80] Aphrodite's intervention in the war could be a relic of her mythical forebear, the warlike Mother Goddess; however, this Iliadic Aphrodite, defeated by a mortal, is far different from her ancestor. Surprisingly, the arrogant taunt of Diomedes (5.348-51) goes unpunished, and it is in the non-formulaic diction of Diomedes' words[81] that we see the poet's careful plan – to make us perceive Aphrodite as powerless in the war. This is similar to Hector's words 'the war will be the men's concern' (πόλεμος δ᾽ ἄνδρεσσι μελήσει, *Il.* 6.492),[82] when Andromache suggests taking up a defensive position by the fig-tree (6.429-39). Diomedes repeats the adjective ἄναλκις again in 349, this time of women. The implication of Diomedes' insult is that Aphrodite is so feeble that she can only exercise her power over women, who are feeble enough to be cheated. It is natural, therefore, that Zeus prohibits her from attending the war at the conclusion of this episode:

οὔ τοι, τέκνον ἐμόν, δέδοται πολεμήϊα ἔργα,
ἀλλὰ σύ γ᾽ ἱμερόεντα μετέρχεο ἔργα γάμοιο,
ταῦτα δ᾽ Ἄρηϊ θοῷ καὶ Ἀθήνῃ πάντα μελήσει.

No, my child, the works of warfare are not for you, rather, concern yourself with sweet works of love and marriage, while all this will be dealt with by quick Ares and Athena (*Il.* 5.428-30)

Zeus confines Aphrodite to the 'sweet works of love and marriage' (429). Granted only the power of love, she is thus deprived of the power of war, political power and, most of all, any mighty all-embracing power, which the Great Mother had possessed.

The second example from the *Iliad* occurs at 14.190 when Hera impresses on us the youthfulness of Aphrodite as a 'junior' goddess:

ἦ ῥά νύ μοί τι πίθοιο, φίλον τέκος, ὅττι κεν εἴπω,

Would you do something for me, dear child, that I [Hera] tell you, (*Il.* 14.190)

Ἥρη, πρέσβα θεά, θύγατερ μεγάλοιο Κρόνοιο,
αὔδα ὅ τι φρονέεις· τελέσαι δέ με θυμὸς ἄνωγεν,
εἰ δύναμαι τελέσαι γε καὶ εἰ τετελεσμένον ἐστίν.

Hera, senior goddess, daughter of great Cronus, speak out whatever is in your mind. My heart prompts me to do it, if I [Aphrodite] can surely accomplish and if it is something that can be accomplished. (*Il* 14.194-6)

The phrase φίλον τέκος used by Hera (14.190) is an affectionate address to a younger person,[83] and Aphrodite, in return, respectfully addresses Hera as πρέσβα θεά (14.194). The word-play on τελέω (14.195-6) would seem to intensify Aphrodite's offer of help to Hera – she wishes heartily for the accomplishment of Hera's plan. It is emphatically demonstrated that Aphrodite is not only under the control of Zeus, but is also an obedient, junior goddess in relation to Hera. In the *Odyssey*, Aphrodite is presented as a shameful goddess in Demodocus' song of her love affair with Ares (*Od.* 8.266-366).

There is, however, one arena in which Aphrodite retains power: when she shows her formidable side to Helen (*Il.* 3.413-20). We see that, although her power is restricted only to the work of love, she is recognised as the mightiest at least in that sphere.

The *Theogony* offers a remarkable relic of Aphrodite's challenge to the power of Zeus, in its account of the birth and death of Typhon (Typhoeus):

αὐτὰρ ἐπεὶ Τιτῆνας ἀπ᾽ οὐρανοῦ ἐξέλασε Ζεύς,
ὁπλότατον τέκε παῖδα Τυφωέα Γαῖα πελώρη
Ταρτάρου ἐν φιλότητι διὰ χρυσῆν Ἀφροδίτην·

VII. The Bitter Sorrow of Aphrodite

Now when Zeus had driven the Titans out of heaven, huge Earth bore as her youngest child Typhoeus, being in love with Tartarus because of golden Aphrodite. (*Theog.* 820-2)

αὐτὰρ ἐπεὶ δή μιν δάμασε πληγῇσιν ἱμάσσας,
ἤριπε γυιωθείς, στονάχιζε δὲ Γαῖα πελώρη·

When he [Zeus] had overcome him [Typhoeus] by lashing him with his blows, Typhoeus fell down lamed, and the huge Earth groaned. (*Theog.* 857-8)

After the defeat of the Titans, Gaia gives birth to Typhoeus as the next challenger to Zeus. In this attempt, Gaia is assisted by Aphrodite (*Theog.* 822).[84] In the *Hymn to Apollo* (334-9), Typhon is the son of Hera who calls upon Gaia, Uranus and the Titans in Tartarus in her prayer for a child, as discussed in the previous chapter. The versions are united by one significant similarity – a chthonic challenge to Zeus' sovereignty. Just as Hera is helped by Gaia, Uranus and the Titans in the *Hymn to Apollo*, so Gaia and Tartarus are helped by Aphrodite in the *Theogony*: all these gods are, to some extent, resistant to Zeus. When Typhon is defeated by Zeus, Gaia groans (*Theog.* 858), but it would be not only Gaia, but also all the other deities in her alliance in the project of producing Zeus' challenger, who must bitterly lament.

Zeus and Aphrodite

The *Hymn to Aphrodite* follows Homer on Aphrodite's parentage and characterisation, but goes still further: even in the work of love, she is now under the control of Zeus. A most ingenious technique of the hymn-poet is to make Aphrodite fulfil the plan of Zeus by accomplishing her *own* desire. As Clay remarks,[85] Zeus utilises Aphrodite's own weapon against her. Zeus reacts not to her power to initiate disruptive love affairs, but to her potential to boast about this power among the gods (47). Zeus, in fact, punishes Aphrodite for the influence that she is able to exert over both himself and the other gods:

καί τε παρὲκ Ζηνὸς νόον ἤγαγε τερπικεραύνου,
ὅς τε μέγιστός τ᾽ ἐστί, μεγίστης τ᾽ ἔμμορε τιμῆς·
καί τε τοῦ εὖτ᾽ ἐθέλοι πυκινὰς φρένας ἐξαπαφοῦσα
ῥηϊδίως συνέμιξε καταθνητῇσι γυναιξίν,
Ἥρης ἐκλελαθοῦσα κασιγνήτης ἀλόχου τε,   40
ἣ μέγα εἶδος ἀρίστη ἐν ἀθανάτῃσι θεῇσι

She even led astray the mind of Zeus who delights in thunder, who is the greatest and has the greatest honour as his portion. She deceived even his intricate mind whenever she wishes, easily uniting him with mortal women and making him forget Hera, his sister and wife, the most beautiful in shape among the deathless goddesses (*Hymn. Aphr.* 36-41)

147

Note the unconventional juxtaposition in verse 37 – repetition with polysyndeton – of Zeus' mightiness with her great influential power.

Her boast, and the punishment for it, are dramatised in an imaginary speech:

> Τῇ δὲ καὶ αὐτῇ Ζεὺς γλυκὺν ἵμερον ἔμβαλε θυμῷ   45
> ἀνδρὶ καταθνητῷ μιχθήμεναι, ὄφρα τάχιστα
> μηδ' αὐτὴ βροτέης εὐνῆς ἀποεργμένη εἴη
> καί ποτ' ἐπευξαμένη εἴπῃ μετὰ πᾶσι θεοῖσιν
> ἡδὺ γελοιήσασα φιλομμειδὴς Ἀφροδίτη,
> ὥς ῥα θεοὺς συνέμιξε καταθνητῇσι γυναιξὶ   50
> καί τε καταθνητοὺς υἱεῖς τέκον ἀθανάτοισιν,
> ὥς τε θεὰς ἀνέμιξε καταθνητοῖς ἀνθρώποις.

> Zeus cast sweet longing into Aphrodite's own heart to be united with a mortal
> man, so that very soon even she might not able to keep away from the bed of
> a mortal man, and that some day the smile-loving Aphrodite might not laugh
> sweetly and boast among all the gods of how she had coupled gods with
> mortal women, who bore mortal sons to the immortals, and how she had
> coupled goddesses with mortal men. (*Hymn. Aphr.* 45-52)

This passage (particularly verse 49) well characterises Aphrodite as a powerful and attractive manipulator of love-making between immortals and mortals, and it is because of this dangerous aspect to her character that she must be punished; hereafter, she is obliged to stop boasting.

The same conclusion is presented in Hesiod's *Works and Days*, but in a quite different way. In the myth of the Heroic Age (among the Five Ages), mortal sons from the union of mortals and immortals are called ἡμίθεοι (*W.D.* 160).[86] They are subject to death but are superior to the men of the present day, i.e. the poet's own time.[87] Zeus made the *hemitheoi* (158), and they were born because men and gods lived on intimate terms in those days.[88] Hesiod gives no explanation for why the Heroic Age had to end, or why the race of *hemitheoi* had to perish – he merely states that grim war and dread battle destroyed them (161). According to the *Cypria* fr. 1, Zeus brought about the war to relieve the earth of overpopulation (schol. *Il.* 1.5); Hesiod may, therefore, imply that it was Zeus who not only made the heroes (158) but also brought about their destruction.[89]

A fragment of Book 5 of the *Catalogue of Women* (Hes. fr. 155 Most [204 M-W]) clearly states that Zeus wanted to separate gods and men:

> ἤδη δὲ γένος μερόπων ἀνθρώπων
> πολλὸν ἀϊστῶσαι σπεῦδε, πρ[ό]φασιν μὲν ὀλέσθαι
> ψυχὰς ἡμιθέω[ν..... ......]οισι βροτοῖσι   100
> τέκνα θεῶν μι[...].[..]ο [ὀφ]θαλμοῖσιν ὁρῶντα,
> ἀλλ' οἳ μ[ὲ]ν μάκ[α]ρες κ[......]ν ὡς τὸ πάρος περ
> χωρὶς ἀπ' ἀν[θ]ρώπων [βίοτον κα]ὶ ἤθε' ἔχωσιν

148

VII. The Bitter Sorrow of Aphrodite

> Now he [Zeus] was eager to obliterate the race of mortal men in order, as he said, that the lives of the semi-gods [*hemitheoi*] should be destroyed ... to mortals the children of the gods ... seeing with their eyes, but the blessed ones ... as in the past should have their livelihood and dwellings apart from men (Hes. fr. 155 Most [204 M-W], vv. 98-103)

According to Thalmann's interpretation, the fragment presents the perspective of the gods – not men – on death: Zeus destroyed the *hemitheoi* once and for all, and prevented the mating of immortals with mortals, because he and the gods could not change the fate of their offspring, and did not want to watch their death.[90] If Thalmann is correct, this offers quite a sympathetic portrayal of the attitude of Zeus and the gods towards humans.

The basic concept of these texts (the *Hymn to Aphrodite, Works and Days*, and the fragment of the *Catalogue of Women*) is the same: once, mortals and immortals enjoyed congress, but at a certain stage it ended, and the race of the *hemitheoi* perished. However, a remarkable feature of the *Hymn to Aphrodite* is that this idea is presented as the consequence of Zeus' punishment of Aphrodite. The story-telling is ingenious: the narration of Aphrodite's power as the reason for her punishment is drawn out through the development of the story of her love-making with Anchises.

The power of Aphrodite

Aphrodite's power is uniquely different from that of the other gods. The most important feature of her power is that it is grounded in the basic necessity for life to continue procreating. No other gods are privileged with this type of primordial power. For example, Athena's craftsmanship and warlike skills, Artemis' hunting and dancing, Hestia's housekeeping skills, Apollo's music and archery, and Hephaestus' smithing are all types of practical skills or techniques of benefit to humans. But Aphrodite's power of love is characterised by its control over the interrelations of *all* living creatures – which inevitably involves the other gods and goddesses. The mode by which her power operates is problematic: her activity directly attacks other gods and, as a consequence, could pose a challenge to the Olympian order. If her power were beneficial or effective for human beings alone, like the skills of the other gods, Zeus could have afforded to be indifferent to her activities. However, the primordial and interrelational nature of her power could cause serious trouble on Olympus. What Zeus objects to is Aphrodite's boast in the hymn (50-52), but Zeus would know that her indiscipline might cause a serious crisis.

Thus on the surface, the text of the hymn simply narrates Zeus' punishment of Aphrodite for her boasting. But if we ask why Zeus should have cared about her boasting, we might notice behind the text his precaution against her overwhelming power. Aphrodite does not fight against Zeus as

149

the male gods do, but she challenges the power of Zeus in her own peculiar way. The punishment by Zeus, who sees the potential for crisis, signifies that Aphrodite's power is too dangerous to be ignored, as it might threaten the power-relations between the Olympian gods.

Zeus' sovereignty rests on a delicate balance of power. If he is to achieve this, and to bring harmony to the divine domain, Aphrodite must lose her pre-eminence. Her suffering – αἰνὸν ἄχος – is thus necessary for achieving this balance of power among the gods. We note, moreover, that her new emotion is, of course, in clear opposition to her earlier laughter (ἡδὺ γελοιήσασα, 49).

Aphrodite can exercise her power even over Zeus, but Zeus can exercise his power over her in exactly the same way (45-52).[91] Thus a balance of power is achieved between the two gods. The hymn poet who celebrates Aphrodite's power nevertheless undermines and restricts this power to achieve a well-balanced relationship between *all* of the gods in terms of the power they each hold. When we read the hymn in these terms we realise that, in the culminating moment which celebrates Aphrodite's most important aspect, it is rather Zeus' power which becomes the focus of the narrative.

The importance of maintaining cosmic harmony also explains another paradox: Zeus, who at the beginning of the hymn plans to subdue Aphrodite, appears as her defender at the end, when she commands Anchises not to reveal that she is Aeneas' mother. She threatens him with the power of Zeus' thunderbolt:

εἰ δέ κεν ἐξείπῃς καὶ ἐπεύξεαι ἄφρονι θυμῷ
ἐν φιλότητι μιγῆναι ἐϋστεφάνῳ Κυθερείῃ,
Ζεύς σε χολωσάμενος βαλέει ψολόεντι κεραυνῷ.

But if you speak this out and boast with your foolish heart to have been united in love with fair-garlanded Cytherea, Zeus will be enraged and smite you with a smoking thunderbolt. (*Hymn. Aphr.* 286-8)

That Zeus, not Aphrodite, will punish him may appear to show their co-operation. In fact, it provides a final, culminating irony, making it appear that Aphrodite, heroine of the hymn, is only such a powerful goddess because almighty Zeus supports her. Other parallel readings might suggest that Aphrodite is also not powerful enough to inflict damage on a mortal; or, that she is not allowed to punish mortals and must leave this to Zeus.[92]

Aphrodite's warning to Anchises presupposes that he might boast of his affair with a goddess. The implication is that, for a human male, pairing with a goddess is regarded in a positive light. We know already, from the beginning of the hymn, that this divine-human pairing is viewed negatively on the divine side (45-52), since the affair is itself contrived by Zeus as a *punishment* for Aphrodite. Ironically, what is sorrowful to a divinity brings honour to a mortal. These two views of the same experience, presented at the beginning and the end of the hymn, function as a framework.

3. The three goddesses at the beginning of the *Hymn to Aphrodite*

The long narrative praising the three goddesses, Athena, Artemis and Hestia, at the very beginning (8-32) is one of the most perplexing parts of the hymn. Many interpretations have been suggested, but not wholly satisfactorily.[93] I suggest that the problem is best explored from the perspective first, of power relations and harmony among the Olympian gods, and secondly, of Zeus' strategy for his sovereignty.

(1) First, Greek myth is strongly preoccupied with kinship and tensions within the family.[94] Indeed, the balance of power among the major Olympian goddesses is particularly important with regard to Aphrodite,[95] if we recollect the origin of the Trojan War in the story of her victory over Athena and Hera in the judgement of Paris. Even from the brief mention of the cause of the Trojan War at *Iliad* 24.29-30, the tension between Aphrodite and the two goddesses, Athena and Hera, is clearly understood:

ὃς νείκεσσε θεάς, ὅτε οἱ μέσσαυλον ἵκοντο,
τὴν δ᾽ ᾔνησ᾽ ἥ οἱ πόρε μαχλοσύνην ἀλεγεινήν.

[Paris] had insulted the goddesses when they came to his sheepfold,
and favoured her [Aphrodite] who offered him dangerous lust. (*Il.* 24.29-30)

Paris insulted the other two goddesses and praised Aphrodite. The sharp contrast between νείκεσσε (24.29) and ᾔνησε (24.30) effectively demonstrates the two goddesses' hostility toward Aphrodite as a consequence of Paris' judgement. Richardson[96] writes that the word μαχλοσύνη (24.30) implies that what *appeared* to be a gift really turned out to be disastrous for Paris and for Troy, since the word usually indicates a *punishment* sent by Aphrodite, rather than a reward. It seems, however, that the unexpected disaster will not only affect Paris and Troy, but also Aphrodite herself. The judgement of Paris appeared to be a glorification of Aphrodite, but it placed her in the most difficult of situations among her fellow goddesses.

Conscious of this ancient legendary motif, the hymnic poet seems to regard the harmonious relation with the three maiden goddesses, Athena, Artemis and Hestia, as being a most joyful and welcoming moment for Aphrodite, since he puts the account of concord with them in the very beginning of his hymn. The poet implies that this relationship is attained as a consequence of Aphrodite's defeat and experience of bitter sorrow, because, as the logic shows, her love affair and the following punishment by Zeus prohibits her from boasting and from imposing her power on the goddesses. Thus in structural terms, the hymn presents us with the result (the harmonious relation with the goddesses) first, and then with the narration of the episode which preceded it and brought it forth.

The *Hymn to Apollo* offers a similar example of this construction:[97] it begins with the reconciliation scene (2-13) – Apollo, disarmed by Leto, receives nectar from Zeus (10). We then discover that this newly established relationship between Zeus and Apollo is the result of what is subsequently narrated – Apollo's defeat of the dragon (356-62). Similarly, in the *Hymn to Aphrodite*, the harmonious unity with the goddesses is celebrated first, as of vital importance, *then* the episode which forms the prerequisite for it is narrated.

A curious tale in the *Odyssey* (20.66-78) implies the harmonious association of Aphrodite and the other goddesses:

ὡς δ᾽ ὅτε Πανδαρέου κούρας ἀνέλοντο θύελλαι·
τῆσι τοκῆας μὲν φθῖσαν θεοί, αἱ δ᾽ ἐλίποντο
ὀρφαναὶ ἐν μεγάροισι, κόμισσε δὲ δῖ᾽ Ἀφροδίτη
τυρῷ καὶ μέλιτι γλυκερῷ καὶ ἡδέϊ οἴνῳ·
Ἥρη δ᾽ αὐτῇσιν περὶ πασέων δῶκε γυναικῶν   70
εἶδος καὶ πινυτήν, μῆκος δ᾽ ἔπορ᾽ Ἄρτεμις ἁγνή,
ἔργα δ᾽ Ἀθηναίη δέδαε κλυτὰ ἐργάζεσθαι.
εὖτ᾽ Ἀφροδίτη δῖα προσέστιχε μακρὸν Ὄλυμπον,
κούρης αἰτήσουσα τέλος θαλεροῖο γάμοιο,
ἐς Δία τερπικέραυνον – ὁ γάρ τ᾽ εὖ οἶδεν ἅπαντα,   75
μοῖράν τ᾽ ἀμμορίην τε καταθνητῶν ἀνθρώπων –
τόφρα δὲ τὰς κούρας ἅρπυιαι ἀνηρείψαντο
καί ῥ᾽ ἔδοσαν στυγερῇσιν ἐρινύσιν ἀμφιπολεύειν·

It was when the stormy winds carried away the daughters of Pandareos. The gods had killed their parents, and the girls were left orphaned in their house. But divine Aphrodite had nurtured them with cheese, sweet honey and pleasant wine; Hera granted them beauty and wisdom beyond all other women; virgin Artemis gave them stature, and Athena taught them splendid handiwork . But when Aphrodite went up to high Olympus to request for these girls achievement of flourishing marriage to Zeus who rejoices in thunder, because he well knows all things, what is fated and what not fated for mortal men, meanwhile the storm-spirits snatched these girls away and gave them to the care of the hateful furies. (*Od.* 20.66-78)

Penelope, having decided to hold the contest of the bow on the following morning, tells this story to illustrate the sudden death (or disappearance) of some girls before their marriage. In the story, Aphrodite raises the orphaned daughters of Pandareus. It is difficult to explain why she would do this,[98] but it is possibly because of her specialised connection with pre-nuptial dressing. Aphrodite dresses herself carefully before she meets Anchises in the *Hymn to Aphrodite* (V: 61-5); and in the *Hymn to Aphrodite* (VI) she wears garments with a fine well-wrought golden crown, golden earrings, and golden necklaces (5-13), and then, importantly, the hymnic poet mentions marriage: 'every one of gods wished to take her home to be his wedded wife' (VI.16-17). In the *Cypria* too (fr. 4, 5 Allen; Athenaeus 682d-f), she clothes herself in perfumed garments, with crowns of flowers, before she goes to Ida. Aphrodite also helps Pandora become attractive, by shedding grace on her (*W.D.* 65-6); Pandora is then sent to marry Epimetheus. In the dressing-scene of Hera (*Il.* 14.169-86), Zeus' wife completes her adornment with Aphrodite's help (*Il.* 14.187-223).[99] Likewise the daughters of Pandareus, with Aphrodite's support, now anticipate their marriage (*Od.* 20.73-5), and the story is well-suited to Penelope's current situation, since she has decided to marry the winner of the bow-contest (*Od.* 19.579).

What is significant in the story of Pandareus' daughters is that the goddesses of the hymn, with the exception of Hestia, appear here too: Aphrodite, Hera, Artemis, and Athena. The powers of the three goddesses are similarly listed – in the form of their presents to the daughters of Pandareus. Hera gives them beauty and wisdom; Artemis, stature; and Athena, skill in handiwork (*Od.* 20.70-2). While the three goddesses are giving them these benefits, Zeus leaves them to do as they like. However, once Aphrodite asks about their marriage, Zeus intervenes.[100] Although the relation between Zeus and the ἅρπυιαι (the storm spirits, *Od.* 20.77) is unclear, it may be implied that Zeus is behind the action of the ἅρπυιαι. In this story, Aphrodite co-operates with the other Olympian goddesses, without infringing on their areas of expertise, just as in the hymn. Zeus presides over everything, acting to check Aphrodite's power – again, as he does in the hymn. It seems that the *Hymn to Aphrodite* and the story of Pandareus' daughters in the *Odyssey* share a constant element, both in the relationship between Aphrodite and the other Olympian goddesses *and* in the relationship between Aphrodite and Zeus. From these accounts, one can perceive that Zeus is cautiously keeping his eye on Aphrodite, so that he would intervene in her activity if she were to exert too much of her power.

(2) Secondly, the virginity of all three goddesses who are praised in the hymn is of great significance. The power relation with them would be important not only for Aphrodite but also, perhaps more seriously, for Zeus, because their virginity is indispensable for his sovereignty. If Aphrodite tried to lure these three goddesses into love affairs, cosmic order could be overthrown. This is the last thing that Zeus wishes, because their possible children, as the result of their love affairs, might become dangerous challengers to the power of Zeus. It has been argued throughout this book that Zeus is always cautious and afraid of the birth of a son who will be mightier than himself, having learned from his predecessors. It is vitally important for Zeus, therefore, that Aphrodite not exert her influence on the virgin goddesses. Against this background we see that Aphrodite's power is especially dangerous for the equilibrium of the Olym-

pian family. The celebration and praise of these goddesses in this hymn implies that Aphrodite would not exercise her powers over them in order to secure Zeus' sovereignty.

Aphrodite, having originated as a Great Goddess in Near Eastern tradition, was eventually incorporated into the Olympian family. In that process she was refined and civilised, but at the same time she had to lose much of her power.[101] As I have demonstrated, her power of love was the first vital power in the creation of the universe in the *Theogony*, as Hesiod puts Eros among the four primordial powers, with Chaos, Gaia and Tartarus (*Theog.* 116-20). Then, almost all of the heavenly bodies, gods and goddesses, are born through the power of love. Aphrodite, as the anthropomorphic equivalent of Eros, holds power of such fundamental and pre-eminent significance that no one can resist. This reminds us of the relationship between the all-embracing Mighty Mother and the other gods. If Zeus is to take over the dominant place held by this Mighty Mother, he must reduce the perilous power of Aphrodite. It is surprising how much change Aphrodite has to suffer, and how much diminished her power is in Homer and the *Hymn to Aphrodite*, by comparison not only with the Mighty Mother but also even with herself in the *Theogony*. It is undoubtedly Zeus' strategy in the hymn, as well as Homer's, to demote Aphrodite, who might cause cosmic strife as a powerful kingmaker; as a daughter of Uranus, she could have taken revenge on Zeus by producing mighty challengers against him through her power of love. However, by his clever and precautionary strategy towards her, Zeus successfully avoids the crisis, as the hymn suggests.

For the hymnic poet, however, even though her power has become restricted, the welcoming of Aphrodite by the Olympian gods, especially the three goddesses, is the main basis of his praise for her. Herodotus quite rightly remarks on this motivation of the poets: 'Homer and Hesiod composed a theogony for the Greeks, gave the gods their titles, assigned them privileges and skills, and described their appearances' (2.53). Within the existing hierarchy, every god has to establish his own sphere of influence. The *Hymn to Aphrodite* celebrates both Aphrodite's properly assigned privileges and her final integration into the Olympian order.

The gods assemble on Olympus as a unity. The effect of this device is to compare the community of gods with the human world as a whole.[102] The festivals in honour of the gods also celebrate civic life, where the solidarity of the community is of major importance. The hymns would naturally be expected to celebrate the harmonious divine world, and to affirm the value of community. The *Hymn to Aphrodite* contributes effectively to this purpose, by representing solidarity in Olympian society.

The value of this hymn, however, lies not only in this theme of social and political solidarity. The hymn deals with profound and universal problems of mortality, love and death, by presenting us with a dualistic picture of Aphrodite's greatness *and* insignificance, in much the same way as we look at the heroes of epic, where both the greatness and the insignificance of human life is narrated.[103] The hymn demonstrates that, like the human heroes, gods, too, have complex natures: they have sublime knowledge and power coupled with apparently all too human weaknesses.

Epilogue

In this book I have proposed new ways of interpreting the enigmatic texts under discussion. As I pointed out in the Introduction, my approaches and conclusions articulate but one coherent hermeneusis amid a wealth of possible alternatives. All along, my aim has been to find ways of reaching a deeper understanding of this material.

I emphasised the function of allusion in the narratives. In particular, I highlighted how difficult it is to distinguish between poetic allusion and poetic innovation or invention. One specific problem is that, almost certainly, the two concepts can co-exist: that is, the existence of one does not negate the existence of the other. The poet can be considered to be innovating in his individual selection and orchestration of allusions and intertexts – in the details and story variants to which he refers. But, as I suggested, the designation of poetic choices as 'inventions' – because of their improbability, inconsistency or lack of other parallel account – can restrict a more sensitive reading of the power and meaning of these deliberate poetic selections. As Buxton points out, 'in view of the patchy nature of our evidence, it is unwise to be so restrictive ... Greek mythical tradition was dynamic: given the right circumstances an innovation would achieve currency, only to lose it later if other versions were found more persuasive.'[1]

Beneath the extant epic tradition, we can distinguish an enormous variety of versions of epic and mythic stories on which the poet could draw: the possibilities for allusion – and innovation – are extensive. It has been a central concern in this book to delve below the extant epic tradition in search of these alternative stories to which the poets alluded, or which resonated in their words,[2] and to seek more profound implications in these texts than have previously been considered.

Some might wonder if the audience of the oral poetry could appreciate such literary techniques as allusions or parallels, which we recognise by means of 'close reading'. However, we should not underestimate the sophistication of the ancient audience. We might compare the example offered by Aristophanes' comedies: it seems that some, at least, of the spectators were attuned to a great many story-variants, and remembered and appreciated the various verses of the tragedies represented and parodied by the comic poet. Like the audiences of these comedies, the audiences of early epic must similarly have possessed considerable knowledge of – and openness towards – the myths and stories which had been

157

passed down to them. It is not too much to presume that, when they listened to these epic tales, they were sensitive to the poets' hints and allusions to other stories, and appreciated their allusive skills and techniques.

Recovering such allusions is difficult, but we should attempt to trace suspected concealed meanings in order to facilitate our access to the ancient reception of these texts. Recognising the underlying 'hidden logic' represented by these poetic allusions broadens our understanding of the scale of the stories and strengthens our sense of the impressiveness of the episodes. It is for this reason that I have exploited the potential offered by 'harder' readings of the function and consequences of poetic allusion.

In following these allusive threads, I have concentrated on one major theme, namely challenges to the power of Zeus. My particular interest was prompted by the fact that many echoes of this story pattern have been preserved in surviving Greek poetry. One reason for their preservation, I suggest, is the audiences' fondness for a particular theme:[3] that is, the concept that equilibrium is obtained only after the overcoming of dangerous enemies. The idea of competition and the desire for victory would also seem to have been particularly important in ancient Greece.[4] Further, there was an interest in imagining the ingenious means and devices by which a conqueror, exploiting both intellectual and physical power, obtained final victory. This is a theme observed in the *Odyssey*: after narrating Odysseus' exciting adventures, the final twelve books narrate for us, at length, how Odysseus successfully regained his kingship at Ithaca. Similarly, Zeus' lengthy progress to victory was apparently a story which held tremendous interest to ancient audiences.

Another theme that has attracted me is that of generational strife, which seems to be a conspicuous and recurrent motif in Greek myth. It constitutes a basic element in many Greek stories, in which the relation of son and father is of great importance. One of my objectives has been to demonstrate how the two themes, challenges to the power of Zeus and generational strife, are ingeniously intertwined as thematic threads woven throughout the texts.

These themes are preserved, and recur in manifold forms, both explicitly narrated and implicitly alluded to or implied in early epic. By following these allusive traces, we gain a broader understanding of the 'logic' of Zeus' victory. In turn, as I have elaborated, we can share something of the amusement and joy with which the ancient audience beheld Zeus' cunning victories.

In conclusion, it is worth recalling Kirk's statement on the nature of myth:[5]

Myths, therefore, are often multifunctional, and consequently different hearers can value a myth for different reasons. Like any tale, a myth may have different emphases or levels of meaning; if these are especially abstract, then the area of ambivalence is increased still further. The consequence is that analysis of a myth should not stop when one particular theoretical explanation had been applied and found productive. Other kinds of explanation may also be valid.

Myth presents us with an innumerable multiplicity of explanations of such attractiveness and allusiveness as to induce us to form manifold interpretations of the same basic materials. Myth, we find, is powerful: all ages and all peoples have been fascinated by the potential offered by myth to provide complex reflections of human activity – or, in other words, a crystallisation of the human soul.

Notes

Introduction

1. There are many deities on the Pylos tablets. This seems to indicate that Mycenaean society, at least in Pylos, allowed variety in religious devotion, although Poseidon is undoubtedly the most important among the gods listed. Because of the scanty evidence, it is difficult to get much religious information at Mycenaean sites other than Pylos, but as Chadwick (1976) 15 points out, 'the homogeneity of Mycenaean culture is so marked, that it would be strange if other parts of Greece behaved very differently.' If this holds true, we might suspect that it was a general phenomenon that a variety of gods were worshipped at Mycenaean sites.

2. The list of the gods and the votive offerings of tablet Tn 316 is as follows. See Duhoux (2008) 321-35; Palmer (1963) 261-8; Gallavotti ed. (1961) *Inscriptiones Pyliae ad Mycenaeam Aetatem Pertinentes*; Ventris and Chadwick (1956) 286-9:

> those who get one golden vessel and two women: the precinct of Poseidon;
> one golden vessel and a man: Zeus, Hermes;
> one golden vessel and a woman: *potinija* (Potnia), the Dove-goddess, *manasa*, *posidaeja* (the feminine form of Poseidon?), *diuja* (the feminine form of Zeus?), *pe-re**82, Hera;
> one golden vessel only: *tiriseroe* (Trishero?), *dopota*, *ipemedeja* (Iphimedeia, the mother of Otus and Ephialtes by Poseidon in *Od.* 11.305?), *dirimijo* (Drimios, son of Zeus?).

3. Duhoux (2008) 370 suggests that these three gods are honoured in the same shrine, and constitute a 'holy family'.

4. Palmer (1963) 265-6 suggests that the operation recorded in this tablet might be human sacrifice at the New Year festival for the purpose of the removal of the previous year's guilt and defilement. Chadwick (1976) 89-90 submits that this document might have been written in the last days of the palace of Pylos, since it is 'the most disgraceful piece of hastily compiled record of offerings'.

5. Es 645, 646, 647, 648, 649, 651, 652, 653, 703, 726, 728, 729.

6. Ventris and Chadwick (1956) 282-4 consider that the tablet records a glorified representation of ceremonial processions.

7. The well-known etymology of Poseidon as 'the Lord of the earth' (*posis-da*) is rejected by Chadwick (1976) 86-7, especially with regard to the latter half of the name, *-da*. He similarly questions the etymology of Demeter (*da-mater*). See further Chapter V, Section 2 below. Cf. Frisk (1972) II, 583.

8. Campbell (1964) 149.

9. For the goddesses of Anatolia, see Gimbutas (1974) chs 8-10.

10. Guthrie (1950) 36.

11. Graf (1993) 95 proposes two periods of oral transmission of Near Eastern myths to the Greeks: the Mycenaean and the archaic periods. Graf considers the latter more likely, because there is no Canaanite influence in Hesiod; if the Greeks had taken over the oriental tales in Mycenaean times, some traces of Canaanite

161

myth would be found, and the Hittite and Mesopotamian myths would hardly have been so prominent. Lane Fox (2008) 103-13 writes about the importance of the site of Al Mina in northern Syria, where the conspicuous traces of Euboean immigration, such as pottery, can be noticed.

12. For Panhellenism, see further Nagy (1979) 9; Clay (1989) 8-9.

13. Rohde (1898) 39.

14. See further, Nagy (1979) 9.

15. Brown (1952) 138.

16. Burkert (1992) 3-5 reviews the history of scholarship on orientalism and anti-orientalism in the late nineteenth century. He explores the dominance of the image of 'pure, self-contained Hellenism' especially among German scholars including Wilamowitz-Moellendorff, and how it was overtaken by three groups of new discoveries: the decipherment of cuneiform writing, the archaeological discovery of Mycenaean civilisation, and the recognition of an oriental phase in the development of archaic Greek art. West (1997) also deals with this subject, pointing out (p. 586) that the Greek poets of the Archaic age were profoundly indebted to western Asia at many levels, such as mythical and literary motifs, cosmological and theological conceptions, formal procedures, technical devices, figures of speech, even phraseology and idioms.

17. In the *Enuma Elish* the strife separates the new generation from the old one, whereas in Greek myth it develops over three generations in a stepwise manner.

18. Dumézil (1968) 168-9.

19. Eliade (1961) 98: the god Varuna has the magic power to bind and unbind men at a distance.

20. For example, Tenes, who was put in a box and carried off to sea as a result of the slander of his step-mother; finally he arrived on the island that was, then, called Tenedos; Corythus, who was killed by his father because of his relations with his step-mother Helen (Parthenius 4); Euryalus, who was killed by his father, Odysseus, at the suggestion of Penelope (Parthenius 3). It should be noted that in all these stories the step-mothers, that is, the females, take the initiative. See further Sourvinou-Inwood (1991) 244-84.

21. The date of the hymns is not easy to determine. I follow AHS (1936) 183, who argue that the *Hymn to Apollo* is the oldest of the hymns. However Janko (1982) 132 dates the *Hymn to Pythian Apollo* to c. 585 – a date later than the composition of the *Hymn to Aphrodite, c.* 700 BC. Cf. Chapter VII n. 2.

22. Taplin (1992) 55.

23. Taplin (1992) 10.

24. The idea of competition and the desire for victory seems to have been particularly important in ancient Greece. The principle of competition prevailed throughout society – in battle, sports, and even in artistic fields. For example, in the *Certamen*, Homer and Hesiod compete in a poetic contest: the quality of the poets' songs is judged. The *Hymn to Apollo* presents the delightful festival in Delos (146-76), where hymns are recited in a contest. In the classical age, it is well known that dramas were performed as a contest. As Nagy (1990) 79 writes, 'the performance of poetry, from the day of the oral poets to the era of the rhapsodes, was by its nature a matter of competition'. In such a competitive society, the idea of gods who fight with each other would have been accepted without difficulty. However, Griffith (1990) 189 points out the ambiguity of the verdict at the contests, giving the example of the contest between Hesiod and Homer, and writes (p. 191) that the game need not come out to a 'zero-sum'. I agree with Griffith (pp. 196-7) that

this 'contest-system' allowed the existence of alternative or contradictory versions of myth.

25. For the extreme case, cf. Todorov (1977) 55 on the 'antidigressive law'.

26. Taplin (1992) 8f.

27. I pursue the problem in a direction similar to that of Slatkin (1991) 8, who writes that 'what we need is ... to recover as much as possible what an ancient "reading" might have been based on; or rather we might say that to gain greater access to what Homer's audience heard in the epics.'

28. Clay (1989) 205.

29. Reception, of course, lies beyond an author's control: see Martindale (1993) 13-16 on theoretical questions associated with the redescribability of texts by the 'implied reader'. I wish here merely to note that I am aware of the considerable pitfalls associated with the use of 'reader', 'hearer' and 'audience' in the context of the Homeric problem. In general, see Rutherford (1996) 9-15.

30. Taplin (1992) 10f.

31. In the fifth-century tragedians we see even more pointed examples of differences from earlier cores of material sources: the powerless Aphrodite of the *Hymn* and the potent Aphrodite of Euripides' *Hippolytus*.

32. Willcock (1964) 147.

33. Willcock (1964) 146 writes that 'where it does seem probable that Homer is inventing is in the detail of the paradeigma itself'.

34. As I also note, the *Hymn* adopts the Homeric account of Hephaestus' parentage.

35. Just as 'the canon' itself is open to innovation. Martindale (1993) 25 points out that 'there is no reason why canons should be regarded as necessarily, or intrinsically, conservative, since texts can be appropriated for different positions'.

36. Lang (1983) 151.

37. Graf (1993) 61.

38. Slatkin (1991) 5.

39. Willcock (1964) 141-54; Willcock (1977) 45-9; also Edwards (1991) ad 20. 67-74.

40. Graf (1993) 63 notes that the epithet of Nestor, ἱππότα, suggests that epic poetry existed about the hero, Nestor. Further, he suggests that Nestor's mythical biography (*Il.* 11.688-761) is closely connected with that of Heracles. Alden (2000) 74-111 discusses the function of Nestor's speeches, and concludes at p. 111 that Nestor's speeches are always relevant to their context, offering discreet advice on the best way of proceeding in the circumstances.

41. Cf. Chapter I n. 1.

42. Kirk (1985) ad 1.399.

43. See Rutherford (1996) 5-6 on this perennial process of acceptance and variation: Homer was 'an active participant in a tradition which thrives on competition and constant reworking of well-established themes'.

I. The Threat of Thetis

1. Particularly Kullmann (1960) 15 n. 2; Willcock (1964) 141-54; (1977) 41-53; and (1978) ad loc.; Kirk (1985) ad loc.

2. Griffin (1980a) 185.

3. I agree with Lang (1983) 163, who points out that 'whether an *Iliad* theme attracted old tales as exempla or an old tale inspired an *Iliad* episode for which the old tale was used as support, each would be liable over time to infiltration of details from the other.' See also Introduction above.

4. *The Power of Thetis: Allusion and Interpretation in the Iliad*, Berkeley and Los Angeles, 1991.

5. For example, Aristotle (*EN* 1124b12-17) explains that Thetis did not tell the story because Zeus, being a god full of μεγαλοψυχία, disliked being reminded of the benefit that he received.

6. Easterling (1991) 147 points out the important function of the women in the *Iliad*, who articulate some of the great issues of the poem.

7. Slatkin (1991) 53.

8. Kuch (1993) 204.

9. Later it becomes clear that Thetis had told Achilles of his fate: a choice of either a short but glorious life, or a long life without glory (9.410-16). He also mentions his proposal to leave Troy – which means a long but inglorious life (1.169-71). Here, however, his words suggest that his short life is ordained, and it is not a matter of choice.

10. The marriage of Peleus and Thetis is mentioned by Pindar (*Isthm.* 8.29-38; *Pyth.* 3.87-92; *Nem.* 3.32-6; 4.49-67; 5.25-37) and Aeschylus (*P.V.* 167ff., 515ff., 755ff., 907ff.); in Homer it is mentioned only once, and not in detail (18.434). I agree with Griffin (1977) 41, who writes that, 'the poet of the *Iliad* is familiar with the story but has suppressed it, preferring unexplained mystery to the monstrousness of metamorphosis and ascription to Thetis of an un-human pixie character'.

11. Kirk (1985) ad loc. notes that 'Achilles could hardly be free from grief in such circumstance; had he been griefless, he would have been out there fighting'.

12. Kuch (1993) 205 also points out that the scene between Thetis and Achilles foreshadows the scene between Thetis and Zeus; and between these two scenes a deliberate use of 'Rückblende' is noticeable.

13. Regarding the narrative function of Briareus, Slatkin (1991) 69 suggests that he functions as a reminder, multiplying the succession myth motif. For the double terminology of Briareus and Aegaion, see Hooker (1980) 189, who concludes that there is no essential difference between the human and divine terms used by Homer.

14. I take γάρ as emphatic, not explanatory, since 'mightier than his father' does not explain the alternative name of Aegaion, as is generally recognised. Cf. Kirk (1985) ad loc.; Slatkin (1991) 70 n. 17. Leaf (1960) ad loc. comments on αὖτε that 'Poseidon, in union with the other gods, was stronger than Zeus, so his son again was stronger than he.' Against Willcock's claim (1964) 147 that this phrase is illogical in the context, I contend that it is a key phrase in the story.

15. Slatkin (1991) 69.

16. Slatkin (1991) 59 observes that Thetis is one figure who does not refer to her own power, since the rescue of Dionysus (6.130-7) and that of Hephaestus (18.394-9) are narrated by those whom she saved.

17. Braswell (1971) 19 n. 2 holds that Thetis does not mention Achilles' story because the audience still has Achilles' speech in mind; but this explanation is unlikely, because there is a well-known example of repetition when Achilles relates the story of Agamemnon and Chryses (1.366-92) to Thetis, even though the audience would certainly remember what had just been previously narrated (1.8-244). Cf. Kirk (1985) 91-3. Willcock (1964) 143 tentatively suggests that Thetis does not think it worth repeating the story because it is sheer invention. But even if it *was* invented, this would not be a satisfactory reason for not repeating it, if to tell the story in detail would serve a persuasive purpose. There would be no reason to suppose that the story would seem fictitious to Thetis or Zeus.

18. Slatkin (1991) 101-3 points out that 'the price of Zeus' hegemony is Achilles' death'.

19. On the question of why Achilles does not appeal directly to Zeus, Leaf (1960), Willcock (1978) and Kirk (1985) offer no comment. Slatkin (1991) 59-61 raises the question without answering it. My view is that it is not an Iliadic way of thinking that gods will always be amenable to the prayers of human beings; heroes' prayers are in most cases partly or wholly rejected in the *Iliad*: the prayer of Agamemnon to Zeus (2.419-20) is wholly rejected, as is that of Hector to Athena (6.311). Indeed, when Achilles directly prays to Zeus for Patroclus (16. 233-48), his prayer is only partially accepted. Here, however, the acceptance of Achilles' appeal is indispensable for the whole plot of the epic. In order to preclude the wholesale acceptance of a human being's (Achilles) prayer, Thetis, instead of Achilles, makes the appeal. In addition, the importance of supplication must be noted. The supplication of Chryses, the priest of Apollo, was successful (1.37-52). As direct supplication to Zeus would not be allowed in Achilles' case, since he is not a priest of Zeus, he might have asked Thetis to make the appeal. What is significant is that Zeus accepted Thetis' supplication at the cost of Patroclus' life. The fact that Thetis' prayer does not prevent the loss implies, again, that supplication by a mortal is not often accepted, even if supported by an immortal. In terms of the epic's plot – on the macroscopic, cosmic level – the intervention of Thetis is, of course, important for the further development of the strife-in-heaven motif.

20. Nagy (1979) 188 writes that 'the wish that the mother of Achilles conveys from the hero to Zeus is phrased from the standpoint of the Oath. ... In this way, the Oath of Achilles is translated into the will of Zeus ... .' For the oath of Achilles and the poetical significance of the *skeptron*, see Easterling (1989) 112-15.

21. Kirk (1985) ad loc.

22. O'Brien (1993) 89 comments that this word expresses Thetis' intimate dependence on Zeus.

23. Kirk (1985) ad loc.

24. Slatkin (1991) 66.

25. We note similar phrases to οὔ τοι ἔπι δέος at *Hymn. Aphr.* 194 (οὐ γάρ τοί τι δέος, addressed by Aphrodite to Anchises); *Il.* 12.246 (σοὶ δ᾽ οὐ δέος ἔστ᾽, Hector to Polydamas); *Od.* 5.347 (οὐδέ τί τοι παθέειν δέος, Calypso to Odysseus); *Od.* 8. 563 (οὔτε τι πημανθῆναι ἔτι δέος, Alcinous to the Phaeacians). In these examples, the phrases are *literally* true, in the sense of consolation or encouragement, because they are employed by a superior to an inferior. However, the case of the present argument (*Il.* 1.515) is unique because the phrase is used by one who appears to be an inferior (Thetis) to her apparent superior (Zeus). Thetis is obviously not consoling or praising Zeus: I suggest that the words can be interpreted as Thetis' ingenious way of threatening Zeus with moral blackmail .

26. Thetis' diction here could be compared with a similar speech of Hera to Zeus (4.53), where she paradoxically speaks of her beloved three cities, Argos, Sparta and Mycenae; 'Sack these, whenever your heart feels strong hatred for them' (τὰς διαπέρσαι, ὅτ᾽ ἄν τοι ἀπέχθωνται περὶ κῆρι).

27. West (1998), in his new Teubner edition, reads τρέψεν φρένας, 'made me change my mind', in 459 (Plut. *Coriol.* 32.5) instead of παῦσεν χόλον (id. *Mor.* 26f.).

28. Hainsworth (1993) ad loc.

29. Devereux (1973) 43-4 argues that castration and blinding are regular alternative punishments for sexual transgression in Greek mythology.

30. The passage is cited only by Plutarch, who states that Aristarchus removed these verses 'from fear' (*Mor.* 26f, ὁ μὲν οὖν Ἀρίσταρχος ἐξεῖλε ταῦτα τὰ ἔπη φοβηθείς). It is widely assumed that the verses are genuine, although Aristarchus (or more probably, an earlier transmitter of the Homeric text) omitted them. Janko

(1992) 28, followed by Hainsworth (1993) ad loc., comments that 'the lines ... are Homeric in style and language'. Griffin (1995) ad loc. writes that v. 460 does not look Iliadic, and considers the possibility that the verses are not original, but derive from a marginal note by some learned reader. It may have seemed to later editors to be an immoral intention for Achilles' preceptor.

31. Since the precise description in the following passage (462-77) seems to reflect ancient custom, I do not agree with van der Valk (1963) 484, who suggests that Homer invents a quarrel between Phoenix and his father in order to give a reason for his taking refuge with Peleus. For the history of the discussion see Scodel (1982a) 128 nn. 1 and 3, who argues (133-6) that this is a negative paradigm: in order to persuade Achilles to remain, Phoenix at first suggests that his own departure was an appropriate event. But this would seem too sophisticated and complicated explanation.

32. Alden (2000) 21 cites this story as an example of 'para-narratives' which make some internal reference to the events of the main narrative.

33. Slater (1968) 132 notes the fear of the mother's procreative power in the myth of revolt. He points out that mature and maternal women are particularly feared by the ancient Greeks, and sometimes are regarded as the most dangerous. Slater (1968) 12: in tragedy it is young women and virginal goddesses who are helpful and benign, and most often the household is 'mother-dominant and father-avoidant'. Caldwell (1989) 161 offers an interesting perspective on the relationship between the mother and the son in generational myth: 'the lesson Cronus has learned from the fate of Uranus is basically misogynistic: he sees that it is the woman as much as the son who is his enemy. His children must be kept separate from their mother'. Cf. Chapter IV, Sections 2 and 3.

34. In terms of story patterns or motifs in Books 5-24 of the *Odyssey,* two motifs dominate the epic: 'the motif of the homecoming of the wanderer' and 'the motif of choosing a husband by bow-contest'. Neither of these motifs necessitates the presence of a son of the wanderer. It seems, therefore, that the poet required some other device to mesh the story of Telemachus with these other motifs.

35. Rutherford (1992) 26.

36. De Jong (2001) ad 21.101-39 comments that the scene offers a different significance for the Suitors as opposed to the narratees: for the Suitors, Telemachus plays the role of a weak and helpless youngster, but for the narratees, he shows his real strength by setting up the axes well. De Jong might be right, but I am reluctant to accept her suggestion that 'Telemachus purposely failed to string the bow', because this interpretation would damage the suspense of the critical scene of Odysseus' nodding. If Telemachus were not serious in stringing the bow, it would not have been necessary for Odysseus to risk his life by giving a nod of warning.

37. For example, the first aim of the Trojan War is to regain Helen, but it is obvious that, for the Greeks, a second and more important aim is to capture the city of Troy and gain its wealth. Likewise, the aim of the bow-contest would naturally be not only to gain Penelope but to win the kingship of Ithaca which Odysseus also possessed. If his father dies, Telemachus will succeed to the palace of Odysseus. However, the kingship of Ithaca seems to be a different question: it would not automatically pass to the son (1.394-8). The suitors also clearly distinguish the ownership of the palace from the kingship of Ithaca; they admit that Telemachus will own his father's property after a husband of Penelope has been selected, but they leave the problem of the kingship of Ithaca (it should be decided by the gods: 1.400-4).

38. I agree with Gadamer (1985) 223 who writes that 'Es ist nichts als seine Arete, durch die sich legitimiert, Sohn seines Vater zu sein'.

39. Dawe (1993) ad loc comments that 'the only prize at stake is Penelope herself'. He doubts the authenticity of line 117, saying that the line is 'a vaunt which has strayed in from some rival version, in which the "prizes" were the iron and bronze'.

40. Hayman (1882) ad loc.

41. Hayman (1882) ad loc.; Monro (1901) ad loc.; Ameis, Hentze and Cauer (1925) ad loc.; Stanford (1948) ad loc.; Russo, Fernandez-Galiano and Heubeck (1992) ad loc.

42. Van Leeuwen (1917) ad loc.; For Dawe's interpretation, cf. n. 39 above. The difficulty of this interpretation lies in the word κατόπισθε (116), which implies a contrast between Penelope's going and Telemachus' staying behind. However, the word could have temporal significance, meaning that 'I remain hereafter'.

43. Stanford (1948) ad loc.

44. Both ἄεθλον and ἀέθλιον could mean 'the contests' in their plural forms, such as at *Od.* 24. 89; *Od.* 24. 168-9. However, at *Od.* 21. 73, ἄεθλον is used in the singular, and the combination with the verb φαίνετ' strongly suggests that ἄεθλον means the prize of the contest, which can be construed as Penelope.

45. Finkelberg (1991) 306 and 315 argues that kingship in heroic Greece is characteristically transmitted by marriage to the royal heiress, and that this is the reason why Telemachus not only cannot assume the position of his missing and presumably dead father, but even has to think of the possibility that the future king of Ithaca is to be found among the suitors. My interpretation of this passage demonstrates how critical and dangerous the situation becomes when Telemachus almost commits himself to it.

46. Gainsford (1999) 190-2 gives a thorough list of the testimonia on the death of Odysseus. On top of the three sources cited above, the following are listed: Eugammon [Proclus]; Soph. *Od. Akanthoplex*; [Lyc.] *Alex* 795-7; Oppian *Halieut.* 2.500-2; Dictys 6.15; Tzetzes on [Lyc.] *Alex.* 805.

47. An additional point of interest is that, according to the *Telegony*, Telegonus marries Penelope, and Telemachus marries Circe. This reveals a curious double relationship: two sons of Odysseus marry two partners of Odysseus.

48. De Jong (2001) 53; West in Heubeck et al. (1988) ad 153.

49. S. West in Heubeck et al. (1988) ad 153 suggests that the eagles rip their own cheeks as a gesture of mourning at events in Ithaca, but she also agrees that this attitude is unlikely for birds. The eagles' unnatural behaviour could indicate the disturbed state of affairs on Ithaca, but this interpretation does not fully explain the entire episode of the eagles' ripping each other's cheeks.

50. Braswell (1971) 23 notes the seeming inconsistency between Hera's attitude to Thetis in Books 1 and 24. However, inconsistency is not a wholly satisfactory reason for postulating invention (as was stated in my Introduction). The poet could certainly allude to different existing stories on diverse, appropriate occasions. For example, Hephaestus' lameness is caused by Zeus at *Il.* 1.590-1 and by Hera at *Il.* 18.395-6.

51. Macleod (1982) ad loc.; Willcock (1984) ad loc. comments that there is no background concerning Thetis' upbringing; Richardson (1993) ad loc. refers to Braswell with no comment.

52. O'Brien (1993) 93 offers a unique interpretation of Hera's upbringing of Thetis: the χόλος of Hera was physically transmitted through Thetis to her infant son Achilles. If χόλος could be transmitted by upbringing, as O'Brien suggests, the χόλος of Oceanus and Tethys (14. 306) would also have been transmitted to Hera, although there is nothing in the story as told by Hera to suggest that Oceanus and Tethys were angry with one another when they were rearing her.

167

53. Willcock (1984) ad loc.

54. The verbs τρέφειν and ἀτιτάλλειν are commonly used for nurture, with no reference to rearing a possible challenger, as in *Il*. 2.548; 5.271; 14.303; *Od*. 7.12; 19.354; *Hymn. Aphr*. 115. However, there are some contexts in which τρέφειν clearly does carry this implication, such as Bacchylides 5.86-8 (τίς ἀθανάτων / ἢ βροτῶν τοιοῦτον ἔρνος / θρέψεν ἐν ποίαι χθονί;) ; Aesch. *Eum*. 57-9 (οὐκ ὄπωπα ... ἥτις αἶα τοῦτ᾽ ἐπεύχεται γένος / τρέφουσ᾽ ...); Aristophanes, *Thesm*. 520-3 (τουτὶ μέντοι θαυμαστόν ... χῆτις ἐξέθρεψε χώρα / τήνδε τὴν θρασεῖαν οὕτω).

55. It is understandable from Thetis' point of view to refuse Zeus' advance out of respect for Hera, although Hera herself wanted Thetis to have a son.

56. *Theogony* 886-929 gives a list of the unions between Zeus and goddesses, some of which openly imply Zeus' compulsion. In other versions, his relations with Metis, Nemesis, Europa, Io and Leda involve deception and/or force. In addition, he allows Peleus to subdue Thetis, and Hades to snatch Persephone at *Hymn. Dem*. 3.

57. The story of Nemesis (Athen. 334 B and *Cyp*. fr. 9 *PEG*) supports my argument: Nemesis transforms herself to avoid marriage with Zeus. The motif of unwilling marriage and transformation is similar to Thetis' story: in both cases they mate under compulsion.

58. Gantz (1993) 61.

59. Hunter (1993) 97.

60. Green (1997) 327; Hunter (1993) 100 remarks that this scene is a powerful manifestation of the gulf between frightened anger [of Zeus and of Hera] and silent suffering [of Thetis].

61. Apollodorus probably took the story from Aeschylus' Prometheus plays.

62. The traditional role of Hera is, of course, that of the jealous wife who prevents and puts obstacles in the way of Zeus' various love affairs (as was mentioned earlier in this chapter). Nevertheless, so great is her hatred of Zeus that, in spite of the implications it might hold for herself, she might risk promoting such an affair if it resulted in his downfall. Compare her great hatred of Troy in *Il*. 4.20-49.

63. The identification of the roles of Themis and Prometheus could be traditional. Gantz (1993) 52 suggests that the prophecy was originally given by Themis, and that Aeschylus (*P.V*. 209-10) invented the story that Themis was Prometheus' mother to give Prometheus some leverage over Zeus.

64. Note that Apollodorus offers the different versions as alternatives without opting for a 'real reason'.

65. Cf. Chapter VI n. 32 below.

66. For further discussion of ἄλλο, cf. Chapter VI, Section 2.

67. Nilsson (1932) 221ff., followed by Griffin (1980a) 186, suggests that the concept of a unified divine society is a creation of the epic, which is influenced by the religious ideas current in the second millennium BC.

68. Janko (1992) ad *Il*. 15.104-12.

69. Janko (1992) ad *Il*. 14.295-6 points out that Hera alludes to Metis with the words ποικιλομῆτα and μητίσεαι (322). Hera's anxiety, therefore, is evidently about the sovereignty of the universe, because swallowing Metis and begetting Athena were contrived by Zeus precisely for that purpose.

70. Edwards (1991) ad loc. makes the point that ἔμβαλον does not imply violence. However, the connotation of this word – and also that of the *Hymn to Aphrodite* 199, βροτοῦ ἀνέρος ἔμπεσον εὐνῇ, which Edwards himself cites – seems to be of an unwilling marriage.

71. I agree with the neoanalytic interpretation of Patroclus' death as paralleled by Achilles'; for example Whitman (1958) 199, Nagy (1979) 292-3, and Edwards (1991) 15.

72. Richardson (1993) ad loc.

73. Macleod (1982) ad loc.

74. Gould (1973) 96 n. 111.

75. Richardson (1993) ad loc. also notes 'the reversal of roles': in the narrative it is the supplicated man who is the killer, and the suppliant who is the rich man.

76. Richardson (1993) ad loc.

77. Lynn-George (1988) 242 notes the language in Priam's statement, pointing out that 'Priam's discourse is constructed as the choice of a word; from among the possibilities recommended by the god, Priam selects one; this word, "father".'

78. Kim (2000) 23-63, esp. p. 33, tries to answer this question by establishing Achilles' pity for Priam as a φίλος. I agree, but my concern is rather with what induces Achilles' pity for Priam.

79. Edwards (1991) 10.

80. Rutherford (1982) 146 also points out Achilles' inability as the archetypal tragic figure: for all his power and greatness, Achilles is unable to dictate or influence the course of future events.

81. O'Brien (1993) 79 explains that Achilles is reconciled with Priam in response to Zeus' new ethic of pity, retreating from Hera's hatred. While this is plausible, I would stress, in addition, Achilles' self-reintegration within his own genealogy.

82. Peleus held Thetis by force to win her: she tried to escape him by changing her shape into fire, water, wind, a tree, a bird, a lion, snake and cuttlefish (cf. Pindar *Nem.* 4.62ff.; Pausanias 5.18.5; Apollod. 3.13.5). This myth suggests that Peleus raped Thetis: but this story also demonstrates the physical excellence required to win a divine bride. It is significant that the *Iliad*'s portrayal of the *elderly* Peleus emphasises his decency as a mediator in domestic problems and glosses over the fact that he married Thetis against her will.

83. Phoenix became ὀπάων of Peleus. For the relationship of ὀπάων, see Hainsworth (1993) ad loc.

84. These images of Peleus imply a parallel with Thetis, who rescued Dionysus (6.132-7) and Hephaestus (18.395-405).

85. Alden (2000) 290 emphasises the rejection of λιταί, giving references such as Chryses to Agamemnon in Book 1; the embassy in Book 9; Priam and Hecuba to Hector in Book 22; and Hector and Achilles in Book 22.

86. Slatkin (1991) 103.

87. I agree with Rutherford (1982) 160 who comments that it is part of human nature to seek to comprehend the course of events even when they are beyond human understanding. The characterisation of Peleus here seems to be a good example of 'the course of events'.

88. Caldwell (1989) 179.

89. Griffin (1977) 48 notes that the Διὸς βουλή applies to the events of the poem as a whole, and also to the plan which Zeus devises with Thetis. I would emphasise the latter.

90. Lynn-George (1988) 38-9.

91. *Cypria* fr. 1; schol. *Il.* 1.5.

II. The Golden Chain of Hera

1. I agree with Janko (1992) ad 15.18-31, who comments that the story has latent cosmic implications.

2. His famous attacks on the gods: 'Homer and Hesiod have attributed to the gods everything that is a shame and reproach among men, stealing and committing adultery and deceiving each other' (fr. 11 D-K)

3. Griffin (1980a) 146 comments that 'the gods of the *Iliad* are in fact the chief source of comedy in the poem; ... the gods of the *Iliad* belong to the conventional world of epic and were understood as such by the audience'.

4. O'Brien (1993) 77.

5. For example, Whitman (1970) 39.

6. Eliade (1961) 123 offers an interesting suggestion: it is only among Indo-Europeans that the 'binding' complex is originally integrated into the structure of 'terrible' sovereignty, both divine and human. In the *Enuma Elish* 1.60-74, Ea binds the primordial monsters Mummû and Apsû with a magic incantation, and then kills them.

7. All of these passages use the word δεσμός with special significance, especially in the case of Andromache's hair-band: δεσμός signifies her peaceful domestic world, since it is used when women do domestic work (schol. bT ad 22.468), whereas κρήδεμνον (22.470) signifies her outer world (and chastity, see Nagler [1967] 299), since it is used when women go outdoors. Accordingly when Andromache throws off both her δεσμός and κρήδεμνον at Hector's death, it signifies the destruction of her whole life, both internal and external, domestic and social.

8. Slatkin (1991) 67 notes that binding is a primary way of asserting divine sovereignty over a potential or actual challenger. See also n. 6 above.

9. Détienne and Vernant (1978) 72-3 note that no mention of binding is offered as long as the story remains on the cosmological level of the relationship between Gaia and Uranus.

10. Edwards (1991) 189.

11. Austin (1966) 309.

12. Hephaestus' laying down his tools in the middle of his task may also signify the enormity of the debt he owes to Thetis, who rescued him.

13. The scholiast is quite right to note the significance of the unfinished work, although the aspect emphasised (the sense of joy in schol. bT, as just mentioned) is different from mine.

14. West (2001a) 191-2 suspects 5.338 for the following reasons: (a) Aphrodite's wound is in her hand, which would not be covered by her *peplos*; (b) 'through her robe' in 338 looks like an afterthought, coming as it does after the mention of the wounding of her hand and the piercing of her skin; (c) the line interrupts the description of the flesh-wound; (d) neglect of digamma of the pronoun οἱ. I regard reasons (a) to (c) as unconvincing: (a) the *peplos* could cover the 'base of the hand' (πρυμνὸν ὕπερ θέναρος, 339, Kirk (1990) ad loc.), since it is nearer to the arm than to the fingers; (b) the description of the *peplos* (or a brief digression on *peplos*) is unlikely to be an 'afterthought'; (c) the effect of the digression is to intensify the significance of the event, although it seems to interrupt the account; cf. Austin (1966) 306.

15. Willcock (1978) ad loc. suggests that this story is a Homeric invention; but I agree with Kirk (1990) ad loc. that it is unlikely. However, Kirk comments that this is too bizarre to be a plausible Homeric invention. I do not believe that whether or not a story is bizarre is a criterion. There are other stories of this sort: for

example, Laomedon threatens to bind Poseidon and Apollo's feet and hands, and even to lop off their ears (*Il.* 21.453-5).

16. For example, van der Valk (1949) 189 argues that Aristarchus' athetesis is prompted by his 'prosaic mentality'; Hayman (1873) ad loc. suggests that the legend originated from a pre-Hellenic nature-myth; see also Heubeck and Hoekstra (1989) ad loc.

17. Kirk (1990) ad *Il.* 5.385-7.

18. However, Ap. *Bibl.* 1.6.1-2 narrates that the Gigantes are large and powerful with long hair and beards and scaly snakes for lower limbs. Gantz (1993) 477 notes that Hellenistic and later writers commonly confuse Titans and Gigantes. West (1966) ad *Theog.* 50 comments that, in Homer, the Gigantes occupy an intermediate position between men and gods, like the Laestrygonians (*Od.* 10.120). For the ambivalent relation between the Gigantes and men, see Chapter V, Section 1.

19. Although it is impossible to get rid of speculative factors, the following are possible reasons for assuming that these passages refer to a single event. First, both are characterised as transgressors of the moral, ritual and spiritual limits of their station. The race of Gigantes is called ἀτάσθαλον in *Od.* 7.60, and this is precisely how Otus and Ephialtes behave in *Od.* 11.305-20: although they are mortal, they bind a god and attempt to ascend to heaven. Secondly, both accounts refer to the lineage of Poseidon: Otus and Ephialtes are sons of Poseidon (11.306-8), while Eurymedon is Poseidon's father-in-law (his daughter Periboia married Poseidon, 7.56-8). Thirdly, Apollo kills members of both groups: Otus and Ephialtes were killed by him (11.318-20), and Rhexenor, fourth generation after Eurymedon, was killed by Apollo (7.63-4). Of course, as Apollo is involved in many human deaths, particularly untimely ones, this could also be a conventional expression for such a death. When we link these two stories (7.58-60 and 11.305-20) with the story of the binding of Ares (*Il.* 5.385-91), a picture of the Gigantomachy could emerge. Eurymedon was the leader of the Gigantes; Otus and Ephialtes bound Ares; Otus and Ephialtes almost succeeded in ascending to heaven, but were too young to do so and were killed by Apollo; Eurymedon and his people were finally defeated by the gods.

20. For example, in Pseudo-Nonnus (*Or.* 4), Ares' battle with them could be read as a separate expedition; in Stephanus (*Ethnica* 168) the battle is located in Crete; and Apollodorus (*Bibl.* 1.7.4) locates their death on Naxos.

21. Isocrates (10.52) and Diodorus (4.15.1) regard all the Olympian gods as united on Zeus' side in the Gigantomachy. However, if we accept that the story of Ares' binding is an event from the Gigantomachy, then we might suggest that the gods fight with each other (as is narrated in general terms at *Il.* 5.383-4).

22. Apollo avoids fighting Poseidon in *Iliad* 21.461-7, saying that οὐκ ἄν με σαόφρονα μυθήσαιο / ἔμμεναι, εἰ δὴ σοί γε βροτῶν ἕνεκα πτολεμίξω / δειλῶν (21.462-4). But they do fight each other in *Il.* 20.54-74; 21.342-520. Cf. Chapter III, Section 3 below.

23. O'Brien (1993) 100. Also Willcock (1984) ad loc. comments that this is a similar form of punishment to that of a Roman slave, hung with heavy weights on his feet as in Plautus' *Asinaria* 301-5.

24. West (1966) ad *Theog.* 722 suggests that ἄκμων is a meteorite. He points out that an ἄκμων is made of bronze, while meteorites are a compound of iron, nickel and stones, but at an earlier stage, people surely could not distinguish bronze from nickel. Janko (1992) ad loc. suggests that being tied with ἄκμονες means that Hera is lashed by thunderbolts, which was what meteorites were thought to be.

25. Or Hephaestus might have tried to stop Zeus from punishing Hera. Whichever the case might be, this seems to be another example of generational strife. In Book 18, Hera is responsible for the fall (18.396). Braswell (1971) 20 suggests that the story in Book 1 came from some pre-Homeric myth, and Homer invented (or modified) the story in Book 18 in order to make Thetis the rescuer, thus providing her with a claim on Hephaestus.

26. The release of Prometheus is not made clear in the *Theogony*. Hesiod does not say that Heracles released Prometheus from chains, but only that he killed the eagle (527). Prometheus is still bound in 616. For further discussion see West (1966) ad 523-33, and Chapter V below.

27. In this version of the myth, Hephaestus was crippled at birth. Hera was disgusted with him, and threw him down from heaven into the sea. After staying in the sea with the Nereids for years, and developing his skills, Hephaestus sent his mother a chair with hidden bonds. See further Pind. fr. 283; Paus. 1.20.3.

28. As the picture on the François Vase (Florence, Mus. Arch. 4209) shows, Aphrodite might have been the reward, instead of Athena, because Aphrodite emerges at the centre of the composition in front of Zeus. See further Gantz (1993) 75-6. Hera also offers a chair, which was made by Hephaestus, as the reward to Hypnus (*Il.* 14.267-8) and, after his refusal, she persuades him by promising the hand of the Grace (Charis) Pasithea (*Il.* 14.267-8). This arrangement has interesting connotations, since the Charites are the handmaidens of Aphrodite. For the interrelation between Hephaestus and Hypnus with a chair and the marriage to a goddess as the rewards, see Janko (1992) ad 14.256-61.

29. *P.Oxy.* 670, ed. Grenfell and Hunt.

30. West (2001b) 1-11.

31. West (2001b) 5.

32. West (2001b) suggests that ἡμέτεροι (l. 19) is not 'of ours', which would not suit Dionysus, but 'of mine', which is a frequent Homeric use.

33. West (2001b) 6.

34. Janko (1992) ad loc. comments that this phrase provokes suspense by making clear that his intervention cannot last. Cf. Chapter III, Section 1.

35. Janko (1992) ad loc.

36. In the Titanomachy, too, the Titans are on high Othrys, and Zeus and other gods fight from Mount Olympus (*Theog.* 629-33). For the antagonism between Zeus and Poseidon, see Chapter III.

37. In the *Theogony*, Zeus is the youngest (ὁπλότατον παίδων ἤμελλε τεκέσθαι, 478), although he is born first. See further Chapter III.

38. These Homeric genealogies fit well with the legendary accounts of Heracles' activities: Heracles' son Tlepolemus of Rhodes and his grandsons Pheidippus and Antiphus of Cos fight against Laomedon's son Priam and grandson Hector. See further Craik (1980) 165.

39. Sherwin-White (1978) 48.

40. P.Köln III 126. Lloyd-Jones & Parsons (1983) 406-7. The epic is quoted in a fragment of Apollodorus' Περὶ θεῶν.

41. Sherwin-White (1978) 48 n. 96 suggests the Hellenistic date because, first, in line 42 the ancient commentator says ἐδόκει δέ μοι τὰ ποιήμα[τα] νεωτέρου τινὸς εἶναι, and, secondly, the pervasive Homeric influence in the poem is a Hellenistic imitation.

42. Janko (1992) ad 14.250-61. Lloyd-Jones (1984) 145-50 discusses the diction and style of the epic and concludes that it dates from the archaic period, pointing

out that οἱ νεώτεροι means, for ancient Homeric scholars, 'poets later than Homer'. Kramer et al. (1978) 24 suggest a date in the second half of the sixth century.

43. For the Meropes as the Gigantes, see Janko (1992) ad 14.250-61.

44. Janko (1992) ad 14.250-61 holds that Asterus must be the same as Asterius.

45. Lloyd-Jones (1984) 144. He also refers to *Il.* 5.311-12, where Aphrodite protects Aeneas from the attack by Diomedes.

46. Kirk (1990) ad loc.

47. Louden (1993) 182-4 calls this type of Homeric narrative technique (i.e. 'and now X would have happened, had not Y intervened') 'pivotal contrafactuals', and he analyses its advantages as (a) emphasising the change of direction of the plot; (b) heightening the narrative in various ways by additional means of emphasis; (c) making an editorial comment on a particular character.

48. Merkelbach's supplement.

49. After 65, the poem immediately changes the subject to Mestra and Sisyphus. Since there is no link to what precedes or follows, Gantz (1993) 446 suggests that the whole of line 65 might be an interpolation. However, the transition is not unacceptable, because the *Catalogue* typically makes abrupt switches of this kind.

50. Janko (1992) ad 14.250-61. Pindar also mentions that Heracles conquered the Gigantes (*Nem.* 7.90).

51. See Janko (1992) ad 14.250-61.

52. According to Apollodorus (1.6.1), mentioned above, Earth tried to prevent the Gigantes from being destroyed. Thinking of the chthonic nature of Hera (*H. Apol.* 340), it is well understandable that she stands on the side of the Gigantes in the Gigantomachy.

53. *The Theogony* (950-55) narrates that Heracles acquired his divine status after his death, and married Hebe the daughter of Zeus and Hera. This story might imply that Heracles was finally reconciled with his stepmother. One might also recall the story of Heracles' infancy (in Ps-Eratosthenes, *Cat.* 44; Lycophron 38-9, 1327-8), that he was once nursed at the breast of Hera; and that the archetype of Heracles was the vegetation god, controlled under the power of the Earth Mother, of which features Hera strongly inherited. The story of the birth of Heracles mentioned in *Il.* 19.95-133 also alludes to the intricate relation between Hera and Heracles.

54. Dindorf (1875) ad 14.295 (MS A) records this variant: Eurymedon raped Hera while she was still being nurtured by her parents, and she became pregnant and bore Prometheus: Ἥραν τρεφομένην παρὰ τοῖς γονεῦσιν εἰς τῶν Γιγάντων Εὐρυμέδων βιασάμενος ἔγκυον ἐποίησεν, ἡ δὲ Προμηθέα ἐγέννησεν. Cf., similarly, Helmut van Thiel's text of the D-scholia.

55. Strabo (10.5.16) offers two versions of the death of Polybotes: he lies beneath either Nisyros or Cos.

56. At 7.452-3, Poseidon says that he and Apollo built the Trojan wall, while at 21.448-9 Apollo tended Laomedon's herds. Kirk (1990) ad 7.443-63 comments that 7.443-63 is an addition, developed not by Homer but by another ἀοιδός. However, I agree with Richardson (1993) ad 21.441-57 who suggests that it is hardly a serious contradiction.

57. Fontenrose (1959) 367 n. 3 gives several forms of Telphousa's name: Telphus(s)a, Tilphus(s)a, Tilphos(s)a, Telphusia, Thelpusa, Tilphos(s)ia.

58. See further Chapter VI.

59. Fontenrose (1959) 395: Heracles used this horse, Areion, in his race with Cycnus.

60. The custom at Onchestus is unclear. AHS (1936) ad *Hymn. Apol.* 231-8 gives several explanations such as the custom of 'a rule of the road' or the horse-race.

Janko (1986) 43 refers to the scholion to *Aspis* 105, which explains Poseidon's epithet ταύρεος from the sacrifice of bulls in Onchestus.

61. Other evidence of Poseidon's chthonic nature: Ge (Chthonia) and Poseidon once held the oracle in partnership in Delphi; and, beside the altar of Poseidon in Apollo's temple in Delphi, is the hearth altar, called *eschara* or *hestia*, which is associated with the worship of heroes and chthonic powers. See further Fontenrose (1959) 394, 397.

62. Whitman (1970) 37-9, followed by Richardson (1975) 70-1; and O'Brien (1993) 101.

63. O'Brien (1993) 101-3 suggests that the battle in which Hera and Hephaestus formed an alliance was against a river god (21.331-41). However, her interpretation does not fit – the account in the *Iliad* is that Hera was punished for her contrivance against Heracles. Moreover, it is unthinkable that Hera and Hephaestus would have received such punishment after a battle against a river god who does not seem to concern Zeus seriously.

64. For example, Stanford (1947) ad 7.59. Erbse (1986) 18-21 notes that the role of Hypnus in the Heraclean story (*Il.* 14.242-68) is an invention of the poet, but offers no conclusions as to the existence of the Gigantomachy.

65. Janko (1992) ad 14.250-61.

66. West (1966) ad loc. leaves the problem open, noting that Hesiod may be imagining something like his own Myth of the Ages (109ff.), where the bronze generation possess several characteristics shared with the Gigantes; but this view does not seem convincing.

67. ed. Allen (1912) 144-7.

68. Huxley (1969) 105-6 gives a summary of this epic: Heracles defeated Eurytus, king of Oechalia, in an archery contest; he therefore claimed the promised prize, the king's daughter, Iole or Ioleia; when Eurytus refused to hand her over, Heracles sacked the city, slew Eurytus, and took Iole captive. Creophylus of Samos was believed to be the composer of this epic, but his date is unknown. For the testimonia on Creophylus, see *PEG* 157-64. For the text and testimonia for *Oechaliae Halosis*, see *EGF* 149-53.

69. Nagy (1979) 165.

70. Edwards (1991) ad loc.

71. For the further discussion on the antagonism between Zeus and Poseidon, see Chapter III.

72. O'Brien (1993) 174.

73. Gantz (1993) 61.

III. The Reordering of the Universe

1. The *Odyssey* is quite different: harmony prevails in the council of the gods, and procedure in the council is quiet and orderly. However, it is worth noting that they decide on Odysseus' return in the absence of Poseidon (*Od.* 1.22).

2. Cf. Griffin (1980a) 162, 'the Homeric epics are poems about the actions and doom of heroes, but we see everything in them falsely if we did not see it against the background of the gods and of the dead'.

3. Andersen (1990) 30.

4. Andersen (1990) 43 n. 30.

5. For example, as Griffin (1980b) 25 writes, although Homer suppressed the hostility of Hera and Athena to Troy, which was connected with the story of the Judgment of Paris, he retained the hostility of the two goddesses.

6. Ares wishes to challenge Zeus (15.113-18), but is immediately checked by Athena (15.121-41). See further Section 2 of this chapter.

7. Janko (1992) ad 358-60.

8. Janko (1992) ad 13.1-3 writes that ὄσσε φαεινώ recurs five times, only in Books 13-21. This proves that the dangerous tension among the gods is increasing towards the Theomachy in Books 20-1. Cf. Sections 2 and 3 of this chapter.

9. Cf. Chapter II, Section 2, n. 34.

10. Janko (1992) ad 13.10-38 notes that the description emphasises Poseidon's purpose and the importance of his arrival, and expresses his three main attributes: earth-shaker, horse-god and sea-god.

11. Compare the description of Athena's preparations at *Il.* 5.733-42 and 8.384-91, where armour, car (horses), whip and spear are mentioned. As these examples demonstrate, the description of arming can be regarded, on the one hand, as formulaic; but on the other hand, each episode has, in itself, a coherent artistic function. Janko (1992) ad 13.21-2 comments that here Poseidon's preparation stresses the idea of imperishability; it also makes the scene glitter. I examine the significance of Athena's preparation in Chapter IV, Section 3.

12. Reinhardt (1961) 279: 'der Gebieter rüstet sich zu seinem Unternehmen wie ein Held zu seinen Aristien'.

13. Leaf (1960) ad loc. denounces this speech as too long, tautological and ill-suited to its position. I consider that this speech becomes significant when viewed from the perspective of Poseidon's antagonism toward Zeus, and is appropriate to the sub-textual context (the war of the gods).

14. Janko (1992) ad loc. comments that this verb is used in the context of 'thirst' in 22.2; 'ship' in *Od.* 14.383; and 'error' in Hdt. 1.167. Leaf (1960) ad loc., following schol. bT ad loc., suggests that 'the obvious reference of this line is to Achilles'. Leaf's interpretation ignores an essential logic: Poseidon encourages the Achaeans to fight bravely even if Achilles is absent.

15. Willcock (1984) ad loc.

16. Cf. a similar phrase in 10.224-5, 'If two go together, one is quicker than the other to see how it is advantageous. Even if a man on his own may see it, his mind is less significant than two, and his resource is weak'. See further Janko (1992) ad 13.237-8.

17. Zeus' isolation and the alliance of the other gods are sometimes mentioned, for example, at 8.210-11; 15.84-5; 15.106; 15.213-17, as discussed below.

18. Willcock (1984) ad loc. explains the two Homeric methods of fighting: close combat, in which the necessary qualities were physical strength, mental endurance and good weapon skill; and, more open fighting, with some fleeing and others pursuing, in which speed of foot was the foremost requirement.

19. For the age of Zeus and Poseidon, see n. 28 below.

20. Edwards (1991) ad 20.31-74 and 67-74 discusses the usual structure of battle. Although he believes that no 'proper' duel occurs in the battle of gods, I propose that this tug-of-war between Zeus and Poseidon functions as a duel in the first stage of the war between the gods.

21. The cord/rope is given different descriptions: in the tug-of-war in Book 8, the rope is σειρή (8.19 and 25), in Book 13, πεῖραρ (13.359). For σειρή and δεσμός, see Chapter II, Section 1.

22. In the variants of the proem of the *Iliad*, Apellicon's version does not mention the wrath of Achilles (Μούσας ἀείδω καὶ Ἀπόλλωνα κλυτότοξον). Aristoxenus' version offers the μῆνις and χόλος of Achilles, but more emphasis is given to Apollo than to Zeus. Cf. Kirk (1985) ad 1.1, who comments that a proem could

easily be varied from occasion to occasion to suit the audience or in accord with the length of the version to be presented.

23. Holoka (1983) 16 analyses the phrase ὑπόδρα ἰδὼν at 15.13, suggesting that it reasserts Zeus' superiority and his entitlement to deference from Hera.

24. Janko (1992) ad 15.72-3 writes that 'the hero's wrath and the god's are brought back into parallel'. For close discussion of the passages athetised by Aristophanes and Aristarchus (56-77) and Zenodotus (64-77), see Janko (1992) ad 15.56-77.

25. Janko (1992) ad loc. comments that 'the contrafactual conditional emphasises the gravity of the crisis'. He also notes the excitement that is so effectively expressed by *hysteron proteron* in 124.

26. Kirk (1990) ad loc. gives the etymology of this word: *ἀ- ϝεπτο- ϝεπής, 'speaking a word that should not be spoken'.

27. There are two variants (-ίζων Zenodotus; -ίξων Aristarchus). I follow West's new edition (2000). Janko (1992) ad loc. comments that the future is more minatory.

28. Zeus is the eldest in the *Iliad*, but the youngest in the *Theogony* (478). This shows the different usage of motifs between the two poems: for the poet of the *Iliad*, Zeus' seniority is an indispensable justification for Poseidon's surrender to him; for Hesiod, Zeus must be the youngest to fit in with the Hesiodic logic of succession in which the youngest son overthrows his father.

29. Cf. Chapter I, Section 1.

30. Burkert (1992) 90-1 discusses Babylonian influence (*Atrahasis* 43) on the Iliadic division of the cosmos. The obvious similarities between the *Iliad* and *Atrahasis* lie in (1) the division into heaven, sea and underworld (whereas in other old epics, the division is between heaven, earth and underworld, or heaven, sea and earth); and (2) the division is made by drawing lots.

31. In the *Theogony*, Zeus deprived Cronus of his βασιληίδα τιμήν (*Theog.* 462, 'honour of kingship').

32. Clay (1989) 12. For the idea of man's will and his lot, see Nilsson (1925) 169-70; Janko (1992) 4-7.

33. Achilles also demands an equal portion in accordance with his work (*Il.* 9.318-22), where he links μοῖρα and τιμή. Dietrich (1965) 209 suggests that Moira in 9.318 is equivalent to 'honour'. The words μόρος and αἶσα are usually understood in the original sense of 'portion', without any connotation of death or fate. See further Leaf (1960) ad 15.209.; Janko (1992) ad 15.209-11.

34. Dietrich (1965) 208.

35. I follow the reading of West (2000): γε Ar D; κε vulg.

36. Janko (1992) ad 15.206-8 and ad 16.49-63, following Lohmann (1970) 274, comments that Achilles' speech to Aias (9.644-55) follows the same pattern.

37. Aphrodite also feels αἰνὸν ἄχος (*Hymn. Aphr.* 198-9). It is worth noting that both Poseidon and Aphrodite surrender to Zeus' power, and both express the same emotion. See Chapter VII, Sections 1 and 2.

38. Allen (1920) and West (2000) read κε, meaning 'would have heard'. I follow Janko (1992) ad 15.224-5., with schol. D and most early codices, in reading τε, 'have experienced'.

39. Nilsson (1925) 159.

40. I agree with Nilsson (1925) 177, who writes that the legacy bequeathed by Homer to tragedy is the humanisation of the gods and the increasing relevance of myth to men.

41. Especially Griffin (1980a) 167, 189.

42. Zeus cannot alter the αἶσα of Sarpedon (16.441-2), nor can Hera change the αἶσα of Achilles (20.127-8). The day of one's death is determined at the day of birth (*Il.* 23.79), regardless of the gods' will. For the metaphor of 'spinning one's destiny', see Dietrich (1965) 290.

43. Griffin (1980a) 143.

44. Détienne and Vernant (1978) 75.

45. Griffin (1980a) 80.

46. I agree with Nilsson (1925) 155, who suggests that the spirit of partisanship affects all the gods, and that they pursue their ends by every means, including cunning and deceit.

47. Leaf (1960) 382 comments that the Theomachy passage in Book 21 is 'the anticlimax' and 'poetically bad'. Edwards (1991) ad 20.67-74 suspects that the passage [20.67-74] was 'added to the monumental poem at a later date', on the grounds of structure (there is no parallel to the listing of combatants in Homeric battle) and language (rare forms including Ἑρμῆς in 72). However, I agree with Richardson (1993) ad 21.383-513, who suggests that the account in 20.54-74 provides a frame for the battle in 21.383-513.

48. Edwards (1991) ad 54-66 comments that the involvement of sky, sea, earth and the underworld in the strife, and the shaking of the mountain beneath the feet of the combatants, echo a standard theme common in description of the Titanomachy.

49. Schol. BE ad *Od.* 8.77 comments that the quarrel is about the tactics to be used in sacking Troy: Achilles demands brave fighting (ἀνδρεία), and Odysseus supports contrivance (μηχανή). See Griffin (1980a) 183-4, who writes that Zeus is like one who enjoys the spectacle of others struggling and being humiliated for his own pleasure.

50. When Apollo accuses Hermes of the theft of his cattle, it is Zeus' laughter, not the scales of justice, which resolves the quarrel (*Hymn. Herm.* 324-89).

51. Aristarchus athetised 475-7 as being inconsistent with the character of Apollo at 468-9. Willcock (1977) 49-50 regards this passage as '*ad hoc* invention', asserting that, 'nothing at all makes it probable that Apollo should have made a practice of boasting in this way'. However, in view of the partisanship of the gods, it is highly probable that Apollo might have spoken thus.

52. For the good terms existing between Zeus and Apollo, see Chapter VI on the *Hymn to Apollo*, esp. Section 3. In the *Iliad*, too, Zeus and Apollo collaborate several times: for example, in 15.220-61, Apollo is sent by Zeus to rouse Hector's strength (232); and Hector is revived by Zeus' will (242); in 17.582-96, Apollo encourages Hector (582), and Zeus shakes the aegis to threaten the Achaeans (593-6). Significantly, Apollo shares the aegis with Zeus (15.229-30, 318-22; 24.20). Also in the *Odyssey* 11.305-20, Zeus' son Apollo defeats the Aloadae, who are Poseidon's sons.

53. For other examples, Hades goes back to Zeus' house after his fight with Heracles (5.398); Ares sits beside Zeus after he is hurt by Diomedes (5.869).

54. Notoriously, Zeus is twice described as 'husband of Hera' (πόσις Ἥρης, 7.411; 16.88).

55. Otto (1955) 31; see also Caldwell (1989) 161. Cf. Chapter IV, Section 2.

56. Griffin (1980a) 169-70 writes that the complex plan of Zeus, which involves helping Troy but not actually routing the Achaeans, leads to ambiguity.

57. Griffin (1980a) 102.

IV. The Birth of Athena

1. Solmsen (1949) 164.

2. It is generally accepted that there are clear similarities between Near Eastern and Greek theologies. See Walcot (1966) 1-54; Caldwell (1989) 80-1; Burkert (1992) passim; Graf (1993) 92-3; West (1997) 279-83.

3. Burkert (1992) 16-19 is persuasive in his discussion of 'orientalising works'; in particular, the bronze shields from the Idaean cave on Crete, some of which have an overtly Assyrian appearance.

4. The Hurrians were active from shortly after 2500 BC until the early centuries of the first millennium BC. The text of the kinship in Heaven is Hurrian, either translated straight into Hittite or freely adapted. Some of the divine names, such as Kumarbi, are Hurrian, while Alalu and Anu are Babylonian gods. See further Walcot (1966) 19-20. I use the translation of A. Goetze: *ANET* (1969) 120-1.

5. Burkert (1992) 94 also offers an interesting discussion on the collective idea of 'gods': in Hurrian myth, the Storm-god banishes Kumarbi and other 'ancient gods', which corresponds to Zeus' defeat of Cronus and the Titans as a collective entity. West (1997) 280 lists the similarities between the Hesiodic *Theogony* and the *Song of Kumarbi,* including that the deity named KA.ZAL issues from Kumarbi's skull, as Athena does from that of Zeus.

6. Solmsen (1989) 413 admits that there are differences, but thinks that they are only 'details' which are, according to him, due to the large number of intermediate stages.

7. For example, [Zeus] βίῃ καὶ χερσὶ δαμάσσας (490), [Cronus] νικηθεὶς ... βίηφί τε παιδὸς ἑοῖο (496).

8. Do they result from the influence of other myths, Hesiodic invention, or other factors? West (1966) ad 453-506 discusses the Near Eastern elements in the story of the birth of Zeus, and concludes that it is impossible to determine a direct relationship between the versions, and hard to say which is the original one.

9. Heidel (1951) 14 dates the original poem, in approximately its present form, to the First Babylonian Dynasty, 1894-1595 BC. But Walcot (1966) 33-9 re-examines the date of the tablets of the *Enuma Elish,* assigning it to 1100 BC. Pointing to the original 'loose end' of the epic, he suggests that Marduk, as the supreme god, might be a later development. Graf (1993) 90 also dates the epic around 1100 BC. West (1997) 282 points out that the *Enuma Elish* is not a theogony in the sense that it attempts a complete genealogy of the gods, as Hesiod does, but rather it is the story of how Marduk came to power.

10. How much of the *Enuma Elish* can be traced to Sumerian sources cannot to be ascertained, but some gods such as Apsu, Anu and Enlil are Sumerian. See further Heidel (1951) 12.

11. I use the translation of Heidel (1951) 1-60.

12. During the battle, Marduk and Tiâmat meet in single combat (Tablet IV, l.94). As Tiâmat is a goddess of the salt-sea ocean, the description of Marduk's fight against Tiâmat (flood) reminds us of Achilles' fight against the river god Xanthos (*Il.* 21.233-327). Thalmann (1984) 40 emphasises the parallel between the *Theogony* and the *Enuma Elish* in Marduk's ordering of the natural elements. For other comparisons between Iliadic cosmology and the *Enuma Elish,* see Burkert (1992) 92-4.

13. Walcot (1966) 33.

14. Cornford (1952) 248 offers the strongest argument for the similarity, concluding that Hesiod's cosmological myth is derived ultimately from the Babylonian – and the discrepancies are less striking than the coincidences; whereas

West (1997) 282 thinks that the parallelism with the Hesiodic narrative is not as close as in the case of the Hurro-Hittite account.

15. Solmsen (1949) 57. I also agree with Caldwell (1964) 186 who writes that 'Hesiod did not invent something entirely new'; cf. Walcot (1966) 31: 'Hesiod was a master and not the slave of the material at his command.'

16. Nagy (1990) 42.

17. Solmsen (1949) 59 suggests that the word, κευθμών, of Gaia, could be cosmological rather than physiological: Hesiodic Gaia is both the goddess *and* the earth as part of the cosmos.

18. I do not agree with Détienne and Vernant (1978) 61-2, who hold that Uranus is not considered to be a king, and that the theme of the competition for sovereignty is introduced from Cronus onwards.

19. West (1966) ad 463 comments that Uranus in this oracular passage appears merely as a complement to Gaia.

20. Lloyd-Jones (1970) ad loc. observes that the Delphic oracle had belonged to the Great Goddess who played an important part in Minoan and Mycenaean religions. Sommerstein (1989) ad loc. suggests reading 'the first oracular deity (at Delphi)' rather than 'the first to prophesy (anywhere)'. Paus. 10.5.5 also writes that Earth was the first possessor of Delphi.

21. As West (1966) ad 465 comments, Cronus was not told 'Zeus has a mind to overthrow you', only 'You will be overthrown by your own son': Διὸς μεγάλου διὰ βουλάς was not part of the original oracle, but Hesiod's explanation.

22. Caldwell (1989) 161.

23. Angier [Sowa] (1964) 340 notes the similarities and explains that they indicate oral variants of one type-scene. Thalmann (1984) 43-4 also points out the similar pattern of Gaia's role in the two passages, stressing the creation of expectation by the repeated motifs.

24. Zeitlin (1995) 61 and 67 thinks that Cronus' swallowing his children imitates pregnancy; consequently Zeus' triumph over Cronus represents the victory of the son over the father, and also the triumph of the father over the mother as a higher form of reproduction. Zeus' swallowing of Metis is a doubly significant event: Zeus also gains intelligence by swallowing her, as is discussed in the next section of this chapter.

25. Thalmann (1984) 42 admits that epithets are mostly conventional expressions, but also notes that 'the recurrence of these phrases (sc. epithets of μῆτις) in the *Theogony* is so persistent and patterned that Hesiod must surely be manipulating their sounds and meanings'.

26. In *Works and Days* 257, Hesiod, with the introduction of Dike as a new goddess, proclaims that Zeus' rule is one of justice. However, in the *Theogony*, Zeus' justice is not emphasised. For example, the story of Prometheus (535-69) shows that Prometheus, not Zeus, seems to have justice on his side. I do not follow Lloyd-Jones (1983) 35 who suggests that 'Cronus gave Zeus provocation, so Zeus overthrew Cronus; since then justice has sat beside his throne'. In the *Theogony*, the Hesiodic idea of justice seems to be expressed in the vengeance of Gaia. Gaia is also related to the Erinyes who ensure that no evil deed goes unpunished. Solmsen (1949) 26 offers the unique and unconvincing idea that a curse runs through the family of Zeus; see also Solmsen (1982) 4 n. 8.

27. According to the analysis of folktale by Propp (1968) 79-80, Gaia could be classified as 'the helper' who gives the solution to difficult tasks and helps the hero to move on to the next step in the narrative.

28. Typhon is a son of Hera in the *Homeric Hymn to Apollo* (349-52).

29. Stevenson (1992) 432 points out that, where superiority is established by force, its maintenance tends subsequently to become a matter of emphasising morality, legality, etc. I agree with Stevenson in general, but I do not think that Zeus' morality is emphasised here.

30. Clay (1989) 13 suggests that, after Zeus' victory over Typhoeus, Gaia finally admits defeat and renounces her opposition by advising Zeus of the danger involved in marriage to Metis. I think that Gaia's defeat is not necessarily implied by her advice, because the content of her advice is similar to that which she offered Cronus.

31. Zeus already has two children, Ares and Hephaestus, but the one is mentally immature and dangerously violent, the other is lame. Ares is despised by the other gods in the *Iliad*: e.g. 5.385-91, 846-98; 21.410-14; Athena says to him, μαινόμενε, φρένας ἠλέ (*Il.* 15.128); Hephaestus is mocked in the *Iliad* 1.597-600.

32. Austin (1989) 81.

33. In antiquity, the head is not the seat of cognition, so we must reject the Stoic interpretation of Athena's birth from the head of Zeus to signify that she is connected with intellect. Athena's intellect should be linked with Metis. See Pope (1960) 114.

34. Jacoby (1930) 41-2 marks lines 886-900 as an interpolation; Solmsen (1949) 67-8 rejects the passage because (a) Themis is Zeus' first wife in Pindar, (b) Zeus' giving birth to Athena from his head is inconsistent with Metis as her mother, and (c) Athena as daughter of Zeus and Wisdom appears to be later allegorical or semi-allegorical theology. West (1966) ad 886-900 suggests the possibility of interpolation, but leaves the question of authenticity open.

35. Schmid and Stählin (1929) 1.1.281; Cook (1940) 3.343-4; Brown (1952) 131. Thalmann (1984) 198 n. 22 persuasively refutes Solmsen's argument, pointing out that Solmsen is dependent on Pindar's account, but Pindar might have changed this traditional story to suit his own purposes. For the defence of the end of the *Theogony*, see also Janko (1992) 202.

36. Brown (1952) 142 concludes that the peculiar birth of Athena is a Hesiodic innovation. I admit that Athena's birth from Zeus' head is especially important for his rule, but it seems difficult to infer this story to be a Hesiodic invention *only* for that reason. The story of the birth of Athena should be considered together with two other peculiar births in the *Theogony*: Aphrodite, born from the sexual organs of Uranus, and Hephaestus, born from Hera without sexual union.

37. I agree with West (1966) ad 886-900, who regards this passage as 'a composite myth'. I cite the passage (895-98) later in this section.

38. Brown (1952) 134 suggests that the unnamed brother of Athena would be considered by Hesiod as a culture-hero type of god. I do not see any reason why the unborn son should be such, although, as Brown claims, in later myth the culture-hero types – Hephaestus, Hermes or Prometheus – attend Zeus' delivery with their axes.

39. One reason for the *Iliad's* silence about the story of Metis could be, of course, the physically abnormal event of Athena's birth from Zeus' head. Cf. Griffin (1977) 40-1 who suggests that bizarre features are not tolerated in Homer. Many scholars think that Homer knew the myth of Athena's birth (for example, Cook 1940: 3.737; Gantz 1993: 83), on the grounds that, when Ares reproaches Zeus for letting Athena do as she pleases, it is implied that Zeus does so because he bore her (σὺ [sc. Zeus] γὰρ τέκες ἄφρονα κούρην, 5.875). Brown (1952) 140 asserts the opposite: the text (5.875) *only implies* Zeus' paternal relationship to mankind.

40. Solmsen (1949) 68 n. 225; Brown (1952) 131 n. 3. The source of Chrysippus'

fragment as quoted by Galen is not known with any certainty. Solmsen (1982) 19-20, esp. n. 65, suggests the possibility that in Chrysippus' day there were copies of the *Theogony* which included the version of vv. 886-901, while others had the alternative Metis story. See also West (1966) ad 886-900.

41. Emended by Hermann, adopted by Evelyn-White. The reading of the Mss. is θεὰ παρέλεκτο Θέμις, in which case Themis made the aegis.

42. Kauer (1959) 42-3. I agree with Kauer's conclusion, although I do not follow some of her argument, as is discussed below.

43. Kauer (1959) 34-5.

44. Kauer (1959) 35 leaves it open as to which text is older. According to her, there are two possibilities: (a) both texts were composed by Hesiod; or (b) the fragment was composed by a minor rhapsode. Solmsen (1949) 68, n. 225 rejects the idea that Chrysippus quoted from a pre-Hesiodic epos. But the concept of 'interpolation' does not necessarily mean *only* that the interpolation is more recent than the main text.

45. The quarrel is related in the *Melampodia* (fr. 211a,b M [275 M-W]): Zeus and Hera had an argument about whether the man or the woman derived most pleasure from sexual intercourse. Teiresias judged that woman did: Hera was so angry that she struck him blind, and Zeus so pleased that he gave him the gift of prophecy. See West (1966) ad 886-900.

46. I do not follow Kauer (1959) 35, who suggests that the main purpose of Hesiod's changing the order (putting Athena's birth earlier than Hephaestus' birth from Hera) is to put more emphasis on Zeus' genealogy rather than on that of Hera. Caldwell (1989) 187 suggests that there is another significant Hesiodic innovation: making the threat to Zeus come not from his son but from the monster Typhoeus. Cf. Chapter VI, Section 2. However, I consider that the threat of an ambitious son prevails throughout Hesiod, and that the challenge of Typhoeus can also be read as an example of generational strife, since he is, in the *Theogony*, a son of Gaia – the grandmother of Zeus.

47. Cf. Chapter VI, Section 2.

48. I agree with Zeitlin (1995) 69 that genealogy is an effective means by which myth can posit a coherent scheme of relations and affinities.

49. The story of her unusual delivery was accepted by later poets: for example, Pindar (*Ol.* 7.33-9) and Aeschylus (*Eum.* 736-8). The importance of the father-daughter relationship of Zeus and Athena seems to have been widely recognised. In the earliest artistic representation of Athena's birth (a relief amphora from Tenos, dating to the first half of the seventh century), Zeus is attended by Eileithuia: the implication is that Zeus' own labour produces the birth. In Attic black-figure painting, the motif of Hephaestus' role became popular: Athena is released from the head of Zeus by the blow of an axe held by Hephaestus (or, sometimes, by Prometheus or Hermes). It is unclear how old the motif of Hephaestus' cleaving Zeus' head is. These paintings presuppose that the birth of Hephaestus is prior to that of Athena. Cf. *LIMC*, Athena 346, 347. For the Hurrian parallel (Kumarbi gives birth to KA.ZAL from his head), cf. n. 5 above.

50. Brown (1952) 134.

51. I do not agree with Caldwell (1989) 186-7, when he writes that Zeus is victorious because unlike Uranus and Cronus, he does not have the role of the archetypal father who suppresses his sons; that is, Zeus does not destroy Apollo, Ares or Hephaestus. Zeus, however, eliminates his potentially mighty son by swallowing Metis, which undoubtedly shows the archetypal aspect of his nature.

52. Caldwell (1989) 179.

53. Cf. Solmsen (1949) 67, who writes that the tale of Metis is the vehicle for a profound idea, inasmuch as Metis stands for wisdom.

54. Arthur (1983) 99.

55. Of course there are other important reasons for Zeus' success, for example his incorporation of intelligence by swallowing Metis: see Jeanmaire (1956) 18; Clay (1989) 13 and others. Also, Zeus' good relationship with the gods of the preceding generation: see Caldwell (1989) 181. However, from the *thematic* point of view, Athena's birth is one of the most important factors in his triumph.

56. Cf. Chapter VII, Section 3.

57. Harrison (1903) 303.

58. The form and use of the aegis is unclear. It has one hundred golden tassels (*Il.* 2.447-9) and is decorated with a Gorgon head (*Il.* 5.742). Kirk (1985) ad 2.446-51 comments that, from its etymology, it is probably a goat skin in some form. Fowler (1988) 112 suggests an association with rain-magic, because Zeus produces rain by shaking his aegis (*Il.* 17.593-6). Janko (1992) ad 15.308-11 comments that the word also means 'squall', and, also in its obvious sense, 'goatskin'; in the bards' imagination it is a primitive shield with a shaggy fringe. Gantz (1993) 84 submits that its primary use would not be as something worn for defence, but that, rather, it was held in the hands and shaken to terrify the enemy – as in *Il.* 15.229-30, 318-22; *Od.* 22.297-8.

59. Apollo is also associated with the aegis: on Zeus' suggestion Apollo uses it to frighten the Achaeans (15.229-30, 318-22) and to guard Hector's corpse when Achilles drags him (24.20-1).

60. Kirk (1990) ad 5.734-7 notes that this passage accords with *Il.* 8.374-6 where Athena enters Zeus' house to arm for war. Cf. Chapter III, Section 1, n. 13.

61. Athena also restrains Ares when he intends to join the war against Zeus' will (*Il.* 15.119-41).

62. Richardson (1993) ad loc. notes the resemblance of this passage to 7.264-5, where Hector hits Ajax with a similar stone. Kirk (1990) ad 7.264-5 suggests that the stone might be meteoritic, because of its colour and shape. Such stones, which may have been what were later understood to be meteorites, might have been thought of as thunderbolts. See Chapter II, n. 24 on ἄκμων, and also Janko (1992) ad 15.18-31.

63. Pope (1960) 125 notes that Zeus becomes far more impartial, dignified and remote, just as his dwelling-place on Olympus is no longer regarded as an earthly mountain.

64. Achilles: five times (1.74; 16.169; 18.203; 22.216; 24.472); Hector: four times (6.318; 10.49; 13.674); Odysseus: three times (10.527; 11.419, 473); once for Phyleus (2.628), Phoenix (9.168) and Patroclus (11.611).

65. Odysseus: thrice (*Il.* 2.169, 407, 636); Hector: twice (*Il.* 7.47 = 11.200).

66. Brown (1952) 135.

67. Jeanmaire (1956) 30-3 illustrates the genealogy of the royal family of Athens, which is strongly connected with professional craftsmen.

68. Pl. *Lg.* 796C: ἃ δὴ πάντως μιμεῖσθαι πρέπον ἂν εἴη κόρους τε ἅμα καὶ κόρας, τὴν τῆς θεοῦ χάριν τιμῶντας. According to Harrison (1903) 302, Athena is 'the incarnation of their life and being', and Shearer (1966) 16 puts it that Athena constantly works 'to redress the balance of power between Olympus and the human race'.

69. Sommerstein (1989) ad loc. offers three possible interpretations: (a) 'I am wholly my father's child; (b) 'I am wholly on the side of the father'; (c) 'I am a faithful follower of my father'.

70. Neils (2001) 229-31 discusses the vase paintings and the relief on the Parthenon which represent Athena and Zeus side by side in similar poses.

71. Cook (1940) 3.189 suggests that Athena might be a snake-goddess of the early Cretans and – in 3.748-9 – the pre-Greek mountain mother. He discusses (3.201-3) the presentation of Hephaestus and Athena as husband and wife in prehistoric times – local equivalents of Cronus and Rhea. In *LIMC* II, the strong linkage between Athena and snakes is noticed in her costume (171, 187, 194, 220, 267, 371, 429, 512, 518 etc.) and in her hair (315, 319, 328, 331 etc.)

72. The epithet Tritogeneia may indicate the existence of an old tradition of the birth of Athena from the sea, like the miraculous birth of Aphrodite. See Brown (1952) 143.

73. Campbell (1964) 149.

74. Slater (1968) 129 points out that Zeus' marital dominance is his major achievement. Cf. Thalmann (1984) 40, who writes that the marriages and children of Zeus characterise his rule.

75. Stevenson (1992) 429. He explains the typically political relationship among the Greeks (and Romans) as that of benefactor-beneficiary.

76. As Arthur (1983) 64 suggests, achieving the patriarchal form of the family is the teleological goal of the *Theogony*.

77. In Sophocles' *OC*, blind Oedipus is led by his daughter Antigone. This also seems to show that the ancient Greeks found their solution and consolation for the conflict between father (Laius) and son (Oedipus) in the relation between father and daughter.

78. Clay (1989) 9; Nagy (1979) 7; O'Brien (1993) 5. The earliest attestation of the word Πανέλληνες in the sense of 'all Greeks' is in Hesiod, *Works and Days* 528. West (1978) ad loc. comments that Homeric use of Ἑλλάς (*Il.* 2.530) denotes only the northern Greeks.

V. Prometheus, God of Forethought

1. West (1966) 307 comments that, 'what we have in Hesiod ... is a combination of three myths, all probably traditional, which could have been told separately'. Philips (1973) 293-4 suggests that the story of the division of the sacrifice belonged to a different story of Prometheus, and was in origin a local myth among the residents of Mecone. Vernant in Détienne and Vernant (eds) (1989) 22 writes that 'Hesiod stitched completely disparate elements together in the same text. To the traditional theme of the theft of fire he would have artificially connected an aetiological myth intended to account for what he found strange in sacrificing practice ... .' Kirk (1970) 271 writes that '... the Greek myths concerning Prometheus and especially the first woman strike me as curiously arbitrary in places'.

2. Philips (1973) 290.

3. Among the claims for the unity and coherence of the myth, see especially Vernant in Detienne and Vernant (eds) (1989) 22-3; Clay (2003) 101.

4. Zeitlin (1996) 72.

5. The aetiological value of the Mecone scene is unanimously recognised. It is obviously designed to provide an explanation for the Greek method of sacrificing an animal. A multiplicity of explanations for the meaning of the first sacrifice have been offered: for example, Burkert (1979) 52, 'according to the serious and outspoken belief of the Greeks, sacrifice is a way to deal with gods'; Vernant in Détienne and Vernant (eds) (1989) 25, 'each category of living creature has the food which

suits it and which it deserves'; Graf (1993) 182, 'it served to define the human condition'; Buxton (1994) 199, 'to follow the procedure inaugurated by Prometheus' founding act is to distinguish oneself ... from the beasts'.

6. Caldwell (1989) 93.

7. Graf (1993) 79.

8. Many features of Prometheus' myth suggest Oriental influence: see West (1966) 313; Kirk (1970) 237; Philips (1973) 292; Pucci (1977) 83; Burkert (1979) 80.

9. Griffin (1986) 17.

10. Zeitlin (1996) 82.

11. Thomson (1941) 317 suggests that the primitive nucleus of this myth is the idea that Prometheus brought fire down from the sun, stored in a stalk of fennel. For the similarities with a Sumerian Sun-God, see Section 2 below.

12. West (1966) ad loc. comments that the word 'belly' is used colloquially to imply hunger.

13. Vernant in Détienne and Vernant (eds) (1989) 60-7 discusses the significance of using the same word in the scene where the sacrifice is divided: mankind's share is wrapped in the ox's belly (καλύψας γαστρὶ βοείη 539).

14. Heracles is mentioned in the *Theogony* quite often: at 289, 315, 318, 332, 527, 530, 943, 951 and 982. This would be natural, because he is a son of Zeus and pre-eminent among all the other heroes. However, his stories are not narrated in detail, but rather mentioned briefly in only a few lines. One of the reasons for this could be Hesiod's attitude towards men, as discussed above: as Hesiod focuses on the powerlessness of men, detailed stories of such a strong hero as Heracles must be truncated.

15. West (1966) ad loc.

16. Clay (2003) 97-9, 113.

17. In the unidentified fragment of Greek lyric (*PMG* 985), the giant Alcyoneus, 'the oldest of the Gigantes', is included among those listed as being the first man. For the relation between the gigantes and men, see Chapter II, Section 1, n. 18.

18. Hamilton (1989) 34 writes that 'mankind's interests are central to the story. Men are integral to all parts of the story.'

19. West (1966) ad loc.

20. The other two sons of Iapetus are also punished by Zeus: Menoetius is struck by Zeus' thunderbolt and sent to Erebus (514-16); Atlas must hold up the heaven with his head and hands (517-18, 746-8). It is not clear from the text of the *Theogony* whether their punishment is related to the Titanomachy or not.

21. The authenticity of the *P.V.* has been much debated since 1856, when Rossbach-Westphal first raised the problem. I do not deal with this problem, and by 'Aeschylus' I mean the 'authour of the *P.V.*' throughout this chapter. For the detailed discussions on the authenticity of the play, see Griffith (1977).

22. Solmsen (1949) 127-30.

23. For example, Hamilton (1989) 39: 'the movement of the work is toward the Titanomachy in the main narrative, and backward away from it to the beginning in the digressions'; also Clay (2003) 100.

24. Lamberton (1988) 87 writes that 'the passage [of the myth of Prometheus] constitutes a sort of window within the larger generational narrative, looking out on a brutal but familiar world decidedly different from the stage of the larger narrative'.

25. The similarities of the stone and the first woman Pandora are often pointed out: Arthur (1982) 72 writes that both are the symbol of the intersection between natural and artificial creation, and between the divine and human realms; Zeitlin

184

(1996) 81 persuasively develops her idea that both are substitutes (the stone is a substitute for Zeus, Pandora a substitute for the stolen fire). Moreover, both are remarkably described as θαῦμα (500; 588).

26. The implication of 527-8 (releasing Prometheus from anxiety) would be that he is freed from the eagle, but not from bondage. See p. 109 and n. 36 below.

27. Hamilton (1989) 40 writes that, in the Proem of the *Theogony*, Hesiod offers us the chronologically latest point (sc. the account of the Muses in Hesiod's own age) at the beginning; so, the beginning is also the end. This technique could be compared to that of the *Iliad* and the *Odyssey*, where the starting points of the epics are chronologically near the end of the story. For the general arrangement of the genealogies in the *Theogony*, see West (1966) 37-9.

28. West (1966) ad loc. explains βουλὰς as 'designs', pointing out that Prometheus tried to fulfil designs which conflicted with those of Zeus.

29. Cf. West (1978) ad 99 of the *Works and Days*: he translates βουλῇσι Διός as 'by the will of Zeus', which illustrates the way in which the plural can have a meaning very similar to the singular.

30. For example, Wirshbo (1982) 107.

31. Philips (1973) 292 adds an interesting note (n. 10) that in the *Enuma Elish* there is a celebration feast of the gods shortly after the creation of man. West (1966) ad loc. also comments that the word denotes a 'settlement' in the legal sense.

32. Stoddard (2004) 103 suggests the latter would be the better interpretation, as the plural form of ἄναξ seldom means gods in Homer and Hesiod. She also notes that Zeus' insult, which is disguised as a compliment, exactly corresponds to Prometheus' offer of a dishonourable portion inadequately disguised as an honourable one.

33. West (1966) ad loc. writes that this is quite typical of Hesiod who inserts the comment to save Zeus' omnipotence and prestige. Clay (2003) 111-13, however, claims that Zeus did see through the contents of the two portions and consciously chose the white bones in order to bring about the separation of gods and men. I do not find Clay's argument very convincing because it cannot explain why Zeus got angry when he found that he had taken the worse portion (554). The logic of the story here seems to demand perhaps that Zeus is deceived.

34. Stoddard (2004) 102 n. 6 comments that, like Zeus, man has no choice when taking a wife: the one who refuses to take a wife (remaining childless) fares as badly as the man who marries.

35. West (1966) ad loc. translates this verse as 'So you are even now intent on trickery'. G.M. Most, in the Loeb edition, translates 'So you did not forget your deceptive craft after all'.

36. Thus the mention of 'releasing Prometheus from anxiety' (527-8) should be understood to mean that he is freed from the eagle but not from bondage.

37. As is well known, this is the most striking difference between Hesiod and Aeschylus. In the *P.V.* of Aeschylus, Prometheus knows a momentous secret, which is enough to serve for his releasing by reciprocity. See Solmsen (1949) 128-9; Caldwell (1989) 170. Slatkin (1991) 75-7 discusses the possibility that the story of Thetis' secret power was known to the poet of the *Iliad*.

38. Chantraine (1968) II.940, s.v. προμηθής.

39. Frisk (1970) II.599, s.v. προμηθής.

40. Chadwick (1976) 86 also explains that Zeus is known as *dyaus pitar* in Vedic, exactly as *Iuppiter* in Latin incorporates the word for 'father'.

41. Ibid. 86-7.

42. Ibid. 86.

43. Roscher (1908) col. 3033-4. Bapp also suggests the Sanscrit *pramantha* as the origin of the name Prometheus, which means 'stalk holder', indicating the stalk of the fennel in which Prometheus concealed the fire; but he himself writes that this etymology is unlikely.

44. This might give a deeper significance to the non-naming of Prometheus in the Proem of the *Theogony*, when there is a puzzle of why Iapetus is named but not Prometheus.

45. Burkert (1979) 80.

46. For the primitive nucleus of the Prometheus myth, see Thomson (1941) 317 (cited in n. 11 above).

47. West (1966) ad 511 points out that the name Epimetheus is evidently invented as the opposite of Prometheus, 'Afterthought' as opposed to 'Forethought'. See also Détienne and Vernant (1978) 18; Gantz (1993) 40.

48. Détienne and Vernant (1978) 18.

49. Prometheus is characterised by late Greek authors as the great benefactor of mankind, and is praised as the inventor of human technology, but this reflects the subsequent reception of his myth, strongly affected by the *P.V.* of Aeschylus.

50. Caldwell (1989) 90 discusses how the myths of Prometheus and Tantalus are virtual duplicates of each other.

51. Pindar says that people are called λαοί, because they are made out of stone (λᾶας, pl. λᾶες), which is surely a false etymology.

52. For other references to the creation of the human race by Prometheus see, for example, Ovid (*Met.* 1.82-8); Lucian (*Dialogi Deorum* 5.5); Pausanias (10.4.4); Juvenal (*Sat.* 14.35); Hyginus (*Fab.* 142); Libanius (*Orat.* 25.31).

53. Dunbar (1995) 430.

54. Philips (1973) 304 also suggests that two incidents, the sacrifice at Mecone and the creation of a woman, are recent additions which Hesiod may have incorporated into the basic plot.

55. Among the many explanations of Pandora's story, the discussions of Gow (1913) 99-109, Philips (1973) 303-4 and Zeitlin (1996) 61-83 seem to me the most instructive and important. For the gender problems in this story, see Arthur (1982) 75-6. For Pandora as an earth-goddess, the article of Harrison (1900) 106-8 remains useful.

56. For classification of the explanations of ἐλπίς, see Gow (1913) 102-3 and Verdenius (1971) 225-6.

57. For example, Pucci (1977) 103 writes that 'we read Zeus' desire for Elpis to remain in the jar as an act that enables man to endure a situation otherwise insufferable'.

58. Gow (1913) 103 points out that the error into which many critics have fallen is that they do not observe that when the lid of the jar was replaced, Elpis was withheld from man.

59. For the interpretation of ἐλπίς at *Works and Days* 96, see Verdenius (1971) 230.

60. West (1978) ad 96 points out the good and bad meanings of the word, suggesting that ἐλπίς in a neutral context, usually implies hope/expectation of good things. But he goes on to stress the dangerous nature of ἐλπίς, which can be bad in the effects that it has. Most (2006) translates as 'anticipation', with a note (n. 7) that 'the Greek word can mean anticipation of bad as well as of good things'.

61. For the other examples of 'bad anticipation' in the *Iliad*, 7.353; 15.110; 16.281; 17.239.

62. There are no examples of ἐλπίς (as a noun) in the *Iliad*. In thirty-one examples of the verb related to this word (ἔλπομαι), it is hard to tell the distinction between 'to anticipate' and 'to foresee'. However, three examples, which are related to the fate of the individuals concerned, are rather like the usage of foreseeing: 15.288, 504; 21.605.

63. Griffith (1983) ad 250. In the later tradition, hopes are typically deceptive or vain (Semonides fr. 1.7W; Solon fr. 13-36W; Pind. *Nem.* 8.45; Aesch. *Per.* 804). For other later references on hope, see West (1978) ad 96; Griffith (1983) ad 250.

64. This verse is omitted in the pseudo-Plutarchean *Consolatio ad Apollonium*, whereas it is presupposed by sch. vet. on 96, and present in *P41* as well as all medieval manuscripts. I agree with West (1978) ad loc. who takes this verse to be genuine.

65. Griffith (1983) 2.

66. Detienne and Vernant (1978) 90.

67. In the *Odyssey*, Iasion was struck down by Zeus with a thunderbolt while he lay with Demeter in a thrice-ploughed field. In the story of the Mother Goddess and her lover, we perceive the pattern in which the Goddess mourns the loss of a loved one, goes on a search, and brings about a form of resurrection. See further Leeming (1990) 134-5.

68. Thomson (1941) 318.

VI. Typhon, Son of Hera

1. Many German critics have argued the separatist view. The earlier history of criticism of the hymn is in Drerup (1937) 81-99; a thorough account of the views on this problem is in Förstel (1979) 20-59.

2. For example, West (1975) 161-5 argues that the poets of D. and P. are different, because of their different geographical outlook and stylistic differences, such as neglect of initial digamma, but that there is a 'conspicuous parallelism' between their opening sections. West (2003) 9-12 analyses the construction and the composition of the hymn; on his analysis, the Pythian hymn is the older of the two (early sixth century BC), and Cynaethus composed the Delian part half a century later, then combined them with some arrangements for the festival on Delos in 523 BC under the leadership of Polycrates. According to Janko (1982) 103-4, dividing the hymn at line 178 commands general acknowledgement, because lines 177-8 are a normal conclusion to a complete hymn, and the geographical outlook and religious interests of the two sections differ profoundly; however, the two parts of the hymn came to be coupled together by Cynaethus who was responsible for the epic performance at Polycrates' grand Delian and Pythian festival. In his review of Clay in *CR* 41 (1991) 12-13, he adopts a more unitarian position. Sowa (1984) 173 and 183 admits religious, linguistic and formulaic differences, but from the point of view of thematic analysis, suggests that the poem presents a continuous unity. Burkert (1979) 61 notes that the Delian-Pythian festival of Polycrates at Delos in 522 BC presented an appropriate context for a combined Delian-Pythian hymn to Apollo, and suggests that a Homerid from Chios in fact composed or arranged the text.

3. Penglase (1994) 117, following Miller (1986) xi.

4. Allen and Sikes (1904) 82 and 113 note that line 114 is perhaps echoed at *Av.* 575, and line 443 at *Eq.* 1016.

5. For arguments on the interpolation see Allen and Sikes (1904) 65; cf. Clay (1989) 64.

6. For example, Janko (1982) 116 describes it as 'clumsy'.

7. As Segal (1971) 5-6 suggests, 'the repetitions allow the parallels or divergences of situation to clarify and develop.'

8. Fontenrose (1959) 468 writes that 'the Telphousa of the *Homeric Hymn to Apollo* is a double of the dragoness'.

9. Clay (1989) 60 notes that 'the spot he (Apollo) finally elects for his sanctuary has no natural attraction', being different from Telphousa's place. She ignores the fact that καλλίρροος qualifies both springs.

10. Schol. D ad *Iliad* 23.346 gives the story that Poseidon was married to Erinys in the shape of a horse by the spring of Telphousa. Janko (1986) 54-5 suggests that Telphousa was once Erinys in the Boeotian version of the myth, and Apollo's treatment of Telphousa symbolises, first, the antagonism between Apollo and Poseidon, and, second, the religious and political depreciation of Thebes. Cf. n. 34.

11. Strab. Fr. 1a Meineke: 'The oracle of Zeus at Dodona answered by signs rather than by inspired speech.'

12. Thalmann (1984) 1 aptly points to a similar all-encompassing dualism (that of barbarism versus civilisation) in the *Odyssey*: 'each (the two extremes of the Phaeacians and the Cyclopes) seems necessary to the other, not only for the sake of mutual characterisation, but also so that together they may give shape to what lies between them'.

13. Austin (1966) 303 remarks that 'a past occurrence is used not merely as an edifying example but as positive proof of a present possibility'.

14. Especially, Aeschylus *Eum.* 1-8, the transfer of the oracle's ownership from Gaia to Themis to Phoibe to Apollo; Euripides *I.T.* 1245-7, Themis protected by the dragon. Sommerstein (1989) ad Aesch. *Eum.* 1-2 comments that the first oracular deity at Delphi is Gaia. Cf. Chapter IV, n. 20.

15. Sourvinou-Inwood (1991) 231 writes that this is the model of a violent take-over leading to a higher order. Clay (1989) 62 also points out that 'by ignoring Delphic tradition and denying any continuity or connection between Apollo's establishment and a prior prophetic seat on the same spot, the hymn proclaims Apollo's oracle to be a uniquely Olympian institution and an essential component of the Olympian dispensation.' Conversely, Alcaeus' *Hymn to Apollo* presents Apollo as the first owner of the Delphic oracle. Paus. 10.5.6-8 gives both versions.

16. The composer of this hymn must have had knowledge of the name of the dragon, considering his conspicuous interest in word-play on this name: πύθευ (363), πύσει (369), κατέπυσε (371), Πυθώ (372), Πύθειον (373) and πῦσε (374).

17. The 'rotting' indicates the attribute of Apollo as the 'sun god', since it is narrated in 374 that 'at the very spot, the piercing power of the Sun made the monster rot'. Further, we note that Ἠελίοιο is emphatically placed as the final word in the closing line. Miller (1986) 89 writes that 'rotting' means that the victim's body is not buried but left on the spot to be devoured by birds and dogs, a typical threat in heroic contests.

18. The claim that Thebes was uninhabited when Apollo was journeying to his oracular place (226) is made for the same encomiastic reason.

19. Further to this, being female, the dragon must be unnamed, since Python – if the composer knew that name – is a male name. Fontenrose (1959) 13-21 gives five versions of the myth of Apollo's combat with a dragon, among which only the version elaborated in this hymn features a female dragon. (The female dragon is called Delphyne by later writers, which seems to be a variant of Telphousa. See ibid., 14 n. 4.) The version featuring the male dragon predominates: for example, Euripides *I.T.* 1245, Apollodorus 1.39 and Pausanias 10.65.

20. Miller (1986) 84.

21. Fontenrose (1959) 91 defines the process of change: dental – vowel – labial to labial – vowel – dental, with the initial consonant becoming unaspirated, the final remaining aspirated, i.e. TUF – PUQ. Although this interchange cannot be fully attested, Buck (1933) 129 gives the example of the word group, θείνω – ἔπεφνον, and points out that the Greeks were unconscious of the actual relation in groups like ποῦ – τίς, θείνω – ἔπεφνον. The labiovelars without dissimilation of aspirates would have been *ghwughw-. Sihler (1995) 162-3 gives several examples demonstrating that *gw becomes both *t* and *p*: this change may partly explain how the two names, Typhon and Python, come from the same root. Cf. also Beekes (1995) 128.

22. Even in antiquity, there was uncertainty whether Arimoi referred to a tribe or a place. Pindar *Pyth.* 1.15 places Typhon under Mt. Etna. Kirk (1985) ad loc. suggests various locations; according to Strabo 13.626, it is near Sardis, in Mysia, in Cilicia, Syria, Mt. Etna, or in Pithekoussai. Further on Arimoi, see West (1966) 250. Lane Fox (2008) 114 suggests the location of Arimoi to be Al Mina in the north Syrian river-plain.

23. Hesiod uses the form of Τυφωεύς here, but he also uses Τυφάων at *Theog.* 306, just as both forms are used in the hymn (Τυφωεύς only once, at *Hymn. Apol.* 367). West (1966) 252 notes that these two forms are equivalent. Allen and Sikes (1904) 111 give the interesting example of M's Τυφωνεύς as a mixture of Τυφωεύς and Τυφών.

24. Janko (1982) 119; Clay (1989) 66; O'Brien (1993) 16.

25. Miller (1986) 87-8.

26. This shifting of emphasis may be characteristic of this hymn: similar examples are observed by Clay (1989) 33, who notes the geographical catalogue of Leto's journey when Hera prevents Apollo's birth (30-49) as 'the instance of the peculiar gliding transitions favoured by the poet'.

27. The phrase ὃν τέκον αὐτὴ (317) is ambiguous. Following Allen and Sikes (1904) 106, Miller (1986) 85, and Clay (1989) 68, I understand this to be 'my very own son'. In *Theog.* 927, Hera is his sole parent. Concerning Hephaestus' parentage, this hymn adopts the Homeric account (*Il.* 14.338, *Od.* 8.312).

28. Janko (1992) 199.

29. Hephaestus is disliked by Hera and thrown down by her (*Il.* 18.395-7; *Hymn. Apol.* 318), and for Typhon's case, see n. 39 below.

30. O'Brien (1993) 101-12. The existence of variant versions on the ejection of Hephaestus shows that the poet of the *Iliad* could choose (or create) the story from the myths. At the end of Book 1 of the *Iliad*, when Hephaestus tries to get Zeus and Hera reconciled, the poet chooses not to go further. Cf. Chapter II, Section 3.

31. Stanley (1993) 8 writes that emphasis falls on the central element in the ring-composition. For the significance of this central element, see also Lohmann (1970) 25.

32. Allen, Sikes and Halliday (1936) ad 317 follow earlier editors in assuming a lacuna between 317-18, and suggest as a supplement *exempli gratia*, αἶσχος ἐμοὶ καὶ ὄνειδος ἐν οὐρανῷ ὅν τε καὶ αὐτή, which would of course strengthen the idea of Hera's disgust at Hephaestus' lameness.

33. Cf. Chapter I, Section 4.

34. Fontenrose (1959) 18 gives another version of the myth: Hera put Earth under oath not to let Leto bear her children, but Poseidon gave Leto refuge on Delos when the dragon was pursuing her (Hyg. *Fab.* 140). This may be connected with the mysterious account of the temple of Poseidon at Onchestus, 230-8. Janko

(1986) 55 notes the power relations between Poseidon and Apollo: Poseidon's shrine is central to Boeotian patriotism, and Telphousa's overthrow by Apollo is the key to the control of the road between Thebes (Poseidon's domain) and Delphi (Apollo's domain).

35. Janko (1992), in his commentary on *Il.* 14.295-6, suggests the existence of a tale of threat to Zeus' rule in which Zeus secretly seduces Metis, since, in the Hesiodic fragment 294 Most [343 M-W], Metis' child *is* greater than Zeus. Cf. Chapter IV, Section 3.

36. West (2003) reads ἥ, in which case, it is the 'she-dragon' who worked many evils.

37. Beating the ground always expresses a desire for revenge. In the Meleager story, Althaia beats the ground in a similar way (*Il.* 9.568-9). The chthonic character of Hera also appears in *Il.* 14.271-9, 15.34-8.

38. Line 349 occurs also at *Od.* 11.294, where ἀλλ' ... δή is similarly used as adversative.

39. A child is handed over for nurture in mythic stories; for example, Zeus is nurtured by Gaia (*Theog.* 479-80); Aristaeus, the son of Apollo and Cyrene, is brought by Hermes to the Horae and Gaia to be nurtured (Pindar *Pyth.* 9.59-63). These stories show that it was a common custom for a child to be reared not by his/her mother, but by a nurse (or nurses). The phrase αὐτίκα ... ἔπειτα (353-4) in the present text, however, emphasises focus on Hera's hurried action, 'taking him (the child) at once', she then gave him to ...', which seems to convey an atmosphere somewhat different from the ordinary.

40. *Theog.* 295-6 echoes 351-2 on Callirhoe's giving birth to Εχιδνα· ἡ δ' ἔτεκ' ἄλλο πέλωρον ἀμήχανον, οὐδὲν ἐοικὸς / θνητοῖς ἀνθρώποις οὐδ' ἀθανάτοισι θεοῖσιν. Gemoll (1886) ad loc. comments that δέ of *Hymn. Apol.* 351 is a reminiscence of Hesiod. For the use of apodotic δέ, see Denniston (1954) 177-81.

41. In order to avoid the abruptness at 355, scholars used to propose emending the text; the most popular suggestion was Wolf's ἥ (to denote the female dragon), but editors are now more inclined to accept the text as it stands. See Càssola (1975) ad loc., but contrast West (see n. 36 above).

42. The repetition of the pronouns, at the same time, makes a strong contrast with the word play that begins with πύθεν (363), as was mentioned above, n. 16.

43. Some other examples of an abrupt transition from a digression to the main story are *Il.* 9.564-5; Pind. *Pyth.* II 37-8.

44. Fr. 93 D-K, ὁ ἄναξ, οὗ τὸ μαντεῖόν ἐστι τὸ ἐν Δελφοῖς, οὔτε λέγει οὔτε κρύπτει ἀλλὰ σημαίνει (The lord, whose sanctuary is in Delphi, does not tell nor conceal, but show by a sign).

45. When the Delphic oracle told him to 'beware of seventy-three', Nero supposed that he was to reign till he reached that year; however the oracle alluded to the age of his successor, Galba.

46. Lane Fox (2008) 310 writes the detailed description of the 'Corycian cave' near the Calycadnus river, as the possible site where Typhon hid the sinews of Zeus.

47. Aesch. *P.V.* 353-74, *Sept.* 511-17 and Pindar *Pyth.* 1.15-20, 8.16, *Ol.* 4.7 follow the version in which Zeus has no great difficulty in overcoming Typhon.

48. Schol. b to *Il.* 2.783 give a different version, where Hera is in league with Cronus: once, in a rage against Zeus, Hera approached Cronus for help. He obliged by giving her two eggs smeared with his semen which he told her to bury underground: the daimon born from them would dethrone Zeus. After she buried them under Mt. Arimoi, Typhon came forth.

49. So in Clay (1989) 68, O'Brien (1993) 96 and Förstel (1979) 262-3. Thalmann

(1984) 44 suggests that 'Gaia should turn against Zeus and contrive the birth and survival of the son according to the precedent she has set. Instead, she remains on Zeus' side, for he swallows Metis.' Cf. Chapter IV, Section 3.

50. A large-scale parallel might be implied in the relationship of mother (opposing the ruler)-son-nurse: Rhea (opposing Cronus)-Zeus-Gaia, and Hera (opposing Zeus)-Typhon-the dragon. Clay (1989) 71 notes the parallel between Zeus and Typhon, but goes no further.

51. Fontenrose (1959) 252.

52. Clay (1989) 74 interprets this scene as 'the violent eruption of the usurping son destined to depose his father'. Apollo appears as a threatening figure, as Clay writes, but it is only when he enters the palace in lines 2-4. The predominant atmosphere of this scene is obviously not fear of violence, but celebration. See also Fontenrose (1959) 252.

53. Càssola (1975) 486 notes that Apollo's action (v. 4) contradicts Leto's disarmament (vv. 6-8), but offers no further discussion.

54. Miller (1986) 69, 72.

55. Austin (1966) 306.

VII. The Bitter Sorrow of Aphrodite

1. Allen, Halliday and Sikes (1936) 351 date it after Homer and before 700 BC. Janko (1982) 180 is more precise: on linguistic grounds, he places the composition of the *Hymn. Aphr.* within Hesiod's own time, between Hesiod's *Theogony* and *Hymn. Dem.*

2. On the divergent datings of the *Hymn* see Janko (1982) 151. Bentman (1955) 154-5 dates this hymn to the Alexandrian period on the basis of the poetic technique of its delicate interworkings (such as the use of repetitive patterns).

3. For example, Wilamowitz (1920) 83; Càssola (1975) 244-5. This belief is reviewed by Smith (1981a) 4 and (1981b) 17-18, who claims that there is no historical evidence for the existence of Aeneadae in the Troad. It is hard to say which argument is right, as the issue is one of probability. Among more recent publications, Faulkner (2008) 10 writes that the lineage of Aeneas is a theme central to the narrative, and regards the hypothesis of historical Aeneadae as a serious possibility.

4. Preziosi (1966) 194. Porter (1949) 254-64 discusses the range of repeated elements in this hymn, such as themes, metre, sound (assonance, consonance), and concludes (p. 272) that the technique of repetition in the *Hymn to Aphrodite* is much more elaborately developed than in the *Iliad*.

5. Janko (1982) 19.

6. Hoekstra (1969) 46.

7. As the result of discussion of the similarities between *Hymn. Aphr.* and *Hymn. Dem.*, Janko (1982) 163-5 concludes that *Hymn. Dem.* was composed later.

8. Walcot (1991) 141.

9. The brevity of mortal life as a theme of this hymn is noted by many scholars. See, for example, Gemoll (1886) 258; Porter (1949) 259; Boedeker (1974) 79; Smith (1981a) 5; Sowa (1984) 40; Parry (1986) 263-4; Clay (1989) 158. Among these, I favour primarily the assessment of Smith.

10. Rutherford (1982) 146.

11. Heitsch (1965) 12 emphasises the defeat of Aphrodite. As the hymn celebrates neither the birth of the goddess nor the founding of her cult, Matthiae (1800) 66 even doubted whether this hymn should be considered a hymn (*Sed mihi*

quidem valde dubium est, an carmen illud in hymnorum numerum omnino refer-endum sit). Clay (1989) 170 posits that this hymn conveys an epoch-making event similar to the themes of the other three long hymns: the last union of a god with a mortal to produce the last hero. Fränkel (1975) 248 also mentions that the conclusion implied in this hymn is that man and goddess must now part for ever.

12. Smith (1981a) 61 views the present tense of ἀποκλίνουσι as a generic, timeless description. Janko (1981b) 285, in his review of Smith, also writes the poet's ingenious use of time.

13. Smith (1981a) 44 writes that such a paradoxical combination of mortal and immortal in their appearance assists the audience's acceptance of their union as lovers.

14. Smith (1981a) 42-3.

15. The parallel between the description of Aphrodite's dressing and that of Hera (*Il.* 14.169-86) has been much discussed. For the Near Eastern parallels, see Faulkner (2008) 20-1.

16. Murnaghan (1987) 14.

17. Bergren (1989) 13 emphasises the ambiguity of Aphrodite's disguise: in the presentation of herself to Anchises, the 'real' Aphrodite comes as an imitation of the real Aphrodite.

18. For example, Apollo leaves Hector (*Il.* 22.213); Artemis leaves Hippolytus (Eur. *Hipp.* 1437-9).

19. Although Walcot (1991) 145 argues that 'the list artfully conceals the true answer', there seems to be no reason why Anchises must 'conceal the true answer' at this stage.

20. Odysseus compares Nausicaa with Artemis, when he first met her (*Od.* 6.151). See also n. 26.

21. I agree with Clay (1989) 175-6 that Aphrodite's speech and disguise are complementary.

22. Richardson (1974) 267 (ad 352) comments that 'they [ἀμενηνός and χαμαιγενής] emphasise the helplessness of human beings'.

23. Parry (1971) 16-18.

24. Later, in 192, he is called κύδιστε καταθνητῶν ἀνθρώπων, also with an ironic implication. Janko (1982) 25 suggests that *Hymn. Aphr.* 108 might have adopted a 'Hesiodic' phrase, along with another doublet ὄρος μέγα τε ζάθεόν τε (*Theog.* 2, and *Hymn. Aphr.* 258).

25. Janko (1981a) 254-5 discusses the distribution of the equivalent formulae φιλομμειδὴς Ἀφροδίτη / Διὸς θυγάτηρ Ἀφροδίτη in the *Iliad* and *Hymn. Aphr.* According-ing to him, the alternatives appear in random fashion in the *Iliad*; but in the *Hymn. Aphr.* strong formulaic association decides the choice in 107 = 191, while in the first part of the hymn the hymn-poet appears to forget about the existence of the doublet. However, the hymn-poet deliberately seems to prefer Διὸς θυγάτηρ. This choice would be explained by the poet's strategy to present Aphrodite to be the goddess under Zeus' control, as discussed later in this chapter, Section 2.

26. Odysseus addresses Nausicaa as follows: θεός νύ τις ἦ βροτός ἐσσι; / εἰ μέν τις θεός ἐσσι, τοὶ οὐρανὸν εὐρὺν ἔχουσιν, / Ἀρτέμιδί σε ἐγώ γε, Διὸς κούρῃ μεγάλοιο, / εἶδός τε μέγεθός τε φυήν τ' ἄγχιστα ἐΐσκω· (*Od.* 6.149-52: Are you some goddess or a mortal woman? If you are a god who live in the wide heaven, I think you are most like Artemis, the daughter of almighty Zeus, in your beauty, grace and noble stature).

27. Clay (1989) 177 suggests that the reason for using a common abduction motif is to titillate and inspire Anchises – to give him 'ideas'. I doubt whether the

element of titillation is included here, but I agree with Clay's point (p. 159) that Aphrodite has made herself appear the weaker of the two.

28. I agree with Smith (1981a) 55 that this conditional sentence recapitulates the main point of Aphrodite's narrative. Smith neatly points out that it does not matter whether what she says is to be taken as true or false; if it is true, there can be no harm; if it is false, he may hope to escape blame by appealing to the literal content of what she said.

29. As Van der Ben (1986) 19 writes, οὐ σάφα εἰδώς could mean either 'having no precise knowledge' – as underlining the idea of θεά – or 'not clearly knowing what he did' (tr. Evelyn-White) – as a qualification of παρέλεκτο. I accept the former interpretation, since the main concern of this passage is not 'what he is doing', but apparently 'with whom he is making love'.

30. For example, Clay (1989) 182.

31. Αἰνείας, τὸν ὑπ' Ἀγχίσῃ τέκε δῖ' Ἀφροδίτη, / Ἴδης ἐν κνημοῖσι θεὰ βροτῷ εὐνηθεῖσα (*Il.* 2.820-1, 'Aeneas, to whom divine Aphrodite gave birth by Anchises, when the goddess lay with a mortal on the spurs of Ida'). This phrase is significant as it also relates to Anchises, and may have been traditional in stories about Anchises and his son.

32. The phrase γυνὴ ἐϊκυῖα θεῇσι is used twice in the *Iliad* (11.638, of Hecamede; 19.286, of Briseis), where the formula seems to be used less appropriately than in this hymn. See further Smith (1981a) 120 n. 59.

33. Nagy (1979) 82 explains the name of Achilles, following Palmer (1963) 79, as 'the one who has ἄχος for and of λαός', suggesting that the Homeric theme of ἄχος reflects not only on the individual nature of the Achilles' figure but also on the collective nature of Achaean λαός. Nagy could have mentioned the aetiology of Aeneas based on αἰνὸν ἄχος. For the etymology of Achilles from ἄχος and λαός (Ἀχι-λαϝός), see also Chantraine (1963) 150.

34. Note the contrast at 173-5; her head reaches to the rafters when she reveals herself as a goddess.

35. In this passage, Odysseus, pretending to be a fugitive from Crete, tells Athena a splendid tale. When he finishes his tale, Athena smiles and caresses him (287-8), as she has enjoyed his cunning skill.

36. So told by Achilles at *Il.* 24.526. Only mortals can be serious, since their lives are short and their abilities limited.

37. Buxton (1994) 74.

38. Many scholars believe the story of Tithonus to be the invention of the hymn-poet: Smith (1981a) 84; Segal (1986) 19. However, Kakrides (1930) 35 and King (1986) 27-8 think that the story is older than the hymn. The story is not narrated in detail either by Homer or Hesiod, but is mentioned, briefly, in *Il.* 11.1; *Theog.* 984-5.

39. King (1986) 18-20, regarding Tithonus' fate as being worse than that of a mortal man, writes that the poet demonstrates the similarity between gods and men who can unite sexually, and tries to re-establish the distance between the two terms, by choosing the experience of old age, because it is unknown to the gods. Segal (1986) 38 criticises King's article, suggesting that she fails to distinguish between the analysis of a myth and the critical study of a literary text.

40. For example, Segal (1974) 208 suggests, from a structuralist perspective, that Ganymede is given the Olympian privilege of eternal life, and Tithonus' horizontal movements to the 'limit of the earth' contrast with the vertical move-ment in the other two [Ganymede and Anchises] episodes; Boedeker (1974) 80 writes that Aphrodite, like Eos, is apparently unable to offer a deathless existence

to her lover of her own accord, since that ability rests with Zeus; Sowa (1984) 40 thinks that, as a fertility goddess, she wanted to make Anchises immortal; Clay (1989) 190 puts the argument that, since Zeus had the power to make his beloved Ganymede immortal, Aphrodite would have to apply to Zeus on behalf of Anchises, but she cannot do it.

41. In this context, the life of Ganymede might be seen as more tragic than it is usually thought to be: first he was carried off by Zeus, which means the life on Olympus was not his own choice but enforced by Zeus; secondly he was not allowed to grow or mature physically and mentally, nor produce his own progeny; thirdly he had to pour wine for the gods forever, which is, again, enforced labour. However, in view of 205-6 and 215-17, his life might have been regarded as blessed by ancient audiences or readers.

42. This story, of course, fits with the myth-tradition in which Anchises remains mortal. I agree with Smith (1981a) 88 that, if this myth is not a fantasy of wish-fulfilment, Anchises' ultimate subjection to death is simply assumed.

43. For example, Sarpedon, dearest to Zeus of all men, had to die (*Il* 16.433, 462-503); Heracles did not escape his doom though Zeus loved him (*Il.* 18.117-19); Achilles is another case in point.

44. Smith (1981a) 90. For Tithonus in the new Cologne papyrus of Sappho, see *Kölner Papyri*, Band 11 (Paderborn 2007) n. 429.

45. As another reason for their juxtaposition, one can indicate their exceptional beauty which is shared by the three, all of whom are the members of the same family. Anchises is beautiful like an immortal (55); Ganymede was snatched by Zeus for his beauty (203); Tithonus is also like an immortal (219).

46. Smith (1981a) 90 offers an interesting interpretation: this repetition supplies the link which bridges the transition: 'the limits of mortality cannot be removed'. I admit that there is a slight gap between 243 and 244, as Smith claims, but I doubt that such verse-end repetition could bridge it.

47. Opstelten (1952) 221.

48. Parry (1986) 264 writes that, for these beasts, erotic *anankê* is simple and merely joyful. Sowa (1984) 82 takes this passage as evidence of Aphrodite's cosmic power as a fertility goddess.

49. Smith (1981a) 58-9 discusses this passage from another point of view: the animal skin on his bed emphasises Anchises' strength, which helps to prevent him from being seen as a hopelessly weaker and inappropriate partner.

50. For bibliography on the history of this theory, see Boedeker (1974) 1 n. 7.

51. Rose (1924) 11.

52. Frazer (1914) 36.

53. Penglase (1994) 15ff. In fact, Ishtar and Astarte are related forms of the same name.

54. James (1959) 184; Burkert (1985) 152-3.

55. Vermaseren (1977) 13.

56. Vermaseren (1977) 13-15. Roller (1999) 31-9, in her thorough analysis, places more emphasis on the importance of domestic animals than on female reproductive capacity in the cult of the Anatolian Neolithic period, pointing out (p. 39) that the key symbol of the Phrygian Mother in prehistory is the image of hunting, and of power and strength found in the lion and birds of prey.

57. All the Greek goddesses, of course, inherited something of the Mighty Mother's features. The goddess of 'the fertile furrow' reminds us of Demeter's 'thrice-ploughed furrow' (*Od.* 5.127); productivity, especially in child-birth, reminds us of Hera; and Artemis is closely associated with animals.

Notes to pages 143-145

58. Cf. Introduction, nn. 1 and 2.
59. The name or title *potnia* can be found almost everywhere in the Linear B tablets that were found at Pylos, Knossos, and Thebes. The characteristics of *potnia* in the tablets are (a) she appears often with modifying words, such as 'of *upoyo*' (PYFr 1225, 1236, PYFn187), 'of *newopeo*' (PYCc 665), 'of *erewijo*' (PYVn 48), 'of the Labyrinth' (KNGn 707), 'of *atana*' (KNV52); (b) the word *potnia* has various kinds of derivatives, such as *'potinijawejo'* (PYEp 613, KNDl 933), *'potinijawejojo'* (PYEq213); (c) the word *potnia* always appears in a singular form. Cf. Chadwick (1976); Bennett and Olivier (1973); Chadwick et al. (1986).
60. Burkert (1992) 17 points out that all the sacred sites which came to flourish by the eighth century – Delos, Delphi and, above all, Olympia – have produced substantial finds of oriental objects.
61. Burkert (1992) 14-15.
62. Frazer (1914) chs I-III, esp. pp. 11-12 suggests that the myth of a goddess and her consort is a major feature of Near Eastern religion. Burkert (1992) 96 notes the parallel between the story of the meeting of Ishtar and Gilgamesh with that of *Il.* 5.330-430, where Aphrodite is injured by Diomedes.
63. Boedeker (1974) 5.
64. Boedeker (1974) 15.
65. Boedeker (1974) 5.
66. See also West (1969) 122, 134; West (1997) passim.
67. For the names of gods, see Chapter V, Section 2.
68. Friedrich (1978) 81-2.
69. Càssola (1975) 237-42 also admits Aphrodite's both Semitic and Indo-European elements. Faulkner (2008) 19-22 discusses the parallel motifs between the *Hymn. Aphr.* and Near Eastern literature, noting that Cyprus must have been a major centre for the transmission of Near Eastern culture to the Aegean.
70. I agree with Allen, Halliday and Sikes (1936) 351, who comment that, in the Troad, Aphrodite was probably another form of Cybele; nevertheless, the hymn-writer follows the Homeric conception, and, for Homer, Aphrodite is far removed from Cybele.
71. For example, she is injured by the mortal hero, Diomedes at *Il.* 5.330-430. For further discussion on this, see at pp. 145-51 below.
72. In the *Iliad*, Διὸς θυγάτηρ Ἀφροδίτη: 3.374; 5.131, 312, 820; 14.193, 224; 21.416; 23.185; Διὸς κούρης Ἀφροδίτη: 20.105. In the *Odyssey*, Διὸς θυγάτηρ Ἀφροδίτη: 8.308; οἱ καλὴ θυγάτηρ: 8.320.
73. Gantz (1993) 100.
74. Sale (1961) 508-9; West (1966) 212.
75. This picture of Aphrodite differs little from Homeric notions. It is difficult to understand why Hesiod derives Aphrodite's origin from Uranus. Sale (1961) 520 suggests that Hesiod combined two kinds of myths: first, Uranus as the father of Aphrodite; and, second, Aphrodite's birth as a consequence of his castration.
76. Friedrich (1978) 82 suggests that Aphrodite's birth from the genitals is connected with her sexual-sensuous functions and contrasts symmetrically with Athene's birth from Zeus' head and her patronage of wisdom. For oriental influences on Greek succession myth see West (1966) 20-8; Burkert (1992) 90ff.; Janko (1992) ad *Iliad* 14.200-7.
77. West (1966) 212.
78. Kirk (1990) ad 5.370-2.
79. Clay (1989) 200; Gantz (1993) 99.
80. Kirk (1990) ad loc. takes γιγνώσκων (331) both as a recognition of the

distinction between god and man, and as a recognition of Aphrodite's feebleness. I put more emphasis on the latter connotation.

81. Kirk (1990) ad loc.

82. Also in Ar. *Lys.* 520.

83. Janko (1992) ad loc.

84. West (1966) ad loc. suggests that the epithet χρυσῆν (822) is problematic, and that verse 822 may not be genuine like other verses (962, 1005, etc.) which include this epithet. But even so, considering the importance of giving birth to Typhoeus, who is the youngest son of Gaia, and the youngest son is the dangerous challenger of the sovereignty of the universe, like Cronus for Uranus, Zeus for Cronus, only a mention of Aphrodite here would be significant. This would imply, at least, that Aphrodite is on the side of Gaia and Tartarus, that is, the chthonic side, against Zeus.

85. Clay (1989) 164.

86. West (1978) ad loc. comments that the word refers to their parentage, used when speaking collectively of the men of the heroic age; the word appears only once in the *Iliad* (12.23), when the heroic age is viewed from the distance of the poet's own time. Scodel (1982b) 40-3 discusses the myth of destruction, noting that the theme of destruction by the Deluge affected the myth of the Trojan War, in which Zeus brings about the catastrophe in order to remove the *hemitheoi* from the world and separate men from gods: this could be to relieve the earth of the burden caused by overpopulation, or to punish impiety.

87. The race of heroes are 'just and better' than men of the bronze race (*Works and Days* 158) and, by implication, than men of the iron age. See further Thalmann (1984) 103.

88. Thalmann (1984) 104.

89. For the heroes who are saved and live in the islands of the blessed at 167-73, see West (1978) ad loc.

90. Thalmann (1984) 105-6 also explains that the poet of the fragment imagined, empathetically, what the gods' feelings must be.

91. Fränkel (1975) 249-50 interprets this passage (45-52) as bringing out the principle of compensation, which is, he thinks, an important notion in this hymn, as it is repeated in the story of Ganymede: the anxiety of Tros is recompensed by the honour that he obtained.

92. Bergren (1989) 7 well defines the complex relation between Zeus, Aphrodite and Anchises, writing that the Hymn attempts to resolve the tension between a cosmos controlled by Aphrodite and a cosmos controlled by Zeus. The result would be a stable hierarchy in which the immortal male 'tames' the principle of sexuality as an immortal female, who herself tames the mortal male.

93. For example, Smith (1981a) 356 comments on the social and institutional side of the three goddesses, as well as on their different attitudes to patronage; Sowa (1984) 53 briefly comments on the word play on ἔργα in this passage; Clay (1989) 159-62 explains the description of the three goddesses by means of a 'complex set of oppositions'.

94. Kirk (1974) 226.

95. Hestia is sometimes not included among the twelve Olympian gods. Hera gets an honourable mention at 40-4.

96. Richardson (1993) ad loc. There was a variant ἤ οἱ κεχαρισμένα δῶρ' ὀνόμηνε (Didymus in A).

97. Cf. Chapter VI, Section 3.

98. Schol. Q.V. ad *Od.* 20. 66 gives the story of Pandareus: Pandareus stole the

dog of Zeus on Crete; he kept the dog near Tantalus; when Hermes, sent by Zeus, came to Tantalos, Pandareus fled with his wife and his three daughters to Athens, and then to Sicily; but Zeus found them and killed him and his wife. At *Od.* 19.518-24 another story of Pandareus' daughters is told, but the relationship between these stories is unknown.

99. Janko (1992) ad *Il.* 14.187-223 comments that neither Aphrodite's aid nor that of Hypnus is essential for Hera's success, but the poet seizes his chance to poke fun at Aphrodite, who is tricked into helping the side that she opposes. Sowa (1984) 75-6 analyses the similarities of the preparation of Hera (*Il.* 14.162-86) and Aphrodite (*Hymn. Aphr.* 58-67): both close the door, bathe, are anointed with ambrosial sweet oil, and put on beautiful clothing and ornaments. According to Sowa, all seductions are ultimately performed by Aphrodite herself.

100. I take v. 76 as 'what is fated and what is not fated', following Russo (1992) ad loc.

101. I agree with Clay (1989) 155 n. 7, who notes that restriction of the power of female goddesses is entirely in keeping with the patriarchal Olympian orientation of the *Homeric Hymns*.

102. Griffin (1980a) 186.

103. Griffin (1980a) 203.

Epilogue

1. Buxton (1994) 16.

2. Lang (1983) discusses how 'reverberation' would have operated in the *Iliad*, and specifically she points out at p.158 that divine binding in the stories of Books 1 and 5 was an echo or reverberation from heroic epic.

3. Many of the early stories are influenced by Near Eastern traditions, as I noted in the Introduction. Unfortunately, these Oriental stories are, in general terms, preserved in fragmentary form. Their survival and transmission is both incidental and accidental, and much affected by the political history of the surrounding lands and countries. But we can say that without some will to preserve the texts, they would never have survived.

4. For the competitiveness of ancient Greek society, see Introduction, n. 24.

5. Kirk (1974) 39.

Abbreviations

AHS = T.W. Allen, W.R. Halliday & E.E. Sikes (eds), *The Homeric Hymns*, 2nd edn, Oxford, 1936.

Allen = Archibald Allen (ed.), *The Fragments of Mimnermus: Text and Commentary*, Stuttgart, 1933.

ANET = J. Pritchard (ed.), *Ancient Near Eastern Texts Relating to the Old Testament*, 2nd edn, Princeton, 1955.

D = E. Diehl (ed.), *Anthologia Lyrica Graeca*, Leipzig, 1942.

D-K = H. Diels & W. Krantz (eds) *Die Fragmente der Vorsokratiker*, 3 vols, 6th edn, Zürich, 1951-52.

Drachmann = A.B. Drachmann (ed.), *Scholia Vetera in Pindari Carmina*, vols 1-3, Leipzig, 1903-27, repr. Stuttgart-Leipzig 1997.

Dindorf = W. Dindorf (ed.), *Scholia Graeca in Homeri Odysseam*, vols 1-2, Oxford, 1855.

EGF = M. Davies (ed.), *Epicorum Graecorum Fragmenta*, Göttingen, 1988.

Erbse = H. Erbse (ed.), *Scholia Graeca in Homeri Iliadem*, vols 1-6, Berlin, 1969-83.

G-P = A.S.F. Gow & D.L. Page (eds), *The Greek Anthology: Hellenistic Epigrams*, vols 1-2, Cambridge, 1965.

Gallavotti = C. Gallavotti, E.L. Bennet & M. Lang (eds) *Inscriptiones Pyliae ad Mycenaeam Aetatem Pertinentes*, Rome, 1961.

K-A = R. Kassel & C. Austin (eds), *Poetae Comici Graeci*, vols I-VIII, Berlin, 1983-2001.

H = Martina Hirschberger (ed.), *Gynaikon Katalogos und Megalai Ehoiai*, München-Leipzig, 2004.

LIMC = L. Kahil et al. (eds), *Lexicon Iconographicum Mythologiae Classicae*, Zurich and Munich, 1981- 97.

Most = Glen W. Most (ed.), *Hesiod: The Shield, Catalogue of Women, Other Fragments,* Cambridge, MA, 2007.

M-W = R. Merkelbach & M.L. West (eds), *Fragmenta Hesiodea*, Oxford, 1967.

PEG = A Bernabev (ed.), *Poetae Epici Graeci*, Pars I, Leipzig, 1987.

PMG = D.L. Page (ed.), *Poetae Melici Graeci*, Oxford, 1962.

PMGF = M. Davies (ed.), *Poetarum Melicorum Graecorum Fragmenta*, vol. 1, Oxford, 1991.

P.Köln = B. Kramer, M. Erler, D. Hagedorn & R. Hübner (eds), *Kölner Papyri*, vol. 3, Opladen, 1978.

P.Oxy. = B.P. Grenfell, A.S. Hunt et al. (eds), *Oxyrhynchus Papyri*, London, 1898-.

SH = H. Lloyd-Jones & P. Parsons (eds), *Supplementum Hellenisticum*, Berlin, 1983.

Abbreviations

S-M = B. Snell & H. Maehler (eds), *Pindari Carmina cum Fragmentis*, Leipzig, 1987-89.

V = Eva-Maria Voigt (ed.), *Sappho et Alcaeus*, Amsterdam, 1971.

Van Thiel = H. van Thiel (ed.), *D-Scholia to Homer*, http://kups.ub.uni-koeln.de/1810/

W = M.L. West (ed.), *Iambi et Elegi Graeci*, vols 1-2, Oxford, 1971-72; 2nd edn, 1989-92.

West = M.L. West (ed.), *Homerus: Ilias*, vols 1-2, München-Leipzig, 1998-2000.

Other abbreviations follow *L'Année philologique,* Paris.

Bibliography

Adkins, Arthur W.H., *Merit and Responsibility: A Study in Greek Values*, Oxford: Clarendon Press, 1960.

Alden, Maureen, *Homer Beside Himself: Para-Narratives in the Iliad*, Oxford: Oxford University Press, 2000.

Allen, T.W. & Sikes, E.E., *The Homeric Hymns*, London: Macmillan, 1904.

Allen, T.W. (ed.), *Homeri Ilias*, Oxford: Clarendon Press, 1920 (3rd edn).

Allen, T.W. (ed.), *Homeri Odysseia*, Oxford: Clarendon Press, 1917 (2nd edn).

Allen, T.W., Halliday, W.R. & Sikes, E.E., *The Homeric Hymns*, 2nd edn, Oxford: Clarendon Press, 1936.

Ameis, K., Hentze, C. & Cauer, P., *Homers Odyssee*, 2.2, Gesang 19-24, Leipzig: Teubner, 1925.

Andersen, Øivind, 'The Making of the Past in the *Iliad*', *HSCP* 93 (1990), 25-45.

Angier, [Sowa] Cora, 'Verbal Patterns in Hesiod's *Theogony*', *HSCP* 68 (1964), 329-44.

Arthur, Marylin B., 'Cultural Strategies in Hesiod's *Theogony*: Law, Family, Society', *Arethusa* 15 (1982) 63-82.

Arthur, Marylin B., 'The Dream of a World Without Woman: Poetics and the Circles of Order in the *Theogony* Prooemium', *Arethusa* 16 (1983), 97-116.

Austin, Norman, 'The Function of Digressions in the *Iliad*', *GRBS* 7 (1966), 295-312.

Austin, Norman, *Meaning and Being in Myth*, University Park: Pennsylvania State University Press, 1989.

Beekes, Robert S.P., *Comparative Indo-European Linguistics: An Introduction*, Amsterdam: J. Benjamins Pub., 1995.

Bennett, E.L. (ed.), *The Pylos Tablets: Texts of the Inscriptions Found 1939-1954*, Princeton: Princeton University Press, 1955.

Bennett, E.L. & Olivier, Jean-Pierre, *The Pylos Tablets Transcribed*, Rome: Edizioni dell'Ateneo, 1973-76.

Bennett, E.L., Chadwick, J. & Ventris, M. (eds), *The Knossos Tablets*, 2nd edn, London: University of London, Institute of Classical Studies, 1959.

Bentman, Raymond, 'The Homeric Hymn to Aphrodite', *CJ* 50 (1955), 153-9.

Bergren, Ann L.T., 'The Homeric Hymn to Aphrodite: Tradition, Rhetoric and Blame', *CA* 8 (1989), 1-41.

Blundell, Mary W., *Helping Friends and Harming Enemies: A Study in Sophocles and Greek Ethics*, Cambridge: Cambridge University Press, 1989.

Boedeker, Deborah Dickmann, *Aphrodite's Entry into Greek Epic*, Leiden: E.J. Brill, 1974.

Braswell, Bruce K., 'Mythological Innovation in the *Iliad*', *CQ* 21 (1971), 16-26.

Bibliography

Bremmer, Jan, 'An Enigmatic Indo-European Rite: Paederasty', *Arethusa* 13 (1980), 279-98.

Bremmer, Jan, 'Jokes, Jokers and Jokebooks in Ancient Greek Culture', in J. Bremmer & H. Roodenburg (eds), *A Cultural History of Humour: From Antiquity to the Present Day*, Cambridge: Polity Press, 1997.

Brown, Norman O., 'The Birth of Athena', *TAPA* 83 (1952), 130-43.

Buck, Carl Darling, *Comparative Grammar of Greek and Latin*, Chicago: University of Chicago Press, 1933.

Burkert, Walter, 'Kynaithos, Polycrates, and the Homeric Hymn to Apollo', *Arktouros, Hellenic Studies presented to B.M.W. Knox*, Berlin: Walter de Gruyter, 1979, 53-62.

Burkert, Walter, *Structure and History in Greek Mythology and Ritual*, Berkeley and Los Angeles: University of California Press, 1979.

Burkert, Walter, *Greek Religion: Archaic and Classical*, tr. John Raffan, Oxford: Blackwell, 1985 (originally published as *Griechische Religion der archaischen und klassischen Epoche*, Stuttgart, 1977).

Burkert, Walter, *The Orientalizing Revolution: Near Eastern Influence on Greek Culture in the Early Archaic Age*, tr. M.E. Pinder & W. Burkert, Cambridge, MA: Harvard University Press, 1992 (originally published as *Die orientalisierende Epoche in der griechischen Religion und Literatur,* Heidelberg, 1984).

Burkert, Walter, *Savage Energies: Lessons of Myth and Ritual in Ancient Greece*, tr. Peter Bing, Chicago: University of Chicago Press, 2001 (originally published as *Wilder Ursprung: Opferritual und Mythos bei den Griechen*, Berlin, 1990).

Buxton, Richard, *Imaginary Greece: The Context of Mythology*, Cambridge: Cambridge University Press, 1994.

Caldwell, Richard, *The Origin of the Gods: A Psychoanalytic Study of Greek Theogonic Myth*, Oxford: Oxford University Press, 1989.

Campbell, Joseph, *The Masks of God: Occidental Mythology*, New York: Viking Press, 1964.

Càssola, Filippo di, *Inni Omerici*, Milan: Fondazione Lorenzo Vella, 1975.

Chadwick, J., *The Mycenaean World*, Cambridge: Cambridge University Press, 1976.

Chadwick, J., Godart, L., Killen, J.T., Olivier, J.-P., Sacconi, A. & Sakellarakis, I.A., *Corpus of Mycenaean Inscriptions from Knossos*, I-III, Cambridge: Cambridge University Press, 1986-97.

Chantraine, Pierre, *Grammaire homérique*, tome II: *Syntaxe*, Paris: Librairie C. Klincksieck, 1963.

Chantraine, Pierre, *Dictionnaire étymologique de la langue grecque*, tome 1-2, Paris: Klincksieck, 1968-80.

Clay, Jenny Strauss, *The Politics of Olympus, Form and Meaning in the Major Homeric Hymns,* Princeton: Princeton University Press, 1989.

Clay, Jenny Strauss, *Hesiod's Cosmos*, Cambridge: Cambridge University Press, 2003.

Cook, Arthur Bernard, *Zeus: A Study in Ancient Religion*, vols I-III, Cambridge: Cambridge University Press, 1914-40.

Corbeill, Anthony, *Controlling Laughter: Political Humor in the Late Roman Republic,* Princeton: Princeton University Press, 1996.

Bibliography

Cornford, F.M., *Principium Sapientiae: The Origins of Greek Philosophical Thought*, Cambridge: Cambridge University Press, 1952.

Craik, Elizabeth M., *The Dorian Aegean*, London: Routledge, 1980.

Davidson, Olga M., 'Indo-European Dimensions of Heracles in the *Iliad* 19.95-133', *Arethusa* 13 (1980) 197-202.

Dawe, R.D., *The Odyssey: Translation and Analysis*, Lewes, Sussex: The Book Guild, 1993.

De Jong, Irene, *A Narratological Commentary on the Odyssey*, Cambridge: Cambridge University Press, 2001.

De Ste Croix, G.E.M., *The Class Struggle in the Ancient World*, London: Duckworth, 1981.

Denniston, J.D., *The Greek Particles*, 2nd edn, Oxford: Clarendon Press, 1954.

Détienne, Marcel & Vernant, Jean-Pierre, *Cunning Intelligence in Greek Culture and Society*, tr. Janet Lloyd, Sussex: The Harvester Press, 1978 (originally published as *Les Ruses de l'intelligence: la Métis des grecs*, Paris, 1974).

Détienne, Marcel & Vernant, Jean-Pierre (eds), *The Cuisine of Sacrifice among the Gods*, tr. Paula Wissing, Chicago: University of Chicago Press, 1989 (originally published as *La cuisine du sacrifice en pays grec*, Paris, 1979).

Devereux, G., 'The Self-Blinding of Oidipous in Sophocles' *Oidipous Tyrannos*', *JHS* 93 (1973), 36-49.

Dietrich, B.C., *Death, Fate and the Gods: The Development of a Religious Idea in Greek Popular Belief and in Homer*, London: Athlone Press, 1965.

Dindorf, G., *Scholia Graeca in Homeri Iliadem*, Tomus I & II, Oxford: Clarendon Press, 1875.

Dodds, E.R., *The Greeks and the Irrational*, Berkeley: University of California Press, 1951.

Drerup, Engelbert, 'Der Homerische Apollonhymnos: eine methologische Studie', *Mnemosyne* 3 ser. 5 (1937), 81-134.

DuBois, Page, 'Eros and the Woman', *Ramus* 21 (1992), 97-114.

Duhoux, Yves, 'Mycenaean Anthology', in Yves Duhoux & Anna Morpurgo Davies (eds), *A Companion to Linear B, Mycenaean Greek Texts and their World*, Leuven: Peeters, 2008.

Dumézil, Georges, *Mythe et épopée*, Paris: Gallimard, 1968.

Dunbar, Nan (ed.), *Aristophanes, Birds*, Oxford: Clarendon Press. 1995.

Easterling, P.E., 'Agamemnon's *Skeptron* in the *Iliad*', in M.M. MacKenzie & C. Roueché (eds), *Images of Authority, Papers Presented to Joyce Reynolds on the Occasion of Her 70th Birthday*, Cambridge Philological Society, 1989, 104-21.

Easterling, P.E., 'Men's κλέος and Women's γόος: Female Voices in the *Iliad*', *Journal of Modern Greek Studies* 9 (1991) 145-51.

Edwards, Mark W., *Homer, Poet of the Iliad*, Baltimore: Johns Hopkins University Press, 1987.

Edwards, Mark W., *The Iliad: A Commentary*, vol. V: *Books 17-20*, Cambridge: Cambridge University Press, 1991.

Eliade, Mircea, *Images and Symbols: Studies in Religious Symbolism*, tr. Philip Mairet, London: Harvill Press, 1961 (originally published as *Images et Symboles*, Paris, 1952).

Bibliography

Erbse, Hartmut, *Untersuchungen zur Funktion der Götter im homerischen Epos*, Berlin: Walter de Gruyter, 1986.

Faulkner, Andrew, *The Homeric Hymn to Aphrodite, Introduction, Text, and Commentary*, Oxford: Oxford University Press, 2008.

Fenik, Bernard C. (ed.), *Homer, Tradition and Invention*, Leiden: E.J. Brill, 1978.

Finkelberg, Margalit, 'Royal Succession in Heroic Greece', *CQ* 41 (1991), 303-16.

Fontenrose, Joseph, *Python: A Study of Delphic Myth and its Origins*, Berkeley and Los Angeles: University of California Press, 1959.

Förstel, Karl, *Untersuchungen zum homerischen Apollonhymnos*, Bochum: Studienverlag Brockmeyer, 1979.

Fowler, R.L., 'ΑΙΓ- in Early Greek Language and Myth', *Phoenix* 42 (1988), 95-113.

Fränkel, H., *Early Greek Poetry and Philosophy*, tr. M. Hadas & J. Willis, Oxford: Blackwell, 1975 (originally published as *Dichtung und Philosophie des frühen Griechentums*, München, 1962).

Frazer, J.G., *The Golden Bough: A Study in Magic and Religion, Part IV: Adonis, Attis, Osiris*, vol. 1, 3rd edn, London: Macmillan, 1914.

Friedrich, Paul, *The Meaning of Aphrodite*, Chicago: University of Chicago Press, 1978.

Frisk, Hjalmar, *Griechisches Etymologisches Wörterbuch*, Band I-III, Heidelberg: Carl Winter Universitätsverlag, 1972-3.

Gadamer, H.G., *Griechische Philosophie (Gesammelte Werke 6)*, Tübingen: J.C.B. Mohr, 1985.

Gainsford, Peter, *Homer's Archetypical Family: A Pattern of Relations*, PhD Dissertation (Cambridge University), 1999.

Gallavotti, C., *Inscriptiones Pyliae ad Mycenaeam Aetatem Pertinentes*, Rome: Edizioni dell'Ateneo, 1961.

Gantz, Timothy, *Early Greek Myth: A Guide to Literary and Artistic Sources*, Baltimore: Johns Hopkins University Press, 1993.

Gemoll, A., *Die homerischen Hymnen*, Leipzig: Teubner, 1886.

Gimbutas, Marija, *The Goddesses and Gods of Old Europe: 6500-3500 BC, Myths and Cult Images*, London: Thames & Hudson, 1974.

Gould, J., 'Hiketeia', *JHS* 93 (1973), 74-103, reprinted in his *Myth, Ritual and Exchange, Essays in Greek Literature and Culture* (Oxford, 2001), 22-72 (with an Addendum, 2000, 74-7).

Gow, A.S.F., 'Elpis and Pandora in Hesiod's *Works and Days*', in E.C. Quiggin (ed.), *Essays and Studies presented to William Ridgeway*, Cambridge: Cambridge University Press, 1913.

Graf, Fritz, *Greek Mythology*, tr. Thomas Marier, Baltimore: Johns Hopkins University Press, 1993 (originally published as *Griechische Mythologie*, 1987).

Green, Peter, *The Argonautika, Apollonios Rhodios*, Berkeley and Los Angeles: University of California Press, 1997.

Griffin, Jasper, 'The Epic Cycle and the Uniqueness of Homer', *JHS* 97 (1977) 39-53.

Griffin, Jasper, *Homer on Life and Death*, Oxford: Clarendon Press, 1980a.

Griffin, Jasper, *Homer*, Oxford: Oxford University Press, 1980b.

Griffin, Jasper, *The Mirror of Myth, Classical Theme and Variations*, London: Faber and Faber, 1986.

Griffin, Jasper, *Homer: Iliad Book Nine*, Oxford: Clarendon Press, 1995.

Griffith, Mark, *The Authenticity of 'Prometheus Bound'*, Cambridge: Cambridge University Press, 1977.

Griffith, Mark, (ed.), *Aeschylus: Prometheus Bound*, Cambridge: Cambridge University Press, 1983.

Griffith, Mark, 'Contest and Contradiction in Early Greek Poetry', in M. Griffith & D.J. Mastronarde (eds), *Cabinet of the Muses: Essays on Classical and Comparative Literature in Honor of Thomas G. Rosenmeyer*, Atlanta: Scholars Press, 1990, 185-207.

Guthrie, W.K.C., *The Greeks and Their Gods*, London: Methuen, 1950.

Hainsworth, Bryan, *The Iliad: A Commentary*, vol. III: *Books 9-12*, Cambridge: Cambridge University Press, 1993.

Halliwell, Stephen, 'The Uses of Laughter in Greek Culture', *CQ* 41 (1991) 279-96.

Hamilton, Richard, *The Architecture of Hesiodic Poetry*, Baltimore: Johns Hopkins University Press, 1989.

Harrison, Jane E., 'Pandora's Box', *JHS* 20 (1900) 99-114.

Harrison, Jane E., *Prolegomena to the Study of Greek Religion*, Cambridge: Cambridge University Press, 1903.

Hayman, Henry, *The Odyssey of Homer*, vol. II: *Books VII-XII*, London: David Nutt, 1873.

Hayman, Henry, *The Odyssey of Homer*, vol. III: *Books XIII-XXIV*, London: David Nutt, 1882.

Heidel, Alexander, *The Babylonian Genesis: The Story of the Creation*, 2nd edn, Chicago: University of Chicago Press, 1951.

Heitsch, E., *Aphroditehymnos, Aeneis und Homer*, Hypomnemata 15, Göttingen: Vandenhoeck & Rupprecht, 1965.

Heubeck, A., West, S. & Hainsworth, J.B., *A Commentary on Homer's Odyssey*, vol. I: *Books I-VIII*, Oxford: Clarendon Press, 1988.

Heubeck, Alfred & Hoekstra, Arie, *A Commentary on Homer's Odyssey,* vol. II: *Books IX-XVI*, Oxford: Clarendon Press, 1989.

Hirschberer, Martina, *Gunaikon Katalogos und Megalai Ehoiai*, Munich-Leipzig: K.G. Saur, 2004.

Hoekstra, A., *The Sub-epic Stage of the Formulaic Tradition: Studies in the Homeric Hymn to Apollo, to Aphrodite and to Demeter*, Amsterdam: North Holland Publishing Company, 1969.

Holoka, James P., 'Looking Darkly (ΥΠΟΔΡΑ ΙΔΩΝ): Reflection on Status and Decorum in Homer', *TAPA* 113 (1983) 1-16.

Hooker, J.T., 'ΑΙΓΑΙΩΝ in Achilles' Plea to Thetis', *JHS* 100 (1980) 188-9.

Hunter, Richard, *Apollonius of Rhodes: Jason and the Golden Fleece (Argonautica)*, Oxford: Clarendon Press, 1993.

Huxley, G. L., *Greek Epic Poetry: From Eumelos to Panyassis*, London: Faber & Faber, 1969.

Jacoby, Felix, *Hesiodi Carmina*, Berlin: Weidmann, 1930.

James, E.O., *The Cult of the Mother Goddess: An Archaeological Documentary Study*, London: Thames & Hudson, 1959.

Janko, Richard, 'Equivalent Formulae in the Greek Epos', *Mnemosyne* 34 (1981a) 251-64.

Janko, Richard, Review of P. Smith, *Nursling of Mortality*, *CR* 31 (1981b) 285-6.

Janko, Richard, *Homer, Hesiod and the Hymns: Diachronic Development in Epic Diction*, Cambridge: Cambridge University Press, 1982.

Janko, Richard, 'The Shield of Heracles and the Legend of Cycnus', *CQ* 36 (1986) 38-59.

Janko, Richard, *The Iliad: A Commentary*, vol. IV: *Books 13-16*, Cambridge: Cambridge University Press, 1992.

Jeanmaire, H., 'La naissance d'Athéna et la royauté magique de Zeus', *Revue Archéologique* 48 (1956), 12-39.

Jebb, R.C., *Sophocles, The Plays and Fragments, Part III: The Antigone*, Cambridge: Cambridge University Press, 1906.

Kakrides, J.P., 'ΤΙΘΩΝΟΣ', *Wiener Studien* 48 (1930) 25-38.

Kamerbeek, J.C., *The Plays of Sophocles, Part I: The Ajax*, Leiden: E.J. Brill, 1963.

Kauer, Sigrid, *Die Geburt der Athena im altgriechischen Epos*, Würzburg: Verlag Konrad Triltsch, 1959.

Kim, Jinys, *The Pity of Achilles: Oral Style and the Unity of the Iliad*, Oxford: Rowman & Littlefield, 2000.

King, Helen, 'Tithonos and the Tettix', *Arethusa* 19 (1986), 15-35.

Kirk, G.S., *The Songs of Homer*, Cambridge: Cambridge University Press, 1962.

Kirk, G.S., *Myth; Its Meaning and Function in Ancient and Other Cultures*, Cambridge: Cambridge University Press, 1970.

Kirk, G.S., *The Nature of Greek Myths*, Harmondsworth: Penguin, 1974.

Kirk, G.S., 'The *Iliad*: The Style of Books 5 and 6', in T. Winnifrith et al., *Aspects of the Epic,* London: Macmillan, 1983.

Kirk, G.S., *The Iliad: A Commentary*, vol. I: *Books 1-4,* Cambridge: Cambridge University Press, 1985.

Kirk, G.S., *The Iliad: A Commentary*, vol. II: *Books 5-8,* Cambridge: Cambridge University Press, 1990.

Kramer, B., Erler, M., Hagerdorn, D. & Hübner, R., *Kölner Papyri*, Band 3, Papyrologica Coloniensia, vol. VII, Opladen: Westdeutscher Verlag, 1978.

Kuch, Heinrich, 'Thetis und die Fesselung des Zeus', *Rheinisches Museum für Philologie* 136 (1993), 203-9.

Kullmann, von Wolfgang, *Die Quellen der Ilias (Troische Sagenkreis)*, Wiesbaden: Franzsteiner Verlag, 1960.

Lamberton, Robert, *Hesiod*, New Haven: Yale University Press, 1988.

Lane Fox, Robin, *Travelling Heroes, Greeks and their Myths in the Epic Age of Homer*, London: Penguin, 2008.

Lang, Mabel L., 'Reverberation and Mythology in the *Iliad*', in C.A. Rubino & C. Shelmerdine (eds), *Approaches to Homer*, Austin: University of Texas Press, 1983, 140-64.

Leaf, Walter, *The Iliad*, vols I-II, 2nd edn, Amsterdam: Adolf M. Hakkert, 1960.

Leeming, David Adams, *The World of Myth*, Oxford: Oxford University Press, 1990.

Lesher, J.H., *Xenophanes of Colophon: Fragments*, Toronto: University of Toronto Press, 1992.

Lesky, A., tr. C. Heer and J. Willis, *A History of Greek Literature*, London: Duckworth, 1966 (1963).

Bibliography

Lloyd-Jones, Hugh, *The Eumenides by Aeschylus*, Englewood Cliffs, N.J.: Prentice-Hall, 1970.

Lloyd-Jones, Hugh, *The Justice of Zeus*, 2nd edn, Berkeley: University of California Press, 1983.

Lloyd-Jones, Hugh, 'The *Meropis* (*SH* 903A)', *Atti del XVII Congresso internazionale di papirologia*, Napoli, 1984, 141-50 (reprinted in *Greek Epic, Lyric and Tragedy, The Academic Papers of Sir Hugh Lloyd-Jones* (Oxford, 1990), 21-9.

Lloyd-Jones, Hugh & Parsons, Peter (eds), *Supplementum Hellenisticum*, Berlin: Walter de Gruyter, 1983.

Lohmann, Dieter, *Die Komposition der Reden in der Ilias*, Berlin: Walter de Gruyter, 1970.

Louden, Bruce, 'Pivotal Contrafactuals in Homeric Epic', *CA* 12 (1993), 181-98.

Lynn-George, Michael, *Epos: Word, Narrative and the Iliad*, London: Macmillan Press, 1988.

Macleod, C.W., *Homer, Iliad Book XXIV*, Cambridge: Cambridge University Press, 1982.

Martindale, C., *Redeeming the Text: Latin Poetry and the Hermeneutics of Reception*, Cambridge: Cambridge University Press, 1993.

Matthiae, August, *Animadversiones in Hymnos Homericos, cum Prolegomenis*, Lipsiae: Libraria Weidmannia, 1800.

Miller, Andrew M., *From Delos to Delphi: A Literary Study of the Homeric Hymn to Apollo*, Leiden: Brill, 1986.

Monro, D.B., *Homer's Odyssey: Books XIII-XXIV*, Oxford: Clarendon Press, 1901.

Most, Glenn W., *Hesiod: The Shield, Catalogue of Women, Other Fragments*, Cambridge, MA,: Harvard University Press, 2007.

Most, Glenn W. (ed.), *Hesiod, Theogony Works and Days*, Cambridge, MA: Harvard University Press, 2006.

Murnaghan, Sheila, *Disguise and Recognition in the Odyssey*, Princeton: Princeton University Press, 1987.

Nagler, Michael N., 'Towards a Generative View of the Oral Formula', *TAPA* 98 (1967), 269-311.

Nagy, G., *The Best of the Achaeans: Concepts of the Hero in Archaic Greek Poetry*, Baltimore: Johns Hopkins University Press, 1979.

Nagy, G., *Greek Mythology and Poetics*, Ithaca: Cornell University Press, 1990.

Neils, Jenifer, *Greek Mythology and Poetics*, Ithaca: Cornell University Press, 1980

Neils, Jenifer, 'Athena, Alter Ego of Zeus', in S. Deacy & A. Villing (eds), *Athena in the Classical World*, Leiden: Brill, 2001, 219-32.

Nilsson, Martin P., *A History of Greek Religion*, tr. F.J. Fielden, Oxford: Clarendon Press, 1925.

Nilsson, Martin P., *The Mycenaean Origin of Greek Mythology*, Cambridge: Cambridge University Press, 1932.

O'Brien, Joan V., *The Transformation of Hera: A Study of Ritual, Hero and the Goddess in the Iliad*, Lanham: Rowman & Littlefield Publishers, 1993.

Opstelten, J.C., *Sophocles and Greek Pessimism*, tr. J.A. Ross, Amsterdam: North-Holland Publishing, 1952 (originally published in Dutch as a doctoral thesis at the University of Leiden).

207

Bibliography

Otto, Walter F., *The Homeric Gods: The Spiritual Significance of Greek Religion*, tr. Moses Hades, London: Thames & Hudson, 1955 (originally published as *Die Götter Griechenlands: Das Bild des Göttlichen im Spiegel des griechischen Geistes*, Frankfurt, 1947).

Page, Denys, *Sappho and Alcaeus: An Introduction to the Study of Ancient Lesbian Poetry*, Oxford: Clarendon Press, 1955.

Palmer, L.R., *The Interpretation of Mycenaean Greek Texts*, Oxford: Clarendon Press, 1963.

Parry, Hugh, 'The *Homeric Hymn to Aphrodite*: Erotic *Ananke*', *Phoenix* 40 (1986), 253-68.

Parry, Milman, *The Making of Homeric Verse: The Collected Papers of Milman Parry*, ed. A. Parry, Oxford: Clarendon Press, 1971.

Penglase, Charles, *Greek Myths and Mesopotamia, Parallels and Influence in the Homeric Hymns and Hesiod* , London: Routledge, 1994.

Philips, F. Carter Jr., 'Narrative Compression and the Myths of Prometheus in Hesiod', *CJ* 68 (1973) 289-305.

Pope, M.W.M., 'Athena's Development in Homeric Epic', *AJP* 81 (1960), 113-35.

Porter, H.N., 'Repetition in the *Homeric Hymn to Aphrodite*', *AJP* 70 (1949), 249-72.

Preziosi, Patricia G., 'The *Homeric Hymn to Aphrodite*: An Oral Analysis', *HSCP* 71 (1966), 171-204.

Pritchard, James B. (ed.), *Ancient Near Eastern Texts Relating to the Old Testament*, 2nd edn, Princeton: Princeton University Press, 1955.

Propp, Vladimir, *Morphology of the Folktale*, tr. L. Scott, 2nd edn, Austin: University of Texas Press, 1968 (originally published as *Morfologija skazki*, 1928).

Pucci, Pietro, *Hesiod and the Language of Poetry*, Baltimore, MD: Johns Hopkins University Press, 1977.

Reinhardt, K., *Die Ilias und ihr Dichter*, ed. U. Hölscher, Göttingen: Vandenhoeck und Ruprecht, 1961.

Richardson Nicholas, *The Homeric Hymn to Demeter*, Oxford: Clarendon Press, 1974.

Richardson, Nicholas, 'Homeric Professors in the Age of the Sophocles', *PCPS* 21 (1975), 65-81.

Richardson, Nicholas, *The Iliad: A Commentary*, vol. VI: *Books 21-24*, Cambridge: Cambridge University Press, 1993.

Rohde, Erwin, *Psyche: Seelencult und Unsterblichkeitsglaube der Griechen*, 2nd edn, Freiburg: J.C.B. Mohn, 1898.

Roller, Lynn E., *In Search of God the Mother: The Cult of Anatolian Cybele*, Berkeley and Los Angeles: University of California Press, 1999.

Roscher, W.H., *Ausführliches Lexikon der Griechischen und Römischen Mythologie*, III-2, Leipzig: Teubner, 1908.

Rose, H.J., 'Anchises and Aphrodite', *CQ* 18 (1924), 11-16.

Russo, J., Fernandez-Galiano, M. & Heubeck, A., *A Commentary on Homer's Odyssey*, vol. III: *Books XVII-XXIV*, Oxford: Clarendon Press, 1992.

Rutherford, R.B., 'Tragic Form and Feeling in the *Iliad*', *JHS* 102 (1982), 145-60.

Rutherford, R.B., *Homer: Odyssey Books XIX and XX*, Cambridge: Cambridge University Press, 1992.

Bibliography

Rutherford, R.B., *Homer*, Greece & Rome New Surveys in the Classics 26, Oxford: The Classical Association/Oxford University Press, 1996.

Sale, William, 'Aphrodite in the *Theogony*', *TAPA* 92 (1961), 508-21.

Sale, William, 'Achilles and Heroic Values', *Arion* II-3 (1963), 86-100.

Schmid, W. & Stählin, O., *Geschichte der griechischen Literatur*, Bd. 1, Munich: Beck, 1929.

Scodel, Ruth, 'The Autobiography of Phoenix: *Iliad* 9.444-95', *AJP* 103 (1982a), 128-36.

Scodel, Ruth, 'The Achaean Wall and the Myth of Destruction', *HSCP* 86 (1982b), 33-50.

Seaford, Richard, *Reciprocity and Ritual: Homer and Tragedy in the Developing City-State*, Oxford: Clarendon Press, 1994.

Segal, Charles, *The Theme of the Mutilation of the Corpse in the Iliad*, Mnemosyne Supplement 17, Leiden: E.J. Brill, 1971.

Segal, Charles, 'The *Homeric Hymn to Aphrodite*: A Structuralist Approach', *CW* 67 (1974), 205-12.

Segal, Charles, 'Tithonus and the *Homeric Hymn to Aphrodite*: A Comment', *Arethusa* 19 (1986) 37-47.

Shearer, Ann, *Athene: Image and Energy*, London: Viking Arkana, 1966.

Sherwin-White, Susan M., *Ancient Cos: An Historical Study from the Dorian Settlement to the Imperial Period*, Hypomnemata 51, Göttingen: Vanderhoeck & Rupprecht, 1978.

Sihler, Andrew L., *New Comparative Grammar of Greek and Latin*, Oxford: Oxford University Press, 1955.

Slater, Philip E., *The Glory of Hera: Greek Mythology and the Greek Family*, Princeton: Princeton University Press, 1968.

Slatkin, Laura, *The Power of Thetis: Allusion and Interpretation in the Iliad*, Berkeley: University of California Press, 1991.

Smith, Peter, *Nursling of Mortality: A Study of the Homeric Hymn to Aphrodite*, Frankfurt: Verlag Peter D. Lang, 1981a.

Smith, Peter, 'Aineiadai as Patrons of *Iliad* XX and the *Homeric Hymn to Aphrodite*', *HSCP* 85 (1981b), 17-58.

Smyth, H.W., *Greek Grammar*, Cambridge, MA: Harvard University Press, 1956.

Solmsen, Friedrich, *Hesiod and Aeschylus*, Ithaca: Cornell University Press, 1949.

Solmsen, Friedrich, 'The Earliest Stages in the History of Hesiod's Text', *HSCP* 86 (1982), 1-31.

Solmsen, Friedrich, 'The Two Near Eastern Sources of Hesiod', *Hermes* 117 (1989), 413-22.

Sommerstein, Alan H. (ed.), *Aeschylus, Eumenides*, Cambridge: Cambridge University Press, 1989.

Sourvinou-Inwood, Christiane, *'Reading' Greek Culture, Texts and Images, Rituals and Myths*, Oxford: Clarendon Press, 1991.

Sowa, Cora Angier, *Traditional Themes and the Heroic Hymns*, Chicago: Bolchazy-Carducci Publishers, 1984.

Spyropoulos, T. & Chadwick, J. (eds), *The Thebes Tablets II*, Minos 4, Salamanca: Universidad de Salamanca, 1975.

Stanford, W.B., *The Odyssey of Homer*, vols I-II, London: Macmillan, 1947-8.

Bibliography

Stanley, Keith, *The Shield of Homer, Narrative Structure in the Iliad*, Princeton: Princeton University Press, 1993.

Stevenson, T.R., 'The Ideal Benefactor and the Father Analogy in Greek and Roman Thought', *CQ* 42 (1992), 421-36.

Stoddard, Kathryn, *The Narrative Voice in the Theogony of Hesiod*, Leiden: Brill, 2004.

Taplin, O., *Homeric Soundings: The Shaping of the Iliad*, Oxford: Clarendon Press, 1992.

Thalmann, William G., *Conventions of Form and Thought in Early Greek Epic Poetry*, Baltimore: Johns Hopkins University Press, 1984.

Thomson, George, *Aeschylus and Athens: A Study in the Social Origins of Drama*, London: Lawrence & Wishart, 1941.

Todorov, T., *The Poetics of Prose*, tr. R. Howard, Ithaca, New York: Cornell University Press, 1977.

Van der Ben, N., 'Hymn to Aphrodite 36-291: Note on the Pars Epica of the *Homeric Hymn to Aphrodite*', *Mnemosyne* 39 (1986), 1-41.

Van der Valk, M.H.A.L.H., *Textual Criticism of the Odyssey*, Leiden: A.W. Sijthoff, 1949.

Van der Valk, M., 'On the God Cronus', *GRBS* 26 (1985), 5-11.

Van der Valk, M., *Researches on the Text and Scholia of the Iliad*, I-II, Leiden: E.J. Brill, 1963-64.

Van Leeuwen, J., *Odyssea*, Leiden: A.W. Sijthoff, 1917.

Vendvik, Eirik, *The Prometheus of Hesiod and Aeschylus*, Oslo; Jacob Dybwad, 1943.

Ventris, Michael & Chadwick, John, *Documents in Mycenaean Greek*, Cambridge: Cambridge University Press, 1956.

Verdenius, W.J., 'A "Hopeless" line in Hesiod: *Works and Days* 96', *Mnemosyne* 24 (1971), 225-31.

Vermaseren, Maarten J., *Cybele and Attis: the Myth and the Cult*, tr. A.M.H. Lemmers, London: Thames & Hudson, 1977 (originally published in Dutch).

Vernant, Jean-Pierre, *The Universe, the Gods, and Men: Ancient Greek Myth*, tr. Linda Asher, New York: Harper Collins Publishers, 2001 (originally published as *L'univers, les dieux, les hommes: Récits grecs des origines* in 1999).

Walcot, P., *Hesiod and the Near East*, Cardiff: University of Wales Press, 1966.

Walcot, P., 'Homeric Hymn to Aphrodite. A Literary Appraisal', *G&R* 38 (1991), 137-55.

West, M.L., *Hesiod: Theogony*, Oxford: Clarendon Press, 1966.

West, M.L., 'Near Eastern Material in Hellenistic and Roman Literature', *HSCP* 73 (1969), 113-34.

West, M.L., 'Cynaethus' Hymn to Apollo', *Classical Quarterly* 25 (1975), 161-70.

West, M.L., *Hesiod: Works and Days*, Oxford: Clarendon Press, 1978.

West, M.L., *The East Face of Helicon: West Asiatic Elements in Greek Poetry and Myth*. Oxford: Clarendon Press, 1997.

West, M.L., *Homeri Ilias*, vols 1-2, Leipzig and Munich: Teubner, 1998-2000.

West, M.L., *Studies in the Text and Transmission of the Iliad*, Munich and Leipzig: K.G. Saur, 2001a.

Bibliography

West, M.L., 'The Fragmentary Homeric Hymn to Dionysus', *Zeitschrift für Papyrologie und Epigraphik* 134 (2001b), 1-11.

West, M.L., *Homeric Hymns, Homeric Apocrypha, Lives of Homer*, Cambridge, MA, Harvard University Press, 2003 (Loeb Classical Library).

Whitman, C.H., *Homer and Heroic Tradition*, Cambridge, MA: Harvard University Press. 1958.

Whitman, C.H., 'Hera's Anvils', *HSCP* 74 (1970), 37-53.

Wilamowitz-Moellendorff, Ulrich von, *Die Ilias und Homer*, Berlin: Weidmann, 1920.

Wilamowitz-Moellendorff, Ulrich von, *Der Glaube der Hellenen*, Basel: Benno Schwabe, 1931-2.

Willcock, M.M., 'Mythological Paradeigma in the *Iliad*', *CQ* 58 (1964), 141-54.

Willcock, M.M., '*Ad Hoc* Invention in the *Iliad*', *HSCP* 81 (1977), 41-53.

Willcock, M.M., *The Iliad of Homer, Books I-XII*, London: Macmillan, 1978.

Willcock, M.M., *The Iliad of Homer, Books XIII-XXIV*, London: Macmillan, 1984.

Wirshbo, Eliot, 'The Mecone Scene in the *Theogony*: Prometheus as Prankster', *GRBS* 23 (1982) 101-10.

Zeitlin, Froma I., 'Signifying Difference: the Myth of Pandora', in R. Hawley & B. Levick (eds), *Women in Antiquity*, London: Routledge, 1995, 58-74.

Zeitlin, Froma I., *Playing the Other: Gender and Society in Classical Greek Literature*, Chicago: University of Chicago Press, 1996.

Index of Passages

Index of Names

Achaeans/Argives/Danaans, 47, 48,
   49, 55, 59, 60, 61, 62, 63, 65, 66, 68,
   69, 91, 93, 177n.56
Achilles
   analogous of, to Poseidon, 67-71
   and Peleus, 13, 35-8
   and Priam, 35-8, 169n.78, n.81
   bitter sorrow of, 69, 176n.37
   mortal son of Thetis, 14-8, 164n.9,
      169n.80
   speaks of human destiny, 140
   timê of, 14, 18, 38, 67, 68, 176n.33
   wrath of, 38, 64, 65, 68, 69, 71,
      175n.22
Aegaion, 15, 164n.14
Aeneadae, 191n.3
Aeneas, 132, 139, 145, 193n.31
Agamemnon, 38, 62, 65, 67, 68, 69,
   73, 74
Ajax, 62-3, 64
Alalu (first king in the Hurrian
   myth), 76-7, 178n.4
Alcyoneus (giant), 51, 52, 184n.17
Amyntor (father of Phoenix), 19
Anchises, 132-42, 150, 194n.42
Andromache, 40, 95, 145, 170n.7
Anshar (grandfather of Ea in *Enuma
   Elish*), 78
Antagoras, 51
Anu (Sky-god)
   second king in the Hurrian myth,
      76-7, 178n.4
   in *Enuma Elish*, 78, 178n.4
Aphrodite/Cytherea, 172n.28, 192n.17
   against Zeus in *Theogony*, 146-7,
      195-6n.84
   and Anchises in *Hymn to Aphrodite*,
      132-42

bitter sorrow of, 139-40, 151,
   176n.37
harmonious relation with other
   goddesses, 151-5
in the Greek epics, 144-7
origin as a Great Mother, in Near
   Eastern or Indo-European
   tradition, 142-4
subordinate to Zeus in *Hymn to
   Aphrodite*, 147-51, 196n.92,
   197n.101
Apollo
   against Poseidon, 73-4
   and Athena, 3, 90-6, 181n.49
   and Telphousa, 118-9
   and Zeus, 120, 129, 177n.52
   in *Hymn to Apollo*, 129-30
   killed the female dragon, 119-21,
      128-9
Apollodorus of Athens, 50
Apsu (Tiâmat's husband in *Enuma
   Elish*), 78
Aranzahas (son of Kumarbi), 76
Areion (horse), 55, 173n.58
Ares, 6, 46, 56, 146, 171n.21, 180n.31
   Athena's target, 91-4, 182n.61
   binding of, 43-5, 171n.21
   challenge of, to Zeus, 65, 67, 93-4,
      174n.6
Arimoi, 122, 189n.22
Aristarchus, 43, 50, 106, 165n.30,
   171n.16, 177n.51
Artemis, 139, 149, 151, 152, 153
   one of the three goddesses, in *Hymn
   to Aphrodite*, 151-5, 196n.93
   reproaches Apollo, 73-4
Assyria(n), 3, 143, 177n.3

215

General Index

succession myth, 3, 13, 14, 15, 16, 20,
29, 26, 38, 40, 76, 77, 128, 129
supplication
of Priam, 36, 38, accepted by
Achilles, 36, 38
of Thetis, 13-8, 38, 165n.19,
accepted by Zeus, 14, 38
rejection of, 38
strife, generational, among the gods,
3-5, 9, 10, 14, 18, 19-28, 37-9, 54,
58-9, 68, 76-9, 87, 90, 91-4, 105,
112, 117, 132, 144, 154, 158,
165n.19, 171n.25, 177n.48, 181n.46
swallowing
in the Hurrian myth, 3, 76-7
of his children by Cronus, 81-3,
179n.24
of Metis by Zeus, 81-90, 179n.24,
181n.51, n.55, 190n.49
technique in narrative, 7, 10, 29, 51,
58, 64, 128, 130, 131, 157, 173n.47,
184n.27, 191n.4
Telegony, 26, 167n.47
Telemachia, 21
timê, 68
of Achilles, 14, 18, 38, 67, 68,
176n.33
of Cronus, 85, 176n.31
of Uranus (Heaven), 81, of Uranus
and Gaia to Zeus, 82, 85
of Poseidon, 68
of Thetis, 18
theogony, non-Hesiodic, 97, 102
Theomachy, in *Iliad*, 5, 71, 73, 74,
174n.8

three goddesses (Athena, Artemis,
and Hestia), in *Hymn to Aphrodite*,
151-5, 196n.93
thunder
Brontes, 89, 90
of Athena, 50
of Zeus, 14, 51, 67, 72, 89, 99, 122,
129, 147, 152
thunderbolt, 89
eastern model, 76
ultimate source of Zeus' authority,
46, 48, 51, 58, 63, 67, 70, 89, 93,
94, 99, 104, 122, 134, 150, 171n.24
Titanomachy, 78, 103, 104, 105,
172n.36, 177n.48, 184n.20, n.23
Trojan and Theban epic cycles, 27
Trojan War, 9, 15, 151, 166n.37,
196n.86
tug-of-war, between Zeus and
Poseidon, 59, 62-4, 175n.20, n.21
woman, creation of, 97, 99, 101, 109,
111, 112-3, 183n.1, 184n.25,
186n.54
wrath, *or* anger, 66, 71, 175n.24
of Achilles, 38, 64, 65, 68, 69, 71,
175n.22
of Apollo, 119
of Gaia, 54
of Hera, 89, 118, 123, 126, 168n.60
of Poseidon, 60, 64, 68, 69, 71
of Telphousa, 118
of Thetis, 38
of Zeus, 18, 64, 65, 108, 122, 168n.60

Printed in Great Britain
by Amazon

75048669R00136